A Jewish Professor's Political Punditry

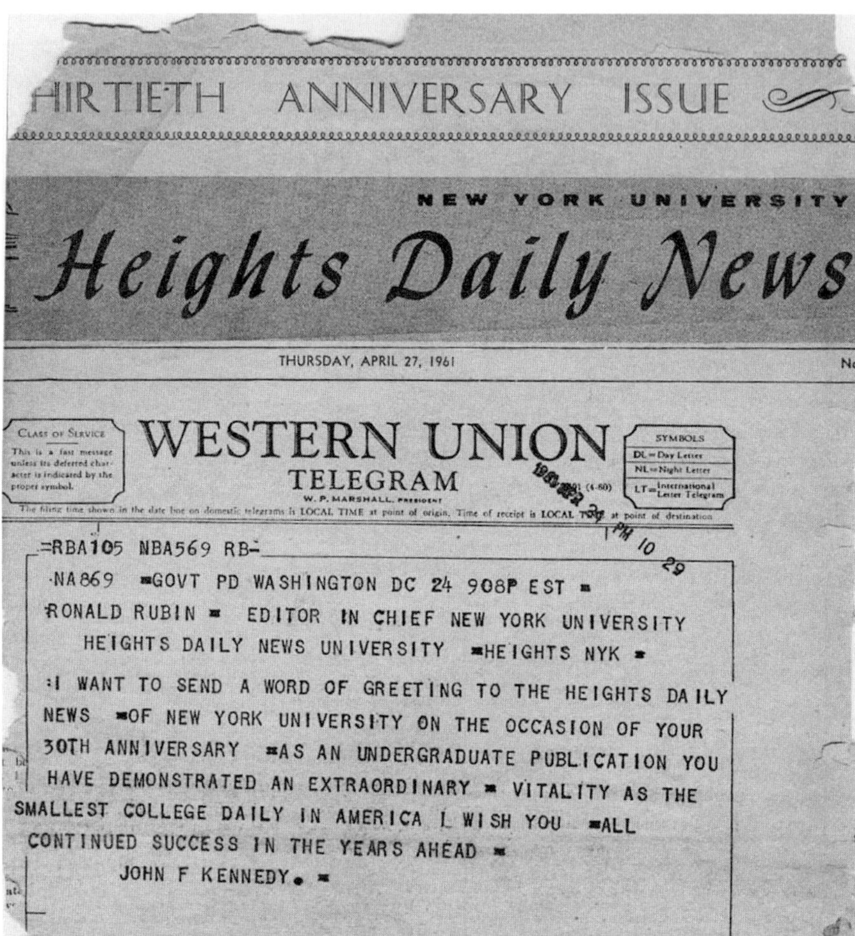

HIRTIETH ANNIVERSARY ISSUE

NEW YORK UNIVERSITY

Heights Daily News

THURSDAY, APRIL 27, 1961

No.

CLASS OF SERVICE
This is a fast message unless its deferred character is indicated by the proper symbol.

WESTERN UNION
TELEGRAM
W. P. MARSHALL, PRESIDENT

SYMBOLS
DL = Day Letter
NL = Night Letter
LT = International Letter Telegram

The filing time shown in the date line on domestic telegrams is LOCAL TIME at point of origin. Time of receipt is LOCAL TIME at point of destination

=RBA105 NBA569 RB=
NA869 =GOVT PD WASHINGTON DC 24 908P EST =
RONAL RUBIN = EDITOR IN CHIEF NEW YORK UNIVERSITY
HEIGHTS DAILY NEWS UNIVERSITY =HEIGHTS NYK =
:I WANT TO SEND A WORD OF GREETING TO THE HEIGHTS DAILY NEWS =OF NEW YORK UNIVERSITY ON THE OCCASION OF YOUR 30TH ANNIVERSARY =AS AN UNDERGRADUATE PUBLICATION YOU HAVE DEMONSTRATED AN EXTRAORDINARY = VITALITY AS THE SMALLEST COLLEGE DAILY IN AMERICA I WISH YOU =ALL CONTINUED SUCCESS IN THE YEARS AHEAD =
JOHN F KENNEDY. =

THE COMPANY WILL APPRECIATE SUGGESTIONS FROM ITS PATRONS CONCERNING ITS SERVICE

Telegram from President John F. Kennedy to Ron Rubin.
Reprinted with permission from New York University Archives;
Photographic Collection and Ron Rubin.

A Jewish Professor's Political Punditry

Fifty-Plus Years of Published Commentary by

Ron Rubin

Edited by Peri Devaney

Syracuse University Press

Cover: Stack of recycled magazines. Copyright: Somchai Rakin. Used under license from Shutterstock.com. *Back Cover (above):* Photograph courtesy of New York University Archives, Photographic Collection; *(below)* Photograph by Robert (Michoe-l) deVaney.

First Edition 2013

13 14 15 16 17 18 6 5 4 3 2 1

∞ The paper used in this publication meets the minimum requirements of the American National Standard for Information Sciences—Permanence of Paper for Printed Library Materials, ANSI Z39.48-1992.

For a listing of books published and distributed by Syracuse University Press, visit our website at SyracuseUniversityPress.syr.edu.

ISBN: 978-0-8156-1020-5

Library of Congress Cataloging-in-Publication Data

Rubin, Ron.
A Jewish professor's political punditry : fifty-plus years of published commentary / by Ron Rubin ; edited by Peri Devaney. — First edition.
pages cm
"This anthology takes a look at the Jewish world of the past fifty-plus years through Rubin's writings. It looks at Judaism, the religion; Israel, the country; Jewish American politics; world politics"—publisher's note
Includes bibliographical references and index.
ISBN 978-0-8156-1020-5 (pbk. : alk. paper) 1. Rubin, Ron. 2. Jewish journalists—United States—Biography. I. Devaney, Peri, editor. II. Title.
PN4874.R7525A3 2013
070.4'82092—dc23 2013005498

Dedicated
In Loving Memory of My Parents

SIDNEY LEVINE (Simcha ben Yisroel haLevi[ע״ה])—1922–2009
A gentle man and avid reader and storyteller, he encouraged me and instilled in me a love for writing.
&
SHIRLEY LEVINE (Sarah bas Moshe v Leah[ע״ה])—1929–1982
A true Aishes Chayil (Woman of Valor), she was a dedicated member and respected leader of Women's American ORT and the Southern Long Island Jewish Community, and she imbued in me a strong connection to Judaism, Israel, and the Jewish people worldwide.

And in Honor of
RON RUBIN,
without whom there wouldn't be this unique perspective on fifty-plus years of Jewish history.

Peri Devaney is an editorial consultant, copy writer and editor, and full-time administrator of the Western U.S. center of Jews for Judaism, an international nonprofit dedicated to empowering Jewish students, the Jewish community, and the community-at-large against peer pressure and deceptive proselytizing. She holds a BA from the University at Buffalo, the State University of New York.

Devaney began her editorial career in the 1970s creating newsletters and brochures as a volunteer for nonprofit groups and as a staff member at a trade association. In the late 1980s, while executive director of an international IT association, AFCOM, she added the role of managing editor and was instrumental in creating AFCOM's highly acclaimed monthly magazine. In 1993 she left AFCOM to develop her home-based editorial, marketing, and administrative support firm, PERIodicals, and under its banner has done extensive volunteer work and, as editorial consultant, rewrote three manuscripts leading to the publication of *Diary of a Dirty Little War: The Spanish American War of 1898* (Praeger, 2000) and *Richmond Pearson Hobson: Naval Hero from Magnolia Grove* (Yucca Tree Press, 2001) by Harvey Rosenfeld, and *Anything for a T-Shirt: Fred Lebow and the New York City Marathon* (Syracuse University Press, 2004) by Ron Rubin.

Contents

Preface

According to the medieval Jewish philosopher, Maimonides, one of the ways for a Jew to find divine forgiveness is by "dismantling for the purpose of building." This term, a play on words, refers to one of the thirty-nine categories of work Jews performed in constructing the Temple in their biblical journey through the desert on the way to the Holy Land.

Spiritually, what Maimonides meant by "dismantling," was that a person should carefully analyze his speech, actions and thoughts as a way to self-improvement. Such critical self-analysis would spur the person to become, in Hebrew, a *breiah chadasha*, a newly made creation.

Ron Rubin, in the selections that follow, has tried adapting this Maimonidian concept to the political arena, namely by examining ("dismantling") political forces and events with the hope that a more secure future would emerge ("for the purpose of building"). The centrality of political power as a tool for Jewish well-being has been Rubin's theme spanning more than a half-century of his writings. No American of his era has written on as wide a variety of subjects touching on the Jew in the political arena and he is among the most prolific writers on the subject of Soviet Jewry.

For more than fifty years Rubin has been writing editorials, cover articles, feature articles, "op-eds," book reviews, serials, columns, papers, and full-length books. His works are in print in periodicals ranging from university dailies to *The New York Times*; from *The Jewish Press* to *The Christian Science Monitor*; from *Columbia Journalism Review* to *New York* Magazine. He has been published around the world—from the United States to London (*Parliamentary Affairs*), Moscow (*America*), Amsterdam (*The Gazette: International Journal of Mass Communications*), Pakistan (*Pakistan Horizon*), and, of course, Israel (*Jerusalem Post*).

Even when his writings carried no overt Jewish connection, the Jewish dimension had been joined. In articles like "USIA—The Muffled Voice" (referred to on p. 65) and Rubin's ground-breaking expose "The UN Correspondent" (p. 13)—where neither Judaism nor Israel were directly mentioned—one need merely read the word "information" as "propaganda," and consider the affect the UN and media have had, and continue to have, on Israel's well-being and the level of security felt by the global Jewish community, and the connection becomes clear. (Despite the critical role these materials play in Rubin's efforts "dismantling for the purpose of building," very little of what he has written on these subjects will be included herein because of the vast amount of material he has written that more directly discusses Judaism, Israel, and modern Jewish history.)

Born in 1942 and educated at yeshivas in the Bronx and at Manhattan's Yeshiva University High School, Rubin was a student at New York University (NYU) by the age of fifteen. "I wasn't brilliant," he noted, "but ambitious. . . . I was actually so embarrassed at my youth in college that I concealed my age as much as possible."

By the age of eighteen, as a senior at NYU, Rubin was firmly ensconced in the world of journalism. Although he had not chosen journalism, but rather political science, as his major, his journalistic prolificacy led to his being appointed editor-in-chief of the University's *Heights Daily News*, at the time the smallest college daily in the United States.

Currently, Rubin serves as a professor of political science at Borough of Manhattan Community College (BMCC), City University of New York. Having taught at BMCC for almost fifty years, he is the college's most senior faculty member. He has also spent a year in Israel as a visiting senior lecturer in political science at Haifa University's invitation. His hands-on political experience includes working in the United States Congress as a legislative assistant in the House of Representatives.

This anthology takes a look at the Jewish world of the past fifty-plus years through Rubin's writings. It looks at Judaism, the religion; Israel, the country; Jewish American politics; world politics; personalities impacting the Jewish world, and more. Included, too, are pieces from loosely related articles about education—the quality of which has always been of vital importance to the Jewish culture—and political communications issues of special interest to Rubin—because of their impact on Israel, the global Jewish community, and the individual Jew. Entwined throughout is a biographical look at the author himself—the life and interests of an Orthodox Jewish political science professor involved in both the religious and secular aspects of Judaism from the mid-1900s through the first decade of the twenty-first century—as amassed during the compilation of this anthology.

PERI DEVANEY, Editor

Acknowledgments

Many fine people were involved in bringing this work to fruition and I would like to thank them all. Shari Glixman, in her gracious observance of *hachnasas orchim* (the commandment to show hospitality to the stranger), began the process when she opened her home in Florida to a professor from New York and mentioned her cousin, an editor in California. After I finished two projects with Professor Harvey Rosenfeld, he gave my name to Ron Rubin as a potential editor for his manuscript about Fred Lebow and the New York City Marathon.

Dr. Rubin has been instrumental in this project since before its inception. In addition to providing a lifetime of material, he supplied whatever long-distance assistance, input, and encouragement was needed. His wife, Miriam, whose sparkle and warmth welcome and calm, has been a "behind-the-scenes" partner throughout.

Mr. Hollander of hollanderbooks.com and the folks at abebooks.com provided details that helped me track down rights holders for some publications whose publishers are long defunct. And Professor Zhana Yablokova recovered a 1973 article by translating it back to English.

All this work could have gone nowhere without the amazing and dedicated crew at Syracuse University Press. Their commitment to producing a quality product is legend, and I am honored to have this second project to work on with them. I especially want to acknowledge Alice Randel Pfeiffer, director; Kelly Lynne Balenske in acquisitions; Kay Steinmetz, production and editorial manager; Mona Hamlin and Lisa Kuerbis in marketing; Lynn Hoppel Wilcox, design specialist; Fred Wellner, senior designer; Marcia Hough, editorial assistant; Michele Callaghan, copy editor; and past acquisitions editors Mary Selden Evans and Annelise Finegan.

On a personal note I would like to thank my son, Keith Hoffman, for his persistence when I was so often unavailable and, of course, my husband, Michoe-l Devaney, for his priceless support, endurance, and care during the long hours, often weeks on end, when I was completely focused on scanning old documents, preparing the manuscript, seeking permissions, and working with production.

And mostly, I want to acknowledge Hashem, Who created the chain of events that brought *A Jewish Professor's Political Punditry* this far. I look forward to seeing where He takes it from here.

Permissions

I would like to thank all the people I spoke with at the many publications that permitted us to reprint articles for which they hold the copyrights, all of whom waived their normal fees in recognition of Dr. Rubin's contributions and this important volume. Following are the permissions granted for reprinting materials used in *A Jewish Professor's Political Punditry*, in alphabetical order by copyright holder. Except where noted, the author of all materials is Ronald I. (or Ron) Rubin.

Reprinted with permission from the March 31, 1967, issue of *The Christian Science Monitor.* © 1967; and "Students Tour Russia with Sputnik" by Ronald I. Rubin. Reprinted with permission from the March 4, 1967, issue of *The Christian Science Monitor.* © 1967 *The Christian Science Monitor* (www.CSMonitor.com).

Commonweal—"Propaganda" © 1966 Commonweal Foundation, reprinted with permission. For more information, visit www.commonweal magazine.org.

Fordham University Press—"The Plight of Soviet Jews," originally published in *Thought: A Review of Culture and Idea—Fordham University Quarterly,* August 1968. Reprinted with permission.

Indiana University Press—"Soviet Jewry and the United Nations: The Politics of Non-Governmental Organizations" by Ronald Rubin, *Jewish Social Studies—A Quarterly Journal Devoted to Contemporary and Historical Aspects of Jewish Life* 29, no. 3(July 1967). Reprinted with permission from Indiana University Press.

Jerusalem Post—"Crock of Presidents." Published in the *Jerusalem Post* in May 1970. (www.jpost.com).

The Jewish Journal of Greater Los Angeles—"Two Finish Lines," March 2005. Reprinted with permission from *The Jewish Journal of Greater Los Angeles.*

The Jewish Press—Originally appeared in *The Jewish Press*: "Joe Lieberman's Jewish Inreach," March 26, 2004; "Unilateralism Versus Post-Nationalism," May 21, 2004; "Fishl's Marathon," November 5, 2004; "Learning From The Master: My Debt To America's Greatest Judaica Collector," April 22, 2005; "Bolton Versus Powell: A Tale Of Two Diplomatic Cultures," May 20, 2005; "Bush Can't Afford Another Blink," July 14, 2006; "Why Lieberman Will Lose," August 4, 2006; "Olmert's Liberal Mindset to Blame for Lebanon Fiasco," September 1, 2006; "Fred Lebow and Pol 101," October 20, 2006; "An Unforgettable Forty-Year Shabbos Journey," December 15, 2006; "Welcoming Israel's Newest Olim," January 11, 2008; "Why Bush May Yet Shock Everyone And Bomb Iran," February 8, 2008; "How About Brownback for Vice President," April 11, 2008.

Jewish Week—"Clinton's Example," November 1998. Reprinted with permission from *Jewish Week.*

New York University—Reprinted with the permission of New York University Archives: "The Philosophy of the Greek and the Jew: A Comparison," *Historian*, May, 1959; "EDITORIAL: The Sin of Omission," *Heights Daily News*, October 25, 1960; "EDITORIAL: Season's Greetings," *Heights Daily News*, December 20, 1960; "EDITORIAL: Adolf Eichmann," *Heights Daily News*, April 11, 1961.

Orthodox Union—Reprinted by permission of the Orthodox Union: "America's Voice in Israel" *Jewish Life*, May 1969; "Israel's Propaganda War" *Jewish Life*, March–April 1970; "American Jews and Soviet Jews" *Jewish Life*, September '70; "Broadcasting in Israel" *Jewish Life*, March–April 1971; "Where Have All The Liberals Gone?" *Jewish Life*, October 1973 and "Israel Center Library Dedicated in Memory of Young Oleh." *Jewish Action*, Summer 1983.

Riverdale Press—"Serving in Army Helped Identity with Israel," first published in *The Riverdale Press* on January 11, 1990.

Ronald I. Rubin—Reprinted with permission from Ronald I. (Ron) Rubin: Originally published in *Forum*: "Israel's Word War," January 1983.—Originally published in *Forward* magazine: "Prince of Ethnicity," October 1999; "Letter from the New York Marathon: Homage to an Unlikely Impresario," October 1999; "Getting to 'President Joe,'" August 3, 2001; "Dawdling Diplomacy Emboldens Terrorists," February 2003, and "The New Powell Doctrine," March 2003.—First appeared in *Hadassah* Magazine: "Student Struggle for Soviet Jewry," December 1966, and "The Real Shtetl." November 1967.—Originally published in *New York* Magazine: "Help for the Republicans: The Jewish Vote," December 1976, "The City Politic" column; "Brooklyn's Hasidim: The Yiddish Connection," March 1977, "The City Politic" column; "Republicans Court the Jewish Vote: GOP? Couldn't Hurt," July 1978, "The Capitol Letter;" "The Most Powerful Rabbis In New York," January 1979 cover article.—Originally published in *the New York Post*: "A Marathon Man's Answer to the Nazi," November 3, 1999.—Originally published in *The New York Times:* "Protests at Soviet Rabbi's Hunter Talk," June 1968, and "To Be Educated, Or More Educated: That Is the Question," April 10, 1976.—Originally published in *Pakistan Horizon 19, no. 3 (Third Quarter)*, "The Persistence of American Isolationism."—Originally published in *Saturday Review:*

"State and the System," June 1967, and "The Promised Land Grows Dim," September 2, 1967.—Originally published in *The Wall Street Journal* "Letters to the Editor" pages: "Political Orthodoxy," August 16, 2000 and "Do Palestinians Really Want a Permanent Peace With Israel? A Response to 'The Gipper's Mideast Playbook' by Richard Haass," April 14 2007.—YIVO Institute of Jewish Research Award Winning Paper: "A Kosher Supermarket Fights the Blue Laws: Gallagher v Crown Kosher Super," 1965.—Unpublished work: "The Statecraft of Condi Clinton," December 2007.

SAGE Publications, Inc.—"The UN Correspondent." Originally appearing in *Western Political Quarterly*, December 1964, the final, definitive version of this paper has been published in *Political Research Quarterly*, by SAGE Publications, Inc. All rights reserved. Copyright © 1964, University of Utah, http://prq.sagepub.com/content/17/4/615.full.pdf+html. "Israel's Foreign Information Program." Originally appearing in *Gazette (International Journal of Mass Communication Studies)*, Amsterdam, Second Quarter, 1973, the final, definitive version of this paper has been published in *International Communications Gazette*, by SAGE Publications, Inc. All rights reserved. © 1973—http://gaz.sagepub.com/content/19/2/65.full.pdf+html

Shma—"Friends in Need of Votes, Friends Indeed?" Reprinted with permission from *Shma: A Journal of Jewish Responsibility* (www.shma.com), October 15, 1976.

Tradition magazine—"The New Jewish Ethnic," *Tradition: A Journal of Orthodox Jewish Thought*, December 1973. This article is reprinted with permission from *Tradition* magazine.

Yeshiva of the Telshe Alumni—"From Telshe-Lithuania to Riverdale," Yeshiva of the Telshe Alumni's Dinner Journal, June 1993. Reprinted with permission from Yeshiva Telshe Alumni.

Young Israel—"Letter to Russia by Shulie Rubin." Reprinted by permission from *Viewpoint* magazine, February 1985, National Council of Young Israel.

Zionist Organization of America—"The New Style of Soviet and Other Jews," *The American Zionist*, May 1971. Reprinted by permission of the Zionist Organization of America (ZOA).

Author's Note

When I was growing up in the Bronx in the 1940s and 1950s, my horizons stretched beyond the boulevard shaped Grand Concourse. I had access to the lives of presidents, great cities, and political movements of the day through the newspapers, biographies, and periodicals that I was exposed to in my boyhood. Since I was raised in a Jewishly observant home and studied at various yeshivas, I naturally looked on current events from the yardstick of a Jewish perspective. The central political issue in those years for me was the survival of the young, vulnerable State of Israel. In addition to following news accounts, I marched at rallies, canvassed the streets with charity *pushke* boxes, and championed the cause of the tiny, beleaguered Israel in letters and appeals to American politicians.

In my transition from reader of newspapers to writer for newspapers, and eventually to political scientist, the person with the most influence in shaping me was my aunt, Rosalyn Yenta Grubart, younger sister of my mother, Blanche. Personally, she was soft and kind. Intellectually, she belonged to the ranks of those unheralded thinkers that the Jewish people have produced over the centuries. She was a student of Greek and Latin in college, and a Shakespearean scholar. Aunt Rozy bought me books for gifts, provoked my thinking, and honed my writing skills. She was a sounding board for my ideas, and my advocate when these ideas sometimes got me into trouble.

The other woman to whom I humbly pay tribute in connection with the publication of this political memoir is my loving and loveable *Ayshet Chail* (Woman of Valor), Miriam. My wife has sharpened my ideas and prevented literary pitfalls. In her persona, she combines joy with the caring and sensitivity of the occupational therapist that she is.

Ron Rubin

Introduction

Strategies of Jewish Survival

Ron Rubin

For two thousand years, Jews exiled from their homeland and lacking political sovereignty were easy targets for elitist rulers on the right and the pseudo-egalitarian mob on the left. When Emancipation came and Jews exited the ghettos, Jewish self-made pitfalls were no less horrific, as many embraced the trendy "isms" of secular society only to spiritually assimilate and disappear from history. Yet despite the persecutions, on the one hand, and the enticements of some host countries' cultures, on the other, *am Yisroel chai*, the Jewish nation, lives. That is . . . at least a blessed remnant lives after its two millennia catastrophic journey.

How did Jews politically survive in the lands of their dispersion despite statelessness and dependency? How were the terms of their struggle transformed in the era of official political and social equality that came in the wake of the European eighteenth- and nineteenth-century Emancipation? Tracing this trajectory further, what political strategies emerged in an increasingly secular America, where Jews defined themselves more as a "people" than as a religion? With the creation of Israel and the trappings of a sovereign state, how did power replace powerlessness for the one nation more than any other branded as a pariah?

Though these are weighty questions all deserving book-length answers in their own right, certain basic traits enabled the Jews to master all of these epochal challenges. Ingenuity, inventiveness, improvisation and guile were the skills with which they triumphed over the threatening political environment. When this adaptation succeeded, those Jews who were inventive enough remained alive for another day, not merely as survivors, but as actors in God's plans. Hebrew University's Eli Lederhendler described Jewish political behavior in that milieu: "Ideologically, Jews viewed pragmatic efforts to maintain the security and stabilities of their communities as consistent with, and therefore legitimized by, their belief that their own efforts mirrored a divine plan for their people."[1]

Jews in the lands of their dispersion survived not because of brotherly love or "multicultural" accommodation but also by making themselves useful or by providing needed services. Often they were wards of their rulers. When Jews depended on local gentiles who held power, they used this relationship optimally, whether as artisans in Spain's Golden Age or as tax collectors in Poland or as bankers in Austria. For their contributions, the trade-off was that Jews were protected by those in power.

But it remained a dependent relationship with Jews never knowing when their powerlessness would be exposed by pogroms, expulsion, or gas chambers. Strategically, Israel's record among the nations also was marked by improvisation, schemes and feats of daring. Agricultural training programs in third world Africa, international medical rescue missions, programs of cultural diplomacy, fighting United Nations "Zionism is racism" resolutions and such were designed so that some tacit international political acceptance, i.e., legitimacy, would replace political isolationism.

Despite the rise of nationalistic sentiment in early twentieth-century Europe, liberal Jewish thinkers found this Jewish powerlessness not a vulnerability, but a blessing. Ruth Wisse painfully showed in "The Brilliant Failure of Jewish Foreign Policy,"[2] how pleased they were "with the sense that their ethical national identity had been purified of the dross of politics." To these upstanding global citizens, the translation of politics into social ethics represented a giant step in human progress.

1. Lederhendler, Eli. *The Road to Modern Jewish Politics: Political Tradition and Political Reconstruction in the Jewish Community of Tsarist Russia,* Oxford University Press, 1989, pp. 33–34.

2. Wisse, Ruth. "The Brilliant Failure of Jewish Foreign Policy," *Azure, Ideas for the Jewish Nation,* Winter 2001.

Thus, Wisse noted, Hermann Cohen, the main spokesman for liberal Judaism in that period, maintained that with the destruction of the Jewish state in 70 C.E. and the end of the political center of gravity in Jewish history, "the development of the Jewish religion alone has to be presented as the driving cultural force. . . . Religion must become politics insofar as it ought to educate the citizens on the duty of love of humanity."[3]

Similarly, the eminent Russian Jewish historian, Simon Dubnow, argued that the Jewish nation had reached its high level of humanity as a result of its being removed from national politics for some two millennia. This progress showed that Jews had transcended an "egotistical" dimension of power and could sustain national unity through institutions of culture. According to Dubnow, "A nationality which lacks a defensive protection of state or territory develops, instead, forces of inner defense and employs its national energy to strengthen the spiritual and social forces for unity."[4]

But Zionists debated among themselves whether such high-minded humanitarianism represented a smart substitute for political passiveness. Wisse cites Haim Hazaz's gripping story, "The Sermon" (1942), as illustrating the argument that the loss of political sovereignty spelled a national disaster. In this piece, the kibbutz philosopher Yudka denigrated Jewish political weakness in the Diaspora. "We didn't make our own history, the *goyyim* made it for us." Yudka ridiculed the notion of these Jewish intellectuals that turned suffering into a virtue:

> Jewish history is dull, uninteresting. It has no glory, no action, no heroes and conquerors, no rulers and masters of their fate, just a collection of wounded, hunted, groaning and wailing wretches, always begging for mercy. . . . I would simply forbid teaching our children Jewish history. Why the devil teach them about their ancestors' shame?[5]

For Zionists on the Left, by contrast, the creation of a Jewish state was not meant to signify an isolated political act, but to reflect a larger utopian

3. Ibid., 119.
4. Ibid., 120.
5. Ibid. Citing Hazaz, Haim. *The Sermon*. 1942.

purpose. For these more secular Jews, a Zionist state would move their people away from cultural backwardness, forge closeness with nature, and enhance the spiritual health that was chipped away by superstitious, separatist, politically passive religious leaders in the ghettos. This Zionist Left dismissed the narrowness in a vision that maintained that a Jewish state must be an end in itself. Instead, argued the Left, a Jewish state carried the responsibility of serving a higher non-parochial purpose, underscoring the universality of the Jewish mission. Martin Buber asserted:

> Our argument . . . does not concern the Jewish state. It does not concern the addition of one more trifling power structure . . . Zion restored will become the House of the Lord for all peoples and the center of the new world.[6]

Ironically, this high-minded "center of the new world" notion only ended up bringing disillusionment to Jews in the 1930s. The extent of Jewish powerlessness that was revealed in response to Hitler's onslaught showed the futility of such quixotic thinking. Lacking a home territory and self-government, Jews saw that they couldn't survive physically, that the traits that had protected them politically until this time no longer assured protection. This time the Jews failed to convince the world to accommodate them. Wisse summarized this definitive Diaspora failure: "The Jews had tried to make a virtue of adapting to foreign power in order to perpetuate their own way of life with the least interference. Instead, their deferment of power engendered unique conditions for genocide."[7]

In the modern period, liberalism has served as the Jewish political religion. Whether in the United States or in Israel, taking the liberal side was considered as more moral, more humanitarian, more in sync with the strategy of how a minority can be best accommodated and cultivate goodwill. (Accommodation, as in medieval times, continued as the Jewish political goal.) Thus, from the American perspective, the American

6. Hazony, Yoram. Citing Buber, Martin in *The Jewish State,* 101. Basic Books, 2000.

7. Wisse, Ruth.

Jewish Committee's Milton Himmelfarb teased, that Jews are the only ethnic group in the nation with the economic profile of Episcopalians, but the voting record of Puerto Ricans.

And what other American ethnic group matched Jews' "open-mindedness" in inviting the anti-Semitic, polemicist former president Jimmy Carter to berate them at Brandeis (a university under "Jewish auspices") on the "apartheid" of Israel and the responsibility of the "Jewish lobby": for the continuing terror in the Middle East?

Similarly, the intellectual foundation for the 1993 Oslo agreement where Israel became the first sovereign nation in history to arm its historic enemy, the Palestinian Authority, with the hope of gaining security, is found in the naïve universalistic vision of Shimon Peres's *The New Middle East*. Taking issue with the notion of Jewish national strength as the guarantor of security, the dream of mainstream Zionists before Israel's founding, Peres argued, "national political organizations can no longer fulfill the purpose for which they were established—that is, to furnish the fundamental needs of the nation."[8] In other words, Israel must clean up its act, before its Middle East neighbors would concede its legitimacy.

What is the source for this liberal image of good global citizenship? One would expect that those Jews who were committed to group survival, vindicated historically by the costs of weakness, would adopt a more independent-minded, self-interested political model.

The case for the Jewish tie-in with liberal forces in Europe in the wake of the tearing down of the ghetto walls was originally made pragmatically—since liberals were more receptive than entrenched elitists to the extension of rights to newly emancipated folks, including Jews, it made sense to align with them. But according to Boston psychiatrist, Kenneth Levin, who studied Jewish powerlessness, Jews failed to distinguish their particular interests from the overall liberal agenda. He claims that in order to diminish their vulnerability Jews tend to identify with more broad and powerful social groups. Their station was supposedly no different from the other fixtures in this new ethnic bandwagon.

8. Peres, Shimon. *The New Middle East*, 80. New York, 1993.

The Jews' attachment to Franklin Roosevelt illustrated such "categorical thinking," noted Levin. Considering themselves "disadvantaged," Jews felt at home in Roosevelt's New Deal coalition. Yet because of that allegiance, Jews hesitated to pressure Roosevelt to rescue their trapped co-religionists in Europe. Rabbi Stephen Wise, American Jewry's main public figure, took to task Jewish critics of Roosevelt's laggard rescue efforts. "[Roosevelt] is still our friend, even though he does not move as expeditiously as we would wish,"[9] declared Rabbi Wise. When the Republican Presidential platform criticized Roosevelt for failing to do enough to save Jews from the raging Holocaust, Rabbi Wise wrote Roosevelt expressing his shame at this "unjust" Republican accusation.

But Levin turned to psychohistory to find the bedrock source of this self-defeating Jewish relativism. The Jewish failure to assess political issues from the view of self-interest, argued Levin in his classic work on the Oslo Syndrome,[10] is a reflection of what psychologists call internalization, the process of how we adopt the attitudes of authority figures. An example of this model is how children who are abused blame themselves for their "bad" behavior.

In his review of Levin's work,[11] Hillel Halkin explained the chain of events that led from the Enlightenment to Jewish self-blame. A class of homegrown Jewish intellectuals, *maskilim*, or enlighteners, came on the scene in the late eighteenth and early nineteenth centuries in both Germany and Eastern Europe. Pro-Emancipation non-Jewish intellectuals were the role models for these Jewish thinkers.

Yet since these same European intellectuals were genuinely hostile to Judaism and its practitioners, both the *maskilim* and the large numbers of Jews who were influenced by them made this hostility their own. From here was born the ego-attacking pathology of Jewish self-blame and

9. Levin, Kenneth. "Diaspora Jews Embracing the Indictments of Their Enemies," *Jerusalem Center for Public Affairs*, jcpa.org, Feb. 1, 2007.

10. Levin, Kenneth. *The Oslo Syndrome: Delusions of a People under Siege*. Smith & Kraus, 2005.

11. Halkin, Hillel. Review of *The Oslo Syndrome: Delusions of a People under Siege*. *Commentary*, Sept. 2005.

self-denigration—a pathology Levin believes lies at the root of a great deal of Jewish politics up to and including the capitulation at Oslo.[12]

By the mid-twentieth century, the shift to American JCC (Jewish Community Center) Judaism from Synagogue Judaism furthered the shift toward liberalism. In their push to the suburbia, Jews were confused as to who they really were—a religion, a people, a culture, or a nation. Abraham J. Karp observed, "The children of the immigrants wanted to be like Gentiles, without becoming Gentiles, while the grandchildren of the immigrants want to be like Jews, without becoming real Jews."[13] Parroting the liberal values of openness and choice espoused by opinion elites, Jews felt more secure in their relationship with the larger American melting pot.

In recent years, two factors continued to cement this Jewish affinity for liberalism. Just as with the *maskilim* of yore, Jews who craved acceptance by liberal intellectualdom were forced to conform to the Left's political agenda, especially its mounting condemnation of Israel's role as a Palestinian "occupier." Jewish self-blame, especially on campus, grew as the Left cast the Arabs as victims, a downtrodden status Jews themselves held before Israel defeated Arab aggressors in the 1967 Six Day War.

In fact, the ranks of self-professed Jews who declared themselves anti-Zionists (and thus recognizable liberals) grew into a movement. Alvin Rosenfeld of the University of Indiana noted that prominent Jewish leftists on campus and in the media have singled out Israel "as a political entity unworthy of secure and sovereign existence. . . . part of a standard discourse among 'progressive' American Jews, who seem to take for granted that the historical record shows that Israel to be an aggressor state guilty of sins comparable to Hendrik Verwoerd's South Africa and Hitler's Germany."[14]

Secondly, as long as Jews saw themselves as besieged and vulnerable, they forged alliances with welfare state expansionists and secularists, failing to realize that Jewish twenty-first-century political strategies (such as

12. Levin, Kenneth. *The Oslo Syndrome: Delusions of a People under Siege*, 77.

13. Karp, Abraham J. *Haven and Home: A History of the Jews in America*, 371. Schocken, 1988.

14. Rosenfeld, Alvin. *"Progressive" Jewish Thought and the New Anti-Semitism*, 16. American Jewish Committee, 2006.

closer ties with Christian Evangelicals, or supporting faith-based government programs) need not imitate what was taken as fashionable two hundred years earlier.

Regrettably, most Jews still have not caught up with the need for creative political thinking despite the downside of the old utopianism. In Israel, the fantasy persists that the surrender of territory will pacify aggressors committed to Israel's destruction. In the United States, Jews gave scant recognition to George W. Bush, the most pro-Israel president in history. He transformed the nature of Middle East political discourse by abandoning the moral equivalence of past administrations. He specifically blamed Palestinian leadership for the terror that undermined peace and refused to even take a phone call from Yasser Arafat. Yet Jews still gave some three-quarters of their votes in 2004 to Democratic presidential candidate, John Kerry. Similarly, polls showed that Jews, more than other Americans, favored an accelerated withdrawal from Iraq. As such, they failed to see that the ensuing power void and spurring of terrorism that would follow such a retreat not only signals disaster for American interests but also for the security of Israel.

Differing from most of their co-religionists, those Jews whose identity was more shaped by religion and historical memory showed greater awareness that in the quest for Jewish security there were no permanent allegiances, no permanent opponents, and no sacred political isms. For them, recognizing these realities across the sweep of history meant that in modern times ingenuity and inventiveness represented too weak a survival strategy for the remnant of the seed of Abraham. Political finessing would not succeed against enemies actively planning Jewish destruction. The strategy must be simple and sovereign, pointing to security through strength. As stated boldly by Rabbi Joseph B. Soloveitchik, "*dam yisroel eino hefker*," Jewish blood is not for the taking.[15]

Political scientists evaluating current American electoral politics cite the "permanent political campaign," in contrast to political campaigns of

15. Soloveitchik, Rabbi Joseph B. *Kol Dodi Dofek (Listen—My Beloved Calls)*. Edited by Jeffrey R. Woolf. Translated by David Z. Gordon. Yeshiva University Press, 2006.

yesteryear, which were confined to a limited few months before the set voting date. Now, politicians continuously put forward their telegenic selves and hunt for campaign cash. Likewise, the campaign for Jewish survival must too be seen as always under way. Jewish survival requires an understanding of political institutions and the dynamics of political policy. For Jews, failing to understand how these forces are driven will prevent them from making smart decisions. For instance, it is not unusual for voters to feel that they are stuck between choosing two unappetizing candidates. Yet by having the right political analytic tools, hidden agendas, corrupt deals, and ideological shallowness can be appraised. By contrast, indifference and naiveté cause the community to lose out in optimally defending itself.

Both Jewish self-denigration and Jewish utopianism represent the same bottom line—a Jewish powerlessness that ignores the lessons of history. Wishful thinking and shutting one's collective eyes will not ameliorate the survival prospects of one of history's most consistent victims. While Jewish political self-preservation must remain the chief goal, this is not to minimize the importance of pursuing social justice and involvement in building a better country and world. This goal of good citizenship ("*Hakaret Hatov*," gratitude for the good) is traceable to the Bible. One such example is the account of Jacob sending Joseph to Nablus to inquire as to the welfare of his brothers (*Genesis* 37:14). Jacob does not confine his request only to human beings. He adds, "and the welfare of the flock and bring me back word." Why a special request about the status of the sheep? Jewish Biblical commentators interpret Jacob's inquiry into the well-being of the animals not as a business request, but as a social request. From here is derived the teaching that a Jew must enhance the welfare of any source, human or animal, from which he gains benefit.

Judged comparatively, democratic institutions have an excellent record in meeting the welfare of all their constituents, Jews and non-Jews. As the great American jurist, Learned Hand, observed in a 1932 speech to the U.S. Federal Bar Association, "Even though counting heads is not an ideal way to govern, at least it is better than breaking them."

Hopefully, a more politically seasoned Jewry will come to better understand the precarious survival mechanisms for overcoming the daunting challenges that lie ahead.

PART ONE

The University Student, 1957–1965

1

An Undergraduate's Entry into Journalism

After graduating from high school in 1957 at age fifteen, Ron Rubin was admitted into the bachelor of arts program at New York University.

"The NYU experience at first felt rather liberating, graduating as I did from Yeshiva University High School which had classes from 9 a.m.–6 p.m., including Sundays," claimed Rubin.

A political science major who often expressed his views in writing, Rubin began looking for vehicles in which to get his materials published. In May 1959, NYU's Huntington Hill Historical Society sponsored its first issue of *Historian*, " . . . to fulfill the need for an undergraduate publication of historical thought and opinion . . . to encourage historical research and examine the recorded experiences of man . . . ," with Ronald I. Rubin as editor-in-chief and "The Philosophy of the Greek and the Jew" a featured article.

As a senior in 1960, Rubin was appointed editor-in-chief of the *Heights Daily News*, the university's official daily paper. With this appointment he was assured a spot for his "political" commentary for a full year. Coming so recently from a yeshiva background, the subjects of education, religion and community—so vital to Jewish survival—remained paramount in his priorities.

In addition to the many editorials he wrote, Rubin initiated a series on "The Future of the American University." Contributors of original essays included U.S. Senator Hubert Humphrey, political theorist Russell Kirk, novelist Leslie Fiedler, and Woodrow Wilson Foundation president Hans Rosenhaupt. Rubin himself wrote the closing installment, an article by the same name as the series.

The Philosophy of the Greek and the Jew: A Comparison [*Historian*, May 1959]

A comparative study of the philosophical attitudes of both the Greek and the Jew can best be understood in terms of their appeal and their particular emphasis. Hellenism appealed primarily to man's intellect and to his appreciation of the esthetic. Hebraism, on the other hand, stressed conduct, rather than abstract philosophical meditation, and spiritual and moral righteousness, in preference to physical prowess. Although in examining their respective outlooks, we may find many incongruities, there is nonetheless inherent in both ways of life a fundamental goal—the betterment and fulfillment of man's potentialities.

In actual belief, the positive, religious tenets of the Jew and the questioning agnosticism of the Greek, were the springboards from which both cultures developed. Hebraic subjectivity was responsible for the development of a continuity in national culture and thought. Righteousness was the aim of this Hebraic life. The objectivity of the Greek resulted in various, often conflicting, shades of thought. As a prototype the beautiful Greek youth, perfect in body and mind, is representative of Greek aspiration, and the quintessence of their philosophy. The Jew dwelt on the perfection of the human heart and actions of love and morality, all inspired by knowledge of the Creator.

This difference of concept in the Greek and Jewish philosophical attitudes may be further illustrated in their mutual ideas regarding wisdom. The search for wisdom was considered by the Greek one of the significant human faculties to be developed. Rarely, however, was he definite about the nature of it. In Jewish eyes, wisdom was not an ambiguous item. Rather, it was concrete, the end of all philosophical meditation; the acquisition of wisdom was tantamount to the service of God: "The fear of the Lord, that is Wisdom." (Job 28.28)

Whereas Hebraism stressed individual behavior and obedience, Hellenism emphasized truth. It is noteworthy that the Jewish codified religion reached all the people of Israel while the Hellenistic philosophers had a relatively negligible effect upon popular thought. Hellenistic civilization was individualistic and self-centered. Foreign to this philosophy was the Jewish view of service to God and man as the paramount purpose of existence.

Another way, and perhaps an oversimplified one, of differentiating the Greek and Jewish philosophies may be to say that to the Greek, the "holiness of beauty" was the underlying idea, while to the Jew, the "beauty of holiness" took preeminence. The Jew worshipped the timeless, with unwavering belief in the prophetic statements. The religion of the Jew was the emanation of a deeply emotional and subjective people. Its stress on belief, on the human heart, and on vindication of human existence through service to one's fellow-man were the salient aspects of its teachings.

Beauty's sacredness for the Greek appealed to his artistic nature. He was an artist grasping the present, employing his reason, mind and thought. From his rational and inquiring spirit developed the Western pursuit of scientific knowledge. To the Greek, the finite (for example, the circle) was beautiful. To the Jew, the infinite was real and perfect.

All human activity, moreover, was judged and presented by the Jew in terms of religion. The Judaic appeal to the conscience, its emphasis on moral principle and divine reward and punishment, resulted in the seeking after justice. Judaism offered positive dogmas enhanced by the concept of divine revelation, while the Greek philosophers conflicted in matters of faith. Hellenism offered nothing paralleling the thorough Judaic explanation of life and historical events. In that respect, the latter was a soulless culture.

Unlike the Greeks, the Jews did not recognize that philanthropy, the love of mankind, and philosophy, the love of wisdom, were each independent and unrelated to the other. They believed that the love of man was based upon divine wisdom. In comparison with the Greek, the Jew knew what he wanted in life, and what his obligations were. Subsequently, the Jews achieved a confidence in their divine mission, and a spiritual tenacity, which the Greeks, collectively, never experienced.

Stoicism, for example, was a principal school of Greek philosophy. It stood for a Puritanism and moral ordering of life, and subscribed to the idea of a universal law of conduct. Judaism resembled it in these respects. Stoicism had a pantheistic view of God, however, and Judaism preached a transcendental monotheism. Moreover, Stoicism worshipped pagan deities. A basic difference relates to the power of man on earth. Judaic thought held that man is blessed through the grace of God, whereas Stoicism believed that man must stand by his own strength. Stoics preached that the law of conduct is found in nature and they went on to formalize this code. Diametrically opposed in view was Judaism which gave paramountcy to a revealed law that was empirical.

In a panoramic sense, the Jew was certain, and clear, about his life and the meaning of it. He was sure he had found the truth. The Greek, however, occupied himself with the quest for truth and relegated its acquisition to a lesser rank. The legacy of Hellenism was its searching out of nature, and the systematic expression of intellectual ideas. It had a creative force that produced an unequalled literature and art, an elegance and stress on physical form. Perhaps the unfortunate decadence of Hellenism resulted from its lack of definite dogma, and its eternal skepticism.

Hebraic achievement was more of an inner and spiritual one. Morality, conduct, conscience, and an established relationship between man and man, and man and God, are its highlights. The Western concept of justice stems to a significant degree from the Hebraic doctrine.

# # #

Editorial: The Sin of Omission
[*Heights Daily News*, October 25, 1960]

How liberal could a liberal education be in a curriculum which bypasses the Bible? For if a liberal education aims to enkindle an insatiable spark of curiosity in those educated, it is wrong to omit the cornerstone of our intellectual tradition. The Bible is this cornerstone, and more; it is acknowledged by the intellect in every age the Matterhorn of literature.

But the Bible "died" at the Heights three years ago with the passing of the beloved Dean Baer.

No doubt he rests uneasily with the knowledge that his colleagues are not mindful of the love he attached to it. No doubt if he walked the campus today he would lament with Jeremiah over his people forsaking the Bible for the pleasures of hi-fi recordings.

Possibly, it is only those Heightsmen who have been introduced to the Bible through their religious training who miss it here. Those who have not, can only stand in distant admiration of its spiritual splendor.

Who can pick it up once and not return again to be challenged by the power of its thought and the beauty of its metaphor? A book as unpretentious as the sun, to understand it does not require a Chaucerian competence or Elizabethan scholarship. For it can be as simple or as profound as the reader.

But we do not plead its case on spiritual grounds. We ask that it be offered by the Department of English as a work of literature.

When, for instance, Job proclaims: "The Lord gave, and the Lord hath taken a way: Blessed be the name of the Lord," Job does not only enshrine the faith of mankind. He fulfills the canons of judgment by which literature is immortalized—height, depth and breadth.

But if the spiritual and literary arguments for the scriptures do not suffice, we offer the practical. If only for the Heightsmen's enlightenment on political theory, the course of history since the Reformation, the philosophy of Spinoza, the genius of Milton, the Curriculum Committee should not commit its "sin" of omission this year.

# # #

Editorial: Season's Greetings
[*Heights Daily News*, December 20, 1960]

The candles of the Christmas tree and Menorah located on the terrace of the Gould Student Center may flood the Mall with light but it is darkening the reputation of the University.

The Christmas tree is a symbol of Christmas, the holiday celebrating the birth of the Christ child. The Menorah represents the Jewish holiday of Channukah, the festival of light.

Apparently, University officials in authorizing the display of both symbols last Friday did so with the intention of highlighting the significance of both festivals in the minds of the campus population.

Now, let us consider, for a moment, the proper significance of both religious symbols.

The Christmas tree has been related for hundreds of years with the celebration of Christmas. While clergymen may differ as to the strength of this relationship, none deny the existence of such a connection. Depending upon one's theological orientation, the relationship between tree and holiday may be either manifest or weak.

The recent secularization and commercialization of Christmas and customs of Christmas do in no way diminish the historical importance of the Christmas tree. For many, especially those without deep ritualistic convictions or background, the Christmas tree represents Christmas.

The religious significance of the Menorah, however, is beyond argument. Jews are obliged to kindle the Menorah candles in commemoration of the victory over the forces of Hellenism. It is a religious commandment, and the Menorah is thoroughly a Jewish religious symbol.

In brief, therefore, the Student Center display by the University identifies it with Christianity and Judaism. And it should be further remembered that while NYU is a "private" University, it is not private in the ordinary understanding of the word.

Ever since the University was founded in 1831, its officers have prided themselves on the non-sectarian character of NYU. This has been our hallmark and the reason for greatness.

The religious display, however, is alien to this tradition. We must not minimize the import of the display by saying, "why make a fuss over nothing." We should make no bones about the hard fact that the University, not a campus religious society, has taken upon itself the responsibility of religious indoctrination and veneration.

If NYU is true to its founding principles, it has no right to espouse either any or all religions. To acknowledge the holidays of Channukah and Christmas is for our three Heights religious societies. The function of the University is secular, not spiritual nor religious.

For the University to permit this display to stand through the holidays is to establish a grave precedent. It will not be any source of embarrassment for the University to acknowledge its error and take down the tree and Menorah.

Furthermore, we believe that this display affronts the religions represented therein. It secularizes both holidays. It is certainly a source of no religious inspiration to see both symbols in their shabby forms. And as one of the most respected rabbis in America pointed out yesterday, the display misrepresents and dishonors the faithful of both religions by giving the impression that both religions are, at this time celebrating the same festival only in different ways. He consequently objected to the display on *religious* grounds.

The News is fairly certain that the parties responsible for the display never took the time to get in touch with a clergyman of any faith and ask his opinion on the propriety of representing the sacred festivals of both religions on the terrace of the Gould Student Center.

There is one final point which we should consider in evaluating the issue. Only two years ago the Heights was embroiled in the very same controversy. At that time we did not have the advantage of experience as a guide. But in December, 1960, we did have experience on our side. Nearly everyone in the Heights Administration here then is still with us. The same holds for the classes of '61 and '62.

Why, then, did not our sober officials take this into account before authorizing this display? What benefits could have accrued to either Christianity or Judaism, if their holy days were the source of a heated debate on principles of Americanism? The people in the high places should have weighed these factors. The student body deserves such consideration.

In summation, our point is that neither University-sponsored sectarian symbols belongs in the Student Center. We do not want our contention to be misconstrued as being an argument against these religions. Indeed we value them too deeply to see them dishonored by such a display. But at the same time we value the reputation and principles of our University to stand silent while some well-intentioned officials unwittingly violate this tradition.

Their actions dishonor their intentions.

# # #

Editorial: Adolf Eichmann
[*Heights Daily News*, April 11, 1961]

Adolf Eichmann goes on trial today in a Jerusalem courtroom for "crimes against the Jewish people and crimes against humanity." The trial promises to be one of the leading news stories of the year, despite protests over Israel's authority to pass judgment on the accused.

For many, the trial will be as tormenting an experience as it is for Eichmann. These people, especially the citizens of modern-day Israel, will relive in their memories his crimes and atrocities. To stand accused for the death of one human being is frightful enough; to answer for the death—the deliberately reasoned death—of six million people is incredible.

We have all, by this time, read and reflected on the accounts of Eichmann's war activity. While we may grow impatient of reading the points of law involved in Israel's spiriting Eichmann away or Eichmann's defense of his killings, on the ground that he was executing orders, we must never forget that in our generation human life was debased to its historical nadir, that thousands, perhaps hundreds of thousands, of these deaths could have been prevented had the allies acted with humanitarian daring rather than military expedience and that education is no guarantee of civilization.

As American college students, too young to remember the demonic ardor with which Eichmann and assistants contrived the mass annihilation of Jewry, we must abandon the blasé attitude to the world about, and consider the magnitude of his atrocity. It is not in our power to rectify the ills of humanity. It is not in our power to guarantee our descendants that the spiritual heirs of Eichmann will not rise again. But if we plague our conscience with the images of babes and graybeards perishing in Eichmann's crematoria, we can faithfully affirm that the security of academia has not lulled us into the complacency of our fathers.

# # #

On the occasion of the *Heights Daily News*'s thirtieth anniversary, Rubin was honored to receive a congratulatory telegram from President John F. Kennedy as the paper's editor-in-chief. As the final semester of his senior year drew to an end, Rubin wrote his last *Heights* editorial, a biographical look back at what his role as editor meant to him. In it he writes that, "The editor of the News is the head of a society in which he alone considers himself close to the truth. . . . The editorship . . . a reproduction in miniature of the whole cycle of human emotion: jubilation and despair, exhilaration and fatigue, pride and pain." He thanks the university for the opportunity after which he shifts roles to "pay my final respects as an undergraduate to my professors, a group which represents to me the pursuit of the most profitable endeavor in life, learning."

In closing, Rubin reflects how "[i]ssue hour draws close . . . the black type meets yellow copy paper for the final time . . . the boundary line between school and college, college and the News, loses all definition. . . . There is only the memory of a period in which was experienced one's first enlightenments in the classroom and pressroom. . . . The circumstances of time and place seem completely interchangeable; one was there for many years, for an instant. All that is gone. . . . One grows old."

2

Postgraduate

In autumn of 1961, Rubin moved on to Brown University where he quickly earned his master's degree. From 1962 to 1965 he pursued a doctorate from New York University's Department of Politics, winning his degree with a dissertation focused on the role of the United States Information Agency (USIA) and the topic of public diplomacy. The dissertation, which was later expanded into a book, *The Objectives of the United States Information Agency: Controversies and Analysis* (Praeger, 1968), brought together Rubin's interest in politics with his interest in communications and journalism.

During his postgraduate studies, and especially while working on his dissertation, Rubin's pen was virtually silent in other areas. Yet two of his works during the time frame received recognition that were major coups for a young graduate student.

The first was a seventeen-page paper on "The UN Correspondent," a path-breaking work published in the December 1964 issue of *Western Political Quarterly*—one of the highest ranked, refereed scholarly journals in its field (renamed *Political Research Quarterly* in 1992). This was an almost unheard of accomplishment for a graduate student, especially one who was only twenty-two years old.

Before the paper's publication, UN correspondents were regarded exclusively as journalists. Rubin's research, which included original interviews rather than mere library research, revealed that these correspondents played an additional role . . . that of political actors in international diplomacy. Because of the historically significant and previously undocumented dimension it reveals of the UN correspondent—and the way their dispatches would so critically impact world public opinion of the Jewish state—an abridged version is included here.

The UN Correspondent
[*Western Political Quarterly*, December 1964, Abridged Version]

The United Nations ranks among the richest sources of information for the world's press. However, the UN correspondent remains one of the most neglected members of the UN "team." Yet, with the possible exception of UN field activities, the UN correspondent serves as the most direct medium between the organization and the people represented therein—the link between the "man on the street" and the diplomatic conference table. Without press reports, the nationals represented at the UN would hardly know of its work; with these reports they at least have a basis for informed judgment.

Thus far, there have appeared no scholarly studies of UN correspondents and the ways in which they serve as an instrument for public understanding of the UN[1]. This study attempts to determine how UN correspondents gather news; their sources of information; the conditions of their assignment; the techniques of their profession; their opinions of the UN; and the impact of their presence on UN diplomacy to demonstrate their importance to the political process of the UN and to suggest means by which political scientists might further explore their role.

1. Richard M. Swift, "The United Nations and Its Public," *International Organization*, Vol. 14 (Winter 1960), discusses the difficulties faced by OPI in obtaining appropriations. There have been no recent studies published on the political roles of American local or national correspondents. An illuminating study of American journalists serving abroad is Theodore E. Kruglak, *The Foreign Correspondents* (Geneva, 1955). Especially worthwhile are chapters iii (The Professional Composition of the Correspondents Corps), and viii (The Performance of the Correspondents Corps). Kruglak's study is mainly concerned with the sociological background of these correspondents inasmuch as this affects their assignments. A speech by Dr. Hernane Tavares de Sa, UN Under-Secretary for Public Information, before the UN Students Association of London University, "The United Nations Before World Public Opinion," appealing to news media to cover UN economic and social activities, indicates the high value the UN places on publicity in the popular press (UN Press Release M1409, May 15,1962).

Interviewed were 21 journalists accredited by the United Nations Correspondents Association, two Secretariat officials, and two members of the United States mission to the UN associated with press relations. Twelve represent American newspapers or wire services. The others represent newspapers and news agencies, two each for the United Kingdom and Poland, and one each for the Netherlands, Egypt, China, Ghana, and Yugoslavia. The correspondents were promised anonymity.

The United Nations and the Press

In his first annual Report, the Secretary General observed: "The success of the UN depends ultimately on the continued support of the peoples of the world, [which] in turn, must be based upon enlightened public opinion and the widest possible knowledge of the problems concerning the United Nations and the procedure used for their solution. This . . . is particularly true at times of crises. Recognition is given to this fact in almost every chapter of the Charter and great stress is laid upon public meetings and the necessity of keeping the people fully informed on all developments."[2]

The following year the world body created the Department [Office] of Public Information [OPI] concerned chiefly with the distribution of press releases and run on a basis similar to that of a commercial newspaper. In the period June 16, 1961 to June 15, 1962, the OPI issued some 3,300 releases to the UN press corps.

The United Nations Correspondents Association was organized on June 30, 1948. Its purposes:

1. To maintain and protect the freedom and prestige of . . . correspondents in all their relations with the United Nations.

2. To promote the interests of its members and facilitate their personal and professional relationships.

2. United Nations, *Report of the Secretary General to the World Organization* (A/65, June 30, 1946, Lake Success, 1946), p. 45.

3. To . . . protect the rights of bona fide correspondents to secure accreditation and unhindered access to [UN] headquarters . . . offices, and . . . facilities, without discrimination.

4. To undertake any other action, when required, on behalf of . . . correspondents accredited to the UN, either at its headquarters or any of its regional offices.

5. To facilitate social contact between its members, delegates from member nations . . . , officials of the Secretariat, and distinguished personalities connected with international affairs.[3]

The UN operates a public education program. Yet the background material it supplies serves only as a means to understanding UN news carried in private newspapers. The Secretary General, in summarizing the year July 1948–June 1949, expressed: " . . . background information without a continuous supply of news makes the United Nations seem unreal, ineffective, even divorced from current realities. . . ."[4]

The UN acknowledges the importance of the press through the facilities it provides correspondents. No national press department is comparable in size and scope and, unlike many member nations, the UN encourages coverage. It is equally hospitable to correspondents irrespective of their nationalities.[5] The UN provides a centralized news service unparalleled in the history of journalism.

3. *United Nations Correspondents Association* 1962 *Directory* (United Nations, N.Y., 1962), p. 2. The Secretary General's Report the following year noted the formation of UNCA. It added that UNCA "has proved very helpful on more than one occasion in its services both to the correspondent and to the United Nations." United Nations, *Annual Report of the Secretary General on the Work of the Organization* (A/930, Lake Success, 1949), p. 140.

4. Ibid.

5. The UN policy on press accreditation is "to encourage as many professionally qualified people from as many countries as possible to come . . . , wherever its meetings may be held, in order to write or speak about its work." The policy of the Organization permits no discrimination among representatives of information agencies on the grounds of "political or religious opinion, language, race, nationality or sex." *United Nations, Yearbook* 1947–48 (Lake Success, 1948), p. 116. The United States and the UN have negotiated "Headquarters Agreement" so that correspondents may be permitted to cover the

The Sources of United Nations News: Formal
OPI

OPI is basic to the work of every UN correspondent, especially to one-man bureaus. All use OPI information as a starting point for their own stories. In the acting OPI director's opinion of the OPI's duty: "We are not allowed to propagandize and can only counter charges with straight answers [so] we urge international civil servants to give the facts first rather than have to counter a misleading story later."

A United States correspondent warned: "You have to know what [OPI] is going to give and what it is not. OPI is not good in itself. A reporter needs an accumulated background to find the material useful," while another United States correspondent noted its impartiality: "When you work through the OPI, everyone gets it. . . . Very definitely the civil service is tight-mouthed; it's the Hammarskjold tradition to put it all through channels."

Meetings. Most UN committee meetings are open to the press to help people globally understand UN activities; however, most correspondents do not regularly attend. They have facilities in their offices for following UN meetings through an OPI loudspeaker system. One correspondent expressed a typical opinion: "I don't go to many meetings. I might listen to a specific speech but rarely . . . the entire meeting. . . . Sometimes because it is put out as a text. . . . I make use of as many short-cuts as I can. . . ."

The representatives of one-man bureaus labor under trying conditions in attempting to cover the UN. Several also serve as their nation's correspondent for the New York area or even the entire United States.

However, two correspondents found value in attending meetings because only through direct observation can they be certain of not missing "color" stories like the Khrushchev shoe-pounding scene and the riots of Lumumba supporters during the consideration of the Congo issue. One correspondent argued that a shrewd correspondent could gain invaluable

---

UN without immigration delays. This agreement grants a "special status to representatives of the press, radio, films and other information agencies." Ibid.

insights from personally attending them. "I know who is good . . . what delegates have a grasp of the issues . . . [and] delegates who are not active in meetings but who seem to have interesting positions."

Both the reading public and the UN lose out by the failure of correspondents to attend meetings regularly. The stories lack thoroughness and the UN itself suffers when public knowledge is incomplete. Stories based on unattended meetings can fail to:

1. witness significant episodes of drama and color.
2. establish continuity with the particular committees.
3. notice activities that do not get reported via the loudspeaker or official transcript, like conversations among delegates who do not have the floor and the expressions of sympathy, boredom or excitement on delegates' faces.

Absence from a meeting weakens a correspondent's story and prevents his sound understanding of future meetings of that committee.

Press Briefings. The United States and the United Kingdom sponsor daily press briefings during the General Assembly session. United States briefings are regarded by all correspondents as an important source of information with Western nations considering them the most objective. A correspondent for a Dutch newspaper voiced: " . . . The United States is involved in most major issues at the United Nations and . . . one . . . expects it to play a major role. . . . [Its] information officer will give you a good day-to-day picture." However, a radio commentator for an American network expressed the unusual opinion that "press offices and officers of the delegations were more often more confusing than enlightening. When they do facilitate the news flow . . . they often propagandize."

In the larger missions correspondents depend on the press officer rather than delegates for their official information. Two correspondents, however, noted that press officers were unwilling to comment on delicate issues. A correspondent for a Chinese news agency observed that the large missions to the UN keep "mum" on most controversial questions. An American correspondent cautioned: " . . . if you are probing, they are not willing to talk."

It is beneficial to note here that the United States mission's policy in aiding UN correspondents is for its briefings to "give the best possible story consonant with the facts." The press officer possesses a list of correspondents he feels free to contact. Names are placed on the list at the request of the correspondents themselves. These relatively few are considered the ones "really interested" in the press office's work. The chief public relations officer noted: "It's not the best practice to leak information. . . . Sometimes, we inform [correspondents] through background guidance. We keep broken confidences in mind and are less frank with them at the next meeting. Give the greatest trust to those who deserve it and the least to those who violate or abuse it."

The Sources of United Nations News: Informal

It is more difficult to evaluate the informal sources of news for UN correspondents since they are irregular and haphazard. Nevertheless, for many correspondents, the informal sources carry more interest. As the UN bureau chief of an American metropolitan newspaper put it, "It's good to have enough friends in the diplomatic corps . . . sources who will confirm or deny something; who will give you facts and not try to sell you a bill of goods."

The Delegates. UN delegates themselves are the leading informal source, the chief news source for those correspondents closely tied with their nations' UN missions; those writing interpretive stories; and those from large bureaus who use informal sources to supplement official sources.

The correspondent whose home government controls its press faces little hardship in gaining the views of his nation's representatives which can only be obtained directly from them. He devotes more of his attention to his nation's views than to others. A correspondent for a Chinese news agency commented that, "[Except] wire services, foreign correspondents are interested primarily in what their respective delegations do or in those questions relating to their delegation," and a correspondent for an Egyptian newspaper noted: "My job is to interpret the meaning of speeches and their impact on the United Nations. . . . [mainly] stories concerning my people and our region of the world. . . . I get a lot of information from my own delegation [and am] interested in the committees on which my nation serves."

The second category of correspondents, mostly from United States newspapers, includes those writing purely interpretive reports. As a prerequisite they develop an acquaintance with the factual events and formal UN sources. To evaluate political trends at the UN, they need a broad base for the scope of their stories. An American wire agency's UN bureau chief explained: "In diplomatic reporting you have more leeway than you do in other assignments." Another American specializing in analytical stories said: "I try to inform my readers why people talk and act as they do in international affairs," not just the politics in which the United States is involved. "I'm interested in determining the mood of the total membership. . . . Other correspondents are not. . . . Most reporters don't have the background for the big stories being discussed."

The third category of correspondent tracks down behind-the-scene events, or "scoops." They follow elastic and highly individualized schedules and attempt to reach representatives by "telephone, meetings, in the lounge and hallways." One such American correspondent waits in the lobby to catch diplomats after they have conferred with the Secretary General and ask them what happened at the meeting. "They usually answer in vague generalities. . . . People don't talk much after seeing the Secretary General." His assignment is " . . . hit and miss. But people probably tell me things they would not tell a stranger. I get most of my information standing around and waiting outside private meetings."

All correspondents recognized the importance of personal contact with diplomats in the informal atmosphere of the delegates' lounge, but for the two latter categories of correspondent, these contacts are indispensable and the delegates' lounge their foremost habitat. Informal exchanges are also carried out at parties, receptions, and dinners away from the UN. The relaxed settings promote easy conversation. An African correspondent called cocktail parties "a very valuable hunting ground for information. . . . to talk with someone off the cuff. At a Soviet party, I got a tip on a document to be released the next day." A bureau chief for an American wire agency expressed: "Any diplomatic assignment is only as good as your contacts. . . . You go to parties and other functions, drink with them in the lounge in the hope and on the theory that they will be of help to you later." The guest lists themselves are revealing, the presence or absence of a particular diplomat may shed light on the relationship between that diplomat's and the host's mission. (The diplomats also find this contact helpful to their UN work as will be amplified later.)

Colleagues. To all interviewed, relationships with their colleagues help them discharge of their assignments. As a Dutch correspondent expressed: "Socializing among the reporters is an important mutual source of information. . . . The help of my colleagues is indispensable. . . . two people always know more than one."

An exception concerns the opinion of correspondents from non-Communist nations about those from Communist nations. They maintained that the latter do not provide helpful advice. A correspondent for a Chinese agency remarked: "I find you cannot have political discussions with Communist reporters." A correspondent for an Egyptian newspaper said, "The [Russian reporters] are a help to no one. No one ever sees them."

The United Nations as a Journalistic Assignment

This study clarifies how the UN is a unique journalistic assignment by comparing methods used by US correspondents with journalistic techniques used in covering a foreign capital.[6]

Nature of the Assignment. What most obviously distinguishes the UN correspondent's assignment from other journalistic assignments is the compactness of the UN operation, located in several interconnected structures. No foreign capital has the press corps so centralized. This physical propinquity affords correspondents more intimacy—with both colleagues and sources—than can any other diplomatic venue.

A UN press liaison officer commented: "Coverage . . . is unique in that [the correspondents] live and work in the house. This gives them a certain intimacy, and it is sometimes hard to tell the difference between a correspondent and the delegates."

The diplomat's notions of the press are most pronounced in the press's propaganda value. An American correspondent maintained: "The United

6. Kruglak, op. cit.

Nations has a great impact on the delegations who use [it] for value in propaganda. . . . [It can] be a primary factor in enabling them to explain their position on a given issue."

The UN is a learning process for correspondents like it is for diplomats.[7] The personal insights and rewards it has brought diplomats are also accrued by correspondents who, in coming in contact in varying degrees with the policies and diplomats of some 111 nations, gain a broader perspective of the complexities of international organization. In meeting the same deadlines as other journalists, the UN correspondent more deeply appreciates the value of cooperation with his colleagues.

Conditions of the Journalistic Assignment. If a journalist is to present a clear story he must be familiar with his subject. It would appear to be helpful that UN correspondents be acquainted with the politics and work of the United Nations and related agencies and the political interests of its member nations. He presumably must possess a wider, if not more intensive, knowledge of world politics than his counterpart in a foreign capital.

In this survey, however, UN correspondents maintained that the UN assignment did not so necessitate. A correspondent for a US wire agency said, "It is more of a [UN correspondent's] personal work habits than anything else in determining how good a reporter he would be. [He] gets a lot of experience in foreign affairs, but not more . . . than he would gain abroad," and a bureau chief for an American metropolitan newspaper explained, "This is just like any other news beat, and you need some foreign affairs training."

However, the chief public relations officer of the US mission to the UN expressed a minority opinion, likening the assignment of a UN correspondent to that of a correspondent covering both the US State Department and the Congress. He noted, "The Charter and procedures are unique to the institution and there are endless ways of approaching its

7. See Chadwick F. Alger, "United Nations Participation as a Learning Experience" (Evanston: Northwestern University, 1962, ditto). Many of Alger's conclusions concerning the unique ways in which diplomacy at the UN increases mutual understanding apply to the press corps as well.

puzzling problems. . . . Most papers leave their men here because it takes a long time to become steeped; the most influential papers leave their men here a long time."

The unwillingness of most UN correspondents to distinguish their assignments from those of foreign correspondents is arresting and incompatible with their previous observations. Earlier, they noted the unique devices they employ at the United Nations—an intimacy and contiguity both among the members of the press corps and between the press and the diplomats. To take advantage of this situation, the correspondent must possess, in this author's judgment, a considerable understanding of the problems and diplomatic methods of the United Nations system. While this study did not investigate the interviewees' educational backgrounds, future exploration should to examine their views as to how their schooling trained or failed to train them for their UN assignments.

The Problems of the Journalistic Assignment. The compactness and centralization of the UN accounts for both the hardships and rewards of the UN assignment. Most of those interviewed maintained this arrangement makes the UN an easier assignment than a foreign capital; however a sharp dissent was expressed by a correspondent for a West European newspaper: "The UN is not close-knit. It's a huge thing. . . . it's much different than a day's job. A reporter has to find out the attitudes of many different countries. In covering a foreign capital, a reporter only has to concentrate on a single government."

Three correspondents compared their earlier journalistic experiences in London with their UN assignments. An African correspondent found the UN position considerably easier: "In London, the press officers and the Foreign Office gave the same dry stuff. . . . It was hard . . . to find sources. . . . A shift in government might happen overnight. . . . Here, I can write better stories. With the charter and the rules of procedure, there can hardly be big shifts. . . . you can keep a finger on the pulse."

An American wire service correspondent noted: "The Foreign Office briefings, handouts, and usually the official press and radio are the means I used to cover London. . . . There was rarely an official press release by the government. At the United Nations, official press releases are provided for all meetings. The OPI is helpful to all reporters."

A correspondent for a Yugoslavian news agency, whose experience included assignments in some forty different nations, conceded that, " . . . covering the UN is easier than most countries. [However,] London was the easiest to cover. The British traditions are helpful. . . . The British Foreign Office is very cooperative and there is a special person to get in touch with for any information one desires. Here it is not so easy; you call on the phone and might not receive any responses."

The doubling of the number of member nations has presented difficulties for UN correspondents. With the admission of each new nation, the conscientious correspondent must familiarize himself with the history and politics of yet an additional subject. With the expansion of the social and economic work of the UN, he is faced with the need to heighten his understanding of yet another undertaking and the people affected by it.

What Determines United Nations News

The UN correspondent cannot report everything because he cannot be aware of all the diplomatic maneuvering, and his newspaper is limited in the space which it devotes to such news. He must place priorities on the significance of developments[8], considering reader interest, national interest, diplomatic controversy and drama.

Non-American Correspondents at the UN. Of the nine foreign correspondents interviewed only three expressed the opinion that international rather than national interest generally governs their dispatches. To most, events were newsworthy in the proportion in which they relate to national interest. A British radio commentator noted: " . . . I cannot help giving

8. Like all newspaper reporters, the UN correspondent faces the constant problem of determining what is newsworthy. For an introductory analysis of this issue see Grant M. Hyde, *Newspaper Reporting* (New York, 1952), chapter xv, "What is News." The author notes: "There is no standard concept of news. No one has ever succeeded in writing a definition of news—in a sentence, a paragraph, or a chapter—that adequately expressed all the various considerations. Most of the attempted definitions are either too broad or too narrow. . . ." P. 178.

more exposition to the British position. The standard changes because of whom you are reporting for."

One correspondent, representing a Yugoslavian press agency, criticized those correspondents interested in UN events affecting only their home countries: "I try to cover activities most important in international affairs rather than events solely concerning my country. . . . Some African and Arab countries are only concerned with events concerning their countries."

American Correspondents at the United Nations. Coverage by United States correspondents is affected by the fact that they represent not only a member nation of the UN, but one of the great world powers whose policy has a broad impact on UN politics. Their coverage also considers the reasons people in the U.S. read newspapers, whether for education, entertainment, and/or information. The UN bureau chief of a metropolitan newspaper expressed: "People don't read newspapers to get educated and anything they learn from newspapers is incidental."

What American correspondents considered most newsworthy were the East-West power struggle, colonialism, and disunity in the UN community. Two noted that the criterion of news "salability" prevented them from adequately reporting important nonpolitical information. One said: "I don't think we cover the economic, social, and legal events adequately. But even if we did . . . , no one would be interested in using the reports. U Thant and OPI are worried about our not devoting enough attention to economic affairs. . . . [But] the resolutions are usually drawn up in . . . vague terms . . . meaningless to the public. . . ."

Similarly, a wire service bureau chief maintained: "A sad part of the UN assignment is the amount of work it does that cannot be fully reported because . . . you don't sell newspapers with stories about UNICEF or WHO."

The problem arising from the reports of American UN correspondents is the political emphasis of such information. American correspondents put weight on United States participation in the UN inasmuch as it relates to "power politics" with comparatively little information about the UN's humanitarian, economic, and social activities. A correspondent for an Egyptian newspaper argued: "No American knows what is going on in the Third Committee. . . . [All] I read in the United States press recently was that an American lady was giving a party; not any news about its accomplishments."

On the basis of reports in the American press, the reader develops a biased interest in the UN. To him, it emerges as one more instrument by which the United States carries on the cold war. When stories do appear on the nonpolitical work of the UN, they are, generally, so watered-down that they hardly add to his understanding of the organization.

Correspondents View the United Nations

The attitude of a journalist to his assignment affects the fashion in which he reports. They do not operate in a vacuum. They maintain strong beliefs concerning UN procedures and philosophy.

With respect to the purposes of the UN, correspondents' views ranged from deeply hopeful to the gravely pessimistic, the most glowing expressed by an Egyptian newspaper correspondent who had been assigned to the UN since 1949: "I have great faith in the UN. I know what it is accomplishing. In the economic, social, and humanitarian fields, the UN is accomplishing more than in the political field. As a result of being at the UN, delegates see themselves in a new fashion. . . . they must be capable in order to represent their countries. . . . The UN turns diplomats . . . into better diplomats and human beings. . . ."

"The UN," he continued, "is the only place in the world where you can get people together to understand each other."

Every correspondent interviewed sympathized with the chief purposes of the UN; however, many regretted the inability of the organization to live up to these purposes. A correspondent for a Chinese news agency responded: "My opinion of the UN has changed since I have been here. At that time, before coming to the UN, I felt that the organization could do quite a lot in political, economic, and social affairs. But now I feel there are terrific limitations on the capacities of the UN to deal with world problems. The UN could do only what its members want it to do. The UN is only an independent organization which reflects the policies of its members."

A wire service correspondent claimed: "The work of a mission here depends on the attitudes of the home government. Some missions . . . require lengthy reports to be sent back home because their governments are very concerned about what goes on here."

As for its actual political potential to strengthen peace and security, most of the correspondents commenting on this point amplified the view stated above, that the organization is limited by the notions of its members towards it. These correspondents held that since the United States and the Union of Soviet Socialist Republics are powerful nations in their own right, they depend to a lesser extent on the UN than do weaker nations. The emerging nations stand to gain most from the UN. A foreign news editor for an American newspaper noted: "The United Nations is a forum for the developing nations. . . . In a given crisis situation the UN could do very little—they can contact both sides of the dispute and the Secretary General, as a middle man, can present the most dangerous aspect and present a formula. Where super-powers are concerned, the UN can do almost nothing. . . ."

The Impact of the Press on United Nations Diplomacy

This study has thus far concentrated upon the UN correspondent as an instrument of world understanding of the United Nations. But what impact does the press corps exert on UN news? Those interviewed maintained that the press corps, collectively and individually, affects the UN. The central impact stems from the very physical presence there of the press. A correspondent for a metropolitan American newspaper observed: "Some diplomats think they could get more done privately; the press keeps them honest. This is not like ordinary diplomacy—there are too many members in the club." Similarly, a wire service correspondent noted: "If it were not for reporters at the UN, delegates might feel they were operating in a vacuum. The delegates make speeches to gain attention in the nations, not just in the committees."

The second form of impact is that of influencing opinion, both among home governments and in the minds of readers, about UN activities. The chief public relations officer of the United States mission attributed to the

UN press a powerful role in this regard: "One of the virtues of a free and diligent press is keeping government on its toes by making them operate in the light of publicity. This is bound to be the case in an institution without armies, which must pass policies through debate, talk, persuasion and sympathy. . . . It's a business of trying to generate a winning opinion. It's a tug-of-war of words; over the choice of a Secretary General, the Russians yielded just as they often yield to public opinion. This is the center of public opinion-making about the UN, and that is why the press corps is so important. That is the reason for the care which is taken in statements made in a meeting."

A wire service bureau chief noted: "The UN . . . needs the support of the people in the member nations; to do this you need an informed public opinion. The press accomplishes this. [It] brings the United Nations before the eyes of the countries' leaders. . . ."

The third respect in which UN correspondents effect UN diplomacy is through their direct, personal contact with diplomats. All have some form of contact with diplomats, but they differed over the extent which these ties influence UN diplomacy. Two from Europe argued that personal dealings between correspondents and diplomats do not affect diplomacy. A correspondent for a Yugoslavian news agency observed: "The correspondents here do not change the facts." A correspondent for a West European newspaper sought to distinguish the personal impact correspondents have on individual diplomats. He contended: "I cannot subscribe to the idea that the press corps seems to have that we are almighty. My point was proven when Kennedy tied us down in the Cuban crisis. A reporter could tell a veteran diplomat, here since 1945, nothing. But a reporter could tell a new guy something."

A contrary view was expressed by an American newspaper correspondent: "Reporters are also asked for information [in a] process of trading information. Diplomats try to get many views about the same subject. For instance a Russian diplomat asked me what I thought of Mr. Khrushchev's speech. They put it together with everything else." In his judgment, the correspondent at the UN serves as a "sounding-board. . . . One of the first things Stevenson wants to know is the reaction of the United States press."

Another American maintained that diplomats often attempt to convince correspondents in the Delegates' Lounge that their position is the correct one: "One reporter I know saved an ambassador from losing his job by changing the wire service report on what the ambassador originally said. Delegates are more interested in giving than getting news."

The arrangement which encourages effective dissemination of propaganda also serves to bring the aspects of diplomacy which are traditionally "secret" out into the public view. When diplomats wish for "secret" diplomacy, they can engage in it, but the UN press corps makes it more difficult to keep such secrets than is the case in negotiations at foreign capitals. If secret diplomacy is considered a good thing, then the press is a damned nuisance.

Through their association with diplomats, UN correspondents have been integrated into the mainstream of diplomatic life. While it remains for another study to evaluate the thinking of the diplomatic corps about the correspondents, the two OPI officials interviewed spoke highly of their skill. The Acting Director of the OPI noted: "In general, I would give [the correspondents] very plus marks on their conduct, but naturally, we have every type of newsman represented. A majority . . . are real pros. They know their business and are students of the UN and serious men."

The UN atmosphere is equally helpful for the correspondent and diplomat. Each group is vitally aware of the other's presence and looks upon the other as an aid in accompanying its assignment.

Projections

Both in scope and depth, this study seeks to introduce a new personality into political and journalistic research: the UN press correspondent.[9] The record of his relations with his assignment and his estimation of UN news and diplomacy has, heretofore, remained undocumented. This study discusses his role as an instrument for public understanding of the UN and

9. The author wishes to acknowledge the assistance of Thomas Germuska of Northwestern University in the conduct of the above interviews.

concerns itself with his professional techniques insofar as they relate to the central theme of the discussion.

The UN correspondent has achieved recognition from the Secretariat and the diplomatic staff. He deserves such recognition, likewise, from the world of scholarship. If anything, this investigation aims at presenting the UN correspondent, politically and professionally, as worthy of further systematic research. The UN correspondent himself would welcome scholarly exploration of his roles in journalism and international organization.

Further study, taking into account the results of this initial investigation, should attempt to elaborate on his professional techniques and political outlook towards the UN. The correspondent should be asked questions which give him an opportunity for personal elaboration. It would prove beneficial to evaluate him in comparison with his colleagues.

It might also be illuminating to analyze the views of correspondents along national lines, to compare their opinions with those of their national political leaders vis-a-vis their public pronouncements about the UN, to discover the extent to which correspondents representing nations allied with one another share similar or different opinions about the UN.

One should study the educational and professional backgrounds of correspondents to determine the degree of their competence to deal with UN affairs. An inexperienced journalist is a poor choice for covering this assignment, and a journalist with weak training in political reporting is not the best means to transmit information which affects the notions his readers maintain about the UN.

It would be valuable, furthermore, to examine the problems UN correspondents face in gathering news, to assess the opinions of UN diplomats on the capability of UN correspondents, and to study the techniques of correspondents in dealing with informal sources of news. Especially noteworthy would be an analysis of the methods in which correspondents cultivate these sources, and the extent to which they develop sources along national lines.

UN correspondents recognize the role the UN plays in the world today. While they interpret this role differently, their opinions often reflect a deep familiarity with the world-wide projects sponsored by the organization. Finally, it would be illuminating to learn the effect of time spent at the UN upon the evolution of one's attitude towards it. The UN is a learning experience for the correspondent as well as the diplomat.

# # #

Rubin's second coup during this period took place during his second year of graduate school in 1965. A research paper he wrote about a kosher supermarket's challenge against Massachusetts' Blue Laws, using research he had compiled during his studies at Brown University in nearby Rhode Island, won first place (and a prize of $200) in a YIVO Institute of Jewish Research's graduate student writing competition.

A Kosher Supermarket Fights the Blue Laws: *Gallagher v Crown Kosher Super* [YIVO Institute of Jewish Research Award, 1965]

The examination of the meaning of the First and Fourteenth Amendments to the Constitution of the United States of America, which provide that "no law shall be made by the Federal government or the states respecting an establishment of religion or prohibiting the free exercise thereof," is proceeding on many fronts.[1] Currently, the leading issues under debate concern the propriety of governmental aid to private schools operated by religious bodies, and Bible-reading or religious observance in the public schools.

But to the Sabbatarian, or particularly the Orthodox Jew, one of the most important of these religious issues was decided by the Supreme Court of the United States on May 29, 1961. Involved was the constitutionality of the so-called "Blue Laws," state statutes which prohibit, under penalty of fine or imprisonment, certain acts on Sunday which, if performed on any other day of the week, would be lawful. In four cases the Court handed down decisions upholding the validity of compulsory Sunday laws in

1. "Nor shall any state deprive any person of life, liberty, or property, without due process of law." *Cantwell v. Connecticut, 310 U.S. 296*, held that the Fourteenth Amendment made the legislatures of the states as incompetent as Congress to enact laws establishing a religion or prohibiting the free exercise thereof.

Maryland, Massachusetts, and Pennsylvania. Two of the cases, *McGowan v. Maryland*, and *Two Guys From Harrison-Allentown, Inc. v. McGinley*, concerned owners of highway discount department stores which were open for business seven days a week. The other two dealt with Orthodox Jewish owners of a Kosher supermarket in Springfield, Massachusetts, *Gallagher v. Crown Kosher Supermarket*, and small retail stores in Philadelphia, *Braunfeld v. Brown*.

This study will discuss the case of Crown Kosher, tracing the litigation in the Massachusetts lower courts, the Supreme Court's opinion, and conclusions which might be drawn from the Court's decision with regard to the Sabbatarian's religious liberty and economic opportunity. The author should make clear, at the outset, his general sympathy with the arguments of Crown that the Massachusetts statutes under attack[2] are unconstitutional because they establish the first day of the week as the religious day; contrary to the appellees in Crown, restrict them in the free exercise of their religion; and deny to them the equal protection of the laws.

For the Orthodox Jew, the observance of the Sabbath ranks among the cardinal religious tenets. Indeed it is "impossible" to be a truly Orthodox Jew without being a strict observer.[3] Due observance of the Sabbath requires total abstinence from business and work. Orthodox Jews may not

2. Crown attacked sections 5 and 6 of the "Massachusetts General Laws, Chapter 136, Observance of the Lord's Day." The general prohibition of work on Sunday is found in section 5: "Whoever on the Lord's day keeps open his shop, warehouse, or does any manner of labor, business or work, except works of necessity or charity, shall be punished by a fine of not more than fifty dollars."

Section 6 contains the various exemptions for activities on Sunday. Among them is the exemption that kosher butchers who observe the preceding day as their Sabbath, may be permitted to sell and deliver kosher meat between the hours of 6–10 A.M. on Sundays. In the litigations, Crown contended that this four hour exemption was unsatisfactory to its business interests. Accordingly, Crown never went to the bother of opening for business Sunday mornings. Likewise, Crown remained closed Saturday evenings following the conclusion of the Sabbath, for it was held that the travelling time for Crown's employees as well as the inconvenient early and late hours for its customers did not justify the additional few hours of business.

3. Meyer Kramer, "Is America a Christian Country?" *Tradition* (Fall, 1961), page 5.

ride in automobiles or even walk extraordinary distances on the Sabbath. During the twenty-five hours of the Sabbath, commencing at sundown Friday night and concluding shortly after sunset the following day, Orthodox Jews may neither shop nor cook. For Judaism, in proclaiming that the unity between G-D, society and man is organic, "does not distinguish between civil and ecclesiastical law, between the law of sacrifices, the law of marriage, and the law of damages . . . is but one aspect of the religious."[4]

The Crown Kosher Supermarket first opened on Aug. 18, 1953. Located at 59 Sumner Avenue, Springfield, Massachusetts, the enterprise was established by ten Orthodox Jews. While the premises were owned by Harold Chernock, who also ran the market's butcher shop, the balance of the supermarket was leased in the form of concessions. These included grocery, dairy, fruit and vegetable, and delicatessen departments. The butcher shop, which sold fresh meat and poultry, was supervised by the Chief Rabbinate of Springfield. In order for the entire Crown market to be granted the approval of Springfield's religious authorities, it was necessary that it remain closed for business on the Jewish Sabbath and Jewish holidays. For Crown to conduct business on these holy days would have meant revocation of religious sanction by Springfield's religious leaders and, as a result, the loss of the patronage of its approximately 2,000 weekly customers who came from as far as twenty-six miles to purchase kosher meat there.

According to a personal interview with Rabbi Moses D. Sheinkopf, Chief Rabbi of Springfield, the grocery concession carried some non-kosher packaged products, but 95% of its merchandise was edible by Orthodox Jews. He noted, however, that the principal "drawing-card" of the supermarket was its butcher shop. All the butchers were members of the Orthodox Jewish faith. Unlike the remaining shops of Orthodox Jews in Springfield, which were closed on both the Jewish and Christian Sabbaths, Crown's butcher business had religious overtones in that its products, from slaughter to sale, required rabbinical supervision.

4. Kramer, op. cit., page 12.

From the outset, Crown Kosher conducted business on Sundays in violation of Sections 5 and 6 or Chapter 136 of the General Laws of Massachusetts. According to Crown's testimony in the various court proceedings, its Sunday trade accounted for some one-third of its weekly gross of $15,000. In the initial legal action, Chernock was convicted by the District Court of Springfield and, subsequently, by the Superior Court of Hampden County. Thereafter, Chernock took his exceptions to the Supreme Judicial Court of Massachusetts. Chernock's exceptions were overruled in an opinion, *Commonwealth v. Chernock*, Massachusetts A.S. 1057, on November 13, 1957.

Following these proceedings, Crown took the rather unusual legal step of asking for the convening of a three-judge District Court under 28 U.S.C.S. 2284, seeking a declaratory judgment and an injunction to restrain Raymond P. Gallagher, Chief of Police of Springfield, from enforcing criminal provisions of the Massachusetts "Lord's Day Act" on the theory that the state statute violated the Federal Constitution.

At this stage, the case of Crown was attracting increasing attention, and the appeal amounted to more than the objections of an Orthodox Jewish merchant to a Bay State Sunday closing ordinance on the ground that his religious freedom was curtailed. Rabbi Sheinkopf entered the case as President of the Rabbinical Association of Massachusetts. Three of Crown's patrons also became litigants. Through the involvement of Rabbi Sheinkopf and some of Crown's customers, its attorneys sought to prove that the Rabbinate, as well as a sizable section of the community, were appealing to the Court.

The chief attorney for Crown throughout the litigation was Herbert B. Ehrman who, at the time, was President of the American Jewish Committee. In all, Crown's counsel included six law firms in Springfield and Boston, Massachusetts, and Hartford, Connecticut. Counsel attacked the Massachusetts "Blue Law" regulations on four principal counts. For one, it was held that those laws were in violation of the First and Fourteenth Amendments inasmuch as they were laws respecting the "establishment" of religion. In support of this charge, counsel cited several Massachusetts law cases in which opinions were handed down to the effect that the purpose of "Lord's Day" statutes was the protection of Christian religious worship. One such case, *Comm. v. White, 190 Mass.* 578, held that the Sunday observance statute "was originally inserted to secure the observance of the Lord's Day in accordance with the views of our ancestors, and it ever since has stood and still stands for the same purposes."

In arguing that the Sunday statutes were more in the realm of welfare than of religious ordinances, Massachusetts substantially based its case on the opinion in *Commonwealth v. Has 122 Mass.* 40:

"It (the Sunday Law) is essentially a civil regulation providing for a fixed period of rest in the business, the ordinary avocations and the amusements of the community."

Secondly, counsel for Crown claimed that the Massachusetts Sunday law was one which interfered with the free exercise of religion and, therefore, a violation of both the First and Fourteenth Amendments. Counsel did not elaborate upon this charge other than to cite the great cases in which the High Court ruled on issues of religious freedom. These references, too, will receive deeper attention in examining the High Court's action. Thirdly, it was argued that the Sunday laws constitute a deprivation of liberty and property without due process of law and are, therefore, in violation of the Fourteenth Amendment. Counsel cited the Case of *Thomas v. Collins* 323 U.S. 516, in which the Court ruled that any attempt to restrict the liberties of speech, press, religion, and assembly must be justified by "clear and present danger." Counsel asked, "In what way does the closing of this store on Sunday promote the welfare and health of the community?" Crown's attorneys went on to argue that owing to the many amendments of the Massachusetts Sunday Law, activities are permitted which made the day far from tranquil, should extra sleep or quiet be sought. Finally, it was argued that the "Blue Laws" represent a denial of equal protection of laws and, therefore, a violation of the Fourteenth Amendment. The result of the statutory exemptions in the Massachusetts law, Crown charged, is a form of discrimination against Crown in that it compels the closing of its store while permitting other stores similarly situated to remain open for business on Sundays. Accordingly, there was no "rational basis" for permitting some stores to remain open and forcing others to close.

By a vote of 2-1, the Court on May 18, 1959, held that the "Lord's Day Act" violated the Fourteenth Amendment. The majority opinion was written by Judge Calvert Magruder. Judge Peter Woodbury concurred. The opinion traced the Sunday statute back to 1653 in which the Massachusetts legislature enacted a statute compelling the community to observe the Sabbath of the dominant Christian religion. In recent times, however, the legislature, in yielding to various pressure groups, had revised the Sunday law to the extent that it almost exists an "unbelievable hodgepodge." With regard to the argument that the statute should be preserved as a health or welfare measure, the opinion noted that Massachusetts has a distinct law establishing one day of rest in seven for all employees.[5]

What Massachusetts has done in the Sunday statute, the Court held, was to furnish "special protection" to the dominant Christian sect, which celebrates Sunday as the Lord's Day, without furnishing such protection to Sabbatarians, and indeed, to the prejudice of Sabbatarians. The Crown market, it concluded, was denied the right to use its property on Sunday and was, accordingly, deprived of liberty and property without due process of law. Rabbi Sheinkopf and plaintiff customers were deprived of liberty without due process of law.

In sum, the Court's opinion was nearly a complete acceptance of the four arguments advanced by Crown. The Court held that the statute, as it existed, represented an "Establishment" of the Christian Sabbath, that it prevented the plaintiffs from enjoying the free exercise of their religion, that it violated the due process clause, and that it was a denial of their additional right under the Fourteenth Amendment to the equal protection of the law.

In his dissent, written seven months following the majority opinion, Judge William J. McCarthy denied that the Massachusetts Sunday Ordinance was unconstitutional on any of the four aforementioned grounds cited by the Court.

5. Chapter 149, section 48 of the "Massachusetts General Laws" provides that "Every employer of labor engaged in carrying on any manufacturing, mechanical or mercantile establishment or workshop in the commonwealth shall allow every person . . . employed in such manufacturing, mechanical or mercantile establishment or workshop at least twenty-four consecutive hours of rest . . . in every seven consecutive days."

In his judgment, McCarthy asserted there was "nothing" in the Constitution of Massachusetts, nor in the law under attack, which supported the Court's decision. Arguing for judicial self-restraint, McCarthy said it was an "unwarranted intrusion" for a Federal court to substitute its judgment on public policy for that of the legislature. Furthermore, to allow Sabbatarians to conduct business on Sunday would be to "disunite and divide," and to dislocate the traditional economic set-up. Finally, he chided the plaintiffs for "using a spiritual garment" to unjustly enrich themselves. McCarthy found the wish of Crown to operate its establishment the same number of days per week as Sunday-observing Christians irreconcilable with the spiritual values for which Judaism has stood. The Jewish people, he said, was seeking to become unjustly wealthy: "who have passed down through the corridors of centuries the precious spiritual values which have served as a foundation stone of respect for G-D would not for one minute support any movement where, under the cloak of religion, a one man corporation."

McCarthy's reasoning differs somewhat from the subsequent opinion of the High Court in affirming the Massachusetts "Blue Laws." He conceded the plaintiffs far less than do either the Warren or Frankfurter opinions. The two United States Supreme Court justices do not rely on the argument of judicial self-restraint to the extent that McCarthy did.

McCarthy, to be sure, arrives at his position for upholding the Sunday laws through paths similar to those followed by Warren and Frankfurter—the tradition of a day of leisure and rest associated with them by so large a portion of the community—but he is far less sympathetic to the economic deprivation suffered by Sabbatarians. Actually, McCarthy seems to accuse Crown of seeking to profit financially from the fact that the Orthodox Jewish Sabbath falls on a different day from the Christian one.

Crown, however, hardly intended to "cash in" on the Sabbatarian precepts it follows. On the contrary, it merely sought the same constitutional rights of property and liberty accorded to the dominant Christian religion.

The Court, on June 12, 1959, granted Crown the decree it had sought in litigation. It declared that Chapter 136 of the Massachusetts General Laws as amended is "unconstitutional, void, and unenforceable as applied to the plaintiffs in this action, insofar as it requires the Crown Kosher

Super Market to remain closed on Sunday after it has remained closed on the preceding Friday night and Saturday."

While the Court's verdict allowed Crown to conduct business on Sunday, Massachusetts authorities forbade a general abandonment of "Blue Law" enforcement.[6] Following the Court's decision, the religious nature of the Sunday laws was further evidenced by the nature of those who promoted and defended them. The Cardinal of the archdiocese of Boston saw the Massachusetts Court's decision as encouraging a deterioration of the spirit of Sunday observance.[7] If the amici curiae briefs filed in the Crown case were any indication of the concern organized religion had in the outcome of the case, it seems that its interest was considerable. Thus, such briefs were filed, on one side, by an association of Seventh Day Adventists, and on the other, by the Lord's Day League and the Archdiocesan Council of Catholic Men. One wonders why, for all the arguments presented by defenders of Sunday "Blue Laws" as welfare and rest measures, not a single

6. In response to a protest from a group of Cape Cod merchants over the "Blue Laws," Edward J. McCormack, Jr., Attorney General of Massachusetts, said that the Sunday statute "must be obeyed by all citizens and enforced by all officers . . . If it is felt that there are inequalities in this law, the remedy is in legislative amendments, not in nonaction by law enforcement officials." *Religious News Service,* June 6, 1960.

It is interesting to note that shortly after the decision, the Springfield Police Commission asked the city to withdraw its appeal to the High Court. Members of the Commission said they believed Crown was being discriminated against. Commissioner James S. Bulkley said, "I object to Crown being picked on when many Gentile merchants open their stores seven days a week and nothing happens." *The Springfield Globe,* June 23, 1960.

7. Discussing the lower court's decision, Richard Cardinal Cushing asked, "Do we want Sunday to become the kind of day that it is in Soviet Russia, where days of rest are opposed by governmental decree and religious activities are officially excluded from all programs of social planning?"

The Cardinal said, "It is in this direction that we are heading once we disassociate Sunday from religious significance. Once we allow business as usual on Sunday, it is but a short step to the complete secularization of the day that was once known as the Lord's Day. When this point has been reached . . . it will become easy to argue that religion itself has become obsolete." *The Pilot,* June 27, 1959.

organization concerned with community welfare filed an amici curiae brief in any of the legal proceedings.

With the setback suffered by Massachusetts in the opinion of the circuit court, the Bay State appealed to the United States Supreme Court. There are only three opinions of the High Court which discuss Sunday closing laws. In *Soon Hing v. Crowley* 113 U.S. 703, the Sunday closing (of laundries) was not involved, although the opinion indicated it would have been valid. *Hennington v. Georgia* 163 U.S. 299, merely raised the question as to whether the Sunday law conflicted with the Commerce clause of the Constitution. *Petit v. Minnesota* 177 U.S. 164, did not involve a seventh day Sabbath observer. All three cases were decided before it was held that the Fourteenth Amendment made the prohibitions of the First Amendment applicable to state statutes.

Prior to the 1961 decision, there was only one High Court case involving a seventh day Sabbath observer, *Friedman v. New York* 341 U.S. 907. Friedman, a retailer of kosher meat, was convicted of opening his store on Sunday. He appealed to the New York Court of Appeals, *New York v. Friedman* 302 N.Y. 75, and then appealed to the High Court on constitutional grounds. His appeal was dismissed per curium for "want of a substantial federal question." Nevertheless, the Friedman case differed considerably from the Crown one. For one thing, the New York law is not as apparent a religious statute as is the Massachusetts one. Nor did Friedman charge serious financial loss because of the statute. Unlike *Crown*, in *Friedman* there was no argument advanced of the unique importance of the store to the Jewish community, of the hardship on customers as a result of the inability of a kosher shop to meet their dietary needs, nor of interference with Orthodox Rabbis in the performance of their function.[8]

8. Rabbi Sheinkopf contended, in a detailed religious argument, which need not concern us here, that the lapse of an extra day from Friday, when an animal should be slaughtered, until the following Monday, hindered the Rabbinate's function of supervising food to be eaten by observers of Jewish dietary laws. If Crown were open on Sunday, he said, it would facilitate the religious requirements in transporting the meat from the slaughterhouse to the butcher shop. As it were, with the Massachusetts Sunday statute, the meat had to remain in the slaughterhouse from Friday afternoon until Monday morning.

The 56-page Brief of Appellees, Crown Super Market, Rabbi Sheinkopf, and three customers, is divided into two parts. The first is "Procedural Points," and the second, "The Lord's Day Act is a Law Respecting an Establishment of Religion or Prohibiting the Free Exercise Thereof."

The Procedural argument opens by seeking to show the interest of Rabbi Sheinkopf in the case, inasmuch as the "Lord's Day Act" prevented him from fulfilling his religious function relating to the dietary laws of Orthodox Judaism. The three customers of Crown claimed interest in the proceedings inasmuch as they contended the Massachusetts statute was a direct infringement of their religious liberties. The brief argued that the customers were at a substantial disadvantage as compared with shoppers whose Sabbath is observed on Sunday, for they can only shop five days in each week. Sunday Sabbath observers, however, may make purchases on six days of each week.

The Procedural argument concluded by introducing evidence that none of the plaintiffs was barred from maintaining the suit and the Massachusetts District Court properly exercised its equitable jurisdiction in passing on Crown's request to restrain enforcement of state statutes. Since the determination of these procedural arguments was not necessary to the disposition of the major issues of religious liberty, this study will not elaborate upon them.[9]

With regard to the second argument of the appellees, counsel attempted to prove that the "Lord's Day Act" was in violation of the "establishment" clause of the First Amendment and "due process" clause of the Fourteenth Amendment. Crown first sought to show that it was by religious tradition and contemporary Christian observance that the Massachusetts statute

9. The Commonwealth of Massachusetts submitted a comprehensive 137 page brief to the High Court. With regard to Crown's procedural argument, Massachusetts said that the state "has no intention of prosecuting any of the individual defendants for disobedience of the Sunday laws. . . . The relation of customers of the corporate plaintiff and of the Rabbi of their faith to the prosecution of the corporation or its functionaries is too remote to sustain this litigation." Furthermore, Massachusetts claimed that Crown had no standing to sue on the grounds that its religious freedom was impaired, for corporations have no "religious belief."

requiring "at least 24 hours of consecutive rest," fell on the "Lord's Day," i.e., the Christian Sabbath. Thus counsel cited recent amendments to the "Lord's Day" act, whose language was intended to stipulate not a day of civil rest but to protect Christian observance of the Sunday Sabbath.[10]

Crown then contended that certain sections of the Act are especially devoted to maintaining the Lord's Day as the Sabbath.[11] It further cited the exemptions contained in the Act as being introduced with the idea of carefully protecting Sunday Church hours.[12]

Following the examination of the Massachusetts Sunday statute, Crown turned to the history of Commonwealth cases concerning Sunday "Blue Law" enforcement. Counsel's argument here was that the previously cited *Has* case, in which the Massachusetts Supreme Judicial Court in 1877 held that the "Lord's Day Act" as merely a "civil regulation" to establish a "fixed period of rest," was at variance with the entire course of judicial opinion in Massachusetts. Among the cases cited were *Davis v. City of Somerville, 128 Mass. 594*, in which the Court held that Sunday: "should be not merely a day of rest from labor, but also a day devoted to public and private worship and to religious meditation and repose, undisturbed by secular cares or amusement."

10. Among the amendments to the Bay State's "Blue Laws" cited by Crown in support of its argument that the laws were designed to further Christian Sunday observance, is the last amendment to section 3 of chapter 136, passed in 1955, and section 4 of chapter 136, the last amendment passed in 1956. Both amendments refer to public entertainment licenses on the "Lord's Day" in keeping with the character of the day and not inconsistent, with its due observance. Counsel argued that necessity in referring to that day's special "character," as well as to its "due observance."

11. Examples cited included section 10, permitting certain parades on the "Lord's Day," but providing that music must be suspended within 200 feet of any place of worship. Also section 22 (last amendment 1928) and section 27 (last amendment 1931) forbidding the issuance of licenses for sports or games "within 1,000 feet of any regular place of worship."

12. Among the exemptions which Crown argued supported the traditional Sunday Church attendance hours are the following from section 6 of the "Lord's Day" statute; retail sale of bread before 10 A.M., transportation of general commodities by motor truck or trailer before 8 A.M., business of bootblack before 11 A.M., and the transportation of petroleum products by motor truck or trailers before 6 A.M. and after 10 P.M.

In another case, *Commonwealth v. McCarthy*, 244 *Mass*. 484, the Court, in considering the legality of the transportation and delivery of bread on Sunday, wrote: "The statute prohibiting the performance of labor, business or work, except works of necessity and charity, on Sunday, was enacted to secure respect and reverence for the Lord's day."

Crown further contended that the Sunday statute constituted a deprivation of liberty and property without due process of law, and was accordingly in violation of the Fourteenth Amendment. Accordingly, Crown questioned whether it is in the police power of the state to provide not merely for one day of rest in seven, but for a fixed day to be universally observed. There is no data, Crown argued, to justify the assertion that the welfare of the community requires all citizens to rest at the same time.

By denying Sabbatarians the right to conduct business in establishments normally not patronized by Sabbath Sunday observers, and by denying them the rights to engage in retail commercial activity which neither directly nor indirectly disturbs the community rest and neither compels those who observe the Sunday as a day of civil or religious celebration to violate the special meaning that day represents for them, does the state not, therefore, compel Sabbatarians to tacitly join in such observance against their will and to their economic disadvantage?

The High Court upheld Sunday bans on commercial activities of the two aforementioned discount shops by an 8-1 verdict. Chief Justice Warren wrote the Court's opinion. Justice Douglas dissented. The vote in the Crown and *Braunfeld* cases was 6-3 in favor of maintaining Sunday closing laws. The voting in the two cases brought by the Sabbatarians was the same, with Warren announcing the Court's judgment in which Justices Black, Clark, and Whittaker concurred. Justices Frankfurter and Harlan concurred in a separate opinion. Justices Brennan and Stewart dissented only in the two Sabbatarian cases. Justice Douglas dissented in the Sabbatarian cases in a separate opinion.

All four opinions rejected Crown's plea that the "Lord's Day Act" constitutes a violation of the due process clause and represents a denial to the plaintiffs of the equal protection of the laws. Both the Warren and Frankfurter opinions, however, conceded that the Sabbatarians had grounds to assert violation of religious freedom since the operation of the compulsory

Sunday laws hindered the observance of their own Sabbath by imposing upon them an economic hardship. Nevertheless, for reasons to be subsequently presented, six of the justices held that the statutes were constitutional even against the Sabbatarians.

The Warren opinion viewed the Crown complaint as resting on two issues: the allegation that the Massachusetts Sunday statute is unconstitutional because it is a law respecting an establishment of religion; and the allegation that the Sunday closing law prohibits appellees' free exercise of religion. With regard to the first argument in defense of the liberty of Crown, Warren said there was no question that the Sunday statutes were originally religious in origin. However that did not require that they be invalid today, if in fact, the religious purpose was no longer in effect.[13]

With regard to the second charge concerning the free exercise of religion for the plaintiff Sabbatarians, Warren referred to the *Braunfeld* decision in which those allegations were extensively considered.

In *Braunfeld*, the Chief Justice said, what was involved in the present Sabbatarian cases is not freedom to hold religious beliefs or opinions[14] but freedom to act, and such freedom, even when motivated by religious convictions, is not totally free from legislative restrictions. Thus, for exam-

13. Warren offered the following opinion with respect to the popular meaning of Sunday as a day of rest in *McGown*: "People of all religions and people with no religion regard Sunday as a time for family activity, for visiting friends and relatives, for late-sleeping, for passive and active entertainments, for dining out and the like . . . The cause is irrelevant; the fact exists."

14. The evolution of the High Court's interpretation of rights guaranteed by the First Amendment has come to mean, it seems to me, that these First Amendment rights hold a preferred position among constitutional rights. The Court has held that First Amendment rights are, indeed, "necessary to the maintenance of democratic institutions." *Thornhill v. Alabama, 310 U.S. 88.*

The Court has always imposed rigorous tests on legislation abridging First Amendment liberties. *Thomas v. Collins, 323 U.S. 516.* Thus Warren seems to shy away somewhat from previous Court rulings demanding strict safeguards of First Amendment rights in emphasizing the pre-eminence of legislative prerogative in that regard.

ple, the fact that polygamy may be a positive command of the Mormon religion does not prevent the government from declaring it illegal and making its practice criminal.[15] Similarly, the Court in the past had upheld a statute making it a crime for a girl under the age of 18 years to sell newspapers or periodicals in public, despite the fact that for a child of Jehovah's Witnesses' faith, it was her religious duty to perform this work.[16]

The freedom of religious liberty in the Sabbatarian cases, Warren argued, is merely indirect and consequential and the Court should not strike down what it found to be a welfare law merely because of this indirect burden on the exercise of religion. With respect to the alleged restriction on religious freedom, Warren said the Sunday statute did not make the holding of any religious belief criminal, nor did it force anyone to say or believe anything in conflict with his religious tenets. I agree with Warren that the religious freedom guaranteed by the First Amendment does not embrace absolute freedom to act. Furthermore, the Crown argument did not invoke the "no establishment" prohibition in support of practices deemed unconstitutional, such as the aforecited polygamy or child labor acts. Any attempt to restrict the liberties of Crown, must be justified by: "clear public interest, threatened not doubtfully or remotely, but by clear and present danger."[17]

The Frankfurter opinion is more comprehensive than the three remaining opinions. In reasoning characteristic of his judicial opinions, Frankfurter lays emphasis on the thesis of the limitation of absolute rights. He traces Sunday legislation from the time of the 1448 statute of Henry VI until the cases at the bar. He argues that, historically, Sunday statues have passed into the realm of civil ordinances. He discusses the value of maintaining such welfare laws and the atmosphere of communal rest and leisure associated with those laws.

15. *Reynolds v. United States*, 98 U.S. 145.

16. *Prince v. Massachusetts*, 321 U.S. 158.

17. *Thomas v. Collins*, 323 U.S.516, 530. See also *West Virginia State Board of Education v. Barnette*, 319 U.S. 624, 639.

Perhaps the strongest argument advanced by Frankfurter for upholding the Massachusetts laws is the practical difficulty which would arise in enforcing alternative days of rest. Accordingly: "employers who wished to avail themselves of the exception would have to employ only their co-religionists, and there might be introduced into private employment practices an element of religious differentiation which a legislature could regard as undesirable."

I sympathize with Frankfurter in the above difficulties he sees in indiscriminate days of rest. I agree with him over the threat and undesirability of making the state inquirers into religious conviction. The possibility of hiring employees on the basis of religious affiliation should such exemption be permitted, is, to me, equally dangerous. I do not see any persuasive answers to any of the practical difficulties cited by Frankfurter. Yet, in my judgment, the undesirable results of hiring by religious rather than personal qualification, and the introduction of the state into the private affairs of religious conscience, should Sabbatarian exemption be legislated, do not apply in the case under consideration. Crown did not attack the "Blue Laws" in general nor did it ask for the disestablishment of such weekly, state-enforced days of rest. Crown was simply arguing that it should be allowed the right to conduct business on Sunday. It did not argue on behalf of all Sabbatarians. Its contention concerned itself, and only its business.

With respect to the introduction of religious examination into hiring procedures, all the employers of Crown were Orthodox Jews. It was also not a situation of the possibility of such employment disrupting families, for the employer and employees all observed Saturday as their day of rest. Moreover, as concerned the danger of state investigation into the honesty of Crown's religious observance, such establishments, under the supervision of the Orthodox Rabbinate, are not allowed to conduct business on the Jewish Sabbath. Presumably, with the intervention of Rabbi Sheinkopf in the litigation, Crown's religious motivations for keeping closed on Saturday are unquestionable. In other words, Crown did not shut down Saturday and ask to open on Sunday to be placed at an unfair competitive advantage with Christian enterprisers. It had no choice but to be closed Saturday.

Frankfurter goes on to deal with the Crown argument that because of the complete irrationality of the inclusions and exclusions, the Massachusetts Sunday Laws constitute a deprivation of liberty and property without due process of law and a denial of the equal protection of the laws in violation of the Fourteenth Amendment.

In the author's judgement, Frankfurter's sophisticated interpretation of the Sunday exemptions uses reason to defend what are essentially unreasonable enactments. That enforcement of these laws is substantially in the hands of the authorities of the individual communities, serves to weaken further any arguments for their universal rationale.[18] While an intricate examination of the individual statutes is not relevant to the broader theses of this study, the author feels that many of the exemptions are capricious and, perhaps, silly. For the police to be arbitrary in their enforcement of these laws, the latter should be clearer and more systematic.

With respect to the dissenting opinions, the Brennan-Stewart opinion, authored by Justice Brennan, was based on the ground that the statutes unconstitutionally infringed upon the religious liberty of the Sabbatarians. Acknowledging that the Sunday laws were, in fact, social welfare statutes, they contended, nevertheless, that they unnecessarily infringed upon the constitutional rights of persons who observe a day other than Sunday as their day of rest.

The Brennan opinion held that the First Amendment, as embodied in the Fourteenth, stresses personal liberty above collective goals. Brennan criticized what he believed was the Court's action in holding that: "any substantial state interest will justify encroachments on religious practices, at least if those encroachments are cloaked in the guise of some non-religious public purpose . . .

18. One example of the capricious enforcement of the Sunday statute is the case of two Bay State District Courts rendering opposite verdicts for identical alleged offenses by automatic laundry service dealers. In Malden, Mass., a judge ruled in favor of a Seventh Day Adventist laundry shop owner on the ground that the shop was a "secular business" whose operation on Sunday does not violate any law. At Fitchburg, Mass., however, three similar offenders were found guilty in District Court and fined $25 each. *Religious News Service,* February 11, 1960.

" . . . their (the laws') effect is that the appellants may not simultaneously practice their religion and their trade, without being hampered by a substantial competitive disadvantage."

Brennan described the Court's view of the difficulties which would characterize Sabbatarian exemptions as "more fanciful than real." The Court's anticipation of inquiries into religious faith, in the event of the institution of Sabbitarian exemption, is:

"no more an infringement of religious freedom than the requirement imposed by the Court itself, that a plaintiff show that his good faith religious beliefs are hampered before he acquires standing to attack a statute under the Free-Exercise Clause of the First Amendment."

In sum, Brennan favored upholding Crown's position chiefly for the reason that the administrative convenience of state-wide day of rest laws does not justify the economic disadvantage suffered by Sabbatarians. He disagrees with the theses presented by Warren and Frankfurter that the "Lord's Day Act" is not a violation of First Amendment religious freedoms for the simple reason that Sunday statutes do not make criminal any act which is, in itself, prohibited by Judaism or other religions. Brennan regards the indirect encroachments of Sunday laws on Sabbatarian religious freedom as a substantial violation of Sabbatarian First Amendment rights.

The Douglas dissent, in the author's opinion, is the most eloquent of the four opinions. Douglas rejects the Sunday statutes on broader grounds than the Brennan dissent. Douglas considers the Massachusetts statute as representing an "establishment" of religion as well as a prohibition of the free exercise thereof.

Douglas views the fundamental question as whether or not the state can impose criminal sanctions on those who, unlike the Christian majority, practice a different religion. To bring across his opinions, Douglas uses stronger language than that of his three colleagues.

"I do not see how a State can make protesting citizens refrain from doing innocent acts on Sunday because the doing of those acts offends sentiments of their Christian neighbors."

In another reference, Douglas argues:

"It is a strange Bill of Rights that makes it possible for the dominant religious group to bring the minority to heel because the minority, in the doing of acts which intrinsically are wholesome and not anti-social, does not defer to the majority's religious beliefs."

I feel that while Douglas rejects the legality of the application of the "Lord's Day Act" to Crown on the broadest and most fundamental ground, the "establishment" clause, he should have answered the social welfare arguments of Warren and Frankfurter. It seems to me that the Douglas argument is weaker than the Brennan one. Douglas rests his case on the theory that the "Lord's Day Act" is intended to protect the Christian Sabbath and therefore a violation of the religious liberty of Sabbatarians.

But if a case can be put forth for the civil rather than religious goals of the Sunday law, Douglas' case does not hold. Surely, the Warren argument would lose its strength if Warren had conceded the contemporary religious motivation of the Massachusetts law. His argument denies the religious element of the Sunday laws, and, in addition, sees merit in them as social welfare measures.

Yet in devoting his opinion to the importance of freedom of religion as guaranteed by the First Amendment, sacred rights with which, indeed, all of the justices would agree, Douglas, to my mind, does not address the central argument posed in the majority and concurring opinions. That argument is: the Sunday laws are welfare statutes which should be upheld for their merits; by not forcing Sabbatarians to observe another religion's doctrine, these statutes do not violate their religious liberty; the maintenance of a communal weekly day of rest is a more desirable end than the granting to Sabbatarians the right to conduct business on that day; and, finally, such exemptions for Sabbatarians would raise problems of administration, religious hiring provisions, and state inquiry into religious belief.

Accordingly, in challenging the "Lord's Day Act" on the basis of religious "establishment," Douglas finds an evil not shared in the minds of the remaining eight justices. Employing the same line of reasoning as in the "establishment" argument, Douglas also finds the "Blue Laws," due to the economic disadvantage under which it places Crown, to constitute a violation of "free exercise of religion."

Again, I feel, he fails to answer the core of the Court's case: that on the scale of constitutional values, the balance swings in favor of the existing Sunday laws as opposed to the Sabbatarian arguments for revision.

In conclusion, with reference to the Douglas opinion, I find that in dealing with the disputable promise that the "Lord's Day Act" represents a joining of church and state, Douglas deals with only a single point of contention in the Crown case. I do not feel, as counsel for Crown contended, that the support of the Massachusetts legislature for the Christian creed vis-a-vis the "Lord's Day Act" is a clear, indisputable act. Indeed as a result of the trend in recent years for the enactment of social welfare legislation, it seems that a reasonable case can be made for the civil nature of what had once been religious ordinances. In granting Warren and Frankfurter their points that the "Lord's Day Act" is a civil regulation, and challenging it subsequently on a First Amendment argument, the Brennan-Stewart dissent stands on more solid ground.

As regards both dissenting opinions, I believe, on the strength of Crown's allegations of infringements of its Fourteenth Amendment freedoms, they left something to be desired. I believe Crown's arguments in opposition to the "Lord's Day Act" on the grounds of Fourteenth Amendment rights are, indeed, weightier than its claim to First Amendment freedoms. I regret that both dissenting opinions did not answer the Warren and Frankfurter opinions in that regard.

Conclusion

The Crown case holds constitutional, political and religious significance.

To many committed to the principle of religious liberty and the separation of church and state, the Supreme Court decision constitutes a decisive setback. Nevertheless, considerable progress in constitutional attacks on Sunday laws has been made in the past decade. The fundamental arguments presented in the Crown case were similar to those presented in the *Friedman* case ten years ago. At that time, the Court deemed these grounds so lacking in merit as not to warrant oral argument. In the Crown case, however, not only did the Court grant oral argument, but one third of the Court sympathized with the Sabbatarians.

Furthermore, the Court's opinion in the 1961 Sabbatarian cases, marked a return to the *Everson* (1947) and *McCollum* (1948) interpretations of the First Amendment. In both cases, the Court interpreted the First Amendment as barring all aid to religion, even non-preferential aid, and as erecting a wall of separation between Church and State.

In *Zorach* (1952), however, Douglas, in his opinion for the majority, asserted that "We are a religious people whose institutions pre-suppose a Supreme Being." This sentence has since then been frequently cited to justify government action in religious affairs for the purpose of aiding religion and has, in addition, been often quoted as overruling the Everson-McCollum interpretations.

Politically, Massachusetts Governor John A. Volpe, shortly following the Supreme Court decision, appointed a 20-member "Governor's Committee to study Sunday Legislation." Professor Arthur E. Sutherland of the Harvard Law School headed the committee. Other members of the committee included representatives of Catholic, Jewish, and Protestant groups, business and labor officials, and civic leaders.[19]

The Sutherland Committee came up with three different reports to the Governor. A majority report received the backing of ten members, a minority report received the support of nine members, and labor's representative on the committee issued a third report, which differed little from the majority report.

All three reports agreed to the need for changing Massachusetts' Sunday ordinances. The differences rested on the degree of suggested change. Whereas the majority draft would "tidy up" the "Lord's Day Act" but would maintain the theory that work and play are prohibited on Sunday unless

19. In reaction to the High Court decision, the newspaper of the Boston Archdiocese urged the Bay State legislature to appoint a "carefully selected committee to review the Sunday laws as they exist in Massachusetts and to bring them into line with contemporary needs while preserving the traditional respect for the Sabbath." Here, too, Roman Catholic officials seem to find the Sunday statute synonymous with a Christian Sunday protection law. *The Pilot*, June 3, 1961.

specifically allowed, the minority would have work and play allowed, with some exceptions.

As regards the majority body's reference to the legality of kosher super markets, such as Crown, to conduct business on Sunday, it would be permissible under the revised Sunday statute. All three parties of the Governor's committee would, in the future, permit Sabbatarians commercial exemptions of Sunday.

The Massachusetts legislature is expected to enact new Sunday legislation in the current term incorporating recommendations of the respective reports. Had Crown not contested the Bay State's "Blue Laws" before the United States Supreme Court, and attracted national attention to those laws, it is doubtful that the laws would be liberalized at all.

The Crown Kosher Super Market is currently closed Saturday as well as Sunday. Rabbi Sheinkopf told the author that Crown is doing less business than it did when it operated on a six-day-week basis.

According to another Springfield rabbi, Rabbi Norman Lamm, the Jewish community during the litigation looked upon Crown as a "local boy making good" with regard to the fight for religious liberty for Orthodox Jews. Having discussed the constitutional and political implications of the Crown case, this study will conclude by evaluating the future of Orthodox Jews with respect to "Blue Laws."

If the majority of Jews in the United States had not given up Sabbath observance as a fact, and, in many cases, as an ideal, the reasoning for Sabbatarian exemptions would be much more persuasive. Since the majority of American Jews are not Orthodox, Christian Americans form their opinions of Jewish observance on the basis of the image that the non-Orthodox present to the community. The majority of American Jews have, in fact, accepted Sunday as their day of rest and recreation. Saturday has become to many of them the leading business day of the week. Accordingly, how should Christians know that there are Jews making substantial economic sacrifices to observe Saturday as the Sabbath?

Therefore, it seems that the first step that Orthodox Jews must take to obtain Sabbatarian exemption from Sunday closing laws is an educational campaign of the existence of a considerable number, although a minority, of Jews who keep the seventh day of the week as the Sabbath.

Secondly, Orthodox Jews, and for that matter other Sabbatarians such as Seventh Day Adventists, Seventh Day Baptists, and Jehovah's Witnesses, should make clear that their goals are freedom of worship, not disestablishment. Orthodox Jews do not endorse the concept of abolishing Sunday closing laws; their sole interest is an exemption for Sabbath observers. The concern of business, labor, and civic groups with the growing number of discount and chain stores which are open Sunday, and have a competitive advantage over businesses closed on Sunday, is legitimate. Both Supreme Court majority opinions as well as the majority report of the Sutherland Committee stressed this fear over the question of turning Sunday closings into an economic battlefield. Subsequently, if Orthodox Jews are to secure Sunday exemptions, they should emphasize to the Christian majority that they do not challenge the concept of "Blue Laws" as they apply to Christians. This point must be made clear to Christian clergymen, and the Roman Catholic Church in particular.[20]

In sum, the campaign for exemption from Sunday closing laws is a challenge to Orthodox Jewry on behalf of its adherents "who keep the Sabbath from profaning it."

20. The hardships in securing legislative enactment of exemption from "Blue Laws" for Sabbatarians is illustrated by the 1958 experience in the New York State Assembly. The bill for such exemptions was defeated because of inadequate support from the Jewish community, the opposition of the Roman Catholic Church *(The New York Times, March 19, 1958)*, and wrong emphasis in justifying the bill. The general Jewish community seemed unenthusiastic for the bill. Since the Assemblyman who introduced the bill, Sidney Asch, sought that such exemption be authorized on a local option rather than state-wide basis, the bill took on the meaning, in the eyes of advocates and opponents alike, as being a "Jewish Bill," designed to allow Jewish merchants in New York City, in particular, the right to engage in business on Sunday, should they observe the Saturday before as their Sabbath.

Leo Pfeffer, director of the Commission of Law and Social Action of the American Jewish Congress, and chief Attorney for the Synagogue Council of America in its amici curiae brief submitted in the Crown case, told the author, in a personal interview, however, that unlike the New York situation, he "expects" the Massachusetts legislature to relax that state's law inasmuch as it affects Sabbatarians. As was the case with Rabbi Sheinkopf, Mr. Pfeffer declined to predict the extent of such exemption.

Bibliography

Books
Leo Pfeffer, *Church, State and Freedom*, (Boston, 1953).
Articles
Meyer Kramer, "Is America a Christian Country," *Tradition* (Fall, 1961)
Journals
United States Law Week, May 29, 1961
Newspapers
The New York Times
The Pilot
The Springfield Globe

PART TWO

A Young Professor in a Young School, 1965–1969

3

Politically Speaking

With his "career" as a student ending, Rubin quickly moved out into the real world of political science, spending time in 1965 as a legislative assistant for United States Representative Jonathan B. Bingham (NY 23rd CD), one of Israel's main champions. During that time he carried out research on legislative-executive relations of the United States Information Agency (USIA), later published as a paper in London's *Parliamentary Affairs* in 1967.

In September 1965, Dr. Ronald I. Rubin joined the faculty of the six-month-old Borough of Manhattan Community College (BMCC) of the City University of New York (CUNY). At the time the college's full program for 500 students was housed in rented quarters on the second and third floors of the American Management Association Building, one block from Radio City Music Hall. (Today, after almost fifty years, Dr. Rubin is BMCC's most senior faculty member and the college enrolls some 20,000 students housed in a structure as long as the Empire State building measured lying on its side.)

For the next few years, Dr. Rubin's prolific writing had two major foci. The first dealt with topics clearly connected with his new role as a political science professor: communications and public opinion, U.S. politics, U.S. foreign policy, and the United Nations. The second dealt with subjects directly related to Judaism and the global Jewish community. From the materials that deal with the first focus, only those that present concepts that, according to Rubin, have the potential to impact world opinion, American policy, and international relations in ways that would greatly affect the Jewish world are included or discussed herein.

Propaganda
[*Commonweal*, May 1966, Abridged version]
Book Review: *Propaganda* by Jacques Ellul

Propaganda, by whatever name it is called, grows in importance as a political phenomenon, both domestically and internationally. Yet we publicly refuse to acknowledge its pivotal role.

Propaganda by Ellul is valuable not only for dispelling our euphemisms for propaganda, but for highlighting its omnipresence. Ellul considers propaganda an indispensable condition for technical progress. He argues that since intellectuals feel compelled to have opinions on all matters of public import, they fall prey to opinions offered them by propaganda, many of which are unverifiable. For the masses, propaganda is needed because they must feel they are participating in the political affairs of the state. Ellul, however, considers the judgment of the masses so variable and fluctuating that the government could never base a course of action on it. Still, a democracy cannot act without the masses, so, what can it do?

"The democratic state, precisely because it believes in the expression of public opinion, must channel and shape that opinion if it wants to be realistic and not follow an ideological dream."

Central to Ellul's thesis is the paradox that the more individualistic society allegedly becomes, the greater is the usage of propaganda and thought control. Propaganda in certain societies (Soviet and Chinese) helps make man's condition more acceptable to him.

Ellul suggests that people recognize the extreme effectiveness of the weapon used against them and be cognizant of their own frailty and vulnerability instead of being soothed by illusions of security.

This is a masterful work; its importance will undoubtedly grow with the passage of time, as its prophetic forebodings are borne out.

# # #

The Persistence of American Isolationism
[*Pakistan Horizon*, July 1966]

Among the significant intellectual byproducts of the American military commitment in South Vietnam is the resurgence of isolationist thought as a leading theme in American foreign relations. While educators, clergymen and authors were in the forefront of American internationalism following World War II, many in these groups now question American military aims in South Vietnam as well as the mutual defence treaties pledging American assistance to scores of other nations.

In view of the popularity of isolationist notions in United States intellectual circles today, it would prove instructive examining the ideological framework of America's most recent major isolationist period: the era between the two World Wars. The role which these isolationists wanted the United States to play in world affairs between the two World Wars does not sharply differ from the notions expressed by isolationists in the 1960's. Indeed, the features which made isolationism a viable and persistent doctrine in American foreign relations between the two World Wars characterize the outlook of those Americans now crusading for an about-face in America's military commitment in South Vietnam.

Despite the new international order which followed the First World War, twentieth century American isolationists reached the same conclusions as they had a century earlier. American foreign policy in the 1920's and through the late 1930's represented a retreat to traditional isolationism, not in the sense of complete withdrawal from world affairs but of refusal to make any political commitments infringing the nation's freedom of action. Isolationists were prepared to use their moral influence in promoting world peace, and in expanding United States economic interests throughout the globe. American policy during this period reflected an increasing emphasis on moral and ethical concepts which ignored the political responsibilities inherent in America's global position.

The twentieth century isolationists argued that Europe was a source of war and militarism. World War I veterans and parents who had never known military service shrank from the thought that they or their sons might be slain on foreign battle fields for issues seemingly remote. The new isolationists insisted that Europe was a source of hatreds, wars, duplicities, and alliances.

In the 1920's, the world had still seemed reasonably safe for democracy. Fascism had not yet become a formidable threat, and communism lacked the militant international force that it would later acquire. President

Coolidge had been able to maintain that American foreign policy could best be described by one word—"peace." Similarly, President Hoover defended the refusal of the United States to consider alliances or any commitment to sanction: It was a belief that somewhere, somehow, there must be an abiding place for law and a sanctuary for civilization.[1]

The isolationist attitude received its most carefully reasoned support, perhaps, from the philosopher John Dewey. He affirmed his sympathy for the idea of cooperation except on its own terms. The League of Nations, he held, was mainly a device whereby Britain and France hoped to secure the cooperation of the United States in maintaining their own hegemony. Dewey criticized the League because it was a League of government and not of peoples, because it was tied up with the inequities of the Treaty of Versailles, and because it contained no effective solution of the "war-breeding issues" of Europe. Dewey believed that America should continue her policy of aloofness until the liberal parties of European countries brought their foreign offices under the control of democratic principles.[2]

Other Americans, oftentime extreme nationalists, espoused isolationism because they distrusted foreigners. Some Americans were chronic British haters. Many new Americans coming from Ireland and Germany were staunch isolationists as well as Anglophobes. These isolationists had little in common other than an innate antipathy for anything English. Senator Robert La Follette's attack on American intervention in World War I on the side of the Allies is typical of the pro-German, anti-English tone of isolationist sentiment. La Follette called Britain:

> a hereditary monarchy . . . with a hereditary landed system, with a limited and restricted suffrage for one class and a multiplied suffrage power for another, and with grinding industrial conditions for all wage workers.

In sharp contrast, La Follette argued the Germans were a nationality who:

1. Herbert Hoover, *The Memoirs of Herbert Hoover: The Cabinet and the Presidency*, New York, 1952, pp. 377–378.

2. John Dewey, *Intelligence in the Moslem World*, New York, 1939, p. 590.

> wherever they have lived have left a record of courage, loyalty, honesty, and high ideals second to no people which have inhabited the earth since the dawn of history.[3]

Even among anti-British isolationists of German and Irish stock, kinship with the land of origin was often not sufficient to overcome loathing for Adolf Hitler. Yet these groups still composed the hard core of isolationist support. It is noteworthy that Americans of these ancestries intensely fought against United States membership of the World Court. Father Coughlin made a last minute appeal to "Keep America safe for Americans. . . . and not the hunting ground for international plutocrats." His broadcast was responsible for a deluge of anti-Court letters and telegrams which swamped the offices of wavering senators. The distinctive anti-English bias in the new isolationism persisted in the United States through its entry in World War II.

Many Americans influential in supporting social and economic domestic reform in this period similarly supported isolationism. The liberal isolationists justified their opposition to intervention by arguing that it stifled reform at home. They also applied an economic interpretation to World War I which reduced it to a war incited by munitions manufacturers and greedy businessmen. In the thirties, there were potent additional factors creating a fear of entanglement. The liberal of the thirties saw the discouraging spectacle of China and Japan locked in a seemingly interminable war in the Far East. The Prime Ministers in England and France were Chamberlain and Daladier, both conservatives. Many liberals believed the foreign policies of these two administrations were motivated by a desire to preserve fascist Germany as a buffer against the Soviet Union. The Munich appeasement of Hitler in 1938 fortified liberal suspicions of Chamberlain and Daladier. Above all, the liberal of the late thirties' was pushed toward isolationism by the deep-seated disillusionment with Wilsonianism.

3. Eric F. Goldman, *Rendezvous With Destiny: A History of Modern American Reform*, New York, 1952, p. 218.

The chief fount of inspiration for liberal Progressive attacks on internationalism was Senator La Follette. Denouncing proposals to involve the United States in the affairs of Europe between the two World Wars, La Follette argued these schemes would require us to surrender:

> our right to control our own destiny as a Nation . . . to emasculate, if not destroy, our form of government by recognizing the right of some assembly or council of nations, in which we have small voice, to interfere with our most vital concerns.[4]

The enthusiasm with which liberals supported isolationism reached a climax in 1934 with hearings conducted by Senator Gerald P. Nye in the Senate Munitions Investigating Committee. Senator Nye presented a documented thesis that executives in the munitions industry and bankers eager to float international loans dragged the United States into the First World War. Disillusioned by the sacrifices and results of the war, by the failure of Wilsonian idealism to draw favour in Europe, and holding bankers in low esteem in those post-depression years, the public readily endorsed Nye's interpretation. If this facile analysis of the events of 1914–17 was accepted, the way to avoid future wars seemed self-evident. According to Foster Rhea Dulles, the effects of the Nye Committee were so far-reaching that:

> . . . seldom has the popular reading—or misreading of history had a more important effect on the making of foreign policy; and the inaccuracy of the lesson drawn from the experience of 1917 was paralleled by the want of logic in its application.[5]

Charles A. Beard, the leading reform historian of the day, broadened the findings of the Nye Committee into a widely followed liberal interpretation. Beard rarely used the term "isolationist". Instead, he preferred

4. Belle Case and Fola La Follette, *Robert M. La Follette,* New York, 1953, II, 993.

5. Foster Rhea Dulles, *America's Rise to World Power,* 1898–1954, New York, 1954, p. 114.

to think of himself as a "continentalist." By this he meant a concentration of interest by the United States, on the continental domain and on building here a civilization in many respects peculiar to American life and the potentials of the American heritage.[6] Beard rejected the accusation that his theory would hinder international cooperation. He argued that, on the contrary, it would encourage it. In Beard's judgment, cooperation could be most fully realized which nations put their own houses in order and organize their economies so that exchange could be carried out on a basis of mutual benefit. The United States, Beard believed, could follow a policy of continentalism principally because wars in Europe and Asia did not endanger the nation.

Beard's isolationism, however, foresaw the United States eschewing trade wars and abandoning both economic imperialism and dollar diplomacy abroad. These arguments ran counter to the thinking of American businessmen wishing to maintain American economic influence beyond the nation's continental borders. They could hardly agree with Beard that the American Government should:

> surrender forever the imbecilic belief that it was her duty to defend every dollar invested everywhere and every acquisitive merchant seeking his private interests everywhere.[7]

During the same period, Walter Lippmann, another liberal with a considerable following, was classifying the United States as "for all practical purposes an island."[8] Lippmann pointed out that if wars had to be fought, they could be conducted at a safe distance from America's homes, churches, hospitals, and schools.

Closely allied to this fortress concept of security was the reasoning advanced by the America First Committee. Presided over by Robert E. Wood, Chairman of the Board of Sears Roebuck and Company, its leadership included such diverse figures as Colonel Charles A. Lindbergh,

6. Charles A. Beard, A *Foreign Policy for America*, New York, 1940, pp. 32–33.
7. Charles A. Beard, *The Open Door at Home*, New York, 1934, pp. 318–319.
8. Walter Lippmann, "Weapon of Freedom", *Life*, IX, 28 October 1940, p. 56.

Senator Burton Wheeler of Montana, and William L. Hutchinson, Vice-President of the American Federation of Labor. The America First Committee expressed its belief in an isolationism based on power and preparedness in the original announcement of its principles. These principles were:

1. The United States must construct an impregnable defence for continental America.

2. A prepared America could successfully resist attacks by a single foreign Power or a group of foreign Powers.

3. American democracy can be preserved only by keeping out of the European war.

With its emphasis on force, the arguments of the America First Committee were the antitheses of pacifism and liberal isolationism. Although Midwestern Progressives were represented on the America First Committee, they did not constitute the dominant element in the membership. Its principal supporters were businessmen who did not feel obliged to disguise their appeal to individualistic nationalism with idealistic declarations. There were strange bedfellows in the ranks of America Firsters. Among its membership were Anglophobes, Roosevelt-haters, anti-Semites, Coughlinites, and fascists. Never accepted by the America First Committee but piously anti-interventionist until June 1941 when Germany invaded Soviet Russia were the Communists.[9]

The Committee to Defend America by Aiding the Allies was the leading organization urging all possible assistance for victims of Nazi aggression. Like the America First Committee, the interventionist group's membership reflected highly varying points of view. The Committee campaigned ardently and effectively in behalf of the destroyer-naval base agreement, Lend-Lease, and repeal of the neutrality laws.[10]

Following the Nazi cessation of the "Phony War", the proponents of American isolationism were losing popular support. Once Hitler had

9. Wayne S. Cole, *America First: The Battle Against Intervention 1940–41*, Madison, 1953.

10. Walter Johnson, *The Battle Against Isolation*, Chicago, 1944.

conquered Western Europe and the Battle of Britain had begun, American isolationism, liberal or conservative, was "collapsing."[11] The country reacted to President Roosevelt's proposal for Lend-Lease as he wanted. Indicative of the shift away from isolationism in the liberal camp was the editorial stand of the *New Republic*. Following the Versailles negotiations and through the Battle of France, the magazine remained isolationist. Now with the Congressional debate on Lend-Lease, the *New Republic* declared:

> The collapse of France and the danger of possible British defeat suddenly brought home to all sensible Americans the fact that the peril was much greater and more imminent that we had previously believed it could be. We do not see how anyone with eyes in his head can dispute the fact that Hitler is a menace to this country and that, to this extent, England's battle is our own . . . The editors of the *New Republic* . . . are willing to admit that they may be wrong; but they feel that when the existence of the country is at stake, it is better to be sure than sorry.[12]

Meanwhile, the governmental machinery was being overhauled to meet the new demands. The extent of the American commitment against the Axis was illustrated in the Battle of the Atlantic. President Roosevelt felt sufficiently sure of his ground to warn his radio audience on 27 May 1941, "Our Bunker Hill of tomorrow may be several thousand miles from Boston."[13] This statement by Roosevelt is decisive, for he tempered whatever sympathy he might have had for the Allies as Hitler's victories mounted with the understanding that American public opinion was sharply divided over American interventionism. Roosevelt would tell his aide Sam Rosenman in this regard: "It's a terrible thing to look over your shoulder when you are trying to lead—and to find no one there".[14]

11. Goldman, op. cit.; p. 293.

12. Ibid., p. 295.

13. Samuel Rosenman, ed., *The Public Papers and Addresses of Franklin D. Roosevelt, 1941*, New York, 1943, pp. 187–90.

14. Samuel Rosenman, *Working with Roosevelt*, New York, 1952, p. 167.

By the Fall of 1941, Roosevelt grew increasingly restive with Axis sinking of American ships. Roosevelt felt that American public opinion was behind him. He protested to a leader of the Anglophobes:

> When will you Irishmen ever get over hating England? Remember that if England goes down, Ireland goes down too.[15]

The attack on Pearl Harbour drove home with compelling force the lesson being so laboriously learned from the rising conflict with Germany in the Atlantic. Its tremendous emotional impact united the country in the realization that the United States was part of a world community with which its own destiny was inextricably bound.

The characteristics of American isolationism between two World Wars are still evident in today's criticisms of America's military role in South Vietnam. The most appealing quality of both isolationisms is their utopianism. The isolationists of the 1930's looked back to a happier world where a fortress America could enunciate Monroe Doctrines and declarations against entangling alliances. Similarly, contemporary critics of America's Vietnamese policy find their beliefs frustrated regarding the ideal conduct of foreign relations. Their utopianism is reflected in the wistful freedom songs of the civil rights movement as well as in their confidence in legal institutions (United Nations pronouncements) for preserving peace.

Another consistent quality of both isolationisms, similar to the desire to avoid trouble with foreign nations, was the wish to steer clear of war. For many Americans in the 1930's and the 1960's isolationism represents nothing more than isolation from war. Isolationists in both periods conceived of war and militarism as immoral roads for national advancement. In this sense, isolationists are at variance with the traditional American attitude toward war. While the United States has had her share of prominent pacifists, she has had more than her share of militarists who have proclaimed the psychological, moral and material benefits of war.

15. Elliot Roosevelt, ed., *F. D. R., His Personal Letters 1928–1945*, New York, 1950, p. 1159.

The ultimate impact of isolationist thought will not be fully realized until the conclusion of the Vietnamese war. The success of isolationism may cause a re-examination of collective security as the means by which the United States could best uphold the national interest in a nuclear age. Nevertheless, it should be stressed that today's isolationist attraction is deeply rooted in American history—an attraction with a political and sentimental following.

###

The June 1967 *Saturday Review* included *State and the System*, Rubin's review of *Anatomy of the State Department* by Smith Simpson. As did the country's renewed interest in isolationism, the State Department's weaknesses surely impacted America's role in the Middle East. "Essentially," Rubin writes, "[Simpson] argues, a combination of obstacles, internal and political, block State from meeting the challenges of modern diplomacy."

"Ten years ago," the review continues, "Simpson's book would have found its way to nothing more volatile than a supplementary list for a college course in American foreign policy. Since the price of State's short-sightedness is greater now than ever before, the book is recommended reading for informed Americans."

Rubin continued the theme of *State and the System* with *USIA—The Muffled Voice* [*Columbia Journalism Review*, July 1967], here addressing the United States Information Agency's inability to successfully reach foreign audiences.

Rubin also wrote three articles addressing Middle East issues during this period. The first reviewed Hernane Taveres de Sa's book, *The Play within the Play: The Inside Story of the UN* [*The Annals of The American Academy*, November 1967], in which the inability to resolve the Suez crisis is one of many criticisms leveled at the UN. The second and third follow:

###

The Politics of the Aswan Dam; A Reappraisal: I
[*Jewish Frontier Magazine*, June 1968]

Humiliated militarily and crippled economically, there is little to offset Egypt's woes other than the prospects of the Aswan High Dam. But like many of the other substitutes for reality Gamal Abdel Nasser has managed to sell his people, Aswan embodies a pipe dream for progress. When completed at a cost of $1 billion in 1969, Aswan will rank among the most expensive—and self-defeating—hydroelectric projects in history.

From the perspective of Middle East power patterns, however, Aswan will be far more than a dam controlling Egypt's water needs. Before generating any electric current, Aswan set off a series of diplomatic convulsions. On one level, the dispute over Aswan's financing brought on the 1956 Suez War—the conflict, which even today, as Hugh Thomas puts it (Suez, Harper & Row, 1967), is "left in a curious no man's land of time; too painful, too close to be reached effectively by the heavy artillery of history; but also a little too far for the snipers of contemporary politics and journalism."

On another level, Aswan is the watershed in which the Cold War is taken into Africa by the Soviet Union. As for Nasser, Aswan marked the apex of his bargaining and bluffing diplomacy. Finally, many of the American State Department's ambivalent attitudes toward Nasser—in which he has been seen at one time or another as enlightened reformer, "poor sport" or Communist "stooge"—took shape in the crisis over financing Aswan. In view of these factors, a reappraisal of the politics of Aswan today is in order.

In the mid-1950's, Egypt ranked—as it does today—as one of the poorest nations in the world. Of its 23 million inhabitants, ninety percent lived in poverty; over seventy-five percent were illiterate and less than half the children of primary school age attended school. Half the population suffered from contagious diseases, and its birth and mortality rates were among the world's highest. Physically, Egypt included 386,000 square miles with its population concentrated into an area of about 13,900 square miles in the narrow Nile Valley. Population density was among the highest in the world.

To the average informed Egyptian the building of Sadd el-Aali, as Aswan is known, represented a panacea of sorts. All hopes for the nation's overcoming its complex economic problems and historic deprivations rested on Aswan. To be sure, the Nasser government encouraged this all-encompassing optimism in making the dam symbolic of future development.

Before treating the economics or politics of Aswan, let us turn to the proposed dam and region in their technical settings. The Nile is the second largest river in the world. Despite the Nile's size, it has not treated Egyptian agriculture altogether favorably. From August to January, the flood period, the overflow of the Nile vastly exceeds the amount necessary for irrigation, and from February to July, the low stage, the river's discharge is inadequate for irrigation.

Aswan will eliminate four main problems in completely controlling the Nile: annual storage to meet normal demand; reduction in losses from the present flow; "century storage" which will increase the amount of water by building up in good years at the source of the river a supply which could be drawn upon in poor years; protection from high floods.

The new dam will rise 365 feet above the surface of the river. Located about 400 miles up the Nile from Cairo, near the site of the present miniature Aswan Dam (built by the British in 1902), it will be over three miles long—the largest dam in the world—as well as create the largest man-made lake in the world. Aswan's reservoir will have a storage capacity of 130 billion cubic meters. The dam will make 1.3 million acres of Egyptian land cultivable. (It is relevant that this gain in crop lands will be wiped out by Egypt's 2.7 percent annual growth in population since the start of Aswan in 1960.)

Aswan will provide a system of perennial irrigation in an area of 670,000 acres previously irrigated by the basin method and producing only one crop a year. In addition, Aswan will generate 6,000 million kwh of power per year, with an almost equal reserve for future development. (At its construction peak, 35,000 Egyptians and 18,000 Soviet technicians worked on the dam.)

In the abstract, these statistics on Aswan's immenseness are not very revealing. Physical setting must be related to political culture: is the nation equipped to carry through a development scheme without damaging its economy? In relative terms, will Aswan really send Egyptian production soaring? What is the dam's regional impact? Each of these answers regarding Aswan holds large doses of the negative.

The political birth of Aswan stems from the Egyptian revolution of 1952. The revolution marked the overthrow of King Farouk and the old order.

As with most power shifts in the underdeveloped world, the revolution's genesis did not come from the oppressed fellahin (peasants) but from a group of army officers headed by General Mohammed Naguib. These revolutionaries originated essentially from the Moslem middle-class—an element from which Nasser drew his chief support—and saw the demise of Faroukian feudalism as a sign of broader opportunity for themselves.

Notwithstanding Aswan's intended role in coping with Egypt's arrested economic development, the revolutionaries saw the dam as a conspicuous gesture to spur enthusiasm for the "popular" revolution. Together with Machiavelli, they well understood that the purpose of politics is to preserve an increase political power itself, and the barometer by which the politician is judged is his success in doing this. Aswan would be a permanent reminder to the grandstands of the revolution.

By early 1956, however, the original liberation movement had dissolved. Nasser succeeded Naguib in an election in which he was the only candidate and headed the only political party. Nasser received 99.8% of the vote. The Revolutionary Council no longer existed as such, but was absorbed into Nasser's Cabinet. The Cabinet functioned in form rather than actual authority. Nasser, then thirty-eight and a clever nationalist, was the man of the hour.

While Nasser in his economic and social reform undertakings was not as daring as he was subsequently given credit or censure for, he attached much weight to constructing Aswan. It highlighted his Egyptian development effort.

Aswan was also seen by Nasser as a ready means to thwart the "imperialistic" powers from frustrating Egyptian industrialization. Always sensitive to the rituals of international propaganda, Nasser emphasized Aswan as a prestige symbol in championing Pan-Arabism—the creation of an Arab empire extending from the Atlantic to the Indian Ocean.

Previous to his foreign campaigning for Aswan, Nasser hoped that his original land reform proposals would be enough to encourage the large Egyptian landowners to invest in industry. Instead they turned to real estate. When Nasser, in turn, established rent controls to drive them out of real estate, they put their money in stocks. When Nasser levied controls on the stock market, they responded with a flight of capital from

Egypt. Accordingly, Nasser well understood that he was not to win assistance in financing Aswan on the basis of the soundness of the Egyptian economy—and would be forced to turn elsewhere for help.

In addition to problems at home, Nasser had to resolve the physical issue relating to the distribution of the Nile's waters. Geography had made certain of Egypt's neighboring nations similarly dependent upon the Nile for survival. Egypt's immediate obstacle here was Sudan.

Until granted full independence in January, 1956, the Sudan was an Anglo-Egyptian condominium. Egypt, for decades in the early 20th century, had been anxious and suspicious over the possibility of British holding the threat of "water politics" over its head in the Nile Valley. The Egyptian fear, in this regard, was seemingly not well-based, for in the Nile Waters Agreement of 1929 (in which Sudan had no part) Britain showed enormous concern for Egypt's fundamental water-needs. Under this agreement, Egypt was guaranteed ninety-eight percent of the flow of the Nile during the period from December to July. It was not until some twenty-five years afterwards, however, that the Sudanese government denounced the treaty (in October, 1955) on the ground that it ignored the future agricultural and industrial needs of the Sudan.

While Egypt for a quarter of a century prior to the overthrow of Farouk had agitated for amalgamation with Sudan, the ouster of Farouk by the revolutionaries marked a considerable shift in the British attitude to the desirability of Sudanese independence. Since Farouk was deposed, the Egyptian government could no longer make the claim that the King of Egypt was the King of Sudan. As a result, Naguib went on to drop the argument for the unity of Egypt and Sudan. On October 22, 1952, the British Foreign Secretary, Sir Anthony Eden, announced (to Parliament) governmental consent to action by the Governor-General to bring the Sudanese self-government statute into force. Throughout the Egyptian campaign for amalgamation with Sudan, Eden urged Sudanese independence. He opposed Egyptian schemes to "bounce" the Sudan into a union not to its liking. He wanted the Sudanese themselves to decide their future.

Friction between Egypt and Sudan is crucial when considering the fact that no plan providing for the use of the Nile's waters for irrigation would be workable unless agreement would be reached between the two nations. Thus, it is well to assess the sharp objections by the Sudanese to the Aswan plan as formulated by the World Bank and Egypt.

By 1955, the Sudanese had grown more demanding in what they considered to be their justifiable Nile rights. Under the previously cited 1929 agreement, Sudan was entitled to four billion cubic meters annually and Egypt to 48 billion cubic meters. Yet Sudan, at the time of the Aswan negotiations, could point to a population of twelve million, one-half that of Egypt's. It therefore considered itself deserving of one-half the amount of the Nile waters which Egypt received. She also insisted that the large evaporation losses should be absorbed out of Egypt's allotted share of the river, and announced its intentions to absorb similar losses from any storage constructed for the benefit of the Sudanese. Furthermore, Sudan wanted a commitment from the World Bank and Egypt as to the future use she would have of the Nile even before work on Aswan started. Finally, the Sudanese argued that Egypt must bear the entire cost of providing the alternative livelihood and transfer of the 50,000 people of the Sudanese town and district of Wadi Halfa to some other part of the Sudan before the water level at Halfa would be raised by the proposed High Aswan reservoir.

Supporting their case, the Sudanese cited a report of the Economic and Social Council of the United Nations entitled "Water Development in Africa." The study stressed the Sudan's need to develop further irrigation with water from the Nile. According to the report, further expansion of the great increase in prosperity in the Sudan which had occurred in the past thirty years would be limited by the amount of water and capital available. (The leading Sudanese commodity, cotton for export, was developed chiefly on irrigated land.) The report went on to praise the Sudanese record in eking out a living from a relatively inhospitable environment.

Irrespective of Aswan's impact on the Egyptian economy and the East-West power struggle, our first conclusion, then, is that the dam would not have been to the benefit of all concerned. As conceived in 1956, Aswan was scarcely in the spirit of regional development. (In 1959, before the Soviet Union started putting up Aswan, agreement was finally reached between Egypt and Sudan. Egypt agreed to pay 15 million English pounds to Sudan for evacuating the population of Wadi Halfa. Sudan was also to receive 15 percent of the Nile waters. While designed to spur Egyptian progress, the dam would have simultaneously deterred Sudanese development. From the perspective of equilibrium in the volatile Middle East, the high dam at Aswan was in 1956 of questionable merit.

Was the Egyptian economy able to cope with a project as formidable as Aswan? In 1956, land reform was glaringly unsuccessful (although as Nasser's dictatorship became more entrenched, by the late 1960's much progress had been made). Following the overthrow of Farouk, one of the first undertakings of the Junta, in September 1952, was to issue the Land Reform Act breaking up Egypt's large estates. Four years later, however, two-thirds of the total land was still owned by six percent of the population. When the decree was issued, the Junta promised to redistribute between 3–4,000,000 acres among landless peasants. But as of 1956, only about 200,000 acres were so distributed. In the judgment of outside foreign aid experts this shortcoming was significant for it bore on Egypt's capacity—or incapacity—to redistribute future land should the Aswan Dam reach fruition and many millions of irrigable acres become available.

Another feature of the Egyptian economy was a pell-mell recklessness in committing limited resources to costly development projects. For instance, in 1953, Egypt announced a development budget of LE 993,000,000 including LE 470,000,000 for the Aswan Dam. But by March 31, 1955, it had actually spent only LE 32 million. The 1955–56 budget for new social and economic development was LE 77,000,000, all of it dependent on sources other than the normal revenues of the country.

In the late 1955 issues of the government-controlled press, schemes cropped up almost daily suggesting new factories to produce cement, fertilizer, jute, porcelain, paper and many other projects. One United States official added up all the proposals appearing in the local papers in a three-week period in 1956 and found that the total exceeded the entire amount budgeted for economic development by the Egyptian government in a full year.

In the face of warnings by the World Bank (which will be subsequently treated) that rigid economic development is essential to successful financing of the Aswan Dam, Nasser had boosted military expenditures in the current fiscal year to twenty-seven percent of his annual budget. Egypt had budgeted upwards of $216 million a year on its military establishment—or about $10 a year per capita in a nation where the per capita income was, according to Nasser himself, $67.20. (The most recent defense budget prior to the 1956 nationalization of the Suez Canal represented an increase of about one-third over the defense budget of the prior two fiscal years which were LE 53 million.) In addition, Egypt had mortgaged a major chunk of its cotton crop for an indefinite period to the Communist bloc in return for arms. This barter deal appreciably swelled, in Western eyes, the gamble of Nasser's repaying whatever funds would be loaned him for Aswan. Accordingly, Nasser's announced $250 million arms deal with Czechoslovakia indicated mounting Egyptian political and economic dependence upon the Soviet bloc.

Meanwhile Egypt's trade pattern, beginning in 1953, was markedly shifting from West to East. In that year, total exports to the Soviet bloc were valued at $48.2 million; imports at $38.6 million. In 1954, exports to the Soviet bloc were valued at $56.3 million; imports were $29.6 million. In 1955, exports to the Soviet bloc rose to 106.1 million and imports, 38.5 million. According to statistics of the International Monetary Fund, nearly twenty-eight percent of Egypt's exports were headed for Soviet bloc countries and Communist China. In return these nations supplied only eleven percent of Egypt's import needs. For more than sixty-five percent of its imports, Egypt still relied upon the West.

Hence, two conclusions emerge from this review of Egypt's internal and external economics: increasing dependence upon the Soviet Union in matters of trade; and enormous Egyptian expenditures on military equipment while at the same time sponsoring capricious "development" programs completely out of line with the realities of its precarious economic position.

Nevertheless, Aswan was paramount among the diffuse Egyptian modernization plans. Nasser first proposed the dam to Eugene R. Black, president of the World Bank, in 1953. Black reacted coolly, replying, "The Bank is not a handout business." However, in 1954–55, the Bank had experts make a five-month detailed study of Aswan's capabilities. The judgment of the Bank was set forth in two documents never publicly released: a report entitled "The Economic Development of Egypt," which was sent to the Egyptian government in August, 1955, and a "Preliminary Technical Report," dated February 28, 1955.

Most striking is the conclusion that the construction of the High Dam at Aswan would impose upon Egypt's people a decade and a half of rigid austerity and in the end give them a standard of living no higher than the pitiful one on which they barely subsided. The best which could be expected from the mammoth project, according to the report, was that it will "at least prevent a disastrous deterioration" in living standards and give the country a "breathing spell which will provide an opportunity for broadening the industrial base of the country." While the Bank expressed doubt over the ability of Egypt's ruling Junta to manage the nation's economy with sufficient skill to prevent any Aswan High Dam investment from crushing Egypt's stability, it was willing to stake $200 million on the project.

Black personally doubted Egypt's capacity to carry out the Aswan project. In a memorandum to the Bank's directors, dated October 21, 1955, Black argued that Egyptian development commitments over the next decade would heavily tax Egyptian economic flexibility. He noted a proliferation of agencies in Egypt charged with development programs and little over-all planning and direction on their part. Supporting his reservations, Black cited the previously announced ambitious schemes involving substantial expenditures on railways, municipal improvements, industrial projects, cultural developments, port works, health, housing, and schools.

In view of the World Bank's objections, Nasser's campaign to finance Aswan with Western assistance did not receive serious attention until his arms pact with the Communist bloc. Indeed, Western diplomats were so surprised at Nasser's daring that they lacked any concerted plan to counter Communist penetration.

# # #

The Politics of the Aswan Dam; A Reappraisal: II
[*Jewish Frontier Magazine*, July–Aug. 1968]

Coupled with the problem of the new Egyptian alliance with the Communist world was Israel's contention that the delivery of Communist arms to Egypt threatened her security. Israel asked the Eisenhower Administration for arms totaling $65 million to offset the Egyptian "build-up." It is interesting to note here, regarding Arab-Israeli military competition, that Nasser signed his arms pact with the Communist bloc despite the fact that the Eisenhower Administration from the outset was relatively consistent in toning down two prominent aspects of America's Middle East policy stressed by the Truman Administration: out-and-out diplomatic and economic support of Israel, and solicitude for British and French interests in the Arab world.

While the new policy of the Eisenhower Administration in the Middle East would result, perhaps, in increased American diplomatic neutrality in that area, it did not, however, satisfy Nasser's quest for arms. The United States on many occasions in 1955 announced its intentions to steer clear of an Arab-Israeli arms race. But Nasser's difficulties in obtaining arms from the West—at one time or another he sought to obtain such equipment from the United States, Britain, France, Sweden, India, Spain, Belgium, and Germany—were traceable in no small part to his capacity for antagonizing all of them at the same time. Had he acted more judiciously, he might have managed to do business with at least one of the Western nations. But it seemed that the Soviet Union was the only power which would tolerate or gamble on his simultaneous aspirations: the shelving of the Baghdad Pact, increasing his prestige among the Bandung nations as leader of the anti-colonial movement, increasing Egypt's foreign trade, and the "showdown" with Israel.

The immediate Western reaction to the arms deal was Dulles's dispatch of George Allen, Assistant Secretary of State, to Cairo. The Allen mission is one of the mysteries of the Aswan episode. In fact, William Wynn, a biographer of Nasser, contends that Allen himself was ignorant of the nature of his mission. According to Wynn, when Allen reached Cairo, he spent long aimless hours awaiting instructions from Dulles. The instructions were never forthcoming. Allen met Nasser, had talks with a few more people, and meekly went home. He had accomplished nothing. Wynn writes, "The Allen mission convinced the Arabs that Nasser had brought the West to its knees."

By mid-December, 1955, the State Department had come to realize the sharp coup the Soviet Union had scored in the Middle East in supplying Egypt with arms. New rumors also loomed that the Soviet Union was interested in financing Aswan. If Communist influence continued mushrooming at this rate—and with Nasser's strident propaganda machine boasting of the soon-to-be-received arms—Washington feared that its Middle East presence would grow steadily irrelevant.

Chiefly through Washington's initiative, the United States and the United Kingdom announced on December 17, 1955, that they were assisting the Aswan project. By then, the World Bank determined that the dam would cost $1,350,000,000. This figure represented an increase in $650,000,000 over the figure first presented to the Bank in 1953. Of the total final amount, Egypt was expected to spend $550,000,000, mainly in its own currency; $400,000,000 by private investors; and $400,000,000 in foreign currency. Of the total foreign grants, the Bank offered a loan of $200,000,000 at five percent interest over a forty-year period. The United States was to provide a grant of $56,000,000 and Great Britain, $14,000,000. The Western allies also agreed to give sympathetic consideration to subsequent grants and loans totaling $130,000,000.

In assessing the Western offer, it cannot be sufficiently stressed that none of the prerequisites laid down by the Bank in earlier negotiations—agreement with the Sudan over the distribution of the Nile waters and over the resettlement of the 50,000 people to be displaced by the inundation of the Sudanese town of Wadi Halfa, and various guarantees as to the future stability of the Egyptian economy—were met by Egypt when the Anglo-American decision to back the plan was announced. The Western aid announcement simply ignored incontrovertible financial facts. If panic were an excuse for diplomatic "hanky-panky," then the aid offer would have been appropriate.

From the outset, the British were cool to the high dam. But they nonetheless tagged along as a weak-sister partner of the United States. Technically, the British preferred a regional system of watershed control encompassing, along with Egypt, all countries of the Upper Nile Valley—Sudan, Kenya, Ethiopia, and Tanganyika (today Tanzania). There was more, however, than disagreement over the physical dimensions of Aswan dividing Anglo-American Middle Eastern policy. Previous to the Egypt-Communist arms pact, the most serious point of dispute between the United States and Britain was the latter's displeasure with American shyness towards the Baghdad Pact. On the one hand, Secretary of State Dulles insisted that a "northern tier" of defense was needed to contain Communism but, on the other, the United States refused to join such a security arrangement. According to Anthony Eden, the United States, having played a major role in creating the Baghdad Pact, was morally bound to join. In his memoirs, Eden called the United States a "borrower and lender in diplomacy" on the strength of America's remaining aloof from the Baghdad Pact. (As for the Arab-Israeli dispute as a factor in dissuading the United States from joining, Eden argued, "no alliance to which we were a part could be described as being against Israel.")

Moreover, the British were irritated with what the United States regarded to be the soundest policy in the amalgamation dispute between Egypt and the Sudan. Eden writes that Britain "continued to be urged" by the United States to recognize Farouk as the monarch of the Sudan. "I reported that we could not yield on the Sudan." According to Sherman Adams, Eisenhower's Special Assistant, the British feared that the President himself "did not grasp the gravity of their predicament." In the wake of the Egyptian-Communist arms agreement, Adams saw the British as spoiling for direct action to keep Nasser in line and, thereby, to protect the Suez Canal and Western Europe's oil supply.

To be sure, John Robinson Beal, Dulles's biographer, acknowledges that the Western offer was a "crash response" by the standard of democratic procedure. Apparently, the offer was designed to persuade Nasser to cancel his arms pact with the Communist world before the weapons would begin arriving in substantial quantities. Basically, the United States wanted Nasser to decide between Aswan and a militaristic pro-Communist course.

In fairness to Dulles, however, his diplomacy in the early stages of Aswan must be credited with consistency. American support for Aswan went deeper than merely beating out incipient Communist advances in the Middle East. Ever since the Farouk overthrow, United States policy towards Egypt was based on the tentative judgment that the military junta was influenced more by genuine desire to improve the people's lot than on lust for personal power. (This factor, tending to discount militarism as a dominant theme of Egyptian foreign policy, marked the State Department's thinking down to the June, 1967, Six-Day War.) As such, Aswan appealed as a worthy investment. Furthermore, even prior to the arms deal, the Administration saw Aswan as a sound mutual-security project that would win Arab backing for the West and keep oil moving through placid Suez waters, the Persian Gulf, and the Eastern Mediterranean. At first, therefore, the Egyptian arms pact strengthened Dulles's conviction that Western willingness to finance Aswan was of high strategic value.

Despite Dulles's good intentions, Nasser saw matters differently. Indicative of Egyptian appreciation of the Western offer was the reaction of Radio Cairo to Eisenhower's State of the Union message. Nasser's radio station called the President's words "hollow" in respect to the courageous "peace campaign" upon which the Soviet Union had embarked. Nasser also objected to requirements laid down by the Bank in agreeing to assist in the project. He told American Ambassador Byroade he feared the Bank would "dictate" Egyptian finances. Nasser called the Western pledge insufficient; he maintained the right to negotiate contracts for the dam as well as the right to delay an agreement with Sudan over sharing the Nile's waters.

Meanwhile, rumors of generous Soviet offers to counter the Western ones on Aswan continued to circulate. There are no authoritative reports, however, of the Soviet Union ever having tendered Nasser a formal aid pledge in this period. There were only hints of such overtures and Nasser encouraged such speculation. As the early months of 1956 passed, it became apparent that Egypt's neutralism had steadily changed to stronger bonds with the Soviet Union and hostility towards the West. The spectacle of Nasser about to win help from the United States on one project, almost as costly as America's entire foreign aid expenditures for 1956, exasperated allies as well as neutrals. Iraq complained to Eden that the Egyptians had done better out of the West by bullying them than they had by cooperating, and Eden sympathized with the Iraqi disgruntlement.

By the spring of 1956, Nasser's tactics became increasingly belligerent. He chose to undercut administrations in Arab countries friendly to the

West and substitute administrations more disposed to him. In Libya, the Egyptian military attaché was expelled for seeking to weaken the authority of the king and install pro-Nasser officials. In Jordan, joint Egyptian-Saudi Arabian pressure produced plots against the king. They succeeded in persuading Jordan to steer clear of the Baghdad Pact, in removing Brigadier General John Glubb Pasha as commander of the British-financed Arab Legion, and considerably weakening British standing in that country. In Iraq, Egyptian intrigues and attempted assassinations again resulted in the recall of the Egyptian military attaché. In Sudan, subversion was intense, here aided by an inflated staff of the Soviet mission. The "Voice of the Arabs" from Cairo blared out hatred to the West and the "lackeys of imperialism."

Nasser's belligerency towards the West was consummated in Egypt's withdrawal of diplomatic recognition of Formosa [called Taiwan since 1945] on May 16 and the subsequent recognition of Communist China. Egypt's lead was followed by Syria and Yemen with significant repercussions in Lebanon and Jordan. Nasser's diplomatic shift on this bellwether issue was decisive in convincing the West to see him more vindictively. His recognition of Communist China was the final stroke in upsetting the British assumption that it was more advantageous than otherwise that Nasser remain at the Egyptian helm. It was on this assumption that Nasser's government could fairly easily be toppled that the British acted for the balance of 1956, including the Suez episode. Dulles, likewise, saw the move without any economic or substantive motive for Egypt—a "petulant" one revealing how far Nasser had departed from his original goal of rebuilding Egypt for the benefit of its people.

Cold-war tension over financing Aswan mounted the following month with the visit of the Soviet Foreign Minister, Dimitli [sic] Shepilov, to Cairo. Nasser was impressed with Shepilov, for the Soviet Union, in his eyes, was defending the Arabs against Western intrigues. Realistically, Nasser sensed that he did not run any serious risk of being subsequently embarrassed over financing Aswan as long as Shepilov restricted his public utterances to vague assurances of friendship.

To Dulles—forever the moralist—Shepilov's visit marked the last insult the United States would suffer from Nasser. He must demonstrate to allies and to neutrals that the United States could not in the future be made a fool of in the sense Nasser had done. By now, however, the Senate had lost patience with Dulles's vacillating Middle Eastern policy. The Senate Appropriations Committee, on July 16, took the unusual—and unconstitutional—step of passing a resolution ordering the Administration to spend no Mutual Security funds on Aswan. Dulles saw this move as attacking his integrity, for he had earlier assured the Committee that no such funds would be granted without first consulting it.

Now an element of high comedy enters the scene. The day following the Senate Appropriations Committee resolution Egyptian Foreign Minister Ahmed Hussein returns to Washington. Unsuspectingly, Hussein travels to Washington to accept finally the Western offer to assist in Aswan's construction. At the time of Hussein's visit, moreover, it was the general American view that the United States had won out in competing with the Soviet Union to build the high dam. Thus, when Dulles announced on July 19, following a fifty-minute conference with Hussein, that the offer was withdrawn, the effect was electric. Britain immediately followed suit (although Eden was shocked at Dulles's abruptness in canceling the offer), and the World Bank announced that in view of the Anglo-American decision, its offer had also "automatically expired."

Dulles's announcement of withdrawal read:

> Developments within the succeeding seven months have not been favorable to the success of the project, and the United States Government has concluded that it is not feasible in present circumstances to participate in the project. Agreement by the riparian states has not been reached and the ability of Egypt to devote adequate resources to assure the project's success has become more uncertain than at the time the offer was made.

Significantly, Dulles omitted his central cause for turning down Aswan: disdain for Nasser's romance with the Communist powers. Rightly or not, Nasser interpreted Dulles's statement as a move designed to destroy world confidence in Egypt's economic position. From the perspective of political survival at home, Nasser (correctly, perhaps) saw Dulles as addressing the Egyptian masses to overthrow him.

A week following the United States aid withdrawal, Nasser seized the Suez Canal. The idea of nationalizing the Canal was by no means a new one. In the early 1920's the Egyptian Socialist-Communist Party had listed the nationalization of the Canal in its published program of objectives. Furthermore, according to a Reuters dispatch from Cairo, quoting the Egyptian weekly, *Akher Siah,* Nasser had decided "five months ago to wage the Suez battle this year." The dispatch carried an August 15 date line. Nevertheless, the Aswan episode furnished Nasser with a timely excuse to seize the Canal—and to thumb his nose at the West. The West had rebuffed the project on which Nasser based his efforts to spur Egyptian progress. The fashion in which it was abruptly turned down made the dam assume much more importance than it actually merited. It put it on a par with the equilibrium of the Suez Canal.

While we are not concerned here with the ongoing debate about the Suez crisis and the subsequent Sinai War, it is noteworthy that Nasser's ostensible aim in seizing the Canal was to divert its profits towards the building of Aswan. In this lay the convenience of the Aswan rejection in what was likely Nasser's greater goal—the nationalization of the Suez Canal. Would Canal revenues have provided Egypt with funds to build the dam? Nasser himself showed the impossibility of this argument when he signed in 1958 the agreement with the Soviet Union to finance Aswan.

By early 1958, the Egyptians—hardly recovered from the Sinai debacle—were coming to realize the oppressive friendship of the Soviet Union. In 1957, three-fifths of Egypt's imports came from the West, while three-fifths of her exports went to the Communist bloc. In the six years since the Revolution, the contribution of Egyptian industry to the national income had risen only one percent from ten to eleven. Clearly, Nasser had not fulfilled his economic reform pledges. His economic problems were onerous. While the Soviet Union in the fall of 1957 had agreed to lend Egypt $175,000,000 for his first five-year plan, which incidentally was the biggest loan it offered any nation outside the Iron Curtain, that amount was in rubles. Nasser well knew that rubles would not buy necessary machinery from the West and, judging from his dependence upon the Soviet Union, there was little the rubles would get him from that source.

From the economic point of view, in mid-1958, Nasser was eager to resume relations with the West. Once more, Nasser showed his first-rate bargaining skill; again the State Department's efforts to use foreign aid as a blandishment to win Nasser back failed. Nasser was clever enough to sense, at this juncture, that if he came to rely on the Soviet Union any further, he would be little more than a puppet and, as a result, never stand a chance of fulfilling his Pan-Arab ideal. Inordinate economic dependence on the Soviet Union would stifle his political mobility.

Nasser approached the United States embassy on several occasions for wheat, for the resumption of normal trade, and the release of $30 million of Egyptian funds still frozen in United States banks as a result of the Suez crisis. While the United States did not then release the funds it fell for Nasser's bait on the other points: it went ahead to approve increased trade with Egypt and, in a surplus wheat agreement, committed itself to supply what were, in effect, about one-half of Nasser's wheat needs for 1959.

The ability to feed Egypt's masses is not enough, of course, to qualify one for leadership of the Arab world. It was evident to Nasser's fellow Moslem nationalists that Nasser was somehow seeking to regain his previous powerful position among the Arabs. At the end of October, 1958, Nasser suffered a bitter humiliation at the hand of Tunisian President Habib Borguiba. Before the Tunisian Parliament, Borguiba attacked Nasser's plans for Arab hegemony. (In the aftermath of the June, 1967, Six-Day War, Borguiba not only took Nasser to task but suggested that he retire from office.) To be sure, Borguiba had strong personal justification for his suspicions of Nasser—Radio Cairo's prediction that he would meet the same fate as Iraq's murdered pro-Western Prime Minister Said. Nevertheless, the Tunisian attack on Nasser would not have occurred had Nasser enjoyed the same security as when he brought the West to its feet over Aswan.

It is instructive that Nasser then used Aswan as a desperate tack to regain fading popularity among the Arabs. Pride and image have always been central to Nasser's politics. (In fact, a credible hypothesis is that Nasser's ongoing confrontations with Israel represent a desire to avenge injured pride rather than reckless military adventurism.) If he were to redo his shattered image—both within Egypt and the Arab world—Nasser needed a victory. Thinking as he does in terms of image and not reality, Nasser was willing in late 1958 to pay a high price for retrieving his pride—even if it meant strengthening dependence on the Soviet Union. Scarcely a day following Borguiba's indictment, Nasser announced Soviet participation in the first section of Aswan to the tune of a $100 million loan. The deal provided the grandstand play Nasser sought. For the time being, Nasser again had effectively manipulated the superpowers. To his countrymen and the larger Arab world Aswan marked—on the surface—another prestige victory for Nasser.

What conclusions emerge from this review of Aswan's politics? For one, Nasser proved his skill as a political maneuverer in getting the Soviet Union to finance Aswan. However, the dam, in the absence of other economies has shown itself to be a self-defeating venture. Egyptian population increases have already overtaken whatever paper gains will be provided by Aswan. Egypt today instead of slowly catching up with Western living standards slowly falls behind.

Could Nasser have stimulated the productivity which would have made Aswan worthwhile? Considering Egypt's economic and social backwardness, this would have proven most difficult. The key to this answer is found, however, not in Egypt's economy but in Nasser's military ambitions. In siphoning off valuable resources on futile military gambles—with Israel and Yemen—Nasser demonstrated that modernization is secondary to aggression.

How has the United States weathered the Aswan experience? Although there is nothing like diplomatic disaster to spur intelligent thought about policy improvements, the United States persisted in erring on Nasser. In 1956, the United States, far less experienced than Britain and France in the Middle East, darted into the contest for Aswan and, despite good intentions, was caught napping, lacking contingency plans for Nasser's maneuvers. Similar unpreparedness in the face of the long-threatened outbreak of hostilities marked the United States experience in the June, 1967, war.

After Aswan, United States foreign policy mirrored earlier miscalculations: the temptation to view Nasser as a social reformer rather than a strident militarist; the illusion that Arab unity is in the best interests of

Arabs, Israelis, and Americans; the failure of foreign aid in toning down Nasser's hostility.

Some encouragement comes from the State Department apparently having learned in other parts of the world that it cannot be victorious in all foreign aid contests with the Communists—that to win a few and lose a few does not show a bad batting average. Aswan points up the lesson that clear, strong, principled action from American officials is the best way to advance strategic interests on the one hand, and to break the absurd spiral of Middle East warfare on the other.

# # #

America's Voice in Israel
[*Jewish Life*, May 1969]

While Phantom jets, boundary frontiers, and desalination schemes figure prominently in Israeli-American relations, little attention has been paid to the role of cultural relations between the two countries. Yet cultural and educational activities that stress shared ideas are the key to lasting Israeli-American bonds. As the young state struggles to resolve its own political identity, there is much to be learned from the American experience.

America's cultural program in Israel goes back to 1949 with the opening of the American Library at Bialik Street in Tel Aviv. One year earlier, the United States Congress passed the Smith-Mundt Act outlining the role of international information as a factor in promoting "mutual understanding between the people of the United States and the people of other countries."

The American Library filled a need in meeting the herculean strains on the new nation. Civil servants and municipal officials were among the first borrowers. The library introduced the open shelf system into Israel; books were loaned at no charge. In Israel's infancy, the library's collection centered on immediate needs—soil conservation, irrigation, cattle. With industrialization, Israelis came to the library seeking material on administration, education, economics.

Although for its first four years the library was run by the State Department, the United States Information Agency took over operations in 1953.

That year the USIA was set up as an independent agency of the executive branch, directly responsible to the President.

Creating a separate agency has many advantages—reflected in subsequent disseminations to Israel—a greater flexibility, a sharper, faster approach and more singleness of purpose.

Two principal factors brought on the creation of the USIA: the sustained Communist propaganda menace; and the revolution in traditional diplomacy (due to burgeoning mass communications) allowing for a more direct role of the "man in the street" in influencing his government's foreign policy.

The information instrument of statecraft is formidable in cultivating the Israeli public. Wide literacy and intellectual awareness give Israelis a close interest in foreign cultures. Volatile Middle East politics (reflected in rapt following of hourly news summaries) heightens Israeli attention to direct communications from foreign governments. The broad power base of Israeli politics, as with any democracy, encourages the ordinary citizen to be a participant rather than observer in world affairs. And ties with America's Jews make Israelis especially sensitive to American cultural trends.

Overall, the USIA communicates with people abroad to make understandable to them United States policies as well as the traditions and values from which these policies flow. It counters distorted images of the United States. It keeps American policy makers informed about foreign public opinion concerning the United States.

Yet with Israel as with some 105 other USIA client countries, a determination of the population level to be propagandized poses ideological and financial problems. Should the USIA strive to gain the support of the Israeli elite or masses? Is the Tel Aviv lawyer to be courted equally with the Algerian immigrant? Underscoring this problem is the awareness that Israelis' political alertness rules out decision making by only a privileged few. As journalist Welles Hangen put it (in terms of India): "The people cannot be defined as a handful of English-speaking editors in the capital who can dine acceptably at the Public Affairs Officer's house and whose views can be congenially cabled to Washington as evidence of program effectiveness."

While it would appear that the USIA would not willingly sacrifice the attention of either the Israeli elite or masses, it is forced to come to a decision as to which group it should cultivate as a result of budgetary considerations.

(During fiscal year 1967, USIA in Israel expended $337,728 in foreign currency and $1,370 in U.S. dollars, for a total budget of $339,098. A large part of this was spent in connection with the building and furnishing of a new cultural center in Jerusalem. The budget for 1968 came to under $300,000, almost all in foreign currency. While small compared with posts in certain Southeast Asian nations, this expenditure is very much more than the early 1950's, reflecting a larger operation as well as the natural rise in operating costs over the years.)

In Israel, USIA has chosen the elite. Selective targeting, in effect, marks the USIA's operations elsewhere today too. Given the lack of rigid social stratification in Israel, USIA policy-makers there hope that government leaders, university faculty and students, senior high school teachers, labor leaders, reporters and senior military officers will disseminate America's views to a mass audience.

USIA activities in Israel are directed to three main purposes:

Providing information on American life and achievements. Concerts, performances, lectures—the Cincinnati Symphony Orchestra, the Paul Taylor Dance Company, Professor James Sykes of Dartmouth's Music Department—are typical programs. But this aim is also accomplished by providing reference and research information. Thus, in May 1967, a single month, the USIA library supplied material on the organization and function of the U.S. National Security Council to a Knesseth committee considering forming a similar body in Israel; information on Medicare and U.S. Social Security benefits was provided to an inter-ministerial committee appointed by the Cabinet studying the problems of the aged. The Israeli National Defense College in Jerusalem also sought data on the pay of enlisted personnel in the U.S. armed forces in connection with a comprehensive survey it had undertaken of soldiers' salaries. The chairman (member of Knesseth and former Minister of Commerce) of a symposium on "The Press in Israel" received material on press laws and freedoms in the United States for his presentation.

Teaching English. While knowledge of English will not assure Israeli support for the United States, it is intended to foster a more respectful judgment of American culture. The USIA library maintains special collections for English teachers, loans multiple copies of texts for beginning and advanced English students and supplies audio-visual aids and language teaching records. A mailing list keeps these teachers informed of new literature.

Gaining support for United States foreign policy. As to Israel's immediate problems, the USIA advocates policies alleged to contribute to peace and to provide the climate for continued progress and stability in the Middle East. Operationally, this involves distributing Presidential statements, background material, and placing film footage on Israeli newsreels. Thus, during the June 1967, Six-Day War, the USIA distributed eighty copies of the United Nations Middle East debate to Israeli theatres. It is estimated that most of the adult population of Israel saw the film.

On a broader scale, USIA propaganda aims at winning Israeli support for American foreign policy positions. In recent years, none has been as avidly pressed as the American case in Vietnam. And this campaign seems to have met success. To be sure, Israelis do not take lightly mutual tributes by Arab guerrillas and the Communist National Liberation Front of Vietnam. Furthermore, Israelis closely follow America's Vietnam policy from the perspective of the latter's pledge to Israel's "territorial integrity." If America's commitment is broken to South Vietnam, why not Israel?

The USIA has shown films on Communist aggression in South Vietnam, circulated reprints, sponsored the visit of Vietnamese author and scholar Hou Van Chi, and even translated into Hebrew the pamphlet "Why Vietnam?"

Significantly, in reviewing "Why Vietnam?" *Maariv*, Israel's largest newspaper, said that Washington "most probably wished to hint to the thinking Israeli reader that not only to Vietnam does the U.S. have obligations and not only these will the U.S. keep . . . Not to full an obligation is an acceptance of aggression . . . Any deviation from the principle of keeping guarantees and fulfilling obligations in one area can influence other areas in the world in a decisive way."

Crisis situations impose special demands on USIA's Israeli objectives. As the official American voice in Israel, the USIA briefs not only the Israeli public and journalists but foreign correspondents as well. With the Six-Day War, some 850 foreign correspondents and cameramen came to Israel, including at least 250 representing American media.

Looking back at the war now, USIA Information Officer Pilti Heiskanen remembers May and June 1967 for its sharp tension. Born in Helsinki, Heiskanen fought the attacking Red Army in Finland in 1939. He fought with the American Army in World War II. He spent seven years in the Middle East, including three in Iran. "But," says Heiskanen, "I don't think I experienced that kind of tension anywhere."

In addition to disseminating United States policy statements to newsmen, Heiskanen helped evacuate some 7,000 Americans before the fighting started. "The Embassy phoned every day 81 hotels asking about American guests."

For his press activities during the Arab-Israeli war, Heiskanen received the Department of State's Scroll of Appreciation.

The U.S. Cultural Center at 71a Hyarkon Street, Tel Aviv, fronting the Mediterranean, is the heart of the USIA's Israeli operations. Quartered in the same structure as the United States Embassy, the U.S. Cultural Center houses the American Library, a multi-purpose 150-seat auditorium, exhibition facilities, meeting rooms and offices.

From here, the Public Affairs Officer (PAO)—the USIA's head officer in any one country—supervises a staff of three other Americans and some twenty-five Israelis. The Americans carry out information, cultural, and press relations. Israelis serve as translators, secretaries, writers, librarians, and film cataloguers. In diplomatic parlance, the PAO is part of the American "Country Team" in Israel—the coordinating body of American diplomatic policy. As such, he advises the United States Ambassador on the effect of American international positions on Israeli public opinion.

The most recent United States PAO in Israel, Jay W. Gildner (1965–1968), came well prepared to this critical assignment. He had directed *Ameriko Haus*, the famed U.S. Information and Cultural Center in Berlin. He also served as an Assistant White House Press Secretary under President Kennedy.

According to Gildner, Israeli cultural sophistication as well as the large number of intellectually aware people, posed heavy demands on USIA facilities. His main problem was meeting this "almost bottomless" demand by selecting only the most relevant material bearing on Israeli-American relations.

Totaling some 20,000 American volumes, the Cultural Center's broad-ranging library collection includes material on American government, culture, economics, and scientific and technological achievements. In addition to its main task of making the U.S. better known and understood, the library, as with USIA collections in other countries, according to former USIA head, George V. Allen, "aims to symbolize and demonstrate the interest of the United States in other nations." One way the USIA accomplishes this purpose is to include books in translation which have had an important impact on American life. Thus, the USIA Tel Aviv library shelves more than 500 American books in Hebrew translation.

Although USIA libraries generally are not intended to rival national libraries, they are often the only institutions to which people can turn for necessary information. Israeli professors often ask the USIA library to carry material (especially in courses involving the United States) to meet their students' course needs.

In Israel, as in other nations, the library fulfills what Allen has called the objective of "taking the lead in introducing modern library techniques into the community." In showing amazement at American generosity in placing books freely at their disposal, Israelis react no differently from visitors in other countries where open-shelf libraries and no charge book borrowing are still novelties.

In addition to books, the Cultural Center contains a film library with over 800 documentaries on subjects ranging from agriculture to science. More than 1,000 records of American music—classical, folk, jazz, spirituals, and English-language speech (plays, poetry, oratory)—are also available for home use.

Meeting Jewish observance, the USIA library shuts down on the Sabbath. Library hours are Monday through Thursday from 11 a.m. to 7 p.m. and on Friday from 11 a.m. to 3 p.m.

The USIA runs a branch at 16 Agran Street, Jerusalem. Its 6,000 volume collection is supplemented by inter-library loans. In Haifa, 2,000 American books were donated to the Israel-America Society at Beth Rothschild on Mount Carmel. In 1956, 1,000 American volumes were donated to Beersheba's Municipal Library. The Community Center in Nazareth also received 300 volumes some years ago.

Outside Israel's principal cities, the Cultural Center's extension services provide book loan and book gift collections. Kibbutzim and Moshavim are included in the extension service's network.

It is worth noting that all USIA disseminations in Israel, unlike those of France and Britain, for instance, are targeted, direct, and practical. French and British cultural programs are more esthetically oriented, stressing their literatures and cultural heritage. By contrast, USIA activities (particularly library collections) concentrate on "how to do it" issues. USIA operations in Israel are more specifically in support of foreign policy objectives than are the cultural programs of other countries.

How effective is the USIA in Israel? To what extent does it influence Israeli public attitudes? To be sure, the tremendously intellectual character of Israel prevents foreign propagandists from passively pursuing their goals. Thus, in recalling his years as USIA Information Officer, Pilti Heiskanen noted that Tel Aviv alone publishes twenty-two daily newspapers in nine languages. Hard decisions must be made as to where to focus the Agency's limited resources.

Moreover, since psychological objectives tend to be broad and long-term, it is difficult to spell out the impact of USIA. The democratic nature of American society—free speech, limited government, separation of powers—also imposes hardships in determining what is the *real* voice of America. While official and governmental, the USIA is still only one of many American voices finding their way to Israel. Tourists, movies, the press

(Hebrew and foreign), even relatives in America, all compete with and, perhaps, contradict USIA statements.

Strategically, the USIA is troubled by problems similar to those besetting the Agency elsewhere: the proper balance between Israeli elites and masses; the shortage of foreign service officers knowledgeable in Hebrew; a library collection ably mirroring American life, but still not large enough to satisfy the voracious Israeli reading public.

Selecting titles for the USIA's library is not only a matter of taste but of politics. Former USIA head George V. Allen's observations on books and the American image apply to Israel:

"Visiting Americans, including historians, educators, musicians, artists, religionists, economists, sociologists, and experts in other fields frequently complain about the lack of books and magazines representing their specialties. Liberals tend to find a preponderance of material on the conservative side, while conservatives see the opposite." Touring Congressmen in ritualistic visits to Israel also communicate ideas on book selection to USIA personnel.

Yet there are evidences of USIA effectiveness in Israel. The popularity of English as a second language is attributable in no small way to the USIA program. This is in spite of a little-known but still effective treaty between France and Israel designating French as Israel's second language. Between July 1966–July 1967 some 120,000 visitors came to the U.S. Cultural Center's Tel Aviv library. In this period, they borrowed over 158,000 books. USIA news material, especially references to America's scientific prowess, is regularly featured in the Israeli press. Film showings and special lectures draw large crowds.

Politically, the USIA can point to its role in winning sizeable Israeli support for America's policy in Vietnam. At his retirement, Lyndon B. Johnson was probably the world leader most admired by Israelis. Prime Minister Levi Eshkol's tribute to Johnson as one of America's "great" presidents reflected Israeli sentiment.

Beyond its propaganda value for the United States, USIA programs contribute to Israel's educational life. Marjorie Fergusson, former USIA Cultural Affairs Officer, cites the information program's role in acquainting

Israelis with the values of American pluralism. Israelis share with Americans, she notes, a "self-critical" attitude. Supplemented by their high ratio of "thought to action," she feels that Israelis are quick to pick up helpful aspects of American culture.

Still in its formative years, it is of great importance, as Yehoshua Arieli, chairman of the Hebrew University's American Studies Program, put it, that Israel "become acquainted with the liberal and the universal values of the American past and the major trends of its contemporary culture." For the "forward-looking dynamic mentality" of America has much to offer Israel as she works out her own life style.

4

The Plight of Soviet Jewry

During the summer of 1966, Rubin had an opportunity to tour the USSR with a Dutch student group, NBBS. As both the only American and only Jew in the group, he was greatly affected. Beginning with the following article about an especially poignant observance during this trip, Dr. Rubin researched and wrote extensively on the subject of Soviet Jewry over the ensuing years. This interest represented his second area of focus during his first few years as a college professor.

Tishah B'Ab in Moscow
[*Christian Century*, September 28, 1966]

In July 1966, I toured the Soviet Union. As a political scientist, I went to see the country firsthand, to talk with its youth and perhaps acquire background for my classroom descriptions of communism. As an Orthodox Jew, I hoped to check on the authenticity of press reports of the past few years regarding Soviet anti-Semitism. Though my observations of political society in the U.S.S.R. may in general have been hurried and fragmentary, I feel that my conclusions on the observance of Judaism there are based on reliable evidence. During my two-week sojourn I spoke with Jews in three cities—Minsk, Leningrad, and Moscow. The most poignant experience of all was the Tishah b'ab I spent in Moscow.

For some 2,500 years Tishah b'ab has been Judaism's national day of mourning. It originally marked the destruction of the temple in Jerusalem—first by the Babylonians in 586 B.C., then (on precisely the same day of the year) by the Romans in A.D. 70. Now it has come to symbolize all the misfortunes and disasters suffered by the Jews throughout their history. It has all the characteristics of the *shibah*, the period of mourning for the dead. Prohibited on Tishah b'ab are eating, drinking, and laughter, even the traditional handshake of greeting in the synagogue.

Normally Tishah b'ab falls in July or August of the Western calendar year. This year it was observed on Tuesday, July 26. In Moscow I attended Tishah b'ab services at the Central Synagogue—one of three in the area. (The others are in the suburbs; together the three serve some 500,000 Jews, about 10 percent of the total population of the area.) Though the Central Synagogue stands less than a ten-minute walk from Red Square, Moscow's chief tourist attraction, the taxi drivers who took me there on my four visits all had difficulty in finding the site—8 Arkhipova Street. Since the drivers were friendly enough, I concluded that their inability to find the synagogue at once was due not to prejudice but to the fact that this part of the city is little known.

The synagogue is a fairly large, plain building with a yellow exterior, its white entrance columns reminiscent of Greek Renaissance architecture. It fronts directly on the street, which, like most Russian side streets, I found to be virtually devoid of automobile traffic. When I attended services in the chapel on July 24 I asked about the cracks and holes in the chapel ceiling. I was told that repairs were under way, and indeed a painting scaffold clung to the front of the building.

Tishah b'ab services began at 8:30 on Monday evening in the main sanctuary. Present were from 150 to 200 men. In the balcony seat sat a few women (since Orthodox Judaism recognizes only certain prayers as incumbent on women, they are generally excused from actual attendance at the synagogue, and when they do come they sit apart from the men).

Most of the men at the services that night were elderly, mainly, I would judge, in their sixties and seventies, though one told me he was ninety-six. Their clothes were threadbare, as indeed were those of the average man I had seen on the streets. The few young men present seemed less able to follow the service than their elders; apparently Hebrew was unfamiliar to them. Instead of the traditional skull cap, some of the young men wore square Tashkent hats—a type of headgear, imported from Tashkent, much in style in Moscow this year.

The synagogue was dimly lit, in accordance with the ritual of this day of mourning. On the platform in front of the sanctuary were several low, unadorned benches—the type of bench used by Jews during the period of mourning for the dead. Recognizable by his attire—black hat and coat—was bearded Judah Leib Levin, Chief Rabbi of Moscow.

For one accustomed to praying in Western synagogues, certain features distinguished the Moscow service. The most telling difference was the scarcity of prayer books. I watched old men stoop over attempting to make out the print in prayer books held in the hands of others. I saw others reading from books disfigured, kept intact by tape. A few had Israeli-made books, identifiable by their small size and distinctive covers.

Prayers for the Tishah b'ab service are not contained in the standard prayer book; recited are special Lamentations, including Jeremiah's bleakest prophecies. Even fewer worshipers had the Lamentations than had the regular prayer books. Yet the paper-covered Lamentations book I had with me had cost only 20 cents in the United States. Three or four men shared the book during the service; one bent from the pew behind to look over my shoulder. Another, an elderly man seated beside me, stroked the little volume fondly.

Another difference from the accustomed Western service lay in the fact that many of the men present—about one-third, I would estimate—did not join in the prayers at all. Why was this so? For some, it was obviously lack of prayer books; for others, lack of knowledge of Hebrew. One of the few young men present—a boy apparently in his late teens—knew only the Kaddish, the memorial prayer for the dead. The farther from the front, the fewer there were who followed the service, and toward the rear, worshipers engaged in whispered conversation.

Still another contrast I noted was the conscious setting apart of certain worshipers from the rest of the congregation. For instance, Israeli diplomats followed the prayers from an area at the front right side of the sanctuary, where the seats were placed perpendicular to the rest.[1] Was

1. Diplomatic relations between Israel and the Soviet Union were broken off after the Six-Day War. —Ed.

the seating arrangement perhaps designed to make personal contact difficult between Israeli and Russian Jews?

Nevertheless, actual recitation of the prayers resembled that in services I had attended elsewhere. The Job-like melody, the dimmed lights, the old men straining eyes and heart, the torn or missing prayer books created in my mind an image of mourning and death. When the ninety-minute service had ended I offered my prayer book to one of the old men who had shared it. Obviously afraid to accept it openly, he looked about to see if anyone was watching, then slipped it into his inside pocket.

Outside the synagogue a group of worshipers gathered around me, conversing in Yiddish and Hebrew. Ours was not a casual conversation; they sought earnestly for information about Jewish life in the United States and Israel. How many yeshivas (religious schools) are there in the two countries? Did I know the whereabouts of this or that relative in Brooklyn or the Bronx? Are young American Jews religious? Are the infants circumcised into the Covenant of Abraham? What about religious divisions within American Jewry? (A week or so earlier a group of Reform rabbis from the United States had visited the synagogue; apparently the Russian Jews have but a vague idea about divisions in the United States.)

There have been no public classes in Hebrew for many years, yet one man in his late sixties told me in fluent Hebrew that he eats meat only on Jewish holidays; the rest of the year he eats only dairy products, fruits, and vegetables because kosher meat is either unobtainable or impossibly expensive. Usually the only kosher meat available at any time, I was told, is poultry. Several people told me that of all the Jews in Moscow only the chief rabbi regularly eats kosher meat.

When I returned the next morning for the remainder of the Tishah b'ab service I found even fewer people present. As the prayers ended I left the synagogue thinking that here was surely the most meaningful place on earth to observe Tishah b'ab, to reflect on the despair and courage that have marked its commemoration by Jews for 2,500 years.

# # #

Student Struggle for Soviet Jewry
[*Hadassah Magazine*, December 1966]

How long must we plead
For the bound to be freed
From the chains that oppress and degrade?
How long? How long? How long?
How long must we wait
While the hour grows late
And our brothers grow faint and afraid?
Too long! Too long! Too long!

The concern reflected in this topical ballad is the motivating force behind a small but growing movement of youth dedicated to a Herculean task—the rescue of Soviet Jewry from cultural and religious extinction.

Over the past two academic calendar years hardly a month has passed without some student protest about the deprivations of Soviet Jewry. Rallies, vigils, marches, fasts, and prayer sessions have dotted campuses across the country. New York City in particular has been the scene of major activity. The largest demonstration on behalf of Soviet Jewry was held there April 8, 1966. Called the *Geulah* (Redemption) March, it drew the participation of some 15,000 students.

These demonstrations are not haphazardly arranged. They are timed to coincide with significant Jewish or Russian events so as to most effectively arouse public opinion. Thus, about 1,000 students silently marched on the Soviet Union's Mission to the United Nations on May Day, 1964. A Menorah March and Rally, drawing 1,000 students, was held during the Hanukkah festival in 1965, and on the eve of Passover 1966 a *Leyl Shemurim* vigil was organized in front of the United Nations.

Typical of the protest demonstrations was the Jericho March of April 4, 1965. A group of 3,000 students assembled one block east of the Soviet Mission to the United Nations, located at 135 East 67th Street. The group was arranged in two great columns. Seven rabbis and Jewish leaders bearing Torahs, followed by seven students carrying shofars, advanced between the columns to the accompaniment of a simple chant. Two rabbis thereupon recited psalms. The seven shofars were sounded seven times and then the march around the Soviet Mission began.

As the demonstrators paraded, they sang the Hebrew verse from Isaiah inscribed on the U.N. plaza: "Nation shall not lift up sword against nation, neither shall they learn war any more," symbolizing their hope that the Iron Curtain between the United States and the Soviet Union would disappear and that the barriers of distrust and suspicion would melt away.

Like protest movements involving other political and social causes, the student effort to rescue Soviet Jewry has given birth to songs. "There's a Fire Burning" is among them:

There's a fire burning brightly in the sky
And the roar of thunder crashing from on high,
I see a nation there awakening
Iron yokes will soon be breaking,
And a nation long oppressed shall arise—
A nation long oppressed shall arise . . .

A trumpet rings through the night,
The dawn appears—we see the light,
We wake the world, we make them see
That our people must be free.

Freedom's train is racing swiftly through the land
And the tide of love is pounding on the sand,
I can hear the whole world crying
For a nation that's been dying,
It will soon hold out its helping hand.

Many of the tactics used by students fighting for Soviet Jewry resemble those used by civil rights groups in the early 1960's. Both the student movement for Soviet Jewry and the student civil rights struggle share one crucial feature: the bypassing of established institutional means for problem-solving in favor of mass demonstrations mobilizing public support.

Wherein lies the uniqueness of the student appeal for Soviet Jewry? The Soviet Jewry protest campaign has captured the imagination of youth to whom the Nazi disaster represents not simply a historical fact but a pressing reminder of the need for Jewish brotherly concern. Fate prevented these students from being alive in the 1930's and early 1940's and they are determined that this horror, in any of its manifestations, not be repeated in their generation. As such, the effort to save Soviet Jewry represents a new focal point for Jewish identification—in addition to traditional religious and Zionist organizations.

The principal student group involved in the protests is the SSSJ—Student Struggle for Soviet Jewry. Their headquarters at 531 West 122nd Street are close by Columbia and the Jewish Theological Seminary. SSSJ has either organized or co-ordinated many of the national youth protests concerning Soviet Jewry in the past two and a half years. Decidedly community-oriented, SSSJ has sponsored numerous adult programs involving major Jewish organizations and provides guidance, films, speakers, tapes, records, and leadership training programs to adult and youth groups alike.

The students' office and activities function on a volunteer basis, with no salaries paid to any of its workers. Most of its donations consist of $1, $5, or $10 contributions. SSSJ has received a few thousand such donations and each supporter is considered a member. The SSSJ symbol, carried on pins and organizational literature, is the shofar. The shofar represents a threefold meaning: a call to the conscience of the world, a call to action, and the hope for the redemption of Soviet Jewry.

Serving on SSSJ's Advisory Council are some younger Yeshiva University faculty members. Among its honorary patrons are Congressman Leonard Farbstein, Senator Jacob K. Javits, and Professor Abraham J. Heschel.

The prime mover and national co-ordinator of SSSJ is Jacob Birnbaum, thirty-seven, a native Englishman. He is the grandson of Dr. Nathan Birnbaum, the nineteenth-century European Zionist leader and originator of the term "Zionism." Birnbaum has been living off his savings since the founding of SSSJ, refusing to accept any salary for his work.

SSSJ's policy of mass demonstrations has four basic aims:

1. To cause the Soviet Government concern about its image due to its treatment of Jews.

2. To convince the White House that the situation of Soviet Jewry is a matter of burning concern to a very large segment of American citizenry.

3. To give much needed encouragement to Soviet Jews.

4. To arouse among Jews a new spirit of concern for the welfare and destiny of the suffering segments of world Jewry.

What have these demonstrations accomplished? Is there a link between student protests and the survival of Soviet Jewry?

There are no ready answers to these questions. Nevertheless, there is ample support for the thesis that the Soviet Union is sensitive to foreign public opinion, especially if such opinion embraces recognized spokesmen for peace. The U.S.S.R. is bent on expanding Communist influence and, accordingly, responds to events preventing such advances. Continuous press criticism of its policy toward Jews, denunciations by Nobel Prize winners such as Dr. Martin Luther King, letters of disenchantment by Lord Bertrand Russell, and pleas of conscience by Christian clergymen all serve to embarrass the Soviet Union. Reports of persecutions of Jews, moreover, strain the Soviet Union's relations with nations facing minority problems themselves. Finally, many Communist parties and publications in the West which otherwise sympathize with the Soviet Union take issue with its efforts to suppress Judaism.

Demonstrations remind opinion makers in the free world of the predicament of Soviet Jewry. They remind the Soviet Union that a vocal and informed public will never rest while it aims at obliterating Judaism. They remind complacent Jews in the West of the doom befalling their brethren—and word of these demonstrations fortifies the courage of this remnant in the Soviet Union. In short, the pickets are the voice of silenced Soviet Jewry.

However, it is a very youthful voice crying out to redeem them. For the initiative in publicizing their plight at the grass-roots level is largely the product of student effort. The adults may pass resolutions at their organizational conferences, they may attend lectures on this distressing subject, even work behind the scenes or publish important literature. But they do not "take to the streets" on behalf of their brethren behind the Iron Curtain. Adults rarely picket with signs or chant the mournful melodies echoing Jewish oppression through the centuries.

What explains the willingness of these young people with the many distractions which beckon them to take up a cause which, in the end, may be nothing more than an exercise in futility and heartbreak? A law student has offered a reply:

> What I do for myself I try to see in the light of what I can do for others. In every generation there have always been those who labored to assure Jewish continuity. I think I am part of a tragically small group which is struggling to ensure the survival of the Jewish people in the Soviet Union.

# # #

Russia and the "Scattered Ones"
[*Christian Science Monitor*, "From the Bookshelf," December 30, 1966]
***The Jews of Silence: A Personal Report on Soviet Jewry*, by Elie Wiesel. Translated by Neal Kozodoy. New York: Holt, Rinehart and Winston, $4.95.**

The Jew is becoming one of the most sought-after tourist attractions in the Soviet Union. For to meet him is to undergo one of the shattering experiences of a lifetime.

By now, informed opinion in the West is familiar with the plight of Soviet Jewry—that while all religions survive precariously in the Soviet Union, Judaism struggles against singular oppression. To review: unlike other faiths Judaism cannot publish prayer books and Bibles; cannot produce devotional articles: cannot have official contacts with co-religionists abroad. In 1956 there were 450 synagogues in the Soviet Union. Today there are some 60–70 synagogues.

Wiesel, a survivor of Auschwitz, visited the Soviet Union during the period coinciding with the Jewish High Holy Days of 1965. His purpose was to penetrate the silence of the three million Soviet Jews (the second largest Jewish community in the world, surpassing Israel's population) who since the 1917 Revolution have lived apart from their people.

But why the Jews? We know "liberalizing" forces are at work in the Soviet Union, and that its relations improve with the United States. Will these Soviet Jews never end complaining?

Wiesel reverses the question: Why not the Jews? Who were the first, the principal victims of the pogroms? The first to be eliminated in the Communist purges of the 1930's? And the first to be murdered by the invading Germans. And in Stalin's years, who were the victims of his mad liquidation program? The first to be victimized, the last to be rehabilitated.

Yet Wiesel does not portray a self-pitying Soviet Jewry. Rather, he stresses the indomitable strength of their belief. His most moving images focus on the students, who by all laws of logic should have spiritually vanished into the mainstream of mother Russia long ago. Don't Soviet apologists keep reminding us that Judaism disappears because of youthful disinterest?

One must spend with these students the one night a year they live not in fear but as free men. That night is "Simchat Torah," the rejoicing of the law, closing the Jewish High Holy Days. During these holidays everyone entering Moscow's Central Synagogue is photographed. Even on the night of "Simchat Torah" the Jews are not to forget that someone is watching, for two gigantic floodlights have been installed illuminating the street.

But the students come in droves, from the university, from the Komsomol Club, from far and near. Twenty thousand, 30,000, Wiesel cannot estimate precisely the total.

Dreaming and sighing, the throng tries to stop the progress of time. Two songs symbolize the occasion: the wistful, "Gather our scattered ones from among the nations, and our dispersed from the corners of the world," and the ringing, even defiant, verse of Jewish continuity, "David King of Israel lives and endures."

Events such as this "Simchat Torah" celebration convince Wiesel that Soviet Jewry can withstand the fear and survive the terror. But they will submit when persuaded that they have been abandoned by the Jews in the West.

The issue is not whether protests in the West ease the lot of Soviet Jewry. The issue is that protests prove to this remnant of Jacob that they are not cut off from the greater community of Israel. If the measure of concern for Soviet Jewry is the vigor of these demonstrations, Wiesel concludes they have been forgotten. "I returned from the Soviet Union disheartened and depressed. But what torments me most is not the Jews of silence I met in Russia, but the silence of the Jews I live among today."

# # #

Minsk Offers Insights into Russian Culture
[*Christian Science Monitor*, March 21, 1967]

Tourists with limited time to spend in the Soviet Union normally visit Moscow, Leningrad, a Black Sea resort, and a showcase Siberian city. Rarely do they see a medium-sized Russian city—an experience which may provide deeper insights into Russian living patterns than visits to the more populous cities.

A visit to Minsk will reveal much of the urban development which has taken place in the Soviet Union since World War II. One of the oldest cities in Russia, Minsk was founded 900 years ago. It is the capital of the Byelorussian (White Russian) Republic, one of the constituent political entities in the Soviet Union. Byelorussia is on the Russian-Polish border. Minsk numbers about 675,000 people, compared with Moscow's population of five million.

Appearance Contrasted

Like many cities in European Russia, Minsk was reduced to a heap of rubble in World War II. A visit to the concentration camp site where 80,000 people are said to have been murdered is part of Intourist's city tours.

Nearly every building now standing on Minsk's main streets was put up since the war. Even today, photos in the hotels and Intourist offices in Minsk compare what the city looked like in the aftermath of the war with its contemporary appearance.

Minsk is a one hour and forty minute flight from Moscow, and the fare is about $15.50. In comparison with air terminals in American cities of comparable population, Minsk's airport is small. There are no more than four ticket counters at the Minsk terminal and refreshment facilities are minimal.

Tourists who have previously traveled by airplane in the Soviet Union will not be surprised at the Minsk terminal's two waiting rooms—one for Russians and the other for foreigners.

The trip from the airport to the center of Minsk traverses wide tree-lined streets. Many apartment houses along the route have been recently erected. Terraces line the exteriors of these buildings. The apartment houses are mostly six stories high, built from yellow-tan colored bricks, a characteristic building material in White Russia.

Design Planned

Lenin Avenue, running for six miles, is the central thoroughfare in Minsk. In the rebuilding of this section of the city after World War II, the streets were designed in symmetrical patterns. Thus, the quaint "undiscovered" streets which tourists seek out in Western European cities are almost unknown in Minsk.

Minsk's few hotels are mainly in the vicinity of Lenin Avenue and Kruglaya Square, one of the three principal city squares. The leading hotel, the "Hotel Minsk," stands at the corner of Lenin Avenue and Kruglaya Square. It is opposite the General Post Office building.

By Soviet standards, the hotel is middle-sized and comfortable. The floors are serviced by elevators, and the rooms contain running water and flush toilets. However, the hotel's less expensive annex, situated around the corner, is far less desirable.

# # #

Students Tour Russia with Sputnik
[*Christian Science Monitor,* March 4, 1967]

While few American students travel to the Soviet Union, a trip there is of great educational value. The Soviet Union's cultural diversity, strategic import, and scientific prowess make it appealing to students of wide-ranging specialties.

To be sure, students do not visit the Soviet Union with the same objectives as they do Rome, Nice, or Paris. It lacks the carefree elegance and experience in attending to tourists needs marking these West European favorites.

In 1966 fewer than 20,000 Americans visited the Soviet Union. There is no available breakdown as to the number of students in this group, but it appears that no more than a few thousand were included. Despite strong educational arguments for touring the Soviet Union, student travel is minimal, possibly for the following reasons: political tensions, language barriers, travel restrictions within the country, and the absence of American-style comforts.

Students, like other American tourists, must obtain visas from the Soviet Embassy in Washington well in advance of their departures. Russia, unlike other East European nations, does not charge a visa fee.

Most travelers to the Soviet Union go in groups instead of alone. Groups get priority over single tourists in securing hotel rooms and in gaining admission to tourist attractions.

Student tours normally travel by trains. All tourists on a limited visit see the same sights. Higher-priced tours provide for better hotel accommodations, a more diversified diet, and perhaps plane rather than train travel between cities.

In past years, universities as well as civic and religious groups have sponsored student tours to the Soviet Union. The National Student Association of the United States organized two tours in the summer of 1966 with a Dutch student organization. Both tours covered the same route—Minsk, Moscow, and Leningrad. They ran 19 days, including two weeks in the Soviet Union, three days in Poland, and the rest of the time spent in round-trip travel between Holland and Russia.

By United States standards, the price of the tours was very low—approximately $200. This covered all travel, hotel, food and sight-seeing expenses in the Soviet Union. It also included train fare both to and from the Soviet Union from Holland.

Student tours to the Soviet Union are arranged with Sputnik, the youth organization of Intourist, the state-run tourist service. Sputnik workers all belong to Komsomal, the youth division of the Communist Party. Sputnik positions pay well; they also enable Soviet foreign-language students to enhance their conversational skill through practice with foreign students.

American students will find Sputnik guides specializing in English literature very well informed as to the classic works. They are less familiar with more recent writings. Most such guides show curiosity about the latest trends in American fiction.

Student tourists unfamiliar with the Russian language will have few opportunities to converse with their Soviet counterparts. Whether or not by design, the Soviet Union fails to encourage "bull sessions" with foreign students. It prefers emphasizing its educational advances by showing physical structures rather than the personal products of these schools.

For instance, Moscow University, the largest Soviet institution of higher learning, is on every visitor's itinerary. Students are particularly interested in visiting the university and assessing the nature of Soviet education. What better way of learning about Soviet education than through discussions with Soviet students?

Soviet students, however, are completely left out of tours to the university. Visitors are taken to the university's observation tower, then to the basement gymnasium, and finally to a typical dormitory room. No arrangements are made by the Soviet hosts for conversations between the university's students and foreign students.

# # #

The Promised Land Grows Dim
[*Saturday Review*, September 2, 1967]

Between Hammer and Sickle, by Ben Ami (Jewish Publication Society of America. 307 pp. $6), reiterates the fear of Soviet Jewry, bedeviled by anti-Semitism, that they have been forgotten by the West. Ronald I. Rubin, a political scientist at the City University of New York, was among the organizers of The Center for Russian Jewry in New York.

Every religious person in the USSR leads a haunted life. However, the three million Soviet Jews—the second largest concentration of Jews in the world—are singularly trapped. Religious and cultural classes are closed down; Bar Mitzvahs rarely take place; observant Jews are hunted down and often imprisoned on trumped-up charges; kosher meat, on a regular basis, is virtually unobtainable. The Jew lives in fear, cut off from his religion, his people, and the other three-fourths of world Jewry.

If he tries to escape the tortured burden of his Jewishness he is also boxed in: he must remain a Jew on his nationality identity card until death. It is safer, the Communists reason, to know just who are the crafty agents of the "International Jewish Conspiracy" than to have them secretly penetrate Soviet ranks. Finally, if he wants to leave the Soviet Union, the Jew is denied an exit permit.

In *Between Hammer and Sickle* Ben Ami, an Israeli writing under a pseudonym, traces the roots of this pained existence: traditional Russian anti-Semitism; the fact that Jews retain family and spiritual ties with the West, including Israel; the Soviet desire not to jeopardize their mounting alliance with the Arabs by permitting the emigration of Jews, many of whom would find their way to Israel, adding to her manpower and technical resources.

To be sure, *Between Hammer and Sickle*, which was an Israeli bestseller, is not the only work to appear in recent years on the plight of Soviet Jewry. Moreover, while it is not intended as definitive history, chronology of Soviet harassment and a reading list would have strengthened the author's case. A particular contribution of the present study, however, is its description of the Jews in Central Asia; most accounts of Soviet Jewry focus on European Russia. The theme and style of Ben Ami's book resemble Elie Wiesel's *The Jews of Silence* published in 1966; both works are marked by moving anecdotes, impressionistic sketches, and poignant conversations.

There is the story of the famous Israeli singer who represented her country at an international festival in Moscow. She sang Hebrew folk songs, a Yiddish folk song, and a Russian folk song that she had memorized without understanding the words. Dozens of Jews and probably some gentiles as well congratulated her on the performance.

As she was leaving the park a young man caught her hand and told her in Russian how impressed he had been with her songs, but it was soon obvious to him that she did not understand. "*Ia Izrail. Ia Izrail.* [I am Israel]," he said again and again. The singer was unsure whether he meant that his name was Israel or that his heart was with Israel or both. He pressed her hand hard, and in good-bye uttered the only Hebrew words that he knew: "*Yom Kippur.*"

Controlling her tears, the singer responded, "*Yom Kippur, Yom Kippur*" (Day of Atonement).

One of the saddest elements running through the pages of Ben Ami's work is the fear of Soviet Jewry that they have been forgotten by the West. In a hundred whispered greetings the plea is the same: "Don't you hear our cries? Do not forsake us." Ben Ami, who stresses the longing of these Jews for Israel, never conjectured the severance of diplomatic relations with Israel by the Soviet Union and the sharpened anti-Semitism provoked by their labeling as Nazism the Israeli victory over the Arabs. *Between Hammer and Sickle* is even more timely today than when it was first published.

# # #

The Real Shtetl

[*Hadassah Magazine*, November 1967]

The Golden Tradition: Jewish Life and Thought in Eastern Europe.
By Lucy S. Dawidowicz. Holt, Rinehart and Winston. 495 pp. $8.95.
Reviewed by Ronald I. Rubin.

Fiddler on the Roof notwithstanding, Jewish life in Eastern Europe was not altogether poverty and piety. There is no undercutting the extraordinary dynamism and pluralism of Eastern European Jewry from the end of the eighteenth century through 1939.

It was here the unresolved issues of Jewish life today were generated: Orthodoxy versus secularism; the intensity of Zionist commitment and the direction of a Jewish state; how "to save" the half-hearted and assimilated Jew.

In addition to the intellectual relevance of Eastern European Jewry to Jewish life today, there are two further arguments for focusing on that world gone by. Millions of American Jews are no more than two or three generations removed from what was then the center of Jewish civilization (and, likewise, from the plight of Soviet Jewry, the last remnant of this heritage). Secondly, the recent fictional and dramatic sentimentalizing of this world—life in the *shtetl*, for instance—has produced illusions deserving closer analysis.

The Golden Tradition is the type of work which should have appeared earlier than now. Lucy S. Dawidowicz, a frequent contributor to *Commentary*, has splendidly filled this void. Her work is charming and thorough, meriting both popular and scholarly attention.

The Golden Tradition consists of some 60 memoirs, most of them translated from the Yiddish by the authoress, touching on different aspects of Eastern European Jewish life. Mrs. Dawidowicz also has written a learned and engaging introduction which, in itself, is a remarkable document of Jewish intellectual history.

What was the fabric of this civilization? While the movements were not cut from the same cloth, they shared certain elements:

Hassidism offered a spontaneous and surging religious commitment. Believers were provided with a *rebbe* to show the way to this fervent spirituality. In the process, Hassidism challenged coldly rationalist rabbinic traditions.

The *Mussar* movement polished Talmudic learning with ethical excellence. Rabbi Israel Salanter, its founder, took issue with routine religious ritual, especially if such mechanical conduct minimized the goodness and centrality of man. The hallmark of Mussar was: "Know thyself." A quotation from the piece, "Truth and Legend About Israel Salanter," is instructive:

Rabbi Israel used to say that every man could improve himself until love of mankind came naturally to him. He used to teach that a man should not desire another's property not because the Torah commanded "Thou shalt not covet," but because one would scorn an ugly distasteful act, much as one would spurn rotten fish. Only by self-discipline can man reach this state.

The Haskala similarly crusaded against established religious authority in an effort to endow Jews with civic equality and the chance to serve the state. Moses Mendelssohn epitomized Jewish acceptance of this "Enlightenment."

In this setting, politics became a means for strengthening Jewish identity and dispelling notions of Jewish defenselessness. In Poland, the Bund enlisted support from working class and lower middle class Jews. In Russia, Jews cast away their religious ties and embraced Populism, the indigenous socialist movement.

Other Jews saw themselves trapped in the anti-Semitism of the day and sought national revival in the return to Zion. As Mrs. Dawidowicz put it, the East European Jews were the "foot soldiers in Herzl's battalions." Russian Jews took to heart Herzl's charisma and dreams: "The Jews who will it shall achieve their State." By the end of the nineteenth century some 5,000 colonists had populated some 25 agricultural settlements in Palestine. By the outbreak of World War I, the number of colonists had more than doubled: about 12,000 in 43 colonies. From these rank emerged the future leaders of Israel.

The drama of East European Jewry never reached its true fulfillment because the actors were cut down in the Nazi disaster. How can we apply the heritage of East European Jewry to current Jewish and secular issues? Mrs. Dawidowicz' comments in this regard would have been provocative.

# # #

Protests at Soviet Rabbi's Hunter Talk
[*New York Times* Letters to the Editor, June 1968]

To the Editor:

Having attended Rabbi Yehuda Leib Levin's Hunter College speech, I wish to dissent from your June 24 editorial ("Lesson in Intolerance") which took issue with the disruptive tactics of the audience.

The aim of the disruption was not to confront Rabbi Levin directly. Himself a victim of Soviet anti-Semitism, Rabbi Levin is in no position—regardless of how roundly he is booed—to ease the plight of his co-religionists.

Disruption for Record

Instead, the disruption was registered for the record. To have remained silent while Rabbi Levin made the outrageous claim that no anti-Semitism existed in the U.S.S.R. and that Jewish cultural and spiritual outlets were available would have implied complacency. The significance of the protest was to show Soviet Jews that we are aware of their tragedy and will not keep still.

Accordingly, it misses the point to look on this incident as hooliganism—much as the challenges directed, for instance, against the Administration advocates of current strategy in Vietnam. Rabbi Levin is outside the Soviet power structure and cannot shape policy. Secondly, no institutional channels are available for Soviet Jews to cry out. We in the free world must serve as their voice and demand that they be granted religious rights.

Finally, Rabbi Levin is not in the United States to engage in "public dialogue" on Soviet anti-Semitism, as your editorial puts it. A question session was not announced in advance of his Hunter talk, and no debates have pitted Rabbi Levin against critics of Soviet Jewish policy. Given this background, by our silence we condone Soviet anti-Semitism; by our noise we condemn it.

# # #

Rubin's early writings on the plight of Soviet Jewry also include the two in-depth studies summarized below and his second full-length book, *The Unredeemed: Anti-Semitism in the Soviet Union* (Quadrangle Books, 1968). *The Unredeemed* was one of the first "alarms" sounded about the horrific plight and potential disappearance of the thousand-year-old Jewish community in the Soviet Union, the largest Jewish community in Europe.

Soviet Jewry and the United Nations: The Politics of Non-Governmental Organizations [*Jewish Social Studies—A Quarterly Journal Devoted to Contemporary and Historical Aspects of Jewish Life*, July 1967—Summary]

This paper evaluates the role of five Jewish NGOs at the Fifteenth Session of the Subcommission on Prevention of Discrimination and Protection of Minorities, which met at United Nations headquarters from January 14–February 1, 1963. The five NGOs, which all enjoyed consultative status with the Economic and Social Council of the United Nations, had a special interest in this Session because it devoted a considerable portion of its agenda to a study on the background, condition and future of Article 13 (2). Article 13 (2) states that "Everyone has the right to leave any country, including his own, and to return to his country."

The paper assesses the NGOs contributions to the session within the context of the Soviet Union's foreign relations and the United Nations' experience in protecting human rights. It notes that, "the record of the 1963 session may well herald a new role for NGOs in assisting the world body to implement the human rights provisions of its Charter."

# # #

The Plight of Soviet Jews
[*Thought: A Review of Culture and Idea—Fordham University Quarterly*, August 1968—Summary]

To open this paper, Rubin states that "The Soviet Jew is a 'shadow' person—his past denied, his present existence qua Jew unrecognized, his future one in which his soul is destined for extinction."

"In this tragedy-shadowed age," he continues, "the Jews of Russia undergo a special martyrdom. Having survived the pogroms of the Czars, the purges of the 1930's, Hitler's death hunts and Stalin's mad extermination schemes, they face slow spiritual strangulation by the technocrats who today govern the Kremlin. If successful, the Soviets will have wiped out the second largest Jewish community in the world . . . the remnant of the two and a half million Jews murdered by the Nazis in the Soviet Union . . . [a] spiritual genocide campaign . . . unparalleled in modern history."

The paper discusses the nature of the problem, the status of Jews in the Soviet Union, and the three courses theoretically open to them—affirmation, assimilation, emigration—all of which are shown to amount to no more than dead ends.

PART THREE

An Established Professor and Author at Home and Abroad, 1970s and 1980s

5

Israeli Communications

Rubin's tenure at the Borough of Manhattan Community College (BMCC) afforded him the opportunity to take a sabbatical year during the early 1970s—a year he spent in Israel as visiting senior lecturer in the Department of Political Science at Haifa University. His writings reflect much of the information he culled while there.

Two of Rubin's main interests, communications and Israel, merge in the following four pieces. The first addresses *Israel's Propaganda War,* or rather, lack thereof, in 1970, citing Israel's changing status after its victory in the 1967 war and the heightened need for an improved Israeli information program, with blueprints for such a program. The second article looks at the structure and programming of radio and television broadcasting in Israel in 1971.

Articles three and four re-address Israel's information program. The first of these, published three years after *Propaganda War,* in 1973, is a research paper detailing the infrastructure, definitions, methods, and vehicles used by Israel in determining how and what to disseminate as overseas propaganda. In the second, published ten years later, in 1983, Rubin clearly states that "the government of Israel seems to fail consistently to pay attention to the propaganda or ideological element." The article highlights Rubin's concerns about the lack of growth and improvement made by Israel in this arena and cites several Israeli actions in the early 1980s that affected public opinion negatively. Because the article so closely echoes the prior two articles on the topic, it is included in an abridged form.

Israel's Propaganda War
[*Jewish Life*, March–April 1970]

As the only country lacking a single dependable ally, Israel knows better than to expect the world's popularity. Extremes are the lot of Israel in international affairs, and as Abba Eban put it, "The only sentiment not aroused by Israel since its establishment is a feeling of apathy."

While most Americans, and probably most West Europeans, still tend to look upon Israel more favorably than upon the Arabs, Israel's support in the West has nonetheless eroded considerably since the June, 1967, war. Many explanations are possible for this, not the least of which is the upgrading of Arab propaganda over the last two and a half years. The time has passed when Israelis could quip that their best propagandists were the Arabs. At home, Nasser may still use Radio Cairo to whip up internal hysteria against Israel, but abroad the Arab approach has become cooler and more rational. As Arab arguments begin to develop a measure of seeming plausibility, certain academic and church groups, some disaffected blacks, the selective humanitarians of the New Left, and the subterranean antisemites of the old right have found less embarrassment in rallying to their support.

Despite Israel's being small and diplomatically without strong allies, since her 1967 victory Israel is no longer seen as the underdog. In an age of political anti-heroes it is unadmirable to win wars: plaudits are the lot of losers. More than magnanimity in victory, according to this notion, is expected from Israel even though it would leave her exposed to a fourth round of war. Particularly in certain intellectual circles which hold a romantic affection for simple peasantry, Israel is looked upon as culpable for her technical prowess in defeating the Arabs.

Moreover, the plight of Arab refugees, it must be granted, lends itself to exploitation. Yesterday's realities such as Arab expectations before the war to drive the Jews into the sea invariably are forgotten in the shuffle of present tragedy. Israelis are not surprised with the new Arab self-righteousness, turning the refugee issue to maximum political advantage. As an Army press spokesman has noted: "Refugees always get *rachmanuth*."

Unremitting one-sided UN condemnation of Israel has also damaged Israel's image in certain circles which regard the world organization as a sort of universal conscience. Under UN bloc politics, the automatic majority of Communists, Moslems, and "revolutionary" Afro-Asian states brands Israel as an international outlaw. Israel's public resents this intrusion which so invariably works against her: as one Foreign Ministry official put it, "There's a debate here about what's the lowest point on earth—the Dead Sea or the UN."

Finally, Israel suffers from a growing trend in the mass media, which, in the interest of audience-building, stresses sensationalism and political aberrations. Numerically small Arab terrorist organizations are represented as mass movements. While there are as many definitions of news as there are newsmen, basic to most views is the element of conflict. Just as trends of racial progress in the United States often go unmentioned in favor of those of racial discord, so too Israel falls victim to press dramatization. Instances of Israel-Arab cooperation since the war, especially in East Jerusalem, receive slight attention while a demonstration staged by thirty girls in Nablus is news everywhere. Likewise, this dramatization works against Israel's image in retaliatory raids on Arabs. Because foreign policy news suffers space limitations, the press cites the military facts of the raid while eclipsing the Arab terror buildup that had caused such a response. Thus the inverted image of a merciless colossus projected by Arab propaganda.

With fairly defensible borders for the first time in her history, why should Israel worry about unfavorable news abroad? As one Israeli Defense Ministry spokesman put it, "It's naive to sit from the Golan Heights to the Suez Canal and try for a good image abroad, especially if but two years ago you were the underdog and twenty years ago the victim of the world." But the fact is that, even if Israel decides it is not worth her while to portray herself in the best light, what she is will not remain a mystery, because the twentieth century communications revolution makes possible the dissemination by others of information about her.

It is possible to project serious problems for Israel should hostile foreign opinion rise. This development could reinforce Arab militants bent on destroying her; discourage Arab moderates and, not least of all, strengthen the hand of those Soviet politicians willing to gamble on Nasser in their bid for mastery of the Middle East. Heightened anti-Israel sentiment will result in more pressure for international penalties, especially support of Soviet-backed Arab demands voiced at the UN for economic sanctions and arms embargo.

Admittedly, Israel contends with excessively hostile forces in her image campaign. The level of attack against this small state rivals those directed only against major powers. Thus, for Israel, wandering words are no less dangerous than wandering mirages. Actually, a failure to clarify objectives is perhaps more keenly felt in the information realm than in other areas of foreign policy, such as interstate relations, where governments knowingly deal with each other in half-truths and concealed facts.

An information program must be sharply targeted because it is directed at an increasingly skeptical public. It was only at the end of 1969, however, that Prime Minister Golda Meir announced that her new government would for the first time include a Minister of Information. Previously, the Israeli Information Ministry was not administratively autonomous but was attached to the Prime Minister's Office. The Minister of Information, Israel Galili (commander of the Haganah during the British Mandate), was one of three Cabinet Ministers without portfolio. It is expected that Galili will head the new independent Information Ministry.

It remains to be seen, however, to what extent the other units of Israel's disorganized persuasion apparatus will be included under the new ministry. Additional official voices emerging from Israel include the following: the Information Division and the Culture and Scientific Division of the Foreign Ministry (Abba Eban has in the past opposed the transference of Foreign Ministry units to an independent Information Ministry); the overseas service of Kol Israel, the state radio; the Army Spokesman reporting on specific military incidents; the Defense Ministry, reporting on background security policy; and the Tourist Ministry, courting foreign visitors. Also heard is the voice of the Jewish Agency, promoting immigration and serving as liaison with foreign Jewish communities. (This is not to cite the multitude of unofficial voices emerging from Israel as a result of free speech and competition among political parties.)

Since no overall direction of Israeli propaganda existed in the past, the results of these independent operations appeared as multiple shots in the dark. Accordingly, in fund raising appeals, Jewish organizations abroad would stress Israel's heroic "365-days-a-year war" but the Tourist Ministry would portray Israel as an ideal vacation spot. Both of the above objectives have their moment and they represent divergent rather than contradictory goals. When lacking overall coordination, however, the specific disseminations of Israel-sponsored voices could work counter to her broad foreign policy, leaving foreign observers confused as to what Israel really wants.

Worse than a propaganda program with diffuse objectives is one with misdirected goals. Israel sees its program to influence foreign opinion as *Hasbarah* (stemming from the Hebrew verb *l'hasbir,* to explain), a dispassionate, perhaps academic, communications style. Israel deliberately avoids "propaganda" which stands for a more aggressive approach. In times of peace, where favorable foreign opinion is a luxury, a Hasbarah-type explanation program is perhaps justifiable. But when confronted by an aggressive foe on the battlefield and in public relations, Hasbarah misses the point.

Hasbarah stems from the belief that it is possible to fight a propaganda war without propagandists. It is too early to tell how the new Information Ministry will conceptually treat the notion of Hasbarah, but up to the beginning of 1970 foreign communications were only small departments in each ministry. Instead of developing specialists, Hasbarah was seen as a temporary stopover in the course of a career. Deprecation of propaganda's worth naturally works against training specialists in foreign opinion. Cultural or information diplomacy calls for liaison abroad with educators, students, interest groups, literary outlets, and, in Israel's case, a given country's Jewish community.

While the task of staffing some ninety missions in seventy counties obviously strains Israel's manpower, communications representation is especially neglected. Only a few major missions have full-time diplomats in communications work. Even then, the information officer's tenure is often a hit-and-miss affair. This is because he has not been trained by the Foreign Ministry (which does train commercial attachés) in specialized areas—such as the psychological and sociological bases of communications, how ideas and myths are generated, and the interaction between domestic and international policy. In dealing with the press, the information officer's inadequate preparation also contributes to what James Reston has called the natural and historic conflict between the men who make the news and the men who write the news. Sound press relations rests not simply on speed in distributing a statement, but rather on knowledge as to how a story is written and how journalistic layout and language work.

For certain key posts (such as Washington, New York, Bonn, Paris, and London), Israel's Foreign Ministry hires Israeli journalists on a contract basis to serve as press officers. Although this arrangement does away with insensitivity to needs of the press corps, it raises other problems. In addition to the hardship of drawing strong personal loyalties to an organization on the strength of a short-term contract, skilled dealing with a foreign press demands more than journalistic knowhow. In the absence of diplomatic experience, this press officer will be unable to relate domestic trends in his country of assignment to Middle East problems. Inexperience also prevents sound contributions to policy-planning decisions in his own mission. Years of service alone do not make for expertise, but they are integral to perfecting diplomatic skill—chiefly an art rather than a science.

The Hasbarah policy fails to realize that effective foreign communications must be geared not only to governments and an educated elite, but to the mass public. Characteristically, following each major raid into Arab territory, the Foreign Ministry's Information Division puts out a heavily documented list of alleged Arab guerrilla incidents which provoked the Israeli response. This tack may be ideal for persuading diplomatic historians, but such material is usually inaccessible and uninteresting to laymen. A targeted program must focus on specific groups of opinion makers who are determined by a given country's political-social culture. It is not simply a question of providing more money for such activity, for more propaganda does not always mean better propaganda. Appropriate strategy based on research weighing the psychological requirements must be determined. According to these results, a country plan is laid out, spelling out objectives, designating target groups, exploiting media.

Thus, in certain Latin American countries labor unions represent democratic forces and Israel's communications should be geared to what such working men can readily understand (for example, a film on Histadruth, Israel's national union). In African countries, where organized labor is not a major force, Israel must focus on university populations (using media showing Israel's educational program for students from underdeveloped nations). In certain underdeveloped nations, a fast-moving soccer team may have sharper impact than a score of Hebrew University lecturers. To be sure, the notion of country plans is followed by the Tourist Ministry, showing that when Israel sees tangible results in store, such as foreign currency of visitors, she could meet the challenge.

Israel must change the implementation of her communications machinery: the after-the-fact nature of Hasbarah prevents it from reacting speedily to the sudden challenges of guerrilla warfare. Hasbarah is keyed to the slow media of periodical publications rather than fast media associated with daily deadlines and immediacy such as photo journalism, radio, and TV. Thus, Israeli decision-makers overlooked the value of photos when they destroyed Egyptian installations in 1969 in order to show the latter's vulnerability should Egypt continue firing across the Suez ceasefire line. Only in the wake of Egyptian denials was the order given to the air force to return to provide photographic evidence of the sabotage. Widespread illiteracy in the under-developed world also makes the publications orientation of Hasbarah particularly misguided. Thus, funds were unwisely suspended for Kol Israel's only radio program to West Africa although the program drew thousands of favorable letters.

Hasbarah ignores the fact that Israel's strategic position in 1970 is not what it was before the June war. Earlier, the world saw Israel as a brave little country resisting efforts to destroy her by the surrounding Arab nations with many times her population and material resources and with mountains of Soviet arms at their disposal. New circumstances have made Israel a conqueror, and in this role she cannot use the same themes she did as victim. In a strange victory which, as C.L. Sulzberger put it, the victor is prevented from "either destroying an enemy or dictating surrender terms," propaganda must be particularly attuned to delicate shifts in the international climate.

Israel's new themes should depict both positive aspects of her national fiber and the benefits which her victory has brought the Arabs. Subjects which lend themselves to this presentation include: the physical renewal of East Jerusalem since the war; unhindered access to the holy sites by people of all faiths; Jew and Arab living and working harmoniously in united Jerusalem; the Israeli civilian soldier; the pursuit of religious study and of art and culture in border settlements in the line of Arab guns.

Since world opinion is invariably more critical of victor than vanquished, Israel needs to create favorable propaganda situations ("propaganda of the deed"). Photos of soldiers on a mission into Jordan evacuating civilians (in stark contrast with Arab murdering of Israeli civilians) show a sensitive and humanitarian army. Rather than merely blowing up Arab homes adjacent to the Western Wall, believed to harbor terrorists, skilled propaganda would ceremoniously have relocated the evicted Arabs.

Instead, Israel plays the new game by dated rules, with propaganda striving to paint the Arabs darkly. The Foreign Ministry's Information Division publishes detailed analyses of Nasser's speeches in order to point out blatant lies: it releases a booklet of anti-Israel and antisemitic cartoons culled from the Arab press; it challenges El Fatah's professed revolutionary commitment by showing the guerillas' connection with Arab monarchies.

Nowhere does the failure to stress the positive emerge as poignantly as in accounts of Israeli retaliatory raids into Arab territory. Since Israel generally aims in her one raid to compensate for a series of guerrilla attacks, the danger in terms of foreign opinion is in the image of overreaction and brutality. Also there is the military's fear that in the interest of public relations security may be undermined; the price of failure being so obvious no modern army is more security-minded than is Israel's. (They joke in Israel about the Army officer so secretive that he refused to tell his taxi driver where to take him.) Often information justifying Israel's military activity is classified as secret. Censorship by the Army stirs resentment in the foreign press corps. Censorship is now a moot issue because any correspondent may telephone his paper directly abroad. Israel is thus the double loser: censorship is circumvented, and the correspondent soured.

Emphasis on immediate military success, however, has elbowed out presenting military matters in terms the world understands. Ironically, the after-the-fact nature of Hasbarah is most suitable (of all of Israel's information services) to the Army when preliminary public relations attacks from this source are thought to tip off potential targets. But so literally does the Army take the after-the-fact nature of Hasbarah that only after-the-fact does it prepare explanations. Thus, the raid on Beirut airport in December, 1968, found necessary to force the Lebanese government to drive out the terrorists they have harbored, put Israel in the position of attacking a country seemingly uninvolved in the Middle East dispute. No supporting material was drawn up in advance on the principle of freedom of the skies and the Arab criminal violation thereof. No photos were taken during the incident to publicize the brave and dangerous evacuation of civilians by Israelis. No statistics were prepared on the importance of El Al airlines to Israel's economy, the attack on whose passengers and planes impelled the Israeli response. No attempt was made, either before or after the raid, to penetrate Lebanon's image as an aloof spectator in the Middle East dispute (preoccupied with commerce, to be sure) by citing its record as a haven for international antisemitic front groups. In response to foreign criticism, Israel in dribs and drabs argued her case, but there is no evidence of her having drawn up in advance contingency plans which need not have divulged secrets nor jeopardized military security.

Before Israeli foreign propaganda is to succeed, it must be taken seriously at home. Taking propaganda seriously means becoming sensitized to the psychological dimension of foreign policy. Politically, foreign reaction must be anticipated before decision-making. Somehow, the notion persists among Israeli officialdom that, as a result of the travel abroad by officials (most of whose time is spent with Jewish communities, to boot), each such official is qualified to predict foreign opinion. What this amounts to, however, is substituting hunches for the work of specialists who carefully monitor editorial trends and statements of interest groups and politicians. Scientific surveys of possible foreign reaction need not change the actual decision. But they could affect the timing, implementation of decisions and, ultimately, how they are revealed abroad.

To take propaganda seriously from an organizational standpoint means abandoning a patchwork of information division within ministries for the centralized structure created by Prime Minister Meir. In such a propaganda ministry, various departments should be responsible for the public relations areas of every ministry and governmental agency, rather than at present where each ministry (such as the Foreign Ministry) deals with its propaganda individually. Thus, propaganda loses its role as a secondary force in a ministry devoted chiefly to other needs and becomes a full-fledged operation. This change frees the other ministries to concentrate on substantive issues directly relevant to their fields. It also ends existing problems stemming from the loose, informal coordination among ministries in the area of foreign communications. As a result of this reordering, program output in the new propaganda ministry will undoubtedly be marked by increased flexibility, initiative, and responsiveness. Assigning this new organization ministerial rank will make easier its job of advising the Prime Minister and other agencies on foreign public attitudes for present and contemplated Israeli policies, programs, and official statements.

But despite these merits, difficulties could loom for this new structure; the Army, suspicious of civilian agencies, may be unwilling to coordinate its work with an agency not primarily concerned with security.

In view of Israel's disappointing experience with her foreign propaganda since the Six-Day War, certain responsible voices in Israel have been raised for change. Israel has gone so far as to engage the New York public relations firm of Ruder & Finn, indicating increased sensitivity to the needs of a scientific approach to propaganda. However, in principle, the contributions of outsiders to improving Israel's image must be limited; as Abba Eban warned, "Our special experience cannot be presented by one who has not lived it, by one who was capable yesterday, and will be competent tomorrow, of representing, with unprofessional concern, our opponents and the advantages of tooth-paste or a better or worse cigarette." Bureaucratically, the advice of commercial firms half-way across the world will have slight impact on the day-to-day work of Israelis in the foreign communications area.

But neither more administrative recognition nor more money assure better propaganda. Conceptually, Israel's propagandists must drop their commitment to Hasbarah. Admittedly, Hasbarah is an approach appealing to certain strains in the Israeli character: it is independent, direct, proud. It smacks of the stubborn Sabra who insists Israel's case is so clearly in the right it needs no sophisticated presentation, and it lends itself to arguments of black and white, right and wrong, rather than the nuances of gray which are the cornerstone of diplomacy.

Shifting the concept of Israel's foreign communications will be possible under the new ministry, cited above. Training will not be along limited terms as at present. Personnel will learn the wider concepts of propaganda—factors affecting receptivity of ideas, who are the molders and propagators of opinion. Such training produces specialists who not only "create" propaganda, but are alert to exploiting existing situations which lend themselves to building a favorable foreign image.

Despite problems of misdirected objectives and sporadic coordination in Israel's foreign communications program, it must be conceded that on the great issues of her security and well-being, Israel's motives, values, and position are supported by very many people beyond her borders. On the strategic issues in the wake of the Six-Day War, there is wide acceptance abroad of her fundamental claim that without peace Israel cannot be expected to change her cease-fire lines. However, this success is due to Israel's having hammered away at this theme consistently, proof that if she wants something badly enough her propaganda will meet the test. Wide acceptance of the invalidity of the four-power peace talks (or other intermediaries), as opposed to Israel's insistence upon face-to-face negotiations with the Arabs, reflects the fruits of Israel's propaganda.

As for daily events, notwithstanding UN Security Council disapproval, the world seems to have grown accustomed to the inevitability of Israeli reprisals. Finally, the image of Israel—her energy, her social experiments, her renewal of the soil and absorption of the dispossessed—remains what it is in spite of conflict. Now, she must reshape this image in light of the conflict, not by diffuse disseminations, but by propaganda for a propaganda war. How much this already favorable picture of Israel mirrors years of patient work by Jewish organizations outside Israel, or the impressions of visitors and the reports of correspondents, or the work of Israel's communications program, is arguable. The study of opinion formation is sufficiently complicated if we confine it to the domestic scene. When we turn our attention to International political communication where the "who" is a complicated persuasion audience in another culture, distinct limits on content analysis emerge. What is clear is that in building her case abroad, Israel must narrow the gap between her ultimate goal of foreign support and the everyday performance of her communications network.

# # #

Broadcasting in Israel
[*Jewish Life*, March–April 1971]

When the Egged bus driver predictably raises his radio volume for the hourly news summary and a hush falls over the passengers, it shows that keeping informed in Israel is more than a casual pursuit. Given its precarious peace, Israelis are among the world's most avid radio listeners. Since Israel's fate also carries international implications, foreign audiences follow Israel's official broadcasts with a degree of concern belying her small numbers.

What broadcasting media does the Israeli listen to? What is the role of her incipient television programming? How does Israel use the airwaves to project her messages abroad?

To be sure, the flick of a radio dial in Israel brings home stations in Cairo, Damascus, Beirut, and Nicosia (Cyprus) as well as Jerusalem. The Voice of America (VOA) and British Broadcasting Corporation (BBC) are also heard at various times of the day. Inasmuch as Israel's lone television network broadcasted only four hours daily at the beginning of 1971 (with an additional half hour to be added in Arabic in the spring), Israelis add to their viewing time by tuning in programs from Beirut, Amman, or Cairo (depending on one's location in Israel).

Before the establishment of Medinath Israel in 1948, broadcasting was controlled by the British Mandatory Government which operated the Palestine Broadcasting Service in English, Hebrew, and Arabic. Meanwhile, various Jewish resistance groups transmitted from secret locations. After Israel's establishment, Kol Israel was born. Its personnel came from the former British station as well as from the underground stations. Although perhaps still popularly referred to as "Kol Israel," the Hebrew name now used for Israel's broadcasting is "Shiddurey Yisrael"—Israel Broadcasting.

Broadcasting House in Jerusalem, a few minutes away from busy Jaffa Road, was designed to be the summer palace for an Ethiopian princess, but the British converted it into radio facilities. The current TV building was originally the center of Israel's diamond industry.

From the time of Israel's creation until 1965, Kol Israel was administratively part of the Prime Minister's Office. Since 1965, radio and television has been controlled by the IBA (Israel Broadcasting Authority). The IBA is not government controlled but rather a public or state authority. Its independence of the government was shown in the bitter Sabbath TV dispute, where IBA went against the wishes of the government as well as overriding the opposition of much of the populace in scheduling broadcasts that day.

As a public body, the IBA has a Board of Governors consisting of thirty-nine persons appointed by the President on the recommendation of the Government. This is a representative body and Israeli Arabs also serve on it. To prevent government control, the founding legislation of the IBA also limited to four the number of State employees permitted to serve (teachers are not included in this category). A series of advisory committees in such areas as music, literature and art, the Jewish legacy, and Israeli values, also aids the Board of Governors.

The Government also appoints an Executive Committee of seven whose function is to plan daily events and to draw up financial plans. Terms for both Executive Committee and Board of Governors run for three years. The Government also names the Director General of the Authority—today, Sh'muel Almog—after consulting with the Board of Governors, for a five-year term.

Although the IBA is not government controlled, the K'nesseth sets certain broad policies such as, for instance, having final approval as to whether Israeli television should permit commercial sponsorship. In K'nesseth debates, the Minister of Education and Labor acts as spokesman for IBA interests.

Objectives

Unlike a commercial network, Shiddurey Yisrael has very pronounced political and cultural objectives, as spelled out in the Broadcasting Authority Law. These include "fostering good citizenship" and reflecting the achievements of the State, deepening the Jewish heritage, promotion of the Hebrew language, and reflecting the life of Diaspora Jewry and broadcasting to it. Included in this law, in addition, is the responsibility of providing broadcasts in Arabic for the Arab-speaking population and broadcasts for promotion of peace and understanding with neighboring states.

The IBA budget is raised through a dual arrangement, depending on whether funds are to be spent on internal or foreign transmissions. The current 1970–1971 total budget, a figure which is first approved by the K'nesseth (originating in the K'nesseth's Finance Committee), is I£ 45 million ($13 million approximately). Nearly all the money for domestic broadcasts is raised by either radio or television license fees and by revenue from advertisements on radio network B, one of the IBA stations. Each household having a radio must pay an annual licensing fee of I£20 ($6) and I£85 ($24) for a television. The fee is not increased for additional radio and television receivers.

The 1971–1972 budget calls for revenue from television licensing to be more than 250% the income from radio licensing. The current radio advertising rate is I£100 ($29) per 30 seconds, although an increase in the fee is a possibility. Net income to the IBA from radio commercials in the 1970–1971 fiscal year was about I£5 million ($1.4 million). According to IBA regulations, only six minutes per hour may be devoted to radio commercials, most commercials being in the form of spot announcements.

Money raised by licensing and advertisements is not used, however, for financing foreign broadcasts inasmuch as the IBA considers it unfair to make the Israeli public pay for such programs. Indeed, up until 1965, the Jewish Agency was directly involved in running such programs. In addition, the Foreign Ministry is a junior partner in financing overseas broadcasts. How much money is provided by the Jewish Agency and how much by the Foreign Ministry depends on the nature of the program; thus the Jewish Agency mainly pays for Yiddish broadcasts, whereas the cost of the transcription service (taped radio programs for broadcasts overseas) is about equally shared.

What radio programs should one expect to hear in Israel? Shiddurey Yisrael, to begin with, is not one network but four and there are good prospects that a fifth will be shortly established, which would include local foreign language broadcasts and increase the time devoted to Arabic broadcasts. Shiddurey Yisrael's networks are on the air currently a total of fifty-two hours a day. Each network is geared to certain audiences, although there is some overlap in domestic programming. Network A during the week is on the air at peak listening hours, beginning at 11:16 A.M. and closing down at 12:05 A.M. the following day. From 3 P.M.–5 P.M., Network A leaves the air. This is a "highbrow" network whose content features serious music, documentaries, talks, discussions, broadcasts to schools, adult education, drama, children's programs, religion ("Lesson in the Book of Tanyah"), and Jewish folklore. All programs on this station are in Hebrew and no advertising is carried. There are also hourly newscasts and a 45-minute news magazine.

Network B broadcasts from 6 A.M., opening with a 10-minute religious service followed by ten minutes of physical exercise. Beginning in April, 1971, this station will be on the air until 1 A.M. the following day. In addition to hourly newscasts (the same as those carried on Network A) and a 90-minute program of news and music, Network B features pop music ("Hebrew Hit Parade"), light tunes, special programs for housewives ("Housewives' Corner"), teenagers, industrial workers, motorists, sports enthusiasts (reports on the main soccer matches while they are underway), and light drama. Although this is the lone network carrying commercials, advertisers have no say in program content.

Network B also sets aside two peak hours (7 P.M.–9 P.M.) for programs for new immigrants. These consist of news in easy Hebrew, followed by a short feature and news broadcasts in Yiddish, Ladino (Judeo-Spanish), Romanian, Russian, Mograbi (the language of North African immigrants), and Hungarian. Future plans call for moving these two hours, however, to the fifth network cited above.

Radio Programming

Considering Israel's small population, the radio audience is afforded a rich variety of program choice. Direct dialing, featuring audience participation, is common to many programs. Disc jockeys have strong personal followings. Other programs are marked by spontaneous performances by guest entertainers.

The variety of recent programs on Networks A and B include "The Curtain Rises," in which foreign language plays are presented in Hebrew; "A Book to Study," reviewing works on Judaica, history, and philosophy; "Sixty Years Today," providing excerpts from Palestinian newspapers of that era; and "popular Radio University," featuring faculty members lecturing over the air.

Many Shiddurey Yisrael programs, in addition to being entertaining, also have educational worth. Illustrative is the highly popular show "Treasure Hunt," in which listeners and guests help one another in locating important sites or documents of Israel.

The IBA features a wide range of Jewish religious programs, ranging from daily Bible readings to talks on the ethics and spiritual values of Judaism. Special broadcasts normally note Jewish holidays such as the reading of the Megillah on Purim eve live from the Tel Aviv Central Synagogue

And the recital of excerpts of the Megillah the following morning according to different Jewish *nusachim*—Ashkenazic, Sephardic, and Yemenite. Other religions practiced in Israel (Moslem and Christian) also have programs devoted to them in the Arabic and English services of the IBA.

Network D, IBA's Arabic station (Dar el Iza'a el Israiliya), is currently on the air 14½ hours daily. It is heard in Israel and neighboring countries. The Arabic service, which employs a considerable number of Israeli Arabs, operates a full schedule including news, music, comments, cultural features, women's programs, drama, and documentaries. Although there are no special programs for the Arabic-speaking but non-Moslem Druze community, Druzes hold key posts in the IBA's Arabic language services (radio and television).

According to Arie Hauslich, Director of External Services of the IBA, there are three groups of Arab listeners: Arabs living in Israel's pre-1967 boundaries; Arabs in administered territories; and Arabs in bordering countries. The aim of the Arab language network, according to the Israel Government Yearbook, is:

> to expound and justify Israel's stand in the Arab-Israel conflict, to dissuade the Arabs of the administered areas from giving aid or comfort to terrorists, to deter the terrorists themselves, to emphasize Israel's aim of peaceful co-existence, and to render essential services by the radio medium.

Despite the Arab-Israel conflict, this network has achieved a high degree of credibility in the Arab world. One of its specialties is broadcasting general news developments among Israel's neighbors. By now, Arabs recognize that these broadcasts have no ax to grind. On many occasions, the Arab press outside Israel cites as testimony statements made on these Shiddurey Yisrael broadcasts. In order to develop informed transmissions, the IBA also monitors all Arab radio stations from the neighboring lands.

Although Network D broadcasts chiefly in Arabic, it carries news and feature programs for one hour each in both French and English. These programs are not aimed at immigrants per se, but at a wide audience including the diplomatic community, non-Jewish clergy, students, UN personnel, and tourists. According to Hauslich, surveys taken following the Six-Day War indicated that a large percentage of the Arab elite on the West Bank regularly tuned in these English programs—an estimated 9% of the urban West Bank population (mainly professionals). Moreover, the IBA has found that an estimated 11% of all Jewish listeners in Israel regularly follow the English program on this network, and 9% the French broadcasts.

Network C, the final station, is the Overseas Service of the IBA. Over fifty staff are employed in this operation alone. Currently, overseas broadcasts are on the air 6¾ hours daily, beaming programs in Hebrew, English, French, Russian, Yiddish, Persian, Romanian, Hungarian, Ladino, and Mograbi. Russian is the language with the largest on-the-air time, 2¼ hours daily. In recent years, the IBA has increased programming in that language, and with the severance of Soviet-Israeli diplomatic relations in the wake of the 1967 war, these transmissions make up the main daily contact of Russian Jews with Jews abroad.

Nonetheless, compared with America's official foreign broadcasting network, Voice of America, Israel's message is not extensively aired, financial limitations being the problem. For instance, VOA broadcasts in Russian daily about eight hours, plus also broadcasting programs in the minority languages spoken in the Soviet Union.

Overseas Broadcasts

The IBA Overseas program stresses transmissions to Europe and secondarily to Africa. It devotes fifteen minutes daily programming to East Africa and Southern Africa, in English. Due to financial considerations, the IBA eliminated a popular program to West Africa beamed from 1960 to 1963. A unique feature of the discontinued West African program was that it specialized in news about Africa rather than, for instance, the Middle East. As a result many Africans turned to the Israeli-sponsored program in order to keep informed on continental news. Israel was the first country to undertake such a broad-based program to West Africa.

Economy reasons also forced the cancellation of an experimental program transmitted in 1969 to North America. During its six-month life, this program proved to be one of Shiddurey Yisrael's most popular productions, drawing about 2,000 letters from abroad in its first three months on the air. Even today, dozens of letters come weekly into its Jerusalem headquarters inquiring about possibly reviving the program. Actually, this program was only of fifteen minutes duration daily and consisted of news, comment and, when time allowed, a disc of Israeli music.

Content-wise, ISA's foreign transmissions fall into two categories. The first, didactic, emphasizes material on Hebrew, Judaism, and Israeli civilization. Thus, on Jewish holidays such as Purim and Tu B'Shevat, the IBA sponsors special programs. The second broadcasting category, informational, features news, talk shows, interviews, and discussions.

A drawback in Shiddurey Yisrael's foreign programming is the relatively loose coordination existing between the radio station and other informational arms (Foreign Ministry , Tourist Ministry) of Israel. Meetings take place among officials in various governmental agencies concerned with Israel's foreign "image," but these meetings basically set overall policy rather than develop coordinated, systematic themes. What Shiddurey Yisrael broadcasts, of course, is no haphazard decision inasmuch as abroad its transmissions are taken as the official policy of Israel. Thus, the IBA script writers check with the Foreign Ministry before writing up sensitive announcements. Such coordination is along informal lines, for instance through a phone call.

By contrast, it seems that United States foreign information arrangements provide for the American broadcasting arm, VOA, to have a more integral and instructed role in American propaganda. The VOA is also administratively part of the overall American information program, whereas the IBA is administratively independent from other Israeli agencies.

In addition to scheduled broadcasts, the IBA operates a transcription service which prepares taped radio programs for foreign distribution. Programs are produced regularly in English, Spanish, French, Portuguese, Yiddish, and Hebrew. According to the Israel Government Yearbook, South America broadcasts weekly fifty-one such programs in Spanish and seven in Portuguese. Uruguay carries the IBA's news program weekly and a weekly concert of the IBA Symphony Orchestra is performed over the Uruguayan and Paraguayan radio networks. Shiddurey Yisrael programs are distributed to 500 stations in the United States, including a weekly review of the Israel press and a monthly magazine on science, art, and theatre. Some 750 programs go out annually to Africa and Asia to some forty stations, mainly in English and French. In all, the IBA today transmits to some 800 radio stations worldwide.

The Transcription Service also produces special programs for Israel Independence Day and the independence days of friendly countries. Since 1965, the IBA has carried its "International Bible Quiz." Contestants in this program were winners in national preliminary contests in such diverse countries as Ghana, New Zealand, Holland, Malta, Ethiopia, and Finland.

Listeners in Israel and abroad regularly hear performances by the Israel Broadcasting Authority Symphony Orchestra. After the Israel Philharmonic, it is the country's leading orchestra and it specializes in pioneering new Israel music in addition to performances of the classics. The orchestra is made up of fulltime musicians on the payroll of the Authority.

To develop broadcasting personnel, the IBA operates a training center which conducts radio classes for people aspiring to enter broadcasting, for its own staff (announcers, script writers, technicians), and for students in the Communications Department of the Hebrew University. Reflecting the IBA's increased attention to Soviet Jews was an announcement in early 1971 about the opening of a training course for Russian language broadcasting. Courses in television instruction are now in their beginning stage.

Indicative of the important cultural status of the military in Israel is the fact that it is the only other national institution having a radio station of its own—Galley Tzahal ("Waves of the Armed Forces") which has a weekday schedule from 11 A.M. to 12:05 A.M. the following day. It broadcasts shows of military interest such as announcements for troops, shows from military bases, and interviews with troops. Its schedule also includes light music, discussion, interviews, and news. Under the Broadcasting Law, Galley Tzahal's non-military programming is under the supervision of the IBA.

TV Upsurge

The phenomenal growth of television in Israel is one of the main cultural transformations since the Six-Day War. Following an eighteen-month period of active on-air preparation during which programs were beamed several times a week, regular daily broadcasts began in May, 1969. By early 1971, with 356,000 sets in the country, nearly every second family in Israel had a television set, according to the Central Bureau of Statistics. Interestingly, only 31% of Israeli families have phones in their homes. One of the main casualties of the growth of TV viewing has been movie houses, many of which have been turned into catering halls.

Currently, the IBA lone television network transmits Sunday–Thursday and Saturday evenings 6:00–10:00 P.M. Friday programs run from

3:30–4:00 P.M. and 6:30–11:00 P.M. Following controversy about broadcasting on the Sabbath, the Supreme Court upheld such telecasts. (The radio stations too transmit on the Sabbath, although following an abbreviated schedule.)

TV scheduling is basically divided into three audiences—children's programs (one half-hour viewing time in the early evening); Arabic programs (currently one hour, but will be expanded another thirty minutes) featuring news documentaries, family shows, and movies ("A Man Named Bogart"); and Hebrew programs (two and one-half hours) carrying news, interviews (an interview with a captured El Fatah frogman received much public attention), films, documentaries (e.g., the changes taking place in the Israeli Druze community; Aztec civilization), and variety shows.

Israeli television also broadcasts programs on Jewish tradition, daily Bible readings, and a program of religious content at the end of the Sabbath, *Hamavdil*. In 1969, the issue of telecasting on the Sabbath stirred bitter debate in Israel. As regards radio, the IBA and its predecessors have always broadcast on the Sabbath, for which it received special permission from the Labor Ministry.* The decision by the IBA to begin broadcasting on the Sabbath was taken by majority vote in plenary session, although the Israeli Cabinet had earlier called upon the IBA to defer action until the matter could be considered by the new Government. An appeal to the Prime Minister against that vote was allowed and statutorily Sabbath telecasting had to await a Government decision. In the face of this requirement, however, on a petition by a private citizen on November 8, 1969, a Supreme Court Justice "issued an order against the Prime Minister to show cause why the appeal in question should not be disallowed, together with an interim order to resume Sabbath eve telecasts pending the Court's final verdict. That verdict upheld the interim order" (Israel Government Yearbook for 1969). Despite the opposition by religious sources, such TV broadcasts are regular fare today.

*This is but one of many instances of "special permission" by the Labor Ministry granting exemptions from legal requirements as to Sabbath observance by industrial and commercial institutions.—Ed.

The growing pains of Israeli television are perhaps more painful than those of other nations just beginning such programming because not only does Israel presently have just one single station to satisfy the different national viewing tastes, but also because of the need to produce multilanguage and multi-cultural broadcasts to meet the demands of both Jewish and Arab viewers.

One of the important reasons for Israel's decision to develop television was the desire of the Government that her Arab population receive the other side of the story and not only view programs from enemy Arab countries. Yet, at present, Arab programs run early in the evening and ending at 7:30 P.M., an hour which, according to Azar Artul of Nazareth, an Arab member of the IBA, prevents them from watching programs in Arabic later in the evening.

Another problem is the fact that some half the material shown comes from abroad (Hebrew or Arabic subtitles are added), financial limitations preventing the production of more Israeli subject matter. The IBA management also complains that cinema owners working hand in hand with film distributors make it nearly impossible to get Israel films for the TV public because of high sums asked by potential suppliers.

During the day, the television station is used for educational programs directed at school classrooms in such diverse subjects as arithmetic, physics, English, citizenship, and technical drawing. Educational television is operated by a trust established by the Rothschild Foundation under the supervision of the Ministry of Education and Culture.

Whether or not to introduce commercials is one of the major controversies associated with Israel television. The main argument in favor of commercials is that the extra money will enable the IBA to present better programs. Secondly, such advertisements, its proponents claim, will spur competition for various products and will ultimately benefit the consumer.

Forces opposed to commercials maintain that they would stimulate further buying, a situation contrary to the Government's current objective of reducing public spending. Despite the recommendation of Education Minister Yigal Allon, the Cabinet and K'nesseth voted in early 1971 against adding commercials.

According to a survey taken in the summer of 1970, some 70% of the Jewish population aged 14 and above watched the television station's daily Mabat newsreel, good testimony to the medium's popularity. Israelis place much credibility in the truth of the IBA's news reports, despite the fact that owing to security considerations these broadcasts may be relatively slow in transmitting certain items (foreign audiences, for example, knew about the devastating Arab toll in the early stages of the Six-Day War before the Israelis). Program announcers (several newscasters are women) have personal followings, and each vacancy for an announcership brings about 1,500 applications. (Pay for such a position is not excessive.) The jump in TV sales also reflects a confidence that such an acquisition—Israelis are taxed highly for TV's, as a luxury item, making the cost at least double of what the same TV would be in the United States—represents a worthwhile investment in family entertainment and education. Abroad, Shiddurey Yisrael must be scoring points, as indicated by the abuse heaped on it by both Arabs and Russians.

# # #

Israel's Foreign Information Program
[*International Communications Gazette*, formerly *Gazette (International Journal of Mass Communications)*, Amsterdam, Second Quarter 1973]

Whatever the origins of the Israeli-Arab conflict, propaganda is a critical instrument in determining how the rivalry is eventually set forth. How does Israel attempt to win over foreign public opinion, what instruments are used, what themes stressed, and what problems arise?

At the outset, it should be stressed that certain hardships, largely external to Israel's foreign information program, result both from Israel's security needs and the nature of world relations in the 1970s. Israel's victory in the 1967 Six Day War placed her in the role of victor in an era when political sympathy abroad is normally the lot of losers. Continuous denunciations of Israel by United Nations organs, although a voting majority of the U.N. stems from Communist, Moslem and certain Afro-Asian states, automatically casts Israel in the role of a pariah.

Israel also suffers from a declining support for internationalism particularly in the United States and other Western countries which Israel looks toward for favorable recognition. Finally, for better or worse, an underlying factor in determining the success of Israel's foreign information program is the reaction to the more basic issues associated with the notion of a Jewish state.

To be sure, many voices emerge from Israel including official state representations as well as the activities of private organizations within Israel. For purposes of this article, however, attention will be devoted to those formal, governmental activities of Israel designed to influence opinion abroad.

Ministry for Foreign Affairs

In the early 1970s, Israel maintained more than 90 permanent missions in over 70 nations. The Ministry for Foreign Affairs contains the Information Division which aims at gaining favorable foreign opinion for Israel. Particular problems which the Information Division stresses in its disseminations include Israel's position on the reunification of Jerusalem under Israeli control (as a result of Israel's victory in the Six Day War); the refusal to return certain territory to the Arabs captured in the Six Day War because of alleged security considerations; the need for more rather than less face-to-face negotiations with the Arab states as a means of reaching a peace settlement; the plight of Soviet Jewry, particularly that they be given the right to emigrate to Israel, should they so wish.

Ministry publications appear in English, French, Spanish and German. Many of these publications are reprints of material originally brought out either by other Israeli governmental units, by organizations within Israel (Israeli Students of Middle East Affairs, The Association for Peace), Zionist organizations abroad and private publications (*Jerusalem Post, The Israel Economist*). A recent innovation was a series of experimental pamphlets, 'Answers and Questions' produced by the Information Division in 1970 and dealing with a central information subject.

While information or public diplomacy is an increasingly important feature of international politics, Israel only has a few Foreign Ministry personnel engaged in full-time information work abroad. As of 1970, such information officers were stationed in the main Western capitals (United States, Canada, France and England). The busy New York Consulate had several staff dealing exclusively in information work, with one officer assigned, for instance, to focus on Jewish organizational affairs in the New York metropolitan area.

To be sure, in this instance, titles may be misleading and the absence of a formal 'information officer' from an Israeli diplomatic mission does not at all imply that such work is neglected. Given the small size of Israeli diplomatic missions (as is the case as well with other small countries), each diplomat wears several hats and a certain role flexibility invariably results. The Information Division is currently engaged in developing a series of regional information centers overseas in order to supply material to its missions.

In Jerusalem, the Information Division in addition to a Director has three Assistant Directors who are simultaneously responsible for both geographic and functional areas. Among the material sent by the Information Division to missions abroad are general instructions, and reprints and translations of documents (such as a speech by the Prime Minister to the Knesset). Each mission, however, is allowed a certain amount of autonomy. For instance, the Israel Mission to the United States after every important event publishes a 'pink sheet', a mimeographed background paper describing the Israeli view. These documents are distributed to 10,000–12,000 Americans, including leading government officials, Congressmen, businessmen and Jewish organization officials.

The Information Division deals with student opinion on various levels and both in London and the New York Consulate there are officers dealing mainly with student and university affairs. Among the publics of the Information Division are Israeli students abroad, Jewish students outside Israel and students who come to Israel for temporary study (i.e. the junior university year abroad, summer institutes and workstudy programs in Kibbutzim).

Work with students involves relationships by the Information Division both with traditional Jewish organizations and the newer radical Jewish groups outside the Jewish 'establishment'. Such activity with student groups is often delicate for the Information Division inasmuch as certain positions espoused by some student organizations run counter to official Israeli policy. The growth of anti-Israel opinion on the part of the 'New Left' is a leading concern of the Information Division.

Activities focusing on student opinion include seminars abroad with visiting Israelis, paid visits to Israel for selected student leaders, aid for Israeli students to attend international student conferences and sharing in the cost of organizing international student conferences and seminars in Israel.

In terms of other activities designed to influence foreign public opinion, the Information Division sponsors Israeli lecturers abroad (including Arabs), mobile exhibits (i.e. the Holy Places, Jerusalem, development, science and agriculture) and visits to Israel by television teams and radio and television commentators. A relatively new emphasis of the Information Division has been Israeli made films for viewing abroad. In this regard, the absence of a highly developed local film industry presents problems. (While many foreign producers come to Israel to make films, these people deal with the Ministry of Commerce and Industry rather than with the Foreign Ministry.) In 1972, the Information Division opened a Jerusalem office which distributes material to visitors from abroad on various world problems facing Israel.

Press Office: Ministry for Foreign Affairs

Since 1967, Israel has emerged as one of the world's chief journalistic datelines, and inasmuch as an estimated eighty per cent of the news in the world's press about Israel is written in Israel rather than abroad, press relations make up an important part of Israel's foreign information program. While before the Six Day War there were few foreigners in Israel representing overseas press interests, by 1971 in addition to the main Western powers, Holland, Sweden, West Germany and Italy had full time correspondents in Israel. To be sure, the foreign press corps is less specialized than the Israeli press, the latter including newsmen concentrating on such subjects as military affairs and the areas occupied by Israel since the 1967 war.

The foreign press corps in Israel includes resident correspondents, free-lancers, 'stringers' (reporters on a standby basis in different sections of the country), television and radio personnel. The Foreign Press Association numbers about 100 accredited resident correspondents of the international media. About one-half of the resident correspondents are based in Tel Aviv and the other half in Jerusalem, the former city's importance based on its being the headquarters of the Ministry of Defense, and the latter the capital and seat of the Foreign Ministry. Before the Six Day War, Jerusalem was not the important press site for correspondents it is today.

In addition to dealing with the Press Office of the Foreign Ministry, correspondents from abroad are also serviced by the Government Press Office in the areas of accreditation, translations, publication of announcements and in the provision of certain office facilities. As a result of a 1970 administrative reorganization, the Government Press Office falls under the supervision of the Israel Cabinet Secretary.

The Foreign Ministry spokesman who directs the Press Office issues communiqués, information and other authoritative background material and deals with questions from the resident press as well as those made by intercontinental phone. On an official basis, the Press Office also arranges meetings between correspondents and Foreign Ministry officials (although, of course, many informal contacts such as at diplomatic receptions take place in addition), and the Press Office claimed to have arranged about 1,000 such official sessions in 1970. In times of relative quiet, the Press Office arranges for tours by correspondents focusing on Israel's creative and non-military side.

The Foreign Ministry spokesman services not only the foreign press corps but Israeli correspondents as well. In 1971, there were two daily meetings set by the spokesman, one for foreign correspondents and the other for the Israeli press. Depending upon particular problems, the Press Office also sets up special meetings for the foreign press corps with Israeli specialists. The Foreign Ministry Press Liaison Officer in Tel Aviv uses an electronic broadcasting device (facetiously called 'Golem', or 'Dummy') to notify correspondents in either their offices or homes about important news developments.

Since Israel ranks today among the world's leading troublespots, many prominent foreign journalists visit it for a short time period. Such visits are often a combination of tours and meetings with top Israeli policy makers. In order to deal with these visiting correspondents, the Foreign Ministry maintains fulltime personnel both in Jerusalem and Tel Aviv. Before the 1970 reorganization of Israel's information services, services for visiting correspondents were provided by the Government Press Office.

According to Israeli policy, considerations of military security require press censorship and the limitation of certain on-scene press coverage. These rules apply both to domestic media and the transmissions of foreign correspondents. According to censorship policy, however, the press is permitted to cite in their stories material either formally or previously barred from originating in Israel (such as estimates of Israeli air power) provided such information was previously printed abroad and the source referred to in the story.

Israeli censorship policy is traceable to the time of the Palestinian Mandate where the High Commissioner for Palestine served as the chief censor, to have been replaced today by the Minister of Defense. As under the British Mandate, there is a wide definition of what constitutes 'public order', the official ground for censorship. Not only does the censorship office carefully sift stories on Israeli troop movements and military installations, but the press is prevented from noting the names of officers in front lines for fear of possibly endangering them should they be taken prisoner.

Headed by a Colonel, the main censorship office in Tel Aviv has a staff of about thirty and it is open 24 hours every day of the year. The Jerusalem censorship office has about ten personnel. The censorship office consists of career army personnel, enlisted men and civilians. Given the need of journalists to 'get the story', and the responsibility of the Ministry of Defense to safeguard military security, differences of opinion on censorship policy invariably arise, particularly in coverage of military incidents. *Newsweek*, for instance, reported the following accusation:

'One blue pencil doesn't know what the other blue pencil is doing,' complains Associated Press bureau chief Hal McClure, who recalls one occasion when a censor eliminated crucial details from his report on a patrol along the Jordan River even though another censor had cleared a filmed report on the same patrol by a European TV cameraman.

A further complaint of the resident foreign press corps is that whereas their dispatches are closely examined by the censors, visiting correspondents after having left Israel could write anything they wish with virtual impunity. In its defense, the censorship office argues that in view of Israel's precarious security situation laws applicable to news reporting in other countries are not relevant and that the censorship procedures are enforced fairly and consistently.

Overseas, the Foreign Ministry engages Press Officers in certain key posts (for instance Bonn, Paris, Washington, London and Rome). Some Press Officers are career Foreign Ministry personnel and others are Israeli journalists hired on a contractual basis.

Division for Cultural and Scientific Relations, Ministry for Foreign Affairs

In an increasingly politicized world, ideas are often seen in terms of their country of origin rather than in terms of their own intrinsic worth. Among the purposes of this division, is to show Israel's contributions toward creative endeavor, an especially important task in view of the fact that so much of the world's news about Israel stresses her military situation. This division also works against attempts to isolate Israel culturally and scientifically such as efforts by Arab nations to prevent Israeli participation at scientific conferences and at international sports meetings.

As of 1970, Israel had cultural agreements with 28 countries covering such areas as exchanges of students and professors. These agreements spell out the obligations of both signatories, indicating, for instance, the number of scholarships to be awarded and how much each nation will pay toward the exchange of visiting professors.

The Cultural and Scientific Relations Division also encourages university lectureships abroad in Hebrew and Israel Culture, the publication of Hebrew books in original and in translation and provides grants for Israeli academics to attend conventions abroad. It also arranges for exchange visits by performing artists and scientists, exhibits of Israeli artistic life abroad and awards stipends for advanced academic study and research.

This office is more of a coordinator than actual executioner of specific programs. Thus, if Israel paintings are to be displayed abroad, the Cultural and Scientific Relations Division appoints the curator on a contract basis rather than directly do the job itself. The division might also make certain that the paintings are properly sent off (perhaps, in addition, providing a grant for the transferring of equipment) and that maximum coverage is given the exhibition's opening. Among the division's direct undertakings, however, is the publication of the Israeli cultural quarterly, *Ariel*, appearing in English, French, Spanish and German.

As in other aspects of Israel's image abroad, the official work of the cultural and scientific division only reveals part of the picture. Many Israeli groups and individuals engaged in artistic and scientific affairs—the Israeli Philharmonic, a Hebrew University professor, a successful author—have contacts abroad and they, rather than the Foreign Ministry, take the initiative in dealing in what is ultimately foreign public opinion.

In Israel, the Division of Cultural and Scientific Relations has specialists in the following fields: cultural agreements, literature, science, the performing arts, the plastic arts and sports. Abroad, only a small number of missions are staffed by separate cultural attachés. Countries to which the Foreign Ministry assigns Cultural Attachés as of 1970 were Argentina, Brazil, France, England and the United States (with Israeli Consulates in Boston, Chicago, Philadelphia and Los Angeles). Most Cultural Attachés are not career personnel in the foreign Ministry, but instead people who have worked in the arts hired on a contract basis.

Division for Official Guests, Ministry for Foreign Affairs

While the development of the information instrument of diplomacy is predicated in large measure on the new found power of the masses in twentieth century politics, opinion leaders remain formidable factors in determining a given country's foreign policy. Since Israel does not operate with a big budget for its foreign information program, it attaches much weight to the visits of influential official guests. In 1968–1969, this division was responsible for the visits of 587 people from 71 countries and in 1969–1970 it invited 708 guests from 73 countries.

As a result of the background understanding these visits aim at developing, the Foreign Ministry feels these opinion leaders will in the future be more sympathetic toward Israeli policy. Furthermore, the very news of their trips to Israel might be regarded as helpful toward Israel's position. The professions of these guests include Heads of State and Prime Ministers, professors and students, journalists, religious leaders, authors and artists.

Normally, the stay of an official guest in Israel is one week. In addition to arranging a tour of the country, the Division for Official Guests sets up meetings between the guest and his Israeli counterpart (a trade union leader might meet an official of the Histadrut, Israel's Federation of Labor) and appointments with suitable Israeli leaders. Since official guests, as any tourist, are at liberty to visit any section of the country, the final impression of Israel is not limited to the official explanations of the Foreign Ministry hosts.

The number of VIP's coming to Israel under this program is only a small part of the total visiting opinion leaders. Israeli institutions (the Hebrew University inviting a professor) also invite guests and certain opinion leaders come to Israel independently (United States political leaders on fact-finding tours).

Ministry of Tourism

Overtly, the overseas promotion of the Tourist Ministry is aimed at bringing visitors to Israel as a means of promoting domestic employment and foreign currency earnings. But such an undertaking is hardly divorced from politics, ranging from the representational work of the Tourist Ministry abroad to the reasons why tourists either choose to visit or to stay away from Israel. The Israel Government Tourist Corporation which raises funds abroad for investments in tourist industries is also affected by public opinion toward Israel.

The Ministry of Tourism runs twenty official offices overseas. Each office has at least one Israeli plus local staff. Tourist information offices are in Argentina, Australia, Belgium, Brazil, Canada, Denmark, England,

Federal Republic of Germany, France, Holland, Italy, South Africa, Sweden, Switzerland, and the United States (Atlanta, Beverly Hills, Boston, Chicago, New York).

Regarding foreign opinion, the work of the Tourist Ministry can be divided into three main activities: stimulating interest in Israel among the travel trade such as by supplying travel agents and airlines with technical information and knowhow; creating favorable opinion for travel to Israel among the mass public using, for instance, television and radio appearances and film evenings; and through direct contact with the public in lectures. Although the two latter methods are ostensibly non-political, questions about politics either by interviewers from the media or the public often arise.

In its campaigns, the Tourist Ministry uses market research and attempts audience targeting rather than to use uniform, diffuse publicity. The ministry also takes surveys of tourists leaving Israel, although information through this source is limited because it reveals the observations of those tourists who came, but not those of potential tourists who did not come.

Indicative of the variety of approaches used by the Tourist Ministry is that in advertisements geared to American Jews, for instance, the religious and historic aspects of Israel are stressed, whereas in socialist Scandinavia the Ministry focuses on the cooperative Kibbutz movement.

In 1971, the Tourist Ministry launched a publicity program designed to encourage tours by foreign professionals in various fields. These tours combine a vacation with a work-study program on the activities of Israel in specific areas. The advantage of this program is that it marks the first time 'that a group of professionals are able to get complete information and guidance on proposed tours in their specific fields of interest from one source.' The Tourist Ministry has drawn up proposals for the professions of agriculture, medicine, law and social work. Future plans call for widening the group of professions to be included in such tours. These programs depart from traditional tourist promotion that in the past stressed physical sites and city-by-city itineraries.

While a record number of tourists have visited Israel since the Six Day War, intermittent hostilities and negative headlines have kept back what the

Tourists Ministry feels might be an even larger number of potential visitors. In order to show that whatever military incidents take place are confined to border areas and to expose visitors to the day-to-day internal situation, the Tourist Ministry invited in 1970 some 1,200 foreign newsmen to Israel. In cooperation with the Ministry for Foreign Affairs and El Al Airlines, the Tourist Ministry has invited other groups. Within Israel, the Tourist Ministry, through its dozen regional offices, pamphlets and special tourist evenings put together by the local tourist offices, disseminated information.

Israel Broadcasting Authority

Since 1965, radio and television broadcasting in Israel has been controlled by the Israel Broadcasting Authority, a public or state authority, rather than a government controlled network. Previously, Israeli broadcasting was administratively part of the Prime Minister's Office and was officially known as 'Kol Israel' (Voice of Israel) instead of its present Hebrew name, 'Shidurei Israel' (The Network of Israel). As a public body, the IBA has a Board of Governors of 31 members (also including Arabs) designed to represent a cross-section of the Israeli population. IBA beams programs in a variety of languages; programs emphasize transmission to Europe and secondarily to other areas of the world. Content-wise, IBA programs feature material on the Hebrew language, Jewish and Israel culture, talk shows, interviews and discussions. Special programs are aired for Jewish holidays.

Of the information instruments cited in this study, the IBA is the only one directly reaching an Arab audience in Arabic. IBA has a special Arab language network (Dar el Iza'a el Israiliya) on the air in 1970 14½ hours daily. IBA's lone television network which is on the air only a few hours daily, devotes one hour to Arabic language programs. These broadcasts could also be seen in the neighboring states (the reverse also being the case, televisions in Israel receiving broadcasts—depending on one's location in Israel—from Beirut, Amman and Cairo).

According to the IBA, there are three Arab audiences: Arabs living in Israel's pre-1967 boundaries; Arabs in the administered territories; Arabs in adjoining countries. Broadcasts in Arabic have a number of purposes, including the presentation of Israel's case in the Middle East conflict, deterring Arab terrorism and emphasizing Israel's interest in a peaceful settlement.

The Army Spokesman

The Army Spokesman's Office based in Tel Aviv provides information on immediate military developments. This office releases information on clashes between Israel and the Arabs. In terms of the press, two important factors involving the Army Spokesman are the speed in which the details of a clash are revealed and the accuracy of the released information. According to the late R. Erfat who served as Army Spokesman, the office in releasing news strives for impartiality among the press corps and assures that news is not given out until the reliability of the facts is determined. 'We will invariably prefer to wait until we get all the facts straight.'

Ministry of Defense

Previous to the appointment of Moshe Dayan to the post of Minister of Defense, Israeli Prime Ministers also served as Defense Ministers. Under the tenure of Dayan, the Ministry has increased its autonomy in the area of public opinion formation. The Defense Ministry deals with background defense policy, overall policy in terms of governing the areas acquired since the Six Day War, the Israeli defense industries and the military assistance program of Israel's foreign aid. The Defense Ministry is also responsible for certain human problems such as the transition of soldiers from military to civilian life.

Jewish Agency

The Jewish Agency focuses on foreign public opinion on various levels. It coordinates the information of other units of the Israeli government in its contacts with Jewish groups abroad. Its youth department deals with Jewish youth organizations overseas. The Jewish Agency helps to guide study missions visiting Israel and works with friendship leagues between Israel and other countries. Among the Jewish Agency's publications are *Israel*

Today, a series of pamphlets on some forty different aspects of Israel life, and the biweekly *Israel Digest*.

Evaluation of Israel's Foreign Information Program

In domestic matters, it is possible to reach certain general conclusions regarding the function of public opinion in influencing decisions. In international communication, however, where the actors are a wide variety of disseminating instruments in one country and an amorphous recipient audience in another country, it is far harder to come to any definite conclusions. In Israel's case, how she is seen abroad is attributable to many official and unofficial factors including the audience's reaction to Jewish religion and history, the work of Jewish organizations in the recipient country, impressions of tourists and reports of journalists, Jewish publications (*Jerusalem Post* and press releases of the Jewish Telegraphic Agency), Israeli products and Israel's cultural and scientific reputation, geopolitical factors (the importance to the audience of Arab oil or the Suez Canal), as well as, of course, the performance of Israel's main official communicators described above.

Regardless of the information instruments used to get Israel's message abroad, they cannot replace actual Israeli action and policy as the main yardsticks in influencing foreign public opinion. As has been often noted, such policy is at times difficult to pinpoint in view of the nature of the Israeli Cabinet government where one Minister could issue a statement, for instance, on the prospects of war and another Minister on the prospects of peace. (In the last analysis, the finality of Israeli foreign policy is fixed by the Prime Minister's enunciation of a position). In addition to genuine internal division within Israel as to policy, her post-1967 position may have seen certain advantages in public vagueness as to policy as a factor allowing for flexibility in whatever diplomatic bargaining might take place with the Arab states.

Coordination on the subject of foreign information exists both within and among Ministries. The Ministry for Foreign Affairs has a 'Maarach Hasbarah' (Information Alignment) consisting of the Divisions of Information, Cultural and Scientific Relations, the Press Office, the Documentation Center and the Department of Public Relations. While arrangements for cooperation among Ministries exist, cooperation is mainly based around ad hoc projects. Compared with larger nations, Israel has far fewer personnel engaged in foreign communications work and informal working relationships take place among them.

Certain organizational changes in 1970 served to tighten administrative span of control. Previously, Israel Gallili, a Minister of Israel's Cabinet without Portfolio, had parliamentary authority for the information program. Under a 1970 reorganization, however, the authority of Gallili's Ministry evaporated when the Ministry for Foreign Affairs became responsible for the foreign information activity previously carried out by Gallili's office, and the Ministry of Education and Culture took over domestic information work which had also been executed in the past under Gallili.

Hasbarah or Propaganda?

An effort to persuade foreign opinion can be called either 'information' or 'propaganda', the former program being mainly educational, dispassionate and politically defensive, whereas 'Propaganda' is more aggressive, targeted and dramatic.

Officially, the Ministry for Foreign Affairs' foreign communications program is labeled 'Hasbarah' (originating from the Hebrew verb le'hasbir, to explain) rather than 'Tamullah' (Propaganda). Although Israel's shying away from use of the term 'Propaganda' (by contrast, so does the United States; the official governmental persuasion program being called USIA, United States Information Agency) is traceable to the derogatory image this word has acquired, more than semantics is shown in Israel's self-description of 'Hasbarah'. As Netanel Lorch has noted, Israel's foreign information program is 'based on the prosaic doctrine that truth is the best policy'. In other words, facts are facts and they should speak for themselves without being doctored. Basic to the Hasbarah approach is the belief that truth will win out because there is a certain fairness and reason among Israel's audience. In its confidence in Israel's ultimate case, the Hasbarah orientation also reflects an independent strain in the Israeli character.

While in principle each nation today would like complete foreign support for its diplomatic positions, financial limitations preclude such ambitious persuasion goals. As a program of Hasbarah or information, Israel generally aims at shoring up confidence in those already committed rather than aggressively seeking converts. Thus, according to the Foreign Ministry, the three main audiences for Israel's information program, in order of priority, are: 1. sympathizers; 2. the unidentified; 3. the hostile.

On the one hand, the drawback of such an emphasis is that 'we reinforce our efforts to give our audience what they want and at the same time reinforce our own belief in what we are saying'. On the other hand, such a program is defensible insofar as Israel, a country, without any dependable international allies, is better off solidifying the support of her loyal publics rather than investing limited funds in risky information programs elsewhere. Nonetheless, Israel's foreign information program distinguishes degrees of hostility—it is considered rather futile, for example, to attempt to win over to Israel's diplomatic camp the Communist bloc, whereas Israel is worried about opposition from the New Left.

In the past, Israel's information program stressed the written or printed word as a disseminating instrument. According to Lorch, the priority scale was as follows: written communications, first; radio and other audial media, second; audio-visual media, third.

Several explanations were responsible for such emphasis, the first being that Israeli diplomacy was based on traditional methods (government-to-government relations) rather than on 'people-to-people' diplomacy, the latter making much greater use of modern communications instruments. Secondly, this media ordering stems in Lorch's opinion, from the condition that Jews as 'the People of the Book, naturally assume other people, to be equally avid readers'. The Foreign Ministry's Information Division recognizes the need of expanding the output of films and television and the future will probably see more utilization of material in these areas.

The Information Program: How Successful?

Given the difficulties of estimating precisely the role of various attitudes both within and outside Israel affecting Israel's foreign image, there are indications of the success of Israel's position. To be sure, as Foreign Minister Eban noted, the measure of the success of an informational activity is not necessarily shown 'by unqualified support in latter, but rather by sympathy for the main objective of our policy'. The failure of the Arab states to isolate Israel either politically or commercially must be given high priority in rating Israel's image.

While Israel tends to enjoy now substantial support in the world, what of the future? As the New Diplomacy's stress on modern communications instruments becomes increasingly the norm in diplomatic conduct, Israel's foreign information program will need strengthening in several areas. Israeli propagandists of the future will need training in the social and psychological foundations of communications, the opinion formation process, and how ideas are generated between cultures. Since Israel has a limited budget for official propaganda, and in the foreseeable future such financing will not change much, she must rigorously choose her audiences, concentrating where possible on elites rather than broad masses.

Israel has made an important beginning in using media communities in foreign countries, and such a program should be expanded. For instance, in the United States the Conference of Presidents of Major Jewish Organizations has set up a Mass Media Committee, and certain of the committee's activities included creating and distributing Israel Independence Day supplements sent to newspapers throughout the country, a monthly listing of new available material about Israel and a consolidated file of journalists who have visited Israel since the Six Days War. Of course, the chief professional publicists of Israel must be Israelis. This policy should apply to the role of foreign advertising agencies. Abba Eban noted:

> . . . Israel can only be represented efficiently by those whose fate is intimately bound up with its fate, whose identification with Israel is unreserved and exclusive, whose roots are in its traditions, and whose whole being is identified with its mission.

Because information work in the future will be more specialized, reappraisal should also focus on the present variety of official agencies attempting to influence foreign opinion. Without advocating any structural change, it is safe to argue that the total message conveyed by Israel abroad would be more effective under a more unified organizational set up. It is also more likely that a tighter propaganda structure would increase considerations of foreign opinion within Israel before the governmental policymakers make decisions.

Certain of the above suggestions would involve more money, but this change alone would not guarantee more favorable foreign opinion for Israel. More basic must be the realization that because public opinion counts increasingly today in world politics, information policy should be no less haphazard than military policy. In his makeup, the future propagandist of Israel should contain the qualities described by Leonard H. Marks, former head of the U.S. Information Agency (stated in regard to American communications specialists, but applicable to Israel as well) of:

> . . . missionary, teacher, publicist, diplomat and a contradictory combination of rugged individualist and loyal organization man.

# # #

Israel's Word War
[*Forum*, January 1983—Abridged]

While the decline in support for Israel by the West may be linked to issues beyond that nation's control, such as the industrial world's dependence on oil, it may also be explainable in part by the lack of Israel's public diplomacy. Yet the government of Israel seems to fail consistently to pay attention to the propaganda or ideological element.

Friends of Israel abroad regularly raise the issue of Israel's PR shortcomings. Chaim Herzog, now the President of Israel and one time Ambassador to the United Nations, observed, "I cannot remember a meeting at which I was not asked why there is no information policy and why Israel is so poor at explaining itself."[1]

[Rubin here reiterates that] conceptually, Israel's failure to make effective use of the propaganda instrument stems from: (1) the *'Hasbara'* (i.e.,

1. *The Jerusalem Post*, 2 October 1979.

"explanation") thrust of its foreign persuasion program, with an apparent lack of regard for foreign public opinion stemming from a strong need for military security and, possibly, from a vision of the world as essentially anti-Semitic, particularly when Jewish well being is balanced with the world's need for an uninterrupted flow of oil; and (2) the organization of Israel's foreign information program, with at least five different government units disseminating propaganda to a general audience and many others specifically directing messages to world Jewry.

Despite Israel's 'image' problems, it has still failed to develop a cadre of professionally trained foreign information specialists. As the New Diplomacy's stress on modern communications instruments becomes increasingly the norm in international conduct, Israel's foreign information program appears more and more to fail the test.

In the pragmatic mode of operations marking Israel's diplomatic service, Israeli political scientist Nissen Oren noted that training in general is downplayed. Oren maintains that Israeli diplomacy places a low priority on planning and troublesome issues are dealt with as they arise.

There are no apparent indications that public opinion considerations serve as serious input factors in foreign policy formulation. Israel's destruction of an Iraqi nuclear facility in June 1981 showed just such an absence of public relations considerations. (This analysis does not focus on the military value of the action.) In his original defense of the raid, Prime Minister Begin maintained it was necessitated by a threat by Iraqi Prime Minister Hussein to destroy the alleged Zionist entity, but based on a check by the U.S. State Department, the threat was never stated by Iraqi leader but was, rather, published by an Israeli newspaper. In addition to embarrassment on this score, Begin further erred when he gave the press a wrong figure regarding how deeply the reactor was embedded in the ground. Clearly, had Israel been more sensitive to foreign information considerations, Begin would have had his facts correct and the state's case would have been strengthened, not weakened.

Israel's air attack, in July 1981, on a heavily populated neighborhood in Beirut where various PLO factions were quartered, again illustrated this scanty attention to public opinion. Bloody scenes of the attack (which *The New York Times* estimated killed 300 people and injured another

800) were seen on TV the world over. Politically, the timing of the raid infuriated officials of the Reagan Administration who just that day—July 17—had prepared a press release announcing the resumption of deliveries to Israel of F-16 fighter bombers—deliveries which had been held up because of the bombing of the Iraqi nuclear reactor a month earlier. Evidently no preparation in the information arena was undertaken in planning the raid. The world was caught unprepared both by the suddenness and severity of the attack. Press accounts show that even Israeli supporters in the American Jewish community did not understand the need to bomb civilian neighborhoods housing PLO members.

Prime Minister Begin invited Harold M. Squadron, then head of the Conference of Presidents of Major Jewish Organizations, to discuss repercussions of the incident. According to *The New York Times*, "Mr. Squadron said that he told Mr. Begin of the public relations need to prepare public opinion for such an escalation of fighting and to have plans and people ready to address the criticism that would follow"—factors clearly absent in Israel's handling of the event.

And finally, in the 1982 Peace for Galilee campaign, Israel permitted itself to be put on the propaganda defensive through its unchallenged response to the "excessively exaggerated" *(The New York Times,* July 14) reports of the International Red Cross regarding civilian casualties in Lebanon. For over a week after the fighting began, the Israeli army prevented foreign correspondents from visiting the areas of heaviest fighting, enabling these exaggerations to flourish, and it took the Israeli Foreign Ministry two weeks to issue its own version of the causalities. By then, the Red Cross figure had been widely accepted.

[Rubin now reiterates and updates additional problems found in his earlier assessments of Israel's use of the "propaganda instrument":] (1) The inadequate attention shown to the foreign press corps supports the notion that Israel is [still] not as seriously concerned as it might be with its image abroad. "The stark fact is that there is not a single person in Israel with the job of suggesting good feature copy for the foreign press corps."

(2) Israel's censorship procedure [continues to serve] as an additional irritant to foreign correspondents. Particularly in time of stress, opinion in Israel may be to increase the scope of censorship. Thus, in 1982, the head

of the Information Division of the Foreign Ministry, Moshe Yegar, proposed that foreign correspondents harboring 'hostile intentions' be barred from entering the country, and that correspondents already in Israel who are "discovered to be preparing a hostile article should be asked to stop and leave the country, and material they have prepared should be examined and if necessary impounded." Yegar's recommendation came in the wake of a highly critical report on Israel's West Bank policies on the ABC television network. However, his proposal was rejected by the Director General of the Prime Minister's Office who termed it "undemocratic."

Another disturbing feature of censorship, in the judgment of certain correspondents, is that although the aim is to enforce military security, censorship occasionally is used as a means to dampen criticism of governmental actions. In 1982, when 13,000 Druze villagers on the Golan Heights went on strike rather than accept Israeli identity cards, Defense Minister Ariel Sharon declared the village off-limits to the press. The unprecedented ban was eventually lifted following protests by the Israel Journalists' Association.

(3) The lack of coordination among governmental information units also [continues to] hurt Israel's effort to court foreign public opinion. Essentially, each governmental unit goes its own way and determines its own policy in the area of foreign information. To its credit, the Foreign Ministry [still] contains a coordination arrangement relating to overseas propaganda—the *Maarach Hasbara* (Information Alignment). But the lack of input of the information element in the foreign policy process undercuts the benefits of whatever attempted unity exists within the Ministry.

There is no overall national plan for projecting Israel's case abroad. Arrangements for cooperation between the ministries are mainly ad hoc. While Harry Hurwitz (information attaché at the Israeli Embassy in Washington in 1983) served as Information Advisor to Prime Minister Begin (beginning May 1978), he arranged meetings of personnel involved in foreign public opinion from the Foreign Ministry, Defense Ministry, Israel Broadcasting Authority and the Jewish Agency, although the benefits from such limited contact have yet to be seen. Each Ministry picks its own themes, audiences and interpretation of political developments for dissemination abroad. Invariably, conflicts, oversights and duplication develop.

To improve the situation the establishment of an Information Ministry has been suggested many times. During the 1977 election, the creation of a Ministry of Overseas Information was among the planks of Menachem Begin's election campaign.

Twice, Israel has tried to provide the overseas information program with greater institutional stature but both efforts failed. [As covered previously,] Prime Minister Golda Meir asked Israeli Galili, a Cabinet Minister Without Portfolio to be responsible for information activities. [After Rubin's previous articles on the subject], Yitzchak Rabin gave Abraham Yariv this assignment. The authority of both men evaporated when it became clear the governmental ministries whose staffs were to be moved to the new information operation—particularly the Foreign Ministry units previously engaged in these activities—opposed the shift.

A more recent effort, in 1979, to set up an Information Ministry also failed when the Israeli Cabinet floated a trial balloon for Moshe Nissim, then a Minister Without Portfolio, to head the operation. Nissim's lack of experience in the information area, his poor use of spoken English, as well as the opposition of those government employees who would have been moved to uncharted waters were all factors causing the proposal to be scratched.

What of the Future of Israeli Information Diplomacy?

In the long term, it can be assumed that the image Israel `projects to the world will have a direct bearing on the outcome of the Mideast conflict. But improving this image depends on certain changes both in terms of strategy and tactics. Israeli policymakers must understand the importance of political communication in international relations. No democracy can ignore informed public opinion in the reaching of foreign policy decisions. Judgments abroad are continually being reached about Israel, as with any other international hot spot, regardless of the attention that Israel's government shows to the information component.

Strategically, Israel's information diplomacy should be clear in its objectives. The passive, reactive *Hasbara* approach is inappropriate for a state caught in continuous political confrontation. Moreover, Israel cannot base its foreign information program on Holocaust guilt-tripping, or on latent sympathy for a fellow democracy, or on single episode heroism, such as the Entebe raid. Sound strategy would also focus more on policies designed to appeal to non-Jews, rather than in reiterating for Jewish audiences self-serving messages such as the religious-historic value of settling Judea and Samaria.

Although an autonomous Ministry of Overseas Information would not eliminate the cacophony of voices emerging from Israel, several sound arguments support its creation. Principally, the existence of such a government body would better assure that the information element would be taken seriously in foreign policy. From the standpoint of both input in policy formation and output in disseminating material, a unified agency of government, sensitive to foreign opinion considerations could not but help how Israel is seen abroad. In such a framework, training for information diplomacy would become more professional. Similarly, an Information Ministry would be likely to determine with more accuracy than is now the case which audiences overseas are receiving Israel's propaganda and which ones would most profitably be targeted for future messages. Finally, Israeli officialdom would have a harder time ignoring the element of foreign public opinion in their own political judgments because the advice of an independent bureaucratic structure focusing on information diplomacy cannot be all that easily overlooked.

In the final analysis, the people of one country form their judgments of the politics of another based on that country's actions, not words. But how these actions are explained and presented affects the actor's credibility, honor, reputation and, ultimately, power. Israel must start to take the opinion of mankind more seriously.

6

American Jewish Political Behavior

In the mid-1970s Rubin began writing about the American Jewish community and its role in American politics. Between 1973 and 1978 his writings addressed the diverging relationship between American Jews and the liberal establishment, the impact of the new Jewish ethnicism and political self-awareness, the controversial role of the new breed of Jewish political consultants, the emerging effort of the GOP to attract the Jewish vote in 1976, and another look, a year and a half later, at the GOP campaign to recruit the Jewish vote.

Where Have All The Liberals Gone?
[*Jewish Life*, October 1973]

Sidney Hook, the New York University philosopher, used to say, "Only the person wearing the shoe could tell whether it pinches." What Hook meant was that despite the notions of social engineers, the man in the street, in his common wisdom, knows where his interests lie.

For American Jews, liberalism by and large was long regarded as the shoe that fits. And everyone knows this tenet of American politics: scratch a Jew and find a liberal. For instance, Mark Levy and Michael Kramer in their work "The Ethnic Factor: How America's Minorities Decide Elections" (Simon and Schuster) title their chapter of Jewish voting patterns, "The Jews: Forever Liberal Wherever They Are." Whether the movement was for trust-busting, for the League of Nations, for the New Deal, for nuclear disarmament, for Federal aid to education—all such causes have won mass Jewish support and in numerous instances have drawn much on Jewish brains and means.

And through election after election, whether local, state, or national, Jewish voters have gone overwhelmingly to the candidates marked liberal.

Recent developments, however, have brought into question the future relationship between American Jews at large and the liberal establishment. Are their paths diverging?

Among white Americans, only Jews in 1972 gave so high a proportion of their votes to Senator McGovern—two-thirds. This heavy margin was despite some forecasts that the Jewish well-to-do, allegedly concerned about McGovern's far-out economic schemes, would forsake the Democratic Party's bellwether liberal candidate. Closer to the mark were predictions that the Jewish rank-and-file, recoiling from the New Left tinge of McGovern's campaign, were more likely to turn from him than those following the fashionable lead of the limousine liberals. However much McGovern scares America's rich, one observer shrewdly put it, the Jews of Scarsdale would give more of their votes to Sen. McGovern than the Jews of Brooklyn. Although "Brooklyn" departed from its long-inured electoral allegiance to a lesser extent than was envisioned, the fact remains that a much larger proportion of Jews voted for the Republican candidate than ever before since pre-New Deal days at least. President Nixon's Jewish votes came from "Brooklyn" rather than from "Scarsdale." It was apparent that a significant change in Jewish political stance was emerging at the grass-roots level.

Was this actually but a momentary variance, or does it point to a cleavage between Jews and liberals that is likely to persist and grow? An examination of this question requires a view of the factors motivating, respectively, the Jewish political course and that of present-day liberal forces.

Why Jews have been identified with social and political liberalism is not an elusive question. Whether as a result of religious teachings or as a result of their having been victimized so often, Jews were drawn to the messianism of American Liberalism. Liberals wanted to perfect the world, to eliminate injustice, and so did the Jews. Liberalism stood for change, for social experiments. Jews, so often up rooted and forced to learn quickly the rules of survival in each new country, were not socially hidebound. All the more so for non-religious Jews in search of some secular raison d'etre after having rejected the disciplines and ordering of life followed by the religiously orthodox. In liberalism, Jews also saw a chance to escape their numerical marginality; by working hand in hand with well-meaning people of all backgrounds, Jews who had given up religion saw themselves as part of the idealistic mainstream devoted toward advancing the common good. And as has been voiced on many occasions, the Jew is like everyone else, only a little more so. Given the fashionability of liberalism, the dominant sympathy of the media for liberalism, the opportunities presented to immigrants and the children of immigrants in an open society, and the presence of legitimate social, economic, and political grievance in the United States one understands why Jews eagerly manned the liberal ramparts.

The particularly strong liberal affinity of American Jews during the past several decades is also easily understood. The Depression wrought havoc among the masses of American Jews, whether wage workers, storekeepers, professionals, or businessmen; the New Deal, offering vista of a better day and way, won the allegiance of all. Then came the black specter of Nazidom, and it was in the forces of liberalism that Jews saw the will to summon America to the defense of freedom. Too, from a practical standpoint, America's Jews before World War II were essentially an "out" rather than an "in" group. They suffered from medical school quotas, antisemitic hiring practices in the corporate world, restrictive real estate covenants. When it came to international matters, the liberals, still smarting from the Senate's defeat of the League of Nations treaty under Woodrow Wilson, were more sympathetic to an ordering of things globally (thus offering solutions of problems burdening Jews) than were the more isolationist conservatives. Being wealthier in general, the conservatives were more sympathetic to the claims of America's oil companies when it came to the Middle East than were the liberals.

However, in matters involving the Communists, conservatives, being rather absolutist in their views of the world power balance, were more skeptical of the Kremlin than were the liberals. Although in the 1950's there still existed an anti-Communist left, time has mellowed much of the liberal truculence to the Soviet Union, totalitarian police state though it was and is. Nonetheless, conservative umbrage with the Kremlin in the 1950's through the present only took superficial note of the problems of the Jews in the Soviet Union. Whether this situation came to bear because Jews were not conservatives or involved in conservative movements, or because the Jewish plight ranked less in the minds of conservatives trumpeting the ills of the "Captive Nations," or a little of both ingredients being present—this verdict belongs to history.

But for that matter, liberal forces through the same period too seemed little concerned about Soviet persecution of Jews, and their reaction to the Kremlin's trampling of freedom-seeking Hungary, Poland, and Czechoslovakia has been not at all impassioned. This notwithstanding, Jews persisted in seeing liberalism as the torchbearer of democracy and social advance and as committed to its very roots against antisemitism.

To be sure, the liberals themselves up until the 1967 Six-Day War (as good a date as any to arbitrarily delineate substantial defections from liberalism) felt for the Jews' predicament. The Jew from World War II through 1967 was seen basically as an underdog in America and the world, and accordingly as motivating liberal support. The literature and drama of the period when portraying Jews, drew them as outsiders, people who wanted in and had been unfairly victimized. Moreover, the Holocaust experience had not been lost on liberal America. Americans of all persuasions, for example, supported the 1948 birth of Israel not so much on logic as a way to atone for Nazi Germany's atrocities.

The Historical Process

Interestingly, Jewish support for liberal positions in the earlier years of American history did not automatically mean backing of the Democratic Party's Presidential candidates as it has come to be seen today. In view of the tolerance and openness of Jefferson, it was not surprising that Jews found themselves happy with his Democratic Party. The Federalist Party in 1815 passed a resolution prohibiting naturalized citizens from serving in Congress; this message was not lost on Jewish voters. Jews started moving over to Lincoln's Republicans after failure of attempts to persuade President James Buchanan to renegotiate an antisemitic commercial treaty with Switzerland which allowed Swiss cantons to expel American Jews in accordance with Swiss law. Although General Ulysses Grant during the Civil War issued the notorious Order No. 11 which decreed that Jews in Tennessee must leave the area within twenty-four hours, Lincoln quashed the order. Grant apologized, and Jews stayed with him in the election of 1868.

From the Civil War through World War I, the Republicans dominated the White House and a succession of Republican Presidents interceded on overseas situations of grave concern for Jews. For example, President Rutherford B. Hayes warned Romania that the United States was concerned about the fate of Foreign Jews. In 1882 President Chester A. Arthur demanded that the Czarist Russian government end the pogroms.

President Theodore Roosevelt, himself a New Yorker, received much Jewish affection. Roosevelt was the first President to welcome to the White House a delegation of the United States Rabbinical Conference. He continued his successors' concern with the plight of East European Jewry. Earlier, as New York City's Police Commissioner, Roosevelt had assigned only Jewish policemen to guard the German antisemitic Herman Ahlwardt when he visited the city.

By the time of Woodrow Wilson, however, many Jews had moved over to the Democratic Party. They were attracted to the humane quality of Wilson's programs. Wilson's Republican predecessor, William Howard Taft, refused to renegotiate a discriminatory treaty with Russia. Also, Wilson's successor in the Presidency was a Republican, Warren G. Harding, who as a Senator was accused of anti-Jewish prejudice as a result of his having voted against the confirmation of Louis D. Brandeis as an Associate Justice of the United States Supreme Court. By 1928, when Alfred E. Smith unsuccessfully ran for President, most Jews elected to Congress were Democrats, whereas ten years earlier the Jewish Congressional delegation of eleven consisted of ten Republicans and one Socialist.

President Franklin D. Roosevelt's New Deal and President Johnson's Great Society mark the high points of the Jewish consensus for liberalism. Although fewer than one of five Jews voted for Nixon for President in 1968, this election must be seen as a watershed in the Jewish-liberal marriage. Significantly, Republicans expected to pick up greater Jewish votes in 1968, but for the wrong reasons. The GOP hoped that the Jewish penchant for liberalism would push them away from Senator Humphrey's

Democratic candidacy because Humphrey was not liberal enough and because while those favoring America's Vietnam policy might see him as too non-committal, those opposing it would judge him as saddled with Johnson's Vietnam past and the behavior of the Chicago Democratic convention. Such anticipations would have proven logical, of course, if Richard Nixon himself had a liberal identity. But in 1968, the Nixon Jews knew wasn't one they liked.

By 1972, it was clear to all that Jews and professed liberals were not as inseparable as in the past. While Jews had certainly not embraced conservatism as a formal movement, and remained governed by a liberal outlook, many of them now viewed with doubt the trends which had emerged among the banner-bearers of liberalism. It was not so much that they had moved away from liberal basics as the feeling among them that the liberal establishment had itself done so. How many Jews we are dealing with here is unclear. What is known, however, is that organizations of Jews espousing stands contrary to the current line of liberalism have formed, that urban, wage-worker, middle income, orthodox, and more ethnic-conscious Jews are the Jews disenchanted with liberalism.

In a sense, a growing Jewish-liberal dichotomy represents a new Jewish ethnicism, similar to the movements among other white ethnics to beat out an identity. But in terms of the Jews, this phenomenon is more basic. To appreciate what has happened, it is necessary to explore what is meant by liberalism.

Liberalism's Turnabout

What is known as political liberalism today stems from the ideas expressed by the British utilitarians, Jeremy Bentham and John Stuart Mill, that man is essentially good, and the best government provides the greater happiness to the largest numbers with each person determining what it is that makes him happy. Liberalism philosophically has great confidence in individual reason. It is an optimistic faith, much more orientated to change than conservatism because of this positive view of man as governed by a tempering reason. Classical liberalism also emphasized free initiative, economically as well as politically. Although John Locke

(Jefferson's spiritual father) posed a case for revolution in England, he felt that revolution would not be incessant because man still has enough good sense to differentiate basic grievances from petty nuisances, the latter being amenable over time.

Over the years, however, the evolution of liberal thinking in response to unfolding events has brought it far from some of its original tenets. The concept of the Welfare State, today a staple of liberalistic doctrine, is scarcely to be reconciled with the teachings of Bentham and Mill. The all-encompassing role of government in the formulation of contemporary liberalism is the antithesis of what was espoused by classical liberalism. Since Jews at large shared in personal experience the social crises which prompted the change from an individualistic to a collectivist philosophy, this in itself could not breach their affinity to liberalism. But when liberals swept by the collectivist current were drawn toward an authoritarian concept of society, and became increasingly selective in the application of such liberal concepts as freedom of expression and in moral judgments, Jews began to doubt the bona fides not of liberalism proper but of those bearing the liberal banner.

To many Jews, the campus explosions and New Left turmoil of the 60's were ominously reminiscent of the scenes that had paved the way to Auschwitz. The tendency of professed liberals to condone and in many cases to actually lend themselves to the orgy of disruption, riot, and terror, to the wholesale intimidation of those of different view and the suppression of academic freedom, was bitterly disillusioning. The fact that Jews were prominent in the ranks and leadership of the "campus revolution" and among its apologists and supporters added a sense of shame to the revulsion among Jews at large. So too in world affairs, when political realities as perceived by concerned Jews made it essential for liberalism to grasp the dynamics of power politics, liberal forces failed to meet the test. The fact of the matter is while liberals, increasingly espousing an accommodation with the Soviet dictatorship, were intent upon winding down American-Soviet rivalries at practically any cost, the Kremlin was tightening its ruthless grip on surrounding nations, spreading its grasp to the Middle East and beyond, moving for the destruction of Israel, and attempting to crush the last vestiges of Jewish life in the Soviet Union.

Jewish Policy Considerations

Fundamental to the Jewish world outlook must be the premise that Jewish security in general and the security of Israel in particular are conditioned on the survival of Western democracy and the building of real world peace, and that a strong United States is the key to these imperatives. Basic to Jewish interest is a world climate in which democracy cannot be ousted by autocracy and in which the Communist powers cannot indulge the lust for world conquest. Distant as most Jews are from the "Cold Warrior" outlook, they, unlike the new order of liberals, cannot fail to view Communist Russia's course of conquest and subjugation with less concern than Nazi Germany's course of conquest and subjugation. They cannot, again unlike supposed liberals, view Communist penetration across the world, whether it be the Middle East, Cuba, or Vietnam, with any less dismay than Nazi subversion of a lesser span of lands. Nor can they react with less horror to the Communist mass butchery of the Tet "offensive" than to the Nazi mass butchery in Lidice. And surely Jews cannot ignore the present reality that Communism directly threatens the spiritual existence of Soviet Jewry and the physical existence of Israel—together comprising nearly half the Jews of the world. In all of these matters, the Jewish stand is entirely consistent with liberalism's stand in the Hitler era; but not at all so is that of today's liberal establishment. Who, then, has in fact deserted liberalism?

It is no coincidence that any advances for Communism represent setbacks for the cause of democracy, for the United States, and for Israel. Now that the Vietnam War is part of history, more and more people are taking a fresh view of its pros and cons. Jews who refused to be bludgeoned into falling in line with anti-Vietnam War propaganda were formerly apt to be denounced—by fellow Jews, too—as governed by no other consideration than Israel's welfare. In so far as Israel's welfare is inseparable from that of the Free World, the charge is one which no Jew, or non-Jew for that matter, need hesitate to bear, although few if any of those so scorned would have been of different opinion had Israel not been affected by the Vietnam situation in any way. As for Israeli support of the United States position, practical as well as moral considerations were decisive.

As the only country in the world lacking a dependable ally, Israeli security depends in large scale on an equilibrium of international power forces, Israel felt that a precipitous withdrawal from Vietnam by the United States would undermine America's commitments to small nations including itself. In such an atmosphere, Arab nations would be more likely to undertake a fourth round in the Arab-Israeli conflict, believing that since the United States failed to follow to its conclusion its commitment in Vietnam, it would likewise abandon previous pledges to Israel.

In addition to this philosophical underpinning for Israeli backing of American purposes in Vietnam was the more immediate fact of the ties and pledges of support between Communist Vietnamese leaders and her Arab enemies. For historic purposes, it is worth citing some references. The Vietcong Afro-Asian Solidarity Committee sent the following telegram to Ahmed Shukairy, head of the Palestine Liberation Organization:

> We strongly condemn imperialist intervention which uses Israel to destroy the national liberation front and thus endangers the peace and welfare of the inhabitants of the Middle East. We back without reservation the Palestine Liberation Organization in her struggle against the twin enemy—American imperialism and its lackey.

Ho Chi Minh, depicted by many American liberals as the George Washington of Vietnam, in an interview with the Egyptian newspaper *Al Matzor* noted the rights of the Arabs "to the return of their stolen homeland from the clutches of the Zionists and the imperialists." Ho referred to Israel as "a base for aggression used by imperialism to weaken the Arab states and to create tensions in the area."

Another reference to the anti-Israel stand of the North Vietnamese and the Vietcong was a news story in the *Christian Science Monitor* of March 29, 1967, reporting the following:

> The Cairo Mission of the Viet Cong is the largest and most active in the area. Its member, have met with Palestinian Arabs to arrange for combat training in North Vietnam for Shukairy followers.

A June 1, 1971, news report of Premier Golda Meir's visit to Sweden well illustrated the reasons behind Israel's support of American policy. In a moving message to young Swedish Jews, the Premier urged them: "Stand upright and tell the world what it means to be Jews. Tell them that Jews have fought and died for thousands of years to remain Jews. Tell your friends about this people that has refused to be trampled down for thousands of years." Then, referring to a prior meeting with a delegation of Swedish Jewish youth who, echoing the official Swedish antagonism toward the United States role in the Vietnam War, criticized her support of President Nixon, Mrs. Meir said: "But no one helps us like Mr. Nixon does. He enables us to buy arms and even speaks up for us, which no one else does. Here they don't even want to sell us arms."

The overwhelming drumfire of agitation and propaganda swept a good many Jews and their organizations in the United States into support of the anti-Vietnam War movement, despite the implications such a policy held, just as it did all but a steadfast few among liberal forces themselves. But other issues were coming to the fore in which the gap between the Jews and the new-day liberals was visible. One in particular related to the plight of Soviet Jews, especially when Soviet Jews made the basic policy decision to risk everything in their desire to emigrate.

From any standpoint, the situation of Soviet Jewry ranks as one of the major human rights tragedies of the day. Here we have the remnant of East European Jewry, a people who today live with the memory of the Holocaust toll of their own families, a community that suffered the pogroms of the Czars and Stalin's insane schemes, and that has suffered ruthless suppression throughout the past fifty-five years. All that they ask is the right either to go to Israel or to be granted the religious and cultural rights granted to other groups in the Soviet Union and spelled out in the Soviet constitution. And where are the liberals? True, the suffering of Bangladesh is a great tragedy and the struggles for self-rule of the indigenous peoples of Southwest Africa and Portuguese Angola merit deep sympathy. And liberals are justifiably concerned about the air we breathe and the food we eat. They are right in seeking to end discrimination against women, American Indians, Chicanos, Blacks, and Hispanics.

Soviet Jewry? Liberal concern for Soviet Jews occupies a very subordinate position to the above when judged by the comparative quantity of articles in liberal publications, talk shows, fundraising, and the overt protest activity such as picketing and demonstrations. Of course, this is not to discount the resolutions and other public statements on behalf of Soviet Jewry issued by established liberal groups. Nor is this to overlook the support for the Jackson Amendment which ties future American-Soviet trade to free emigration for Soviet citizens. Such support, it should be remembered however, has stemmed in large measure from Jewish politicking and the dramatic, courageous risks of Soviet Jews to secure emigration permission.

Previous to the Six-Day War, liberals provided Israel with much moral and political support. Now, however, when Israeli and Diaspora Jews fall victim to Arab highjackings, kidnappings, and assassinations, liberal outrage remains muted. Although liberals still refer to the United Nations as the "last best hope of man," informed Jews know the type of justice the Communist-Arab-Afro-Asian coalition renders to Israel. This author remembers, in this connection, a joke heard in Israel: What is the lowest point in the world? Answer: The Dead Sea? Wrong—The United Nations.

Lines of Divergence

The divergence between the liberal mentality and Jewish self-interest is best shown by the stands of Senator J. William Fulbright, chairman of the Senate Foreign Relations Committee. Admittedly, Fulbright represents an extreme case, but inasmuch as the Arkansas senator is regarded as one of the stalwarts in the liberal pantheon, his views are worth noting. Had Eugene McCarthy been elected President in 1968, Fulbright would likely have been named Secretary of State. In a McGovern Administration, Fulbright would also have figured prominently.

Senator Fulbright has been the Senate's most outspoken critic of alleged Jewish pressure on Congress to back the Jackson Amendment. According to Fulbright, such Congressional action on behalf of Soviet Jews signifies a basic conflict with the professed United States national aim of fostering *detente*. In 1952, Fulbright opposed Point IV aid to Israel, but he urged Secretary of State Dulles to go along with Nasser's plans for building the Aswan Dam. When there was a move in Congress to cut off aid to Saudi Arabia because of its discrimination against Jewish military personnel stationed at American bases there, Fulbright defended the Saudi Arabians as "our friends." Following the Six-Day War, Fulbright in an interview with the *Christian Science Monitor* claimed that the chief obstacle to peace in the Middle East was Israel's refusal to compromise its occupation of Jerusalem. Such occupation by Israel, he asserted, resulted in denials to the Arabs of access to their holy places.

Senator Fulbright, needless to say, has never signed a petition on behalf of Soviet Jews. When President Nixon nominated political scientist Robert Strauz-Hupé as United States Ambassador to Morocco, Fulbright in the Foreign Relations Committee confirmation hearings maintained that Strauz-Hupé was too involved with Israel to carry out his job effectively.

In pressing domestic issues, the liberal voice has similarly failed to be raised on Jewish behalf. Originally, the merit system bringing about civil service was a liberal reform. Symbolic of the notion of a faceless applicant for a post was the statue of lady justice, her eyes blindfolded in order to eliminate preferences. But preferential treatment programs at all levels of government negate the merit principle and the equal rights provisions of the Constitution. Under such preferential treatment "Affirmative Action" programs, institutions, especially educational institutions, were to set up numerical timetables in terms of future hiring. At first government officials denied it, but eventually the Secretary of Health, Education and Welfare, Casper Weinberger, acknowledged that the distinction between numerical goals advocated in Affirmative Action programs and ethnic quotas was slight. One writer pungently described liberal criticism of Jewish protests against Affirmative Action programs as making it appear that the merit system was a "Jewish conspiracy."

Stemming from Thomas Jefferson, liberals, in the American experience, have shown an interest in local government. Only recently in urban areas has the notion of community control been advanced as a means of involving citizens in neighborhood matters and secondly as a way of reducing bureaucratic inefficiency. The record of the Forest Hills Scatter

Site housing project has been well documented elsewhere. What was particularly onerous for Forest Hills residents was the liberal hypocrisy in their selective advocation of community control. On the one hand, liberals advanced the notion that those who wear the shoe deserve to decide whether it pinches, but when it came to participatory democracy for Forest Hills residents, their communal will was overruled.

Antisemitism, ideologized Jew-hate, is one evil which liberalism has denounced unequivocally throughout modern times—until it emerged in radical Black circles. Diatribes of Jew-hate from the mouths of Black extremists at public meetings and conventions, in radio programs and in published articles, have found at most but mild rebuke from liberal channels and more often than not have actually received extenuation from these sources.

Fighting poverty is an issue integral to Jewish ethics regardless of who contemporary advocates of this issue might be. Given current estimates of Jewish poor as numbering between 400,000–800,000, poverty guidelines from the federal Office of Economic Opportunity were not very applicable to indigent Jews. Since most Jewish children are born to wedded couples, and Jewish poor are generally dispersed rather than concentrated in particular districts, their poverty, in the eyes of liberal bureaucrats who drew up these guidelines, was found wanting. Criticism against government policy makers in this connection, however, must be tempered by the realization that Jewish agencies themselves only belatedly called attention to the plight of the Jewish poor.

Historically, the widening of the franchise has stood out as a commendable goal of liberalism. Yet when Jews complained against poverty elections being set on the Sabbath, rather than on a day convenient for all voters, the American Civil Liberties Union was nowhere to be heard. Similarly, Jewish groups nearly exclusively protested New York State's 1973 voting registration laws, which because of designated resignation days falling on Jewish holidays would serve to disenfranchise otherwise eligible Jewish voters.

Thus current liberalism appears to be moving away from fundamental Jewish political interests just as it has departed from positions fundamental to liberalism proper. Jews in their turn, having taken the cue, are leaving liberalism. In the 1973 Mayoral Democratic primary in New York City, the most professed liberal candidates failed to win the great Jewish majorities they would have expected in the past. In the 1969 New York City Mayoral election John Lindsay, candidate of the liberal forces, failed to win a majority of the Jewish votes. Although in New Left circles Senator Henry Jackson of Washington may be condemned as a "Cold Warrior" (despite his leadership in social and economic reform), Jackson numbers a substantial following among informed Jews.

While many white ethnics are moving away from what passes for liberalism today, because of liberalism's apparent failure in answering the questions it posed, its apathy toward middle class problems and social naiveté, Jews have reasons of their own. Certain events have spurred Jews into becoming more ethnic and less secular in assessing social issues. Israel's example since the Six-Day War, the brave defiance of Soviet Jews, and the coming of age of the children of the post–World War II Jewish immigrants to the United States, Jewishly committed in large part, these are factors which have served to weaken the Jewish embrace of current fashionable social outlooks and to turn more inward.

As American Jews become more ethnic-conscious the attraction of present-day liberalism wanes. To be sure, such diminution would be true not just of liberalism but any political policy seeming to conflict with greater group assertiveness and its sense of right. Jewish ethnicism is new and should be contrasted with ethnocentrism, the latter signifying a concern for one's group and its own welfare. Jews have always been ethnocentric because they have always worried about fellow Jews. What is taking place now, by comparison, in Jewish ethnicism goes beyond the concern and worry for other Jews expressed by ethnocentrism. Ethnicism stands for the pursuit of Jewish strength and the use of Jewish political clout. Ethnicism is the aggressive use of the political process on behalf of Jewish concerns.

The View Ahead

The growing cleavage between the current direction of the liberal establishment and Jewish concerns stand in marked contrast to the contributions that liberalism has made in the past to Jewish well-being, from the New Deal through the Great Society. As a result of the policies of these programs in widening and cutting down on discrimination, Jews share with other segments of the American populace strengthened security. Furthermore, there are many specifics on the liberal agenda which are of direct benefit to Jews, as to others, such as greater funding of poverty programs, increased aid to education, and the channeling of more funds for public housing. Nor should Jews as a result of confrontation tactics with Black extremists submerge that compassionate part of their heritage which in the past, to their credit, found them in the vanguard of movements to achieve racial equality.

Finally, the increasingly bitter experiences with liberalism does not mean that Jews will or should automatically do a complete about face and enlist en masse in conservative ranks. There is much lacking, from a Jewish political standpoint, in the stance of American conservatism. From the philosophical elitism of conservatism to its lukewarm attitude toward social welfare programs which only now are beginning to trickle down to Jewish agencies, conservative interests and Jewish interests are not identical. Conservatives in general stand for a fixed ordering of classes and react with a turned up nose to the social diversity which is basic in order for Jews in the United States to remain inconspicuously competitive. And as has been pointed out by others, extreme conservatives and radical liberals, alike marked by distrust or reason, intolerance, and dogmatic insistence on positions based on a supposedly higher moral order, share many of the same values.

Chaos and upheaval are not foreign to Jews in the Diaspora. It is safe to say that in the minds of many Jews there is underway a reassessment of previously accepted political norms. In fact, the main characteristic of this phenomenon is not the establishment of new patterns of political affiliation among Jews but the weakening of existing ones without the clear cut substitution of new attachments. Ideally, Jews, after this realignment is concluded, should come away with enough leverage so that their worries and needs are taken seriously by both liberal and conservative camps—or whatever new groupings might emerge. As with nations, so Jews or any other group seeking power and influence should be guided in external relationships by the time-tested premise that there exist neither permanent friends nor permanent enemies, only permanent interests.

# # #

The New Jewish Ethnic
[*Tradition: A Journal of Orthodox Jewish Thought*, December 1973]

Whatever currency America as a melting pot sociology enjoyed in the past has been eroded by the ethnic forces which surfaced in the late 1960's. While factors such as age, education, wealth and religious observance mark which Jews join America's growing ethnic bandwagon, clearly there exists a movement of Jews as Jews seeking power for themselves.

Even casual observation shows the rise of Jewish political ethnicism—a new breed of yarmulka-wearing activists highly visible in the media; an aggressive Jewish political clout forcing previously indifferent politicians to take their measure; the mushrooming of spontaneous grassroots organizations challenging both the political style and strategy of the Jewish "establishment."

As is well known, Jews more than any other American group were America's liberals *par excellence*. The objectives of this country's liberal "vital center" were seen by most Jews as running parallel with their own. Why liberalism? Explanations for this behavior run the gamut from Milton Himmelfarb of *Commentary* magazine linking political liberalism with Jewish good taste (i.e., Mario Procaccino, regardless of his positions on the issues, failed to win much Jewish support in New York's 1969 mayoral election because of his *prust* (crude) mannerisms), to more standard theories based on religious messianism and heritage of anti-Semitism (i.e., liberalism presumed to stand for a high degree of social justice and fair play) to a Jewish desire to belong, to be *au courant* (liberalism being fashionable politics). How valid these arguments, or whether or not liberalism served the interest of American Jews in the past better than, let us say, conservatism or moderation does not concern us here.

Nonetheless, Jewish liberalism from World War II through the dawn of the "new politics" of the late 1960's stood for a wide use of governmental power as a means for securing Jewish rights and advancing American society in general. This stance meant Jewish support for political reforms, civil rights, civil liberties, and internationalism. Political reform stood for fighting the urban "bosses" (most of whom were not Jewish), civil rights meant Negro voter registration and anti-discrimination laws (such statutes were also seen as fighting anti-Semitism), civil liberties provided more protection of the rights of the individual (free speech) versus those of society, and internationalism endorsed an activist United States foreign policy, particularly support for the United Nations. The main elected Jewish officeholders in that period—Senators Lehman, Javits, Ribicoff—backed these programs and liberal goals Jews felt squared with their own power interests. Furthermore, as Harvard sociologist Nathan Glazer reminds us, the dominant liberal intellectual thought in that period was positive towards America and its government, and the national Jewish organizations, which over the years have taken the tenets of liberalism more seriously than most Americans, saw anti-Semitism declining in this climate of increased governmental activism.

What brought on the falling out between the Jewish ethnics (ethnics here defined according to sociologist Andrew Greeley as "a human collectivity based on an assumption of common origin, real or imaginary") and liberalism? Basically, the pulling up of roots by Jews was not an isolated event, but part of the overall decline of the Old Left consensus. By the early 1970's, the Old Left was in a withered state. They were divided by the New Left on issues such as anti-Communism, the role of the university, the work ethic, the media's relations with politics and most importantly where Jewish ethnics were concerned, the growing insecurity of urban Jews. In other words, the tenor of American politics had changed, and while after the reshuffling many Jews still told themselves they marched under the familiar liberal banner there were fewer and fewer issues where they could stand together with liberalism's recognized new spokesmen. To be sure, many Jews, perhaps most, did not share the discomfort of the ethnic Jews with liberalism's changed rhetoric.

How could Jews have moved away from the plight of the Blacks? For one, as has often been cited, Blacks, in their own ethnic emergence, increasingly sought to determine their future, rejecting a leading role by "outsiders," however helpful they may have been in the past. Secondly, Jews and Blacks were pitted against one another by politicians outside their own ethnic groups. The attempts by such outsiders to rectify wrongs committed against Blacks in the past were interpreted by Jews as undermining their employment prospects in the civil service and schools through the adoption of tacit ethnic quotas. Thirdly, through an unfortunate set of circumstances, Jews saw themselves threatened by the Black movement to economic and social autonomy. Bewildered not only by apparent Black rejection of their past help, but also by their alleged new role as competitors with Blacks, Jews retrenched. The conflict between Jewish conscience and ethnic self-interest was well put by William Wexler, former president of B'nai B'rith, who said on the one hand Jews didn't want "to reject the black man's quest for justice," nor, on the other, to ignore "discrimination in reverse" against Jewish businessmen, educators, social workers and others who are "visible and vulnerable in Black communities."

More than other Americans, Jews advocated non-discrimination in housing. But as soon as their neighborhoods declined they moved out. This was in contrast to other white ethnics who refused to abandon familiar turf. While erosion of urban areas did not begin in the 1960's, such decline in earlier years was steady, consistent and to that extent evolutionary." In contrast to such slow, ongoing "evolutionary" processes, another development encouraging neighborhood change might be termed "revolutionary"—that which by dramatic events accelerated a process already underway. Here specific large-scale headline-catching phenomena were at work—tanks rolling down streets in the wake of riots, predictions of "long, hot summers"—to hasten Jewish migration from the cities.

The Forest Hills low income scatter-site housing conflict in the early 1970's illustrated the "revolutionary" process. In the minds of opponents, to construct a large low-income development in the relatively new neighborhood of Forest Hills represented unnatural, forced decay or "revolutionary" change. How did the Jewish ethnic reaction to Forest Hills differ from previous experiences with neighborhood deterioration? In the past, self-interest was seen in individual terms—those who could afford it picked up and ran. Here, collective action served self-interest and Jews fearing that the Forest Hills project threatened their neighborhood were forced into joint action.

Likewise, the principle of collective action as serving self-interest was shown in a new Jewish aggressiveness in competing for public anti-poverty finds. Previously, Jewish poverty was regarded by Jews themselves as a private, Jewish communal problem, and the Jewish poor were seen as a relatively small part of the Jewish population. Indicative of the failure of Jewish national organizations to cope with the poverty problem before the surge of ethnicism was the dearth of comprehensive data on poverty among Jews, an especially telling omission given currently accepted estimates of Jewish poor as numbering between 400,000–800,000.

Accordingly, pressure in the early stages for more recognition of Jewish poverty came spontaneously from the Jewish poor themselves rather than from the initiatives of national organizations. To be sure, certain factors militated against attention to poor in addition to the fact that the term "minority group" no longer in the popular mind seemed to refer to Jews. Setting up geographic bases for poverty eligibility, especially in New York City, under a system of local poverty councils hurt Jews living outside the designated areas. Since an estimated two thirds of Jewish poor are believed to be over 65 years of age, not much political activism necessary to win places on local community councils could be expected from this source. Finally, guidelines from the federal Office of Economic Opportunity as to poverty status were not applicable to the overwhelming solid family makeup of Jews.

Nevertheless, attention to Jewish poverty surfaced in Congressional hearings as well as in the grudging admission by the Office of Economic Opportunity that the charge that Jewish poor were systematically excluded from New York City's anti-poverty program "while imprecise is not totally devoid of validity." The formation of the Association of Jewish Anti-Poverty Workers as well as the cancellation of elections for poverty councils on the Sabbath also reflected the growing recognition of Jewish poverty.

Jewish institutions responded to this heightened ethnicism by taking a turn toward more parochial matters while reducing their traditional concern with secular, universalist social justice causes. Developments both within and without the Jewish community forced this shift. Organizational accountability was a watchword in the late 1960's, whether such accountability referred to students asking a greater share in university policy, in accusations against a government "credibility gap," or in consumerism. Sensitive to current political rhetoric, Jews likewise assessed their organizations from a "what's in it for us" stance. Previously, most American Jews were content not to exert too much pressure on their Jewish organizations. Describing such a Jew, Howard Singer wrote:

> He is usually a member not out of persuasion but out of gregariousness, and a group insurance and cut-rate travel plans loom larger in his mind than some press release put out by the national office. If he has a complaint, he must remember to submit it to the resolutions committee three months before the convention opens next year . . .
>
> The typical member will not go to chapter meetings. He will be content to mail his check once a year, serenely confident that the organization is "doing something for Jews and Judaism." But the handful of volunteers and professionals at the top have their own axes to grind. (*Bring Forth the Mighty Men: On Violence and the Jewish Character*: New York, Funk and Wagnall's, 1969).

Confrontation was the name of the game and the established Jewish organizations mired in well-worn tactics of the press release and private representations were out of their league. Even had they wanted to fight with the new public relations instruments, most Jewish groups lacked the activist mass memberships necessary for gaining media attention. Moreover, the passiveness of most members made it easier for organized dissidents to force the professional staff who really run the Jewish "establishment" (as opposed to lay executive boards) to redirect their priorities.

Jewish critics of Jewish organizations became standard fare. They accused their organizations of not being Jewish enough. The ethnics' heaviest assault focused on the alleged lack of emphasis of Jewish education by Jewish communal federations. Critics accused the Jewish federations of putting disproportionate value on community centers, hospitals and other social services, serving Jews and non-Jews compared with the needs of Jewish education. Challenging the religious integrity of Jewish federation fund raisers, some critics demanded that all organizational leaders prove their personal commitments to Judaism by participating in Jewish studies courses. According to the Jewish Defense League's Rabbi Meir Kahane, "At a time when the Jewish youth can look forward only to the farce of the afternoon Hebrew School which leaves him looking upon Judaism as a travesty dreamed up by a Bar Mitzvah caterer, status-seeking parents and a glittering but empty Temple, the Federation refuses to recognize the need for a maximum Jewish education."

Adding insult to injury in the minds of critics was that while major secular American Jewish organizations refused to support the burgeoning Jewish Day School movement, they also took exception to increased government support to Jewish education on grounds of church-state separation. Rabbi Hillel Levine, a graduate student at Harvard, claimed, "the priorities of organized Jewish philanthropies favor a greater mobilization of resources to combat one crack-pot anti-Semite than to deal with the Jewish illiteracy of millions of Jews."

Given this intensified ethnicism, not only was the Jewish "establishment" forced to become more "Jewish," but a proliferation of Jewish youth groups which never before existed sprung up. Spontaneous, unforeseen and often lacking centralized coordination, these groups took everyone by surprise, most of all the older Jewish organizations themselves. Marking this new inwardness were Free Jewish Universities, a Jewish student press service and the offering of courses in Jewish studies for credit in some 185 universities by the end of 1971.

Purist in ideology, the new Jewish youth groups stressed Jewish pride, the joy of being a Jew, Jewish education and culture (Yiddish dramatic offerings), religious observance and Jewish fellowship. They derided supposed Jewish materialism, the extravagance of Jewish social affairs and secular universalism—"Uncle Jake" (the Jewish Uncle Tom) busy fighting other people's battles while neglecting his own. *Kadima*, the Jewish student paper at the University of Illinois, bitterly protested, "Bombing the tracks of Auschwitz alone would have saved 100,000 Jewish lives. But then American bombs cost money, and you must remember that Jewish flesh is cheap. And did your father open his mouth? Even once? Why get involved, right? How about you? Like father, like son?"

Stress on denominationalism, these youth held, weakened Jewish unity. "There is a suspicion that the major divisions serve organizational rather than religious purposes," claimed William Novak, editor of *Response*. The Synagogue, argued James Sleeper, a Harvard graduate student, "is simply an appendage to middle class suburban culture that arose out of the assimilationist needs of a previous generation. The young Jew today has already seen the American dream come true, and he's sick of it."

What brought on the ethnic consciousness of these youth? The awareness stemmed both from the times and the admired actions of other Jews. While there is no underestimating the lesson of Black ethnicism in igniting Jewish consciousness (as it also spurred ethnic awareness in other groups), these youth were, after all, adolescents trying to resolve on a personal level the question "Who am I?" The Jewish ethnics by and large rejected drugs and opted for identity in terms of the group. The Jesus movement among Christian youth attested to the general religious revival from which the Jewish consciousness arose. Israel's amazing victory in the 1967 Six Day War and the courage of Soviet Jews in defying the Kremlin in order to gain exodus to Israel, gave the Jewish youth heroes of their own. The drama of contemporary Jewish survival battle spurred a fascination with the Hitler Holocaust.

Jewish youth had not abandoned liberalism; they simply redirected it to a new target-Judaism. They "sat in" as they had in the past, but in new quarters, the Jewish offices. They confronted, but this time it was the Jewish "establishment." To be sure, most of their fellow young Jews remained committed to secular causes rather than Jewish ones, but the movement was unprecedented in American Jewish history, and the fervor of the believers was there to remind assimilated Jews that the tents of Jacob could still accommodate the reform spirit.

While preaching Jewish spiritual renewal, Jewish ethnicism was forced to put first things first by providing for Jewish self-protection in the decaying cities. High crime neighborhoods saw the appearance of Jewish defense and escort groups. Such moves sometimes spurred police action such as in New York City where police decoys posed as Hassidim. Other

Jews having lost confidence in civic authorities turned to vigilanteeism. The Jewish Defense League, most prominent such body, capitalized on the fashionability of violence as well as the natural tendency of people to seek simple answers when threatened by complex, unmanageable forces. The JDL's entrance on the Jewish scene was eased by the fragmentation of American Jewish organizational life as well as an already existing criticism of the "establishment's" failure to protect Jewish interests in earlier episodes, such as New York City's teacher strike in 1968.

The JDL and the young Jewish ethnics shared many complaints—the complacency of Jews toward other Jews, the alleged unaggressivneness of the Jewish "establishment," the urgency of Jewish physical self-protection. Both factions stressed the need of *aliya* (emigration of Jews to Israel), although for the JDL's Rabbi Kahane settlement in Israel had not only religious and cultural importance, but was necessary for Jewish physical survival. "I believe in the marrow of my bones that the days of the Jews in the United States are numbered and that there is coming a storm of physical brutality that portends a holocaust."

JDL's support of violence, harassment and physical threats towards Soviet officials as a legitimate means for aiding Soviet Jews was not accepted by most young activists. While Kahane was mistakenly labeled a conservative because of his anti-Communist and anti-New Left stands, he shared the view of left-of-center activists that a right-wing backlash loomed as the ultimate threat to American Jews (Kahane arguing that the right would have been sufficiently provoked by left-wing extremism).

It is no accident then that the emergence of Jewish ethnicism was paralleled by a rejection of familiar battle cries. On international issues, Jewish support for the United Nations waned as Israel faced impossible odds in receiving justice from the world body as a result of the Arab-Communist-Afro-Asian coalition. The failure of most of the American Christian community to answer more positively to Israel's case following the Six Day War came as a bitter pill to Jews championing ecumenicism. The New Left likewise fell into disrepute among the ethnics as a result of its affinity for the Arabs.

Voices arose in the American Jewish community urging a new self-interest in judging the White House—that Presidents be evaluated not only on their Southeast Asian or domestic policies, but on how many Phantoms they allowed Israel to buy. President Nixon's gains among Jewish voters in the 1972 election are attributable in no small degree to steadfast support of Israel during his first term. As for the Soviet Union, American Jewish ethnics did not minimize their protests on Soviet anti-Semitism merely to fall in line with Washington's basic goal of building bridges to the Kremlin.

The new political reality was clearest in New York City, traditionally the country's most liberal city. By the time of the 1969 Democratic Mayoral primary, Jewish distaste with "limousine liberals" for discarding their interests was so strong that Mario Procaccino bettered the showing of Abe Beame, a Jew, four years earlier in certain largely Jewish Assembly Districts. John Lindsay running in 1969 as the most liberal of the three Mayoral candidates received less than one-half of the Jewish votes cast and no doubt this figure would have been smaller, perhaps resulting in Lindsay's defeat, had he faced opponents with better media images. The 1969 election vote was a landmark because it was the first time New York's Jews forsook liberalism on behalf of ethnic self-interest. A good case could be made, too, for the national publicity given the largely Jewish protests over the Forest Hills housing project as being the deathblow for Lindsay's 1972 Presidential ambitions.

Where will Jewish ethnicism lead? To begin with, growing Jewish desertion from the melting pot portends more than simply one small population group beating out an identity. If Jews, who despite such strong past support for American universalism, seem to be closing ranks, other traditionally less outward looking ethnic groups probably are even more disaffected. In fact, one of the bad effects of Jewish ethnicism might be that as parochial affairs assume a higher priority, Jews (as other ethnics) will be deflected from general obligations to the body politic. As of now, this danger has not materialized.

While it is hard to judge how many Jews even loosely fall under the ethnic heading, American Jewish ethnicity did not begin with today's touted new pluralism. Jewish survivalists, Orthodox Jews who pray for the welfare of fellow Jews, Zionists and Yiddishists had trained antenna for spotting the Jewish component of current events long before the revision of melting pot sociology.

However thoroughgoing this new Jewish ethnicism, there is still the Jew on the other extreme who as a result of the breakdown of old communities, secularism and mobility flees anything Jewish. The ethnic sees these assimilated Jews as knee-jerk liberals who in their trendiness forsake not only 3,000 years of Jewish continuity, but ultimately endanger their own survival. Most Jews, however, fall somewhere in the middle rank, eschewing both ethnicism and secularism. While few of these middle level Jews take to the streets or carry placards, America's increasing ethnicism has made almost inevitable their taking note of their minority of Jewish activists. Furthermore, certain urban Jews who may not in the past have defined their political interests by their Jewishness—the poor, the aged, the civil servant, residents of blighted neighborhoods—have begun to accept as favorable for them also the positions the ethnics espouse. Many Jews in such vulnerable situations regard the ethnics as an idealistic vanguard, something akin to the following Black Panthers or Young Lords have among their communities, and on key issues (which politician is best for Israel) the advice of the ethnic leaders filters down.

Some analysts, in criticizing Jewish ethnicism as standing for the status quo, misunderstand this phenomenon's complexity. In asking for more governmental financing for parochial schools, increased public housing, the strengthening of anti-poverty programs and a tougher hand combatting crime, Jewish ethnics are clearly advocating change—and on these issues they have forged alliances with other ethnic groups. Status quo thinking appears, however, in the ethnics defense of an internationalistic American foreign policy, as opposed to neo-isolationism which they fear endangers Israel, in opposition to quotas which they see as prejudicial to Jewish interests and, particularly from more Orthodox quarters, hostility to the personal and family morality positions of the fashionable counter culture.

The achievements of the ethnics include a revival of Jewish learning, the exposure of the plight of the Jewish poor, introducing a new sensitivity by politicians to Jewish problems, the spurring of older Jewish organizations to discard yesterday's weapons in fighting today's battles, a new interest in co-religionists abroad, and a greater sense of commitment to community rather than to self. Where an unknown future threatens to replace America's dying social accommodations, the response of the Jewish ethnics has been to shift the focus from universalism to "What's in it for us?" Nevertheless, the extent to which they succeed in substituting ethnicism for the slippage of the center will depend on how well America's open, tolerant society will be able to balance the demands of its many subgroups with those of the nation.

# # #

Friends in Need of Votes, Friends Indeed?

[*Shma: A Journal of Jewish Responsibility*, October 15, 1976. Written jointly with Evelyn Rubin]

In November, Jews and other interest groups will take their scorecards and rate the candidates. It doesn't require any extensive amount of probing for a politician seeking national office to determine how to satisfy Jewish voters—Israel's future, Soviet Jewry, and the legitimacy of Arab boycotts constitute the chief issues, issues which are neither obscure to the general electorate nor newcomers to the American political scene.

The beginning of political wisdom is to reward friends and oppose enemies. Thus, the politicians who championed your cause the last time around will have incentive for future challenges, whereas those who were lukewarm or hostile will draw a blank. That's the way the game is played; performance, not smiles, triggers votes. The bottom line of politics in a democracy is to pull the lever for the politician who has been most steadfast.

Despite this political axiom, the 1976 campaign has seen a new exposition of Jewish political strategy. Simply put, this scenario advocates a yarmulka in every candidate's camp. According to Elkanah Schwartz ([*Shma*, vol. 6, page 114]) Jews should hedge their bets by assigning yarmulkas to every passing political bandwagon. Such a "cover-up" is the height of opportunism and self-defeat.

By the time someone seeks the White House, is it asking too much that he hold positions on the key international issues affecting Jews? After all, we're not talking here about election to a city council or state legislature post where the political impact on Jewish destiny is minimal. When a Presidential aspirant has either a zero or *parve* track record on bellwether Jewish issues, is it for want of a yarmulka-clad advisor? Has it been ignorance or expedience which stood in the way of such a candidate? If time existed to crisscross every hamlet, plunge into any crowd larger than three and chit-chat on third-rate talk shows, it also existed to take positions on these basic subjects.

A *Caveat: Be Selective with Our Support*

In addition to being opportunistic, the argument that Jews should keep their options open by working *qua* Jews for any professed Presidential aspirant is also dangerous. The fact is that certain politicians have shown great loyalty over the years to crucial Jewish issues. It's not only sound politics but simple decency to support their campaigns for higher office, as contrasted with rivals who were either never there or suddenly pretend the need to be "educated." We give our allies scant encouragement by proposing such a cynical distribution of yarmulkas. Moreover, the appearance of a yarmulka in every candidate's entourage deceives those voters who are less politically aware into believing that all the office-seekers carry the same quality *hechsher* (validity).

Finally, the well-meaning yarmulka'd statesman would do well to, recognize the difference between serving as the Jews' spokesman to a candidate and the candidate's spokesman to the Jews. Ironically, certain Jewish political activists who allegedly came to "educate" political office-holders and -seekers ended up by being put into service by the politicians to "educate" their fellow Jews.

The presence of yarmulka'd advisors provides politicians with convenient excuses and front-men in reply to accusations that they are failing Jewish interests. There is a danger that in the ethnic euphoria of current politics a new type of court Jew might emerge. Simply because a yarmulka is pressed into commission there is no guarantee that to a politician its message is any more than skin-deep.

# # #

Help for the Republicans: The Jewish Vote [*New York* Magazine, "The City Politic" Column, December 1976]

The Jewish voter is sending a message—it's no longer *trayf* (nonkosher) to vote Republican. In 1972 Richard Nixon captured 40 percent of the Jewish vote. This time, according to CBS, Gerald Ford got 32 percent of the Jewish vote to Jimmy Carter's 68 percent.

These results are in sharp contrast to Jewish backing for other recent Democratic presidential candidates. In 1960 Kennedy drew 82 percent of the Jewish vote; in 1964 Johnson won 90 percent; in 1968 Humphrey's total was 83 percent.

A trend is under way that provides potentially handsome dividends to the floundering Republican party: An important slice of the Jewish vote is up for grabs.

Why should the Republicans court the Jewish vote, especially that of ethnic Jews, who represent a small percentage of an already small bloc? A fair question on the face of it. But among the could-have-beens of this presidential election, an overlooked but intriguing possibility is what would have happened if one out of every nine Jews who voted for Carter had shifted to Ford. Such a switch would have returned Ford to the White House by putting New York in the Republican column—an entirely plausible prospect, given the candidates, the issues, and the nature of the Jewish electorate.

Consider this arithmetic: Carter won New York's 41 electoral votes by a popular-vote margin of about 250,000 votes out of some 6,300,000 cast. Of New York's 2.5 million Jews (14 percent of the population), about 1.75 million are eligible voters. Given the standard Jewish turnout of 80 percent of registered voters (the highest of any voting group in the state), about 1.4 million Jews went to the polls on November 2. Based on a 68-32 split between Carter and Ford, 1 million Jews went for Carter. If Ford had changed one out of nine of these votes, he would have assured his election.

Jews had no special reason to be fond of Carter in the first place; many of them resented him from the beginning. Here was the spoiler who nuzzled out their two favorite Democratic presidential candidates. If you were a Jewish liberal, you went with Udall; if you were a Hasidic Jew, Jackson was your favorite. Even after Carter wiped out Udall and Jackson, Jerry Brown swamped him in the Jewish precincts of Maryland and California.

Along the road from Plains to the Atlanta statehouse to the Madison Square Garden nomination, Carter had no real scorecard on issues crucial to Jews. Once or twice, in fact, Carter made equivocal statements about the PLO that alarmed Zionists. Also, bitter encounters with Christian messianic movements in history made some Jews instinctively raise their guard against Carter's revivalism.

Along with the shift in Jewish voting patterns in the past two presidential elections, a new type of Jewish civic consciousness emerged. As any streetwise New York City politician knows, there is no *one* Jewish vote; the monolithic New Deal Democrat Jew is a relic of the past. In the late sixties and early seventies, a new Jewish ethnicity surfaced that took the measure of politicians based on "What's in it for us?"

The Forest Hills project, the teachers' strike, and the subterfuge of affirmative-action programs that seemingly kept eligible Jewish kids out of medical schools drove many Jews to rethink their politics. Neither the Democratic party nor conventional liberalism were sacrosanct—what counted was how the individual politician fitted into the ethnics' scheme for Jewish survival.

As far as foreign policy went, the abuse meted out to Israel at the U.N. marked the end of the support by these ethnics of save-the-world visions. Coalesced in the ranks of the Jewish ethnics were the Orthodox, the Zionists, the Jews whose peoplehood was ignited by the resistance of Soviet Jews, and the old and the poor locked in ghettos in their apartment-prisons.

What did in Ford in New York, then, was not the absence of a Jewish constituency bent on shedding past Democratic loyalties if Jewish self-interest seemed to require it, but rather Ford's incapacity to capitalize on such a voting bloc. In particular, Carter's refusal to dump pollster Pat Caddell, who also enjoyed a six-figure retainer from the Saudi Arabian king, added to the ethnics' earlier suspicion of the Georgian. In addition, Carter's tax-reform schemes raised questions about his fiscal acuity in the minds of many Jews. But, thanks to Ford's fumbling on the Arab boycott and General Brown's bad-mouthing of Israel, when the moment of truth came, many Jews gambled on their well-worn Democratic party credentials, if not on Carter himself.

Now, Democratic apologists might claim that the GOP can't count on future windfalls based simply on the results of the presidential voting shift among Jews in 1972 and in 1976. True enough, had the Democrats in those races put up such veteran mouthpieces for Israel as Humphrey and Jackson, heavy defections to the Republicans would not have taken place. But history cannot be erased—a sizable minority of Jews *did* pull the Republican lever the past two times out, no doubt resulting in a change in the political self-perceptions of many who did so.

The conclusion is obvious: If the Republicans are willing to allocate the needed outlays in positions, in time, and in party presence, Jews can be edged even farther from the Democratic spectrum. For the record, we must note, naturally, that most Jews are not about to move en masse to the GOP. Most Jews are too liberal, too humanitarian to abandon their support for the social underdog as identified with the stands of your characteristic Democratic officeholder. Most Jews, true to *Commentary*'s Milton Himmelfarb's observation, will continue to hold the social status of Episcopalians, yet vote like Puerto Ricans.

Not so the Jewish ethnics whose political purpose is to save other Jews before saving the world. The real intent of the Republican party should be to continue to diminish the pull of the Democrats on the Jewish ethnics. This represents a goal not without political precedent. It might be hard to believe, on the basis of today's voting patterns, but in most of the presidential elections between Lincoln and Coolidge, Jews preferred Republican White House aspirants to the Democratic ones. Not because Jews were rich or secure in America then, which they weren't, but because they were drawn to the tough positions taken by national Republicans on anti-Semitism in czarist Russia during that period.

And this is as good a cue as any for the Republicans of today who wish to drive the wedge farther between the Democrats and the Jews. Despite Ford's fear of inviting Solzhenitsyn to the White House, the Republicans—when compared to the Democrats—are more resolutely anti-Kremlin and are more partial to priming the Pentagon. As Pat Moynihan will attest, that's already 99 percent of what ethnic Jews want from Washington.

In New York the Republican case is even stronger. The Republican cast, consisting of Jacob Javits, Louis Lefkowitz, Richard Rosenbaum, and Roy Goodman, is already assembled, only waiting to be handed a script. Next year's mayoral election sets the stage for the cast's debut. In the big things, there is not much that's left for the mayor to decide. But in some of the others, like how to respond to the phenomenon of one or two elderly Jews being murdered in the ghettos each week, some room for mayoral maneuvering exists. Simply because Nixon and Agnew, the head-thumpers of the sixties, proved inadequate to the *pro forma* Republican anticrime spiels is no reason why Roy Goodman, bedecked with a *yarmulkah*, should be denied the constituency that Abe Beame's inaction warrants.

Both in regard to Israel and to the safety of Jewish blood in New York City, Jews are caught up in high-risk politics. On Delancey Street and on Ocean Parkway the ethnics have told us that they are bereft of political considerations other than "What's good for the Jews." They are warming up to the idea that the politics of survival and the local Democratic clubhouse are not automatically synonymous. Richard Rosenbaum, are you listening?

# # #

Republicans Court the Jewish Vote: GOP? Couldn't Hurt [*New York* Magazine, "The Capitol Letter" Column, July 1978]

Sunday, May 21, was a big day for GOP heavy hitters. With a Soviet Jewry Solidarity rally at Battery Park in the afternoon and a dinner of the Union of Orthodox Jewish Congregations of America that night at the New York Hilton, Bill Brock, Bob Packwood, and Chuck Mathias knew where to zero in on the yarmulke-wearing voters they were looking for. The Republican stampede for the Jewish vote had begun.

Six days earlier, thanks to President Carter's intense lobbying, the Senate had approved America's first sale of jet fighters to Saudi Arabia. The Republicans were here to cash in on Jewish fallout, and New York Jews didn't disappoint them. When Bob Lifschutz, President Carter's counsel, rose to address the Soviet Jewry rally, he found staring him in the face a hand painted bed sheet: God Forgive Us For Voting For Carter. Only after

Ed Koch lectured the hecklers about the dictates of courtesy did Lifschutz meekly finish his message.

Under a midday sun, ripples of shifting political alignments could be detected as the crowd gave its heartiest cheers, not to a Jewish-establishment type or a champion of Jewish causes from the urban East, but to Bob Packwood, a senator from Oregon who represents 7,000 Jewish constituents.

Egged on by chants of "Dump Carter" from the crowd, Bob Packwood, also chairman of the National Republican Senatorial Committee, exclaimed, "I'm so damned sore at the State Department," and accused it of "longstanding and blatant" anti-Jewish bias.

Though the 1980 presidential race is still a while away, the Republican party, for the first time in modern history on the national level, is waging a deliberate campaign to woo the Jewish voter, proportionately America's heaviest-voting ethnic group. Because over 80 percent of American Jews live in eight states (New York, California, New Jersey, Florida, Illinois, Ohio, Pennsylvania, Massachusetts) that hold 80 percent of the electoral vote necessary to capture the White House, driving even a minor wedge into Jewry's long-standing loyalty to the Democratic party might result in the election of a Republican president.

"I think there is an opportunity to earn Jewish support, providing we put forth a sincere and concentrated effort," says Republican National Committee chairman Bill Brock. And Kansas Senator Bob Dole, who himself has emerged as an increasingly popular speaker on the Jewish lecture circuit, notes, "Whereas in the past not many doors in the Jewish community were open to us, a lot of Jews are now willing to listen."

The main technician responsible for edging Jews closer to the GOP camp is Larry Goldberg, a hard-driving Rhode Islander who first appeared in national politics in the 1972 election, when he engineered Richard Nixon's total of 40 percent of the Jewish vote.

Educated at Brown and Harvard Law School, Goldberg has a three-year arrangement with the Republican National Committee, between 1978 and 1980, for the purpose of wooing Jewish voters. "The Jewish community is not organized the same way a congressional district is laid out," he says. "Republican candidates may not know where Jewish voters live, how to find local people, which forums are available in the Jewish community, and what issues beyond the obvious ones Jews are interested in."

Currently, Goldberg, aided by five staffers and a budget of between $100,000 and $150,000, plans to scout the Jewish terrain on behalf of a hungry GOP. The budget covers Goldberg's winging across the country to advise Republican candidates and speak with Jewish voters, and his reproducing of nasty articles about Democrats.

"I'm a superactive Jew," says Goldberg. "For me this is a labor of love." Before attempting to bridge Republican politics and Jewish activism, Goldberg was a businessman; he put together a chain of 83 toy-and-sporting-goods stores based between Massachusetts and California. After leaving the business to a conglomerate in 1971, Goldberg found himself "looking for something different to do."

He was able to convince Detroit's Max Fisher, one of the wealthiest Jews in America and a mainstay of Republican politics, of his fitness for the launching of a separate drive in the 1972 presidential campaign for the Jewish vote. Fisher was impressed with Goldberg's volunteer work in Rhode Island politics and his having the right credentials—membership on the national cabinet of the UJA's Young Leadership Cabinet, the vice-presidency of the Jewish Federation of Rhode Island, a leadership role in the Anti-Defamation League of B'nai B'rith.

In 1972, Goldberg pitched his campaign to all strata of the Jewish community, but the real target population was the urban middle and lower middle class. Storefronts sprang up in Borough Park, Nixon campaign vans crisscrossed Williamsburg, and blue-and-white buttons bearing Nixon's name in Hebrew were seen on Hasidim along Ocean Parkway.

Despite such diligence, Goldberg did not escape the more heinous elements in the Nixon administration. Under consideration for a position there, he was investigated by satraps of John Dean because of his opposition to the 1969 Rogers Mideast peace plan and his activism on behalf of Soviet Jewry. Their report raised doubts about the appointment. It also included information based on an illegal use of Goldberg's tax returns, according to later allegations in the House Impeachment Committee's indictment case against Nixon. Ultimately, though, he did get the job.

After working on the White House staff under Jim Lynn, Goldberg left Washington in 1973 to become vice president of development at Brandeis University. In Gerald Ford's administration, Goldberg reappeared as assistant director of the Federal Preparedness Agency in charge of the strategic materials group.

On his 1978 calendar, Goldberg has penciled in over 40 House races, senatorial elections in Massachusetts and New Jersey, and a sprinkling of gubernatorial contests. But by 1980, he will be ready for the big kill—slicing off, he hopes, a big enough piece of the Jewish vote to elect a GOP president.

Because Goldberg knows how rare registered Jewish Republicans are right now, he's going after Jewish independents and Democrats. "We say to such Jews, we know you're interested in political life—here's a candidate sympathetic to your causes and positive on the issues, who also happens to be a Republican. If such a Jew finds himself voting more often for Republicans, and the party is open to him, eventually he'll register as a Republican, even run for office someday as a Republican."

In Goldberg's view there exist major differences between current overtures to Jewish voters and his efforts back in 1972 on behalf of Nixon. "Haldeman's group didn't take this seriously," says Goldberg. "By contrast, Bill Brock is hospitable and highly cooperative. I've spoken with other Republican national chairmen, but Brock is the only one who has wanted to do something to reach the Jewish voter."

Unlike their New Deal–era parents, many of today's Jews are asking pols, "What's in it for us?" Says Dr. Jack M. Sable, former New York State human-rights commissioner under Nelson Rockefeller, "We Jews have always been an issue-oriented bloc; now we're voting as a bloc on the issues."

So, selling the GOP message nationally goes beyond latching on to Jewish support for Israel. "There's a 50-year tradition of Jews' being with the Democrats," notes Oregon's Senator Packwood. "We have to expect only gradual gains at first, but in order to bring this about, we must raise other issues."

Domestically, Brock maintains, the GOP has a better case to make for Jewish voters than the Democrats—by opposing quotas and by "providing the individual with greater economic opportunities," reducing taxes and government regulation. Again, Brock trusts that Jews as a competitive middle-class minority will go for such GOP stands.

One GOP figure going for the jugular as far as the Jewish vote is concerned is Senator Lowell Weicker of Connecticut, who argues that Zbigniew Brzezinski has deliberately accused American Jews of constituting a roadblock to hamper the administration's foreign policy. Brzezinski's version of world order, according to Weicker, "always seems to require that certain groups be trimmed off in the interests of neatness. We know from history that time and again, when national leaders ran into difficulties, they found it convenient to blame their problems on the Jews. . . . If I were president and had a national-security adviser who singled out American Jews as an impediment to my policies, I would have his resignation before sundown and his reputation for breakfast."

Closer to home, Perry Duryea, who last week was in Israel as part of his gubernatorial campaign, hopes to reap gains among Jewish voters by stressing an alleged Carey-Carter connection. His staff will urge Jewish voters to show how dissatisfied they are with the administration's foreign policy by electing a Republican governor in the state with the largest Jewish population.

Even without prompting from Larry Goldberg, New York Jews are spontaneously beginning to appear in GOP circles. George Klein, a Brooklyn manufacturer and former adviser in Gerald Ford's 1976 presidential campaign, is seen as one of the GOP's leading connections with Jewish voters. Sheldon Farber, the state senator from Queens's 10th District (Kew Gardens, the Rockaways), proudly hangs his diploma of Orthodox rabbinic ordination in his office; Lew Lehrman, a founder of the largest retail-drug chain in the Northeast, put together the 1978 New York State Republican platform.

How do the Democrats view such Republican proselytizing? Evan Dobelle, a Jew, who was recently elected treasurer of the Democratic National Committee, praises Carter for his "sincerity" in pursuing Mideast peace. As for Democrats who may be unhappy with the Saudi Arabian plane sale, Dobelle reminds them that Carter "has more senior Jewish staff members than any other president."

One other major Jewish Democratic fund raiser who also accompanied vice president Mondale on his trip to the Mideast this month similarly predicts no "massive changeover among Jews as a result of Carter. Many Jews are still more comfortable with the Democrats for all the traditional reasons. I myself am confident that Carter won't let Israel down." But whether other Jews feel the same way about the president is an open question, and with other domestic issues bothering this largely middle-class voting bloc, Larry Goldberg might just turn out to be the Hamilton Jordan of 1980.

7

Political and Communal Personalities

Rubin began writing—and reviewing books and responding to articles—about personalities in or affecting the Jewish world. His political and communal interests ranged from the world's top political and religious figures to the local Jewish councilman covering his own community and the honorees at his own congregation's annual banquet.

Crock of Presidents
[*Jerusalem Post,* May 1970]
Book Review: *Memoirs* by Arthur Krock
[Abridged, focusing on the sections addressing Israel and world Jewry]

Arthur Krock's account of 12 American Presidents, from Theodore Roosevelt to Richard Nixon, is a formidable contribution—both as history and as entertainment. A declared agnostic born to gentle but not wealthy Jewish parents in Kentucky, Krock rose to become a leading member of the U.S. "Establishment." He was the "N.Y. Times" Washington Correspondent for 30 years (during which he won three Pulitzer Prizes). As such, he became a focus of great attention, and as his book reveals, he emerged on many occasions as both confidant and virtual partner to government decision-makers. He not only meets Presidents at press conferences; he also exchanges social visits and memos with them; he is a dinner guest; from some such as Lyndon B. Johnson he receives gifts (deer sausage); and he was such an intimate of the Kennedys that he was sometimes asked to give them literary advice, and even wrote a law school recommendation for Bobby. So these recollections are not a paste-up of secondary material, but the impressions of a man who was really there. Furthermore, Krock kept careful personal memos of certain major episodes, many of which are presented in toto.

Stereotypical Teddy

Theodore Roosevelt, whom Krock hardly knew, is portrayed no differently from his stereotype: direct, forceful, decisive and individualistic, a man who, according to Krock, "aroused hostility and returned it with interest." In 1 1/2 pages, Krock cites the tragedy of William Howard Taft who "was thrust into that (presidential) arena because T.R. believed Taft would carry out his own policies to the letter, and he was eliminated by the thumbs-down of the same hand."

Woodrow Wilson is also presented as in standard textbook accounts—an idealist who never saw his grand visions realized because of an austere bearing and a refusal to play politics. Krock finds Wilson wrong in not compromising on the text of the League of Nations covenant, but on the basis of his leadership of the Allies in World War I and his domestic reforms, Krock rates Wilson a "great man and a great President."

Warren Harding, who promised a "Return to Normalcy" in the wake of American participation in World War I, is dismissed with a few paragraphs. "He was a handsome man: no one ever looked more a President than he did." Too genial ever to say no to his corrupt friends, Harding died discredited.

Calvin Coolidge, Harding's successor, is pictured as the greatest practical joker ever to occupy the White House. Krock argues that Coolidge was a victim of his own taciturnity in his famous statement "I do not choose to run in 1928," thereby inadvertently eliminating himself from renomination.

The euphoria of the Gay Twenties, when Americans believed that an end to poverty was in sight and two cars would soon sit in every garage, also brings Herbert Hoover into office. Hoover promised too much, according to Krock, but he was still undeservedly maligned. In brief, he presents Hoover as a victim of hard luck. According to Krock, Hoover "initiated sound measures" to halt the depression, and if re-elected he might have even "succeeded earlier and better" than Franklin D. Roosevelt.

Roosevelt's tenure covers a big part of Krock's career. Krock's description of Roosevelt must be weighed in terms of the author's confession earlier in the book of his expectation that a President should "rise above the politics that put him in the White House." Thus, he accuses Roosevelt of "cynical" politics, particularly through his alliance with "even more cynical city bosses." In a balance sheet he drew up four months after Roosevelt's death, Krock listed FDR's virtues and defects.

Among the distinguishing qualities of Harry Truman, according to Krock, was that he was the only President about whom Krock wrote critically but who never held it against Krock personally. Truman had great determination, but his character, in Krock's estimate, combined pettiness with greatness.

Students of Middle East history will find noteworthy Krock's references to the views of James V. Forrestal, the first U.S. Secretary of Defence. Forrestal's tragic decline until he jumped to his death is recounted by Krock. Forrestal lost favour with Truman because of objections to the President's endorsement of the U.N. recommendation to set up a Jewish State in part of Mandatory Palestine. Forrestal argued that the creation of a Jewish State would threaten the flow of Middle East oil to the West. Krock writes that Forrestal predicted a Third World War would result from the creating of such a state "surrounded by enemies" and calling for the U.S. to guarantee its existence. The U.S. would give such a guarantee, and out of expediency would not redeem its pledge—as a result of which its pledged word "would ring hollow in the world." Near his end, Forrestal saw Zionist "spies and assassins lurking in doorways near his residence, bent on revenge for his attitude toward the Palestine partition."

Krock's references to the Eisenhower Presidency are more sympathetic than is now fashionable. America, Krock claims, both wanted and needed a progressive conservative endowed with Eisenhower's qualities—modesty, high intelligence, innate strength of character, warmth and generosity. In foreign policy, Krock maintains, Eisenhower amassed a first-rate record: Formosa was protected, the Korean War ended, Lebanon denied to anti-American forces, and stronger alliances were developed with the German Federal Republic and France. Among the blemishes on Eisenhower's record, however, was the pressure to withdraw from Suez in 1956 . . . Israel alone, according to Krock, could "probably" have kept Suez Canal traffic to all nations, overthrown Nasser: as a result the defeated Arab states would have been more inclined to make peace.

Krock draws the John Kennedy he knew as an intelligent and graceful youth, deeply interested in all sorts of information, perhaps a would-be teacher of history or political science. He reminds us that John in his maiden Senate speech, discussed the plight of the French in Indo-China, yet in his Presidency he made the first substantial commitment of American troops in Vietnam.

There are some interesting references to Bobby—the Kennedy with the most intensity. Krock credits his, dynamic activism, but is critical of Bobby for thinking of the Presidency as a "family fief."

Lyndon Johnson receives a mixed verdict from Krock as a hard-working President, but crafty and childish, anxious and frustrated. He attacks Johnson for more "reckless deficit spending" than any of his White House predecessors. He writes that Johnson made too many promises, especially on the Negro issue (Krock says Johnson acknowledged this mistake).

There is no separate treatment of Richard Nixon, but passing references indicate that Krock clearly sees him as intelligent, "thoughtful and well informed," and as having a rare ability to weigh objectively political problems in which he is personally involved.

At the end of his journalistic tenure, Krock sees a country brought to ruin by liberals. Streets are unsafe, self-reliance is in sharp decline and licentiousness dominates literary and personal life. Because an alliance of special interests controls the government, Krock writes, Americans correctly have less and less faith in the "integrity" of what government does.

Finally, in foreign policy the United Nations has not fulfilled the hopes of the post–World War II era.

# # #

Brooklyn's Hasidim: The Yiddish Connection
[*New York* Magazine, The City Politic Column, March 1977]

The last time you were rushing to a luncheon appointment in Manhattan, were you stopped by a pair of bearded, black-hatted Hasidim inviting you—"if you're Jewish"—to step up and pray in one of their *mitzvah* vans that comb the midtown streets?

These Hasidim—followers of an ultra-Orthodox mystical approach to Judaism centered in a *rebbe*, a leader revered for his holiness—are worried about the lost souls of their fellow Jews. If you have guessed that in matters religious these dark-suited missionaries offer an old-fashioned purism alien to today's standards, you have guessed right.

In addition to following all the codes of Orthodox Judaism—such as the Sabbath laws and dietary laws—the Hasidim, who originated in Eastern Europe, adhere to further restraints in many areas of their personal life. Separation between the sexes is so strict that a man is forbidden to touch or even shake hands with any woman other than his wife. Modesty in dress is extreme—even in 90-degree heat, you'll see Hasidic women wearing long sleeves and, if married, keeping their heads covered.

But if you also guessed that in matters political Hasidim are naïve, watch out. Don't be misled by side curls, a black caftan coat, or a sometimes distracted otherworldly look. The sect remains tightly knit, politically uniform, and family-oriented—sandwiched in a city where everything else seems unpredictable. But the Brooklyn-based Hasid knows that the bottom line of democratic politics is the lever in the voting booth on election day. Be assured that the pols will come acallin' on the 75,000 constituents of the city's various Hasidic dynasties.

Between now and the September mayoral primary, the pols will be beating a path to the Hasidic *rebbes* in Crown Heights and Williamsburg, ostensibly to pay homage and seek encouragement. But they will really be fishing for the city's biggest bloc vote. While an Albert Shanker or a Victor Gotbaum may mouth pledges about delivering their rank and file, only the Hasidim produce close to a 100 percent turnout for their candidate.

In the last mayoral outing, Mario Biaggi had to cool his heels for a month before being squeezed in for a late night appointment with the Lubavitcher *rebbe* of Crown Heights, one of the key Hasidic leaders. Biaggi wanted to report on how—when he was in Moscow at the police ministry—he traded on his reputation as a retired cop to raise the issue of Jewish emigration. Being a sought-after place for such celebrities, the Lubavitcher *rebbe's* ground-floor office at 770 Eastern Parkway is protected by an around-the-clock New York City police guard—thereby tacitly according the site semi-official diplomatic status.

Almost never does the Lubavitcher *rebbe* of Crown Heights or the Satmar *rebbe* of Williamsburg—the other major Hasidic leader—deign to give their personal seal of kosher to a candidate. But to politicians in the know, points are scored by how much time the *rebbe* spends with a visitor and how often he consents to see him. And some politicians never get through the front door—Al Lowenstein, though a Jew, running for Congress against the late John Rooney in Williamsburg, drew a *trayf* (nonkosher) rating from Satmar because of his new-left views.

Rabbi Chaim Stauber, editor of the Satmar weekly *Der Yid (The Jew)*, is an important Hasidic power broker. He regularly puts aside his talmudic tomes to follow *Congressional Record* debates and Albany and City Council roll calls. As one of its leaders, Stauber recommends candidates to the Satmar-controlled United Jewish Organizations of Williamsburg. (On the Sabbath before election day, the sextons of Satmar synagogues in Williamsburg announce the UJO's endorsements from their pulpits to thousands of attentive worshipers.)

Stauber is typical of the half dozen or so Hasidic cognoscenti whose political judgments are endorsed by their respective sects—the Satmar of Williamsburg and the Lubavitch of Crown Heights. He boasts of the strides his community has taken since World War II. The Satmar *rebbe* came to Williamsburg as a refugee from Hungary in 1947. He opened a yeshiva in a basement, enrolling four students. Today, the Satmar sect enrolls 5,000 students in its Yiddish-language schools; the community also operates a pharmacy, an ambulance service, and medical and dental clinics.

The thrust of the Hasidic leaders' political involvement is rarely for personal gain or patronage. They're zealous about job training, housing, day care, and other broad-based communal self-help programs tailored to the Hasidic community. Politicians experienced in bargaining with Hasidim know that the lure of an assistant commissionership will not do when a computer-training program is sought.

Illustrating this symbiotic relationship between the pols and the Hasidim is the Steingut family. Bob, Brooklyn's councilman-at-large, relates, "My Grandpa Irwin, then New York State Assembly speaker, journeyed to the White House to win over FDR's support for admitting the Lubavitcher *rebbe* to the United States as a war refugee." Because of Roosevelt's consent, these Hasidim followed Steingut to his Crown Heights district. They still remain there in close-quartered enclaves. Hasidic sects encourage their members to live close to the *rebbe*, to pray as a unit, and to send their children to special yeshivas.

So, while many whites abandoned Bedford-Stuyvesant, Brownsville, and East New York, the Hasidim of Crown Heights stayed on, guaranteeing themselves an eventual base as one of Brooklyn's largest white ethnic groups. More assimilated Jews fled down the Long Island Expressway. The Hasidim—in contrast—decided to hold their turf, based on the greater communal good.

"If we moved," says Rabbi Mendel Shemtov, president of the Crown Heights Jewish Community Council, "we would be abandoning our old people who couldn't afford to put down new roots. For us that would be a terrible sin." This same Rabbi Shemtov typifies a Hasidic sociological phenomenon. He emigrated here from Russia in 1951, became a successful plastics manufacturer, and today boasts of his eldest son, a rabbi who seeks to reach out to wayward Jewish youth.

Hasidim, following a biblical prohibition against birth control, not infrequently have a half dozen children or more. With a population bursting at the seams, their territory in Crown Heights and Williamsburg strikes them as ever shrinking. Jews recently won over to Hasidim also want to move in, close to the *rebbe*.

Expanding population, well-defined communal goals, high voter turnout—a formula that translates into political clout. At every Lubavitcher festival (there are four or five important ones a year), you'll usually spot among the guests at least one mayor, a United States senator, a half dozen congressmen. One *simcha* (party) last year saw personal greetings from Jerry Ford delivered to the *rebbe* by a member of the White House staff. And every December, a planeload of top-ranking Washington bureaucrats who fund the Satmar economic-aid programs come to share stuffed cabbage and gefilte fish at the yeshiva's dinner.

Hints of a second stage of Americanization are appearing. A few younger Hasidim advocate taking to the hustings—for themselves this time, not for the Democratic machine. Asks Yankel Goldstein, a wiry 30-year-old ordained Lubavitcher rabbi, "Instead of spending our time bargaining with politicians, shouldn't we become the politicians ourselves?" Goldstein served as an aide to John Lindsay, advance man to Mario Biaggi in the mayoral run four years ago, and headed the Jewish desk in Jim Buckley's reelection effort last year. He believes in the last analysis, that only a Hasid can reliably represent Hasidic interests.

For the moment, though, Hasidim are focusing their energies not on gaining Albany or City Council posts, but on getting elected to local community boards, poverty corporations, and school-district offices. Representation on these boards assures the safety of the millions of dollars that the Lubavitcher and Satmar sects have invested in communal institutions.

Bitter past experiences, claim the Hasidim, have underscored for them the need to assert themselves in local councils. "Whenever the few Hasidim on Community Board 8 got up to propose something, even if everyone would benefit," says Rabbi Israel Rosenfeld, executive director of the Crown Heights Jewish Community Council, "the other ethnic groups would shout us down."

The opportunity they were looking for locally presented itself last year. Under charter revision, city-planning-board lines were redrawn—and the Hasidic proposal for creating a compact district centering on Crown Heights was overwhelmingly backed by the Board of Estimates. Rabbi Samuel Fogelman was elected chairman of Community Board 9. He is a former Lubavitcher yeshiva principal who says of his council, roughly evenly divided between whites and blacks, "Together we'll bring the community the services we all want."

Not so, claims Dr. Vernal G. Cave, a dermatologist who heads the Black Community Council of Crown Heights. He sees the heightened Hasidic political presence as part of a deliberate effort to "take over" Crown Heights. "If they can do it to us, the Hasidim can come into any black community and tear it apart."

Dr. Cave waves an accusing finger at his ex-neighbor Shirley Chisholm, who sold her President Street home, two doors away from his, to a Hasidic family. He feels that Shirley should vigorously oppose the alleged Hasidic efforts to "force out" blacks from Crown Heights.

Territoriality is also the main political issue vexing the Satmar community of Williamsburg, a neighborhood of aging brownstones and housing projects where Hasidic children can be heard speaking Yiddish as they play. But here the point of contention isn't over district lines but over who—Hasidim or Hispanics—gets to live in a city-built project, Clemente Plaza. Hasidim argue that since the project is situated in what's known as the "Hasidic triangle," they deserve priority. Opponents claim that in order to maintain ethnic balance in the community, the population of the project should be 75 percent Hispanic and black.

Rabbi Stauber, in advocating the Hasidic case for Clemente Plaza, argues that the only other option for expanding the Hasidic turf is "the East River or the Brooklyn-Queens Expressway." The Satmar leader attributes the thwarting of Hasidic aims on this issue to a 1974 Albany redistricting of the Williamsburg Hasidim into two assembly and two senate districts with the supposed goal of paving the way for more nonwhite legislators. Earlier this month, *oy vays* were sounded throughout Williamsburg as the Supreme Court turned down a last-ditch appeal by the Hasidim to reverse these boundaries.

At least one of his neighbors who "would be delighted" to see the Satmar out is Father Bryan Karvelis, pastor of the Transfiguration Catholic Church and head of Clemente Plaza's board of directors. Because they are "totally turned in on themselves," Reverend Karvelis feels that other Williamsburg residents gain no benefit from the Hasidic "enclave."

The political coming of age of the Hasidim has ramifications beyond Williamsburg and Crown Heights. To a Brooklyn Democratic machine already weakened by losses to Reformers, further erosion by Hasidic voters, the backbone of the organization's support in the past, could send Meade Esposito back to the insurance business full time. And well he must know this. In midterm last year Esposito booted out Borough President Sebastian Leone to a judgeship, replacing him with City Councilman Howie Golden. With a name like Golden heading the machine's slate in the September primary, Esposito hopes to stem defections to possible ethnic Jewish candidates.

Meanwhile, the Hasid sets his antenna to pick up the vibes of politicians who will guard his turf and bring in government money to his community.

So the lesson, Messrs. Beame, Sutton, et al., is that if your script for a visit as a mayoral candidate to 770 Eastern Parkway is limited to donning a yarmulke, drinking a slivovitz, and commiserating over the plight of Jews in Russia, Rumania, Syria, and Iraq, don't bother crossing the Brooklyn Bridge.

# # #

The Most Powerful Rabbis in New York
[*New York* Magazine cover article, January 22, 1979]

Last May more than 500 rabbis from across the country got together for the annual celebration of the founding of the state of Israel. What made last year's party memorable, however, was that it was held on the lawn of the White House. The congregation of rabbis was the president's way of appeasing American Jewry in the period before the Camp David talks, but it also signaled a Jewish power shift. For the first time at the White House, rabbis—rather than the lay leaders and professionals who run the Jewish national organizations—had been invited in force to represent Jewish voters. The American rabbi had arrived.

Previously occupied only with preaching, teaching, and other pastoral activities, the rabbi is becoming increasingly important as a political activist, community organizer, and deliverer of social services. Testifying before public groups, as two Orthodox rabbis did late last year in opposing a gay-rights bill being considered by the City Council, was always a function of a Jewish leader. But such activities as quizzing gubernatorial candidates at public hearings, taking over the office of the president of Lehman College to protest a threat to a Jewish-studies program, demonstrating before the Borough Park police station, and keeping up with the guidelines for HEW [Department of Health, Education, and Welfare] grants illustrate a new activist role for rabbis.

By involving themselves in social and political projects, present-day rabbis forge a link with those Jews who first carried that title 2,000 years ago. The rabbis who wrote the Talmud, in addition to being teachers and interpreters of Jewish law, almost always had other jobs and were intimately involved with problems confronting fellow Jews.

"We are witnessing a return to the classic role of the rabbi," says Rabbi Marc H. Tanenbaum, national interreligious-affairs director of the American Jewish Committee. "The rabbis of old earned their authority based on services to their people. Rabbis of the past never felt they deserved honor because they had a special relationship with God."

Nowhere is the rise of the socially active rabbi more visible than in New York City. Twenty years ago most of New York's rabbis and politicians saw one another only when the rabbi asked the Democratic district leader for a traffic light near the synagogue, or when the local city councilman put in a token appearance at the *shul's* annual dinner.

Now many rabbis and politicians constantly keep in touch, discussing such issues as funding for senior-citizens' centers, plans to halt urban blight, and the agendas of the community planning boards. "The politician realizes that it's important to cultivate the local rabbi," says Rabbi Elkanah Schwartz, an assistant to Deputy Mayor Herman Badillo. "Beforehand, the politician went after the men's-club president; now he knows that the rabbi is the real power."

Early last November, the Jewish newspapers carried a political advertisement containing the names of 80 rabbis; it discussed the stands of Hugh Carey and Perry Duryea on crime, aid to yeshivas, and the rights of Sabbath observers. One ad in the *Jewish Press*, signed by three rabbis in the 9th Congressional District in Queens, backed the Democratic congressional nominee Geraldine Ferraro because of the alleged "outspoken hatred for Israel" by her opponent, GOP Assemblyman Alfred DelliBovi.

Ironically enough, the wholesale courting of rabbis by politicians goes back to John Lindsay's mayoralty, a period in which the hackles of many middle- and low-income Jews were raised over His Honor's support for school-decentralization schemes and for scatter-site housing in Forest Hills. In his successful 1969 re-election campaign, guided by his assistant, former CUNY political-science professor Marvin Schick, Lindsay was the first candidate to pursue the Jewish vote not merely by gathering endorsements from Jewish-establishment types, but also by appearing at any synagogue that would have him.

Lindsay also began the practice of using rabbis to serve as liaison officers with the Jewish community. While Abe Beame and Ed Koch have generally shied away from this approach, Rabbi Mendy Shayovich, the special assistant to the governor for New York City and community affairs, advises Hugh Carey on Jewish and other urban matters. The Jewish campaign desk, manned by a yarmulke-wearing aide who woos the local rabbis, has become standard in city and statewide electoral contests.

Besides advising politicians on how to stay kosher with the Jewish voter, rabbis have taken to the hustings on their own behalf. Sam Hirsch, a lawyer and an ordained rabbi, represents Borough Park in the Assembly; he defeated the Democratic-organization nominee in a 1977 primary. Sheldon Farber, who retired in December as the GOP state senator from the Rockaways, was also ordained by the Orthodox yeshiva before entering the real-estate business. (Farber, Hirsch, and Shayovich do not use the title "rabbi" in public life.)

This increased rabbinic political involvement seems surprising, since the city's Jews are steadily declining in wealth and number. The Jewish population here dropped from an estimated 2.1 million in 1957 to 1.2 million in 1974, and the total today is probably about 1 million. And, according to Malcolm Hoenlein, executive director of New York's Jewish Community Relations Council, some 250,000 Jews, many of them elderly, exist either at or below the poverty level, making them the third-largest poverty group in the city.

The shifts in the economic and social climate that bring heightened insecurity to the Jewish have-nots make them more and more likely to turn to their rabbi, who is the community figure closest to the poor and elderly. Rabbis also find themselves worrying about how long their own synagogues will be able to survive continued urban decay. (The city's largest—and wealthiest—congregation, Temple Emanu-El on Fifth Avenue, has not been troubled by such pressures, and so remains relatively inactive politically.)

Orthodox Jews, who need to live in cities in order to be close to their synagogues, have become an increasingly large part of New York's affiliated Jewish population in the wake of the exodus to suburbia by less traditional Jews. Generally uncomfortable with secular Jewish organizations, which in their eyes often appear to be concerned with saving the world rather than with Jews in particular, these Jews worked through rabbis or set up Orthodox-sponsored social agencies to obtain the federal funds which became available to cities in the 1960s.

"The national-defense-type Jewish organizations never courted urban Orthodox Jews, and Orthodox Jews in turn were suspicious of such non-religious leadership," says Dr. Jack M. Sable, who headed the state's poverty and human-rights agencies under Nelson Rockefeller. Jewish-sponsored programs today receive about 1 percent of all such funds earmarked for New York City.

The growth of ethnic pride during the past decade also spurred the new rabbinic activism. After having demonstrated for Israel and imprisoned Soviet Jews, rabbis turned to problems closer to home. Rabbis were key figures in setting up some two dozen Jewish community councils in New York, mainly found in poor and middle-class neighborhoods. In 1964 the late Rabbi Samuel Schrage, a Lubavitcher Hasid, formed one of the city's first anti-crime patrols, the Maccabees, to combat crimes against Jews in Crown Heights.

Who are New York's most influential rabbis, the religious leaders of the most influential community of Jews ever to live in the Diaspora? If influence means a broad following from fellow Jews, many, many rabbis—heads of congregations, teachers, communal leaders—merit inclusion. Yet after weighing the different areas of rabbinic influence—spiritual, social, political—we found that a few names kept reappearing in interviews with Jews and non-Jews. *New York*'s list also tries to show various areas of rabbinic influence—in Talmudic scholarship, ecumenical relations, social work, and public affairs. All the rabbis are professionally engaged in serving other Jews, and, in most cases, their influence is also felt outside the Jewish community.

Rabbi Moshe Feinstein

Does Judaism countenance test-tube babies? May one twin be killed so that another may live? Does Judaism's ban on posthumous surgery apply in the case of plutonium-powered cardiac pacemakers, which are required under federal guidelines to be removed after death?

These are among the scores of technical questions for which Jews daily turn to 83-year-old Rabbi Moshe Feinstein (affectionately called "Rev Moishe" by his followers), one of the world's leading authorities on Jewish law. While the Lower East Side "world of our fathers" belongs mostly to the past, Rabbi Feinstein's East Broadway yeshiva, Mesivtha Tifereth Jerusalem, continues to hold a pivotal place for devout Jews. A joke among clergymen is that at the back of every young rabbi's ordination certificate, for a quick answer to any religious question, is Rabbi Feinstein's phone number.

In tackling the problems posed by the new technology for observant Jews, the rabbi has left his imprint on Jewish life for generations to come. His five books of responsa—answers to contemporary questions of religious observance—form a link in the chain of Jewish law beginning with the Torah, the Five Books of Moses, and continuing with the Talmud and succeeding commentaries. Indigenous to each work, regardless of the century in which it was written, is the belief that the Torah is as immutable today as when it was first given by God on Mt. Sinai.

Rabbi Feinstein's responsa treat subjects ranging from sex therapy and artificial insemination to the use of automated elevators on the Sabbath. (One recent decision, for instance, was that Orthodox Jews, who may not use appliances on the Sabbath, may set a timer to turn on a lamp—because light is necessary for the holiness of the day—but they may not use it to turn on a dishwasher or oven.) The rabbi's writings are the best guide for a religious Jew seeking to uphold the letter of the law despite complex scientific challenges.

Rabbi Alexander M. Schindler

In the spring of 1978, the low point of American-Israeli relations since the creation of the Jewish state, it fell to Rabbi Alexander M. Schindler, the cigar-smoking Reform rabbi, to challenge the Carter administration's pressures on Menachem Begin to be more accommodating to Anwar Sadat's peace blueprint.

"In March I had the feeling that the administration was beginning to orchestrate a campaign against Begin. I didn't want Jimmy Carter to bamboozle the Jewish community the way FDR had. I decided to go straight to the Jews of America to alert them that trouble was ahead."

At this time, Rabbi Schindler, president of the Union of American Hebrew Congregations, found himself chairman of the Conference of Presidents of Major American Jewish Organizations (the Presidents' Club), an umbrella group whose purpose is to bring unity to the Jewish community on questions relating to Israel.

"When Brzezinski, in response to my charge that the administration was bringing undue pressure on Israel, claimed that if Jews don't agree with you, they call you an anti-Semite, I saw a signal that the White House planned to use blunt force on Begin."

In retrospect, Rabbi Schindler believes that his warning, and the response that it precipitated from the American Jewish community, caused Carter to back down. "Beneath everything," Rabbi Schindler says, "Carter is a politician. He has some very fine instincts, but the desire to be re-elected is overriding."

Having helped Israel weather the crisis which he believes eventually paved the way for the Camp David talks, Rabbi Schindler now devotes more time to running the congregational arm of Reform Judaism. But his earlier performance has caused him to be regularly mentioned as a possible czar for Israeli information programs in this country.

Rabbi Menachem M. Schneerson

Jews who tried to stroll casually home with Christmas trees last month risked reproaches from the Hasidic Jews driving "mitzvah mobiles" in the midtown area. The bearded, blackhatted followers of the Lubavitcher rebbe, 76-year-old Rabbi Menachem M. Schneerson, invited passersby to step into their vans, pray, and ask any religious questions.

Lubavitcher Hasidim consider it a paramount religious duty to reclaim the souls of wayward Jews. The Crown Heights section of Brooklyn, the home of these young missionaries, has seen a sharp rise in its Hasidic population since the Lubavitcher rebbe's father-in-law, the previous leader of the movement, settled there in 1940 with a handful of European refugees.

Followers of the Lubavitcher rebbe, as is the case with other Hasidic sects, want to live close by Rabbi Schneerson, a leader venerated for his holiness, judgment, and mystical attachment to God. Under his leadership, synagogues, schools, shops, and daycare centers have sprung up in Crown Heights. The last are particularly important: Hasidim frown on birth control; this phenomenon is responsible for the doubling of their population every ten years.

To 770 Eastern Parkway, office of the Lubavitcher rebbe, stream not only followers from around the world, but politicians and other celebrities for *yechidas* (private audiences). Politicians hope that getting a foot in the door will help on Election Day, although the rebbe absolutely refrains from giving endorsements. Some politicians have been identified with the movement, however: Rudy Boshwitz, who has just taken office as a Republican senator from Minnesota, and State Attorney General Robert Abrams, whose daughter was named in the Lubavitcher *shul*.

Rabbi Marc H. Tanenbaum

As a child in Baltimore, Rabbi Marc Tanenbaum, now director of national interreligious affairs of the American Jewish Committee, would walk with his father to synagogue every Saturday morning. They would cross the street rather than pass the church along the way. The father was haunted by the memory of how a priest in his native Ukraine had led a mob of congregants after services on Good Friday, dragged his brother to the town lake, and ordered him drowned as revenge on the alleged Christ killers.

Rather than perpetuate the bitterness his father had felt toward religious persecution, the 52-year-old Rabbi Tanenbaum has devoted his life to serving as an apostle to Christians, emphasizing the Jewish roots of Christianity and the indivisibility of human rights. Last year, in a poll of American religion editors, he was voted the fourth "most respected and influential religious leader in America"—after Jimmy Carter, Billy Graham, and University of Chicago theologist Dr. Martin Marty.

As the only rabbi present at Vatican Council II, Rabbi Tanenbaum profoundly influenced Catholic statements repudiating anti-Semitism and calling for a dialogue between Christians and Jews. "By identifying the sources of anti-Semitism," says Rabbi Tanenbaum, "we know how to uproot it." The foremost Jewish ecumenist in the world, this Conservative rabbi speaks annually to live audiences of hundreds of thousands of Christians.

Illustrating the shift in Christian perceptions of Jews, Rabbi Tanenbaum says that "not a single Catholic textbook" used in schools today carries anti-Semitic references. "I can go into any city in the United States and find Jews and Christians meeting not as Jews and Christians but as friends and neighbors. In the past 15 years, we have made more progress at understanding each other than in 1,900 years."

Rabbi Shlomo Riskin

Whether chaining himself to the White House gates to protest an arms sale to Saudi Arabia, battling with the local community board last month for permission to erect a menorah at 72nd Street and Broadway, or lecturing at his Lincoln Square Synagogue on the Jewish attitude toward war, Rabbi Shlomo Riskin sees as his mission the bridging of Orthodox Judaism and the modern world. To further this, he founded two yeshiva high schools in Riverdale; they now draw students from the entire world.

In the 1960s a new brand of Orthodox rabbi appeared on the American scene, stressing the relevance of Jewish law for modern life, and willing to take to the streets when Jewish interests seemed at stake. As the leading figure of this "reach out" school of Orthodoxy, the 39-year-old Rabbi Riskin serves as a model for scores of rabbis and rabbis-to-be. He draws inquiries from intellectually inclined Jewish youth on such subjects as business ethics and homosexuality, and he has awakened other rabbis to the educational needs of women. "There are two types of Jews," says Rabbi Riskin, "the religious and the not yet religious. Every Jew owes it to himself to study his tradition as it has been studied for thousands of years."

Rabbi Riskin is entitled to *kvell* over his revitalization of Jewish life on the West Side—four different Sabbath services attract 1,000 people, half of whom are under 30, and an adult education program draws 1,200 students weekly. The synagogue also runs two yeshivas for college students and graduates who have never studied Torah before.

Yet the rabbi despairs for the future of Judaism in America. "More and more the axioms of American society are not in accord with our own," he says. "The family is in disarray, sexual conduct is not governed by moral standards, and any sort of restraint, whether in print or on the TV screen, is rapidly disappearing."

As a result, he plans in the near future to spend six months a year in Israel building a model community, Efrat, where he hopes 5,000 families will live by 1999.

Rabbi Joel Teitelbaum

An afternoon stroll down Lee Avenue in Brooklyn's Williamsburg section finds Hasidic women with long sleeves and covered heads pushing baby carriages, Yiddish-speaking children playing outside the aging tenements and brownstones, and bearded, dark-suited men wearing shirts without ties. The Hasidic men go tieless to show that a Jew's dress—as everything else in his life—should be different from a Gentile's.

These Williamsburg Hasidim, followers of the 91-year-old Satmar rebbe, Rabbi Joel Teitelbaum, are the Jews apart. When he arrived here in 1947, the rabbi was accompanied by 70 other refugees from the town of Satmar, Hungary. Today, 30,000 followers inhabit Williamsburg's "Hasidic triangle," sharing the crowded community largely with Hispanics. Satmar yeshivas educate more than 6,000 children; medical and dental clinics with Yiddish-speaking personnel serve the community; a bus service connects Williamsburg's Hasidim with other sect members in Borough Park; and a weekly newspaper, *Der Yid (The Jew)*, contains Satmar news, such as the name of a newly appointed *shochet* (ritual slaughterer). The cultural signposts of contemporary America—TV, movies, the media—are banned as worthless tools of assimilation. In fact, Satmar Hasidim study nothing outside the Torah except for what they need in their professions, such as diamond cutting and computer programming.

Although the Satmar Hasidim are intense in their devotion to the Jewish community, they do not, ironically, support the idea of a Jewish state.

According to the Satmar rebbe, the recreation of Israel in 1948 was a violation of God's will. The Jewish destiny, he claims, is to pray for redemption—the coming of the Messiah—rather than to seek it through political activity.

There is, however, no objection to political involvement closer to home; indeed, every Satmar Hasid of voting age in Williamsburg goes to the polls, a message not lost on office seekers from presidential candidates on down. The reapportionment of Hasidic Williamsburg in the early seventies into two New York State Assembly and Senate districts, which the United Jewish Organizations of Williamsburg unsuccessfully fought to the Supreme Court, has somewhat diminished the influence of the Satmar Hasidim, but they are still powerful, and their support is not to be taken for granted. In 1972 Al Lowenstein found this out when he was defeated in his congressional race by John Rooney, who had provided the Hasidim with the benefits of federally funded programs.

Rabbi Seymour Siegel

Two major social reappraisals have been in the air in American Jewish life in the past decade—the love affair with political liberalism and the role of women in synagogue life. Rabbi Seymour Siegel, professor of ethics and theology at the Jewish Theological Seminary, has been in the forefront of both.

Rabbi Siegel sees nothing inconsistent in his advocacy of a Jewish political shift toward conservatism as well as liberalized religious practices, such as the ordination of women as rabbis and their inclusion in the traditionally male *minyan,* the prayer quorum of ten.

The late 1960s marked a period of deep political disillusionment for Rabbi Siegel, who since his youth in Chicago had dabbled in Democratic-party politics. Having marched in civil-rights demonstrations with Dr. Martin Luther King, he recoiled when black politicians began to urge racial quotas. The Columbia University riots, which he witnessed from his seminary office across the street, and the rise of what he felt was an accommodationist philosophy toward left-wing governments by McGovern Democrats caused Rabbi Siegel "to reassess political liberalism as an automatic Jewish reaction," he says. "The weakness of liberalism in the face of attacks on the very roots of democracy became apparent. Jewish self-interest demanded a more conservative position."

As an adviser in the campaigns of James Buckley, Richard Nixon, Gerald Ford, and Perry Duryea, Rabbi Siegel has emerged as the most prominent rabbi in support of the GOP, a political stance he finds colleagues increasingly taking. As chairman of the Committee on Jewish Law of the Rabbinical Assembly, which interprets the law for the Conservative movement, Rabbi Siegel played a major role in the 1973 decision allowing women to be included in a *minyan* in Conservative services. "The reasons for excluding women in the past are no longer valid today," he maintains. "It's only fair that they be included as members of the praying community." At the convention of Conservative rabbis later this month, Rabbi Siegel plans to argue for the ordination of women rabbis. If this position is adopted, it will mean that only the Orthodox will still officially adhere to a strict definition of sex roles in religion.

Rabbi Morris Sherer

A seemingly incongruous collection of photos line the office of Rabbi Morris Sherer—autographed pictures of Presidents Johnson, Nixon, Ford, and Carter on one wall, and, facing them, portraits of the seven bearded yeshiva directors who compose the Council of Torah Sages. The latter group sets basic policy for Agudath Israel of America, the Orthodox organization Sherer heads.

In the 35 years he has been with Agudath Israel—more than half its history in the United States—Rabbi Sherer has shown a masterful skill in persuading the men who run the country to adopt policies that benefit those who run the yeshiva. Laws guarantee that Jewish hospital patients will receive kosher food on request, that periodic threats against kosher slaughtering practices are beaten down, and that employment rights of religious Jews in the civil service are safeguarded.

"Orthodox Jews have unique concerns," says Rabbi Sherer, "and they, rather than Jewish secularists or those who believe that being Jewish is as easy as chewing gum, should represent their cases before governmental bodies."

Following this principle, Rabbi Sherer has formed a close alliance with Catholic educators, who advocate greater government funding for parochial schools. Agudath Israel's government-funded job-training program has already served 18,000 people, including one out of every three recent Jewish refugees from the Soviet Union.

While he claims that politics amounts to "only 1 percent" of his job, the rest being spent administering the religious, educational, and social-service programs of Agudath Israel, Rabbi Sherer has invested his time wisely. Jacob Javits, Abe Beame, and Henry Kissinger consider themselves his friends.

Rabbi Sherer's political influence amply explains his popularity: The rabbis of the Council of Torah Sages, in whose name he speaks on political issues, are revered by hundreds of thousands of Jews. He has, besides, devoted much effort to cultivating political friends, the most prominent among them being Hugh Carey, whom he has known since 1961, when Congressman Carey argued for increased governmental aid to parochial schools. Carey is in the rabbi's debt for his help in delivering the religious-Jewish vote last year despite a strong pro-Duryea effort by the *Jewish Press.*

Rabbi Isaac N. Trainin

Rabbi Isaac N. Trainin's phone doubles as a hot line for desperate Jews—a rabbi inquiring if a bed can be found at Mt. Sinai Hospital for a congregant dying of cancer, the police precinct at East 67th Street with a runaway teenager asking for a rabbi, a Yiddish-speaking Hasid whose son can no longer control his drug problem, an alcoholic seeking an A.A. group with a Jewish membership.

Hardly a Jew in New York at one time or another will not pass through one of the 130 agencies—hospitals, old-age homes, community Y's, summer sleep-away camps—composing the Federation of Jewish Philanthropies. After founding, and serving for 26 years as head of, the federation's Department of Religious Affairs, responsible for this one component of the world's largest local charity, Rabbi Trainin claims, "I have dealt with more rabbis than any other Jew in history."

Rabbi Trainin was hired as a public relations assistant in the early 1950s when the federation was engaged in a bitter dispute with New York's religious Jews as to whether the Long Island Jewish-Hillside Medical Center, then under construction, should have a kosher kitchen. Jews outside the federation saw Rabbi Trainin as an apologist, and secular federation officials saw him as a troublemaker.

Rabbi Trainin looks back on a career of religious firsts for the federation, ranging from the changeover to kosher food of nearly all federation camps, to the establishment of the Metropolitan Council on Jewish Poverty, to the launching of task forces on subjects such as Jewish medical ethics, drugs and Jews, and black Jews.

But as the federation's spokesman to religious Jewry, he has increasingly found his role under attack by more militant types—including his nephew Rabbi Meir Kahane, former head of the militant Jewish Defense League—for the agency's alleged shortchanging of Jewish education. While predicting that the federation's priorities will change as the city's Jewish population becomes smaller and more traditional, Rabbi Trainin defends the agency's broad-based services to all Jews. "The number of Jews, for the time being, may be shrinking," he says, "but the future belongs to those who care. Judaism has survived for almost 4,000 years because enough Jews cared."

# # #

Israel Center Library Dedicated in Memory of Young Oleh [*Jewish Action, Magazine of the Orthodox Union in Israel*, Summer 1983]

The Yair Landau Memorial Library, established in memory of a 23-year-old American *oleh* killed in action last year during Israel's "*Shalom HaGalil*" campaign, was dedicated on June 14th at the Orthodox Union/NCSY Israel Center in Jerusalem.

The library is a new major educational tool of the Israel Center, which offers a variety of services to Americans living, visiting and studying in

Israel. According to current plans, funds raised for the Yair Landau Memorial Library will go towards providing 1000 basic works, both in Hebrew and English, on Jewish history and the land of Israel. Funds will also be earmarked for a copying machine, and air conditioning and soundproofing for the library. In addition, funds will be sought for the salary of a librarian and the ongoing cataloging of new materials.

Yair Landau, one of the six children of Vivian and Julie Landau, came on *aliyah* with his family in 1970 from Silver Spring, Md., and was a student at Jerusalem's Yeshivat HaKotel. Yair had previously been involved in a number of NCSY activities, and was scheduled to lead NCSY's Israel Summer Seminar in the summer of 1982. Instead, he was called to the front two weeks before the group's expected arrival.

The young soldier was mourned by the entire ISS group, which participated in a ceremony marking the *sheloshim* at his grave, and set up a daily *seder* of Torah study in his memory.

A *Goal of Teaching*

According to Yair's mother, Vivian, "the role of a library at the Israel Center fits in with Yair's goal of teaching and bringing people closer to Judaism." His father, Julie, sees the library as a means of helping others "feel as he felt about a life of Torah and the land of Israel. He wanted to establish a dialogue with those who were not religious, and also with those who lived abroad."

Both of Yair's parents were successful professionals in Jerusalem. Julie, a former chairman of the Washington Council of Orthodox Congregations, previously worked at the Library of Congress in Washington, and now heads a public relations firm. Vivian, a nurse at Shaare Zedek Hospital, embarked on her training in nursing after she had already joined the ranks of grandmotherhood. Previously, she had a career as an Israeli tourist guide.

One year after his death, Yair's mother remembers him as a sensitive person, able to relate to others because he knew "what it means to feel strange. His direction became *chinuch*, primarily to work with kids from overseas. He never compromised the *halachic* point of view while at the same time avoiding making kids feel he was shutting them out. People felt comfortable with Yair because he believed one can never convince another person through the hard sell."

In addition to the library at the Israel Center, the Landau family, through a foundation it had established, hopes to endow a small garden situated alongside Binyani Ha'ooma near the entrance to Jerusalem, in memory of Yair. Under the auspices of the Jerusalem Foundation, such a corner bearing the name of Yair Landau, would "make him an integral part of the Eternal City," his parents say.

The Orthodox Union/NCST Israel Center, centrally located at 10 Strauss Street in the heart of Jerusalem, offers lectures, classes, leadership training, Shabbatonim, Melava Malkas, counseling, *aliyah* information and numerous other services. Contributions to the Yair Landau Memorial Library may be made payable through a check to the Orthodox Union.

8

The Plight of Soviet Jewry Continues

Rubin's continued interest in Soviet Jewry was echoed by the second oldest of his five daughters, Shulie, in a touching *Letter to Russia*, the winning entry in the 1984 National Council of Young Israel's National Youth Essay Contest, which is used as an introduction to this chapter. Another "winner" in the chapter is *The Soviet Jewish Problem at the United Nations*. Published in the 1970 *American Jewish Year Book*, this paper is included in the prestigious Berman Jewish Policy Archive at NYU Wagner.

Letter to Russia
Shulie Rubin
[As published in the *Young Israel Viewpoint*, February 1985]

To my Jewish Brother/Sister in the Soviet Union,

Sometimes, I sit and wonder, What am I doing here?

Why is it that I am not helping any of my fellow Jews behind the Iron Curtain? What is the reason that I, a twelve-year-old girl am sitting here in America, and another twelve-year-old Jewish girl, just the same age as me, is living in fear and terror in Russia. Clearly, it is not because I deserve any more special privileges than my counterpart trapped in the U.S.S.R. I am no different than she.

But yet, I am living in the United States of America, where one of the main rules we abide by is freedom—freedom of speech, freedom of the press, freedom of religion. I am not really able to understand with my scanty knowledge of the workings of HaShem and His ways, why a young Jewish girl, just the same as me is not here and I am not there.

But we have not forgotten you. Just today, about one hour ago, I attended a rally in front of the Soviet Embassy. It was an emergency rally, called because of the death of Yuri Andropov. We protested the continued imprisonment of Anatoly Sharansky and we were spoken to by Mrs. Avital Sharansky, his wife. And just as Anatoly Sharansky is a modern Jewish hero, you too are the modern Jewish heroes of our time.

Throughout our history, we have been persecuted and jailed so often, simply for the fact that we were innocent Jews. But we have not died out. We are the only nation that has continued a clear, unbroken path all the way from the time of Avraham Avinu. We have been crushed and trampled upon, and we have been slaughtered and forced to move from our homes, but HaShem has always put us back on the top! Always. For we are the ones that carry His Name through the world. We are the ones to glorify His Being!

And you, our Jewish brothers and sisters living in the Soviet Union, represent a people that will never die. I believe that it is because of such great and holy people as you that HaShem leads us, the Jews, to survival. Have Emunah [faith] in HaShem and Moshiach—for it will come soon—in your honor.

I hope to meet you soon in Eretz Yisroel, where no torture or pain can be inflicted upon us. I will meet you in front of the third and final Beit HaMikdash.

L'Hitraot B'Eretz Yisroel [Until We Meet in the Land of Israel]. B'Ahava U'veChavod Rav [With Love and Great Honor],

Shulie Rubin
Young Israel of Riverdale

# # #

American Jews and Soviet Jews
[*Jewish Life*, September 1970]

Although political scientists cannot precisely estimate the impact of non-governmental pressure groups on another country's policies, there is plausible evidence that protests on behalf of Soviet Jews in the late 1960's and through 1970 have at least slowed the Kremlin's plans to send its Jews to spiritual oblivion. Among indications of the Soviet discomfort are the following: a trickle of Jews, for the sake of family reunion, have been permitted to emigrate (mainly to Israel); a limited printing of prayerbooks and the promise of expanding the number of books authored in Yiddish; the visit of Rabbi Yehuda Levin to the United States in 1968; the numerous stories put out by Novostoi, the Soviet foreign propaganda agency, contending that the Jews in the U.S.S.R. are in good shape.

In addition to showing that the Soviet Union is, within limits, responsive to hostile foreign opinion, these developments raise questions about the connection between Jewish-interest group protests and the desired response from the Soviet government. What are the characteristics of pressure groups acting on behalf of Soviet Jews? What methods have been used and what are their relative effectiveness? Could the goals of these groups be pursued more effectively?

There are, to be sure, compelling reasons why American Jews should be concerned with their Soviet brethren. Many American Jews have relatives in the Soviet Union (only two or three generations separate most American Jews from the East European Pale of Settlement). Soviet Jews are the main survivors of the once great East European Jewish community and silence on their fate would represent a rerun of an earlier response to Hitler's program. According to Jewish law, there is no holier project than Pidyon Shevuyim ("Every moment one postpones the redemption of captives," writes Rabbi Yoseph Karo in the Shulchon Oruch, "It is as though one commits murder.") Moreover, the 3,000,000 Soviet Jews (this is not to argue that all are so inclined) are a prime source for much-needed Aliyah to Israel.

Nonetheless, certain factors in American Jewish life encourage avoidance and misunderstanding of Soviet Antisemitism. While Jews in the United States have shown more political assertiveness and sophistication since the 1967 Six-Day War, strong traces of what Israelis defiantly call the "Goluth Mentality" still persist. The latter approach, defensive, appeasing, and hesitant, stresses universalistic social concerns and reticence on Jewish issues. The "Goluth Mentality" is marked by reliance on Shtadlonim (worldly successful Jews who presumably know how to win the sympathy of the non-Jewish elite) who are expert in "quiet diplomacy" and behind-the-scene intervention. In the "New Politics" of the 1970's, however, where group strength is measured by activism and dramatic mass demonstrations, "quiet diplomacy" is relatively ineffective in aiding Soviet Jews. (Coincidentally, public protests are of short-term importance to Soviet Jews in impressing on them that they have not been forgotten.)

While it is wrong to disparage the bulk of American Jews who, after all, by education and temperament may not be at home with the sensationalism of the "New Politics," it must be stressed that in the 1970's signing a check alone will not very much help Soviet Jews—nor other political issues affecting Jews. Soviet Antisemitism is one of the problems in the Jewish world today not highly soluble by donations. Money helps indirectly by tooling protest and educational programs, but Soviet policy officially forbids foreign supplying of the religious and cultural needs of Jews (prayerbooks, Jewish calendars, etc.).

Further detracting from American Jewish protest potential is the large loss of the most activistic population element—youth. Considerable evidence has shown that in the absence of a strong sense of Jewish identity, Jewish youth find social commitment not in "Jewish" causes but in their peer group culture—and contrasted with American foreign policy in Indochina and the fate of the environment, Soviet Antisemitism does not rate.

Many American Jews feel they fulfill their responsibility to the Jewish people by supporting Israel, particularly in view of Israel's more precarious military position today. Although Israel's survival and Soviet Antisemitism are both pressing matters, and ideally the Jewish conscience should be sensitive enough to both claims, the reality is that most Jews do not have an unlimited reserve of emotional energy and time.

Not only does the immediacy of Israel's fighting and time detract from concern with Soviet Jews, but it is more exciting to help build a nation than to fight against the death of a people. On the political level, it is much harder to determine a cause and effect relationship in urging a policy on the Kremlin than on one's own government. Philanthropy offers the donor tangible results—a forest, a school—whereas the needs of Soviet Jews cannot be so packaged. Also Soviet Jews (with the exception of the brave men and women who smuggle out appeals and the youths who dance in front of synagogues on Simchath Torah) are not visualized as in tune with today's romanticized picture of the self-reliant Jew—the tanned, strong, independent Kibbutznik. Soviet Jewry conjures up the image of the East European Jews huddled together begging for rights.

Finally, the failure of most American Jewish organizations to alert their members (particularly those under 30 to whom Stalinism is but a word) to the meaning of Communism reduces awareness of the fate of Soviet Jews. These organizations neglected to part ways with the dominant liberal notion of "convergence"—that the United States and the Soviet Union are becoming increasingly similar and over the years will converge from different poles. Had those organizations stressed the dangers of Communism to freedom-- its totalitarian, police state anti-individualism and forced conformity—more American Jews would, as a corollary, have been ideologically prepared for the tragedy of Soviet Jews.

Given the foregoing influences, as well as the fragmentation of American Jewish organizational life, it is understandable that various responses have emerged to the problem of Soviet anti-Jewish policy. In terms both of membership size and public importance, the major pressure group response has been through the American Jewish Conference on Soviet Jewry. Created in 1964 by 25 national Jewish organizations (a 26th has since joined), the Conference marked the first concentrated undertaking set up by American Jews to deal with the plight of Soviet Jewry. This step marked a notable change from the competition characterizing these organizations' efforts in issues of Jewish survival.

On the one hand, such a coordinating body underscored the urgency of Soviet Antisemitism. On the other, it revealed the fairly total inaction of American Jewish organizations on this problem through the 1950's and the early 1960's. Of course, certain national Jewish groups during that period undertook isolated steps in response to specific crises. But none had mounted a systematic, deliberate campaign devoted exclusively to Soviet Jews. By 1964, the Soviet Jewish situation became increasingly desperate: Stalin had destroyed all Jewish cultural-communal institutions and his successors would not permit their restoration; the number of synagogues had been reduced from 450 in 1956 to an estimated 100 in 1963; Jews were scapegoated in the early 1960's for "economic crimes," punishable in certain cases by death; Trofim Kichko in 1964 published his notorious "Judaism Without Embellishment."

The orientation of the Conference has been that of a service body operating through established groups rather than that of an activist organization working directly with the "man on the street." Ideally, the Conference, as an umbrella group, was set up to plan overall strategy and to allow the established Jewish agencies to fill in the details, but in effect the Conference lacked the resources to mount a dynamic, thoroughgoing, innovative drive. Contrasted with other issues of injustice, with which the plight of Soviet Jews must of necessity compete in the media, the Conference has been unable to apply the new technology of professionalized pressure group activity—scientific opinion sampling, targeting of messages, etc.

In its early years, the Conference had many earmarks of an *ad hoc* undertaking. Even today it lacks a separate listing in the Manhattan phone directory. From 1964–1966 professional guidance for the Conference was rotated among the constituent agencies. In 1966, NCRAC (the National Jewish Community Relations Advisory Council), itself a coordinator of Jewish community relations groups, assumed full-time responsibility for Conference activities. The Conference's mailing address is at NCRAC headquarters in New York, and it still lacks an office of its own. The Conference is headed by a part-time Chairman (a post rotating usually among its constituent groups) and an NCRAC staffer devotes nearly all his time to Soviet Jewish affairs.

Yet the Conference as of 1970 was neither financially nor structurally equipped to give the issue the attention it demands. Financially, besides the office and personnel expenses defrayed by NCRAC, all the Conference activities were self-sustaining. Thus, for a Conference-sponsored advertisement in *The New York Times* on December 6, 1966, in which 90 United States Senators condemned Soviet Antisemitism, each of the constituents of the Conference was assessed $300. (Likewise, lobbying for this ad was carried out by a lobbyist on the staff of one of the Conference's constituents.) By 1970, the Conference decided to endorse a permanent budget—a sum exclusive of NCRAC support and of special projects expenses. However, this upgrading was far short of satisfying the massive educational campaign which young dissidents had sought from the "establishment."

Structurally, the Conference has also been unable to develop systemic, coherent policy. Conference policy is set by specific subcommittees consisting of professionals of its 26 constituent agencies. Lacking a permanent staff, the formulation of policy runs into obstacles an ongoing structure would not encounter. The present arrangement compounds delay, adds to red tape, and detracts from the thrust of Conference activities. Moreover, this arrangement runs counter to a basic bureaucratic law, namely, that members of a temporary task force show less loyalty to the coordinating structure than they do to their home office.

Defenders of the foregoing arrangement argue that it represents a necessary evil: if the Conference were to be strengthened, the Jewish agencies might scale down their work for Soviet Jews maintaining, for instance, their need to stress Israeli-centered activities. Secondly, since such strengthening would decrease the Conference's dependence on the Jewish agencies, top policy-making officials in the 26 Jewish agencies would be less involved in Conference work.

Because the Jewish agencies on their own have not undertaken, thus far, ambitious programs for Soviet Jews, there is no great risk that an invigorated Conference would upstage them. Furthermore, a strong Conference, mapping general strategy and pressing local communities to implement programs, need not preclude programs geared to the backgrounds of their memberships on the part of permanent Jewish organizations.

The Conference's limited funds permitted few grassroots campaigns. Among the Conference's major grass roots projects have been demonstrations. Previous to 1964, most American Jews had been content to stress "quiet diplomacy" and to restrict their efforts to low-echelon Soviet officials who denied that there was any Jewish problem in the U.S.S.R. These demonstrations, normally held in connection with Jewish holidays touching on themes of freedom (Pesach, Channukah), toward the late 1960's reached their highlight on Simchath Torah—a spectacle of solidarity with the young Soviet Jews who sang and danced on that day in front of the Moscow synagogue. The turnout for these demonstrations hardly ever matched attendance at public rallies on behalf of Israel. However, on Simchath Torah in 1969 fifty-two American communities (plus eight in Canada) held rallies—as compared to thirty-five communities in 1968, and three in 1967.

In terms of publications, another vehicle for alerting the Jewish masses, the Conference has stressed background, supportive material. It has distributed a "Fact Sheet on Soviet Jewry," a "Program Manual," and prayers to be recited for Soviet Jews at the Passover Seder ("Matzoh of Oppression" and "Matzoh of Hope").

Essentially, because of insufficient manpower, the Conference has been geared to such background, feature type of disseminations rather than being able to react to sudden changes (especially since late 1968 when Soviet Jews began to smuggle out petitions). Conference press releases on new developments in the Soviet Jewish scene are sent mainly to Jewish leaders across America who, presumably, would alert local media. The Conference never developed a direct, ongoing tie-in with the nation's media. The most serious shortcoming in this area, however, has been the failure to put out a publication dealing exclusively with Soviet Jewry. With the mounting internal protests of Soviet Jews from 1968–1970 a monthly magazine would have been in order.

In its governmental representations, the Conference has urged United States officials, with some success, to press demands for better treatment of Soviet Jews. The Conference has provided the Voice of America with broadcast material. Conference officials have met many high political office holders and, while the full records of these meetings are understandably confidential, both President Eisenhower (previous to the Conference's founding) and President Kennedy took up the issue with Soviet diplomats. Despite these and other meetings, the results should not be overemphasized. According to Gunther Lawrence ("Three Million More?" 1970, Doubleday), who served as public relations consultant to the Conference:

> . . . Jewish leaders here during this period assumed that their constant pressure resulted in American ambassadors raising the question at the

> Kremlin. No substantive corroboration was forthcoming, although in 1959, Llewellyn Thompson during his first tour as ambassador to Moscow saw to it that about one hundred Yiddish books and periodicals were included in an American book exhibition in the U.S.S.R. Thompson was reluctant to take more direct action and later advised Kennedy to have businessmen raise the issue with Soviet leaders. I was told at the State Department that Ambassador Fay D. Kohler never spoke about the Jewish issue to anyone in the Soviet upper echelon, either, but confirmed his discussions to Soviet intellectuals at social functions.

The Conference cites many pronouncements on Soviet anti-Jewish policy for American politicians, such as the 1968 Republican National Platform, statements by a large number of state Governors in connection with Human Rights Day 1969, and the signature of a large majority of Congressmen on its advertisements. Admittedly, increasing attention has been paid to this issue by American politicians—Senator Eugene McCarthy and Theodore Sorenson brought up the subject of Soviet Jews in visits to the Soviet Union the past year—although no accurate judgment can be made as to whether this recognition is a response to Soviet Jewish restiveness or to American Jewish protests, or both. However, the reaction of American politicians has reflected more of tokenism than substance. Criticism of Soviet Antisemitism is not hard to obtain—which American interest group finds such statements offensive? If the test of commitment is whether the plight of Soviet Jews is an electoral issue (as is American policy toward Israel) even in heavily populated Jewish constituencies, the answer is no. As Yale political scientist Robert A. Dahl notes:

> When I say that a group is heard 'effectively' I mean more than the simple fact that it makes a noise; I mean that one or more officials are not only ready to listen to that noise, but expect to suffer in some significant way if they do not placate the group, its leaders, or its most vociferous members.

To its credit, the Conference has brought to the attention of the United States Mission to the United Nations the plight of Elizaveta Kapshitzer and her son Vitold who was expelled from the Soviet Writers Union because of his Jewish sympathies. The American representative to the Commission on Human Rights raised this case, to the Soviet Union's displeasure. In 1968, the Conference presented to the UN a petition said to contain some 250,000 signatures of Americans protesting Soviet Antisemitism.

Tactically, the Conference has approached the issue of Soviet anti-Jewish policy as a human rights, moral problem. Many of its criticisms of Soviet deprivations have been from the standpoint of "conscience." The Conference has purposely avoided politicizing the problem such as, for instance, attributing it to Communist doctrine or calling for boycotts against Soviet goods or performances by Soviet artists visiting America under official cultural exchanges. As a result of growing attention to the Soviet Jewish issue, however, certain independent American Jewish groups (as well as the Victorian Board of Deputies in Australia) have urged boycotts.

As a coordinating body short both on money and manpower, the Conference expects its constituents to carry on the case for Soviet Jews on an ongoing basis. While the 26 components of the Conference represent a wide range of purposes (religious, cultural, educational, Jewish defense), they all officially acknowledge the high priority of fighting Soviet Antisemitism. (These conclusions are based on questionnaires returned to the author by the organizations.) These organizations have passed resolutions on the Soviet Jewish plight and it increasingly appears on their foreign or international affairs subcommittees agendas. Individually, certain national organizations have exposed antisemitic references in Soviet publications and other such offensive activities. They have raised the problem with national politicians and other opinion leaders and, where applicable, these organizations have communicated developments on this score to their international affiliates. Certain members of the Conference, through non-governmental organizations, have argued the issue before the UN.

However, constituent organizations share the same basic shortcoming as the Conference, namely that their *ad hoc* approach prevents the development of systematic plans and detailed implementation procedures. Over the years, these groups have communicated with district chapters or lodges through headquarters personnel for whom Soviet Jewry represents only one of many responsibilities. No national organization has a staff member dealing exclusively with Soviet Antisemitism.

Thus, in the absence of money, staff, and training these organizations are deficient both in terms of input and output.

Regarding the input, they are unable to put together the impact of ongoing changes in the Soviet Jewish scene. They must rest content with familiar responses and are unable to anticipate and to project scientifically what lies in store. Since they lack contingency plans, they are caught off guard by new perils. In 1970, for instance, these organizations were unprepared for Soviet accusations against Leningrad Jews for allegedly attempting to hijack a plane to Israel, nor did they ever respond creatively (other than through traditional press releases) to the statement by fifty-two prominent Soviet Jews attacking Zionism, and to the brave reply of thirty-nine Moscow Jews challenging this pronouncement.

The output failings follow from the input weaknesses. Despite recognition of the cause of Soviet Jewry in national organizational priorities, this piecemeal approach results in lessened thrust by the time material reaches local chapters. While articles on Soviet Jews have appeared in the publications of these organizations, an independent publication on this issue would be much more effective. These organizations must also be prepared to send either their officers or selected groups to tour the Soviet Union, on a regular basis. By 1970, the heads of most of the Conference constituents had visited the U.S.S.R. at least once. These organizations should give incentives to Jewish-minded American youth to tour the U.S.S.R. in large numbers.

In the last analysis, however, the Soviet Jewish protest campaign rests on success in stimulating awareness and response on the local level. With the assistance of the National Jewish Community Relations Advisory Council, this author sent out questionnaires to some eighty Jewish community councils across the country which hold membership in NCRAC. Since only twenty-six communities answered, and the responses were returned in early 1968 (nationally, interest in Soviet Jewry has risen appreciably since then), it is difficult to reach conclusive judgments on the basis of the current situation. However, it is possible to draw certain conclusions from this sampling.

As of 1968 (it must be recalled that certain hardships imposed on Jews such as the economic trials and the matzoth baking ban date to the early 1960's), most respondents ranked Soviet Jewry in a Number Three priority, usually following Israel and "civil rights" or "local issues."

Certain communities had active programs for Soviet Jewry marked by special meetings, exhibits, wide use of non-Jewish media, interreligious activities, and local publications dealing only with this topic. In other words, relatively active communities undertook special projects, supplemented Conference issuances, and extended themselves to the general community.

Less active communities, by comparison, relied mainly on Conference mailings, focused their work mainly on Jewish leaders, and had limited special projects. Significantly, many of the lesser active communities (in terms of the foregoing criteria) sent delegates to such national conclaves as the Eternal Light Vigil of 1965 in Washington, D.C., and the Conference Biennial in 1966, thus indicating that even if a community participates in a few national conferences it is not enough to spur grassroots efforts.

In response to a question dealing with the respondents' "general observations about the programs dealing with Soviet Jewry, and suggestions for the future direction of these programs," some officials noted the difficulty in stimulating interest. "This is one of the toughest issues to deal with I have seen in over a quarter of a century," one agency official wrote. Another respondent wrote of the need "to arouse our people out of their lethargy on this issue. No one seems to care." He recommended "more dramatic printed materials" and visual aid materials as a response to the problem.

Another suggestion was "to put more emphasis toward youth in order to obtain their creative ideas in the problem of finding new ways to tell the same story over and over again." The executive of a community sponsoring one of the most active programs called for a "monthly newsletter on Soviet Jewry which would serve as an important tool to develop public opinion. It is my feeling that not enough ongoing material is made available to communities in order to develop and maintain public understanding of the issue."

What emerges from these questionnaires is the conclusion that under the present arrangement between most communities and the American Jewish Conference on Soviet Jewry, the former are unable to develop long term, systematic programs. The Conference's main tie-in with local communities was through mailings, but literature alone had a limited effect. At the time of the sampling nearly all communities had inadequate budgets for Soviet Jewry programs most spent a few hundred dollars a year exclusive of staff time. The Jewish Community Relations Council of Cleveland appropriated $7,500 for this activity, and the other extreme was a city (which shall remain nameless) of 450–500,000 Jews which spent $150–$250 a year, exclusive of staff time, mainly for mailings, although it was reported that a larger budget was in the offing.

In order to stimulate local activities, the Conference must redirect its efforts from mailings to personal leadership. Regional coordinators, familiar with the communities they serve, should be named. Nationally, the Conference should appoint permanent staff in the areas of youth, publications, and visual aids who would backstop the coordinators. As with other pressure group causes, the cause of Soviet Jewry requires decentralized administration.

A rising concern for the welfare of one-fifth of the world's Jews together with dissatisfaction in some quarters with the objectives of the American Jewish Conference on Soviet Jewry have led to the formation of other organizations. The Conference on the Status of Soviet Jews is a blue ribbon group of writers, educators, clergy, and civil rights leaders concerned with Soviet Jews. Moshe Decter, an authority on Soviet Jews, is the organization's Executive Secretary and the Conference on the Status of Soviet Jews operates out of the same mailing address as Jewish Minorities Research which Decter heads. The group has issued studies (in 1970 it co-sponsored with the American Jewish Conference on Soviet Jewry a pamphlet "Redemption: Jewish Freedom Letters From Russia" containing the appeals and petitions smuggled out by Soviet Jews since 1968), statements, and advertisements. In 1966 it convened an Ad Hoc Commission on Soviet Jews as a public tribunal of Jewish life in the U.S.S.R., among whose members were Supreme Court Justice William O. Douglas, Walter Reuther, and Dr. Martin Luther King.

The plight of Soviet Jews lends itself to the concerns of academics in view of the heightened assertiveness of the campus in pushing for political and social reform. It was only in 1968, however, that the Academic Committee on Soviet Jewry was formed. In calling for the "moral internationalization" of the Soviet Jewish problem, the Academic Committee's orientation is similar to that of the American Jewish Conference on Soviet Jewry in that the Academic Committee has variously sponsored advertisements and publications with them.

Operationally, the Academic Committee has been a service, background group rather than one directly involved in forming chapters on campus. Compared with the American Academic Association for Peace in the Middle East (a pro-Israel pressure group a year older than the Academic Committee), the Academic Committee has shown less energy and initiative. The Middle East group sponsors a steady stream of publications, fact sheets, and newsletters. It has active chapters on many campuses, it has sponsored fact-finding tours to the Middle East (not only Israel), and it has arranged for briefings of American professors by Israelis.

The Academic Committee, like the American Jewish Conference on Soviet Jewry, does not have an independent headquarters, and is in the B'nai B'rith Building in New York. In 1968 and in 1969 (also in 1970), the Academic Committee sponsored conferences drawing well-known speakers such as Dr. Leonard Schapiro of London and Elie Wiesel. Professor Hans Morgenthau now chairs this body, and his predecessor was Professor Nathan Glazer. While it has released certain material to the press, made some government representations, and published a few studies, it has not developed a systematic, deliberate strategy. It has failed to publish a newsletter, to set up a speaker's bureau, to systematically develop articles for appropriate scholarly journals, to schedule presentations at scholarly conventions, to set up information booths at scholarly conventions, to draw up syllabi for courses, and to sponsor fact-finding trips to the U.S.S.R. It might have been worthwhile for the Academic Committee to politicize the problem by publicly pressuring for the cancellation of academic congresses set for the Soviet Union (a tack applied across the board, for instance, concerning the *apartheid* policy in the Union of South Africa).

Student Struggle for Soviet Jewry (SSSJ), an activist group led by Jacob Birnbaum and Glen Richter, is predicated on the belief that the Jewish "establishment" has inadequately met the issue. Moreover, SSSJ feels it can reach quick policy decisions, whereas it is hard to move the wheels of the 26 national groups comprising the American Jewish Conference on Soviet Jewry. Set up in 1964 and supported largely by student contributions, SSSJ in 1970 consists of a main office in Manhattan and five branches (two outside of New York City–Boston and Syracuse). It published frequent newsletters and other educational material. SSSJ mobilizes youth quickly, and its demonstrations show dramatic flair—imprisonment in chains outside the Soviet Mission to the UN to mark Tisha B'Av and a "guerrilla theatre" production of the trial of the imprisoned Soviet Jew, Boris Kochubiyevsky. In terms of demonstrations sponsored by "establishment" Jewish groups, SSSJ has operated on the periphery; it enlists student participation while it is often critical of alleged inadequate funding.

On a local level, other activist groups have arisen which aim to apply more direct pressure on the Soviet Union. Mainly composed of students, these groups are critical of the "establishment" for allegedly failing to mount necessary protests. Beyond the specific issue of Soviet Jewry, it is possible to attribute the disaffection of these youth to general criticisms of older Jewish organizations as being too "fat" and complacent.

Such groups now exist in Los Angeles, San Francisco, Florida, and Washington, D.C. Among the activities undertaken by these groups were interrupting the performances of visiting Soviet artists, boarding a Soviet ship docked in California (although in this case the "establishment" also participated), locking up in a room visiting Soviet newsmen, sending greeting cards directly to Jews in the U.S.S.R., and reproducing replicas of the internal passports Soviet Jews must carry. The San Francisco group was responsible in 1970 for offering the first course on Soviet Jewry for college credit at the University of California at Berkeley. This group has also seen to it that the issue of Soviet Jewry is represented permanently among the other protest tables in the plaza at Berkeley.

The Jewish Defense League (JDL) has emerged among the most potent and publicity-rich organizations regarding Soviet Antisemitism. Founded in 1968, JDL's attitude toward this issue stems from its thesis that "The time has come for Jews to say loud and clear that he who seeks to give the Jew the short end of the stick may end up getting that stick over his head." JDL sees Soviet Jewry not as an isolated human rights problem, but as an outgrowth of Soviet "tyranny" and Communist despotism.

In December, 1969, JDL drew attention to the plight of Soviet Jews in simultaneous raids on the offices of TASS, Intourist (the Soviet travel agency), and Aeroflot (the Soviet airline). The Soviet offices were decorated with such slogans as *Am Yisroel Chai* (the people of Israel lives). JDL argues that such violence has three merits: it impresses Soviet Jews that outsiders are willing to "suffer the consequences of illegality on their behalf;" it focuses much-needed publicity on the fate of Soviet Jews; it marshals latent anti-Soviet and anti-Communist feeling in the United States to pressure the American government to protest. JDL also attacks the cultural exchanges between the United States and the U.S.S.R., and it plans to pressure travel agents to turn down tourist bookings for the Soviet Union.

Critics of JDL hold that their tactics actually are harmful in the long-run for Soviet Jews. Although the media is hungry for sensationalism, such as represented by JDL anti-Soviet violence, critics argue that the American public which must be drawn to the side of Soviet Jews regards JDL tactics as similar to those of the Communists and thus subsequently disregards the fate of Soviet Jews.

Another agency involved with the problem is the International League for the Repatriation of Russian Jews, which argues that the thrust of American Jewish activities should be securing emigration rights for Soviet Jews who seek to leave. It has sponsored speaking tours in the United States of Jews who managed to emigrate to Israel from the Soviet Union. Whether or not recent Jewish immigrants should join the campaign of publicizing the situation of Soviet Jewry has been a political dispute in Israel.

According to Abba Eban, recent immigrants were not the best people "to carry this message forward because we don't want them to be the last."

Clearly, the groups which have formed recently to protest Soviet Antisemitism fill a vacuum stemming from the inadequate response of the major Jewish organizations. Undoubtedly, current activism is a factor in the desire of these groups to "do their thing" for Soviet Jews, but as the daring of Soviet Jews rises (experts agree it will) more concerned Jews will examine their own response. The main channel for new activity must come through the "establishment"; it represents the vast majority of American Jews who look to it to fight Antisemitism in general. But the "establishment" in terms of the American Jewish Conference on Soviet Jewry has not dealt with the problem systematically. The Jewish response has overwhelmingly been one of jumping from one crisis to another rather than in providing for overall planning. An institutional arrangement demands methods of planning and implementation which would gather the best ideas and information available both in the Jewish community and in the political world.

Underscoring policy making in this area must be the recognition that world Jewry and the Kremlin are at war over the future of one-fifth of the world's Jews. American Jews know that war is a serious business as far as Israel's security goes, but they do not see the plight of Soviet Jewry similarly. In contrast, Israel recognized that on this score alone the Soviet Union was its adversary even before the latter began constructing SAM-3 [surface-to-air missile] sites in Egypt.

An effective policy on behalf of Soviet Jewry must be creative. This means developing anticipatory, imaginative procedures for reaching the five target groups concerned: Soviet Jews; the Soviet Government; the United States Government; American Jews; American non-Jews. This in turn requires enlisting professionals on a fulltime basis who bring to bear scholarly training in the fields of public opinion, communication, and politics. Unaided, the generalists who man the Jewish organizations will fail.

Intelligent policy making also demands a determination of the facts. Incomplete information distorts reality and prevents the formulation of contingency plans. What is really happening to Soviet Jews? How could the Kremlin be persuaded to ease up, to let Jews who so desire emigrate? What is non-Soviet Communist opinion on this issue? Lacking a common structure to pool information and sift theories, the answers must remain incomplete. Academic scholarly expertise on Soviet Jewry must increase. There is probably no scholar attached to a university who devotes a major portion of his time to studying current trends on Soviet Jews.

Finally, there must be effective implementation procedure. American public opinion must be convinced that Soviet Jewry is not too far gone and that the future will be determined, in good measure, by how this message comes across to the Kremlin. This goal requires men who will have regional responsibilities in educating public opinion, in stimulating awareness in different opinion groupings. UJA, Israel Bonds, and other Jewish fundraising campaigns are so organized. Why should the cause of Soviet Jewry be denied the same option?

How the Kremlin will react is unknown, of course. But while Soviet Jews tell outsiders in a hundred different ways "*Shum, Shum*" (make noise, make noise), can we reject their martyrdom?*

# # #

The Soviet Jewish Problem at the United Nations [*American Jewish Year Book,* 1970]

The emerging outspokenness of Soviet Jewry and the growing protest campaigns in the West continue to focus attention on the issue of Soviet antisemitism. An examination of the record of the United Nations in this area is therefore very much to the point. The questions to be considered are: How does the Universal Declaration of Human Rights, rich in provisions of justice and equality, lend itself to the predicament of Soviet Jews, some 73 years after its adoption? How do member nations view the UN as

*The concluding concepts for improving decision-making on Soviet Jewry are based on the foreign policy analyses of Henry A. Kissinger (see "Comment by Henry A. Kissinger," Committee on Government Operations, U.S. Senate, March 3, 1970.)

a forum for focusing on Soviet antisemitism? How has the Kremlin treated accusations of Soviet antisemitism made in the UN?

In addressing these questions, certain political realities should be made clear: Despite the homilies of moralists, the UN is inherently a political body, and the drive for national power marks UN politics, as it does other arenas of international relations. The problem of Soviet Jewry is only one of many ideological and political contests between the superpowers, the United States and the Soviet Union, at the UN. Superficially, the fate of Soviet Jewry appears on the agenda as a human rights question; however, above and beyond human rights considerations, this issue is deeply rooted in cold war politics.

It should also be stressed that, procedurally, the UN cannot function while lacking agreement by the superpowers. Its impact on Soviet antisemitism will be marginal (as with both Vietnam and the Middle East) as long as Moscow and Washington are at odds in this area. Moreover, the human rights provisions of the UN Charter, while relevant to Soviet Jewry, remain unenforced because of the tendency of states to guard jealously the domestic jurisdiction clause (contained in Article 2, Paragraph 7 of the Charter) and to object to foreign criticism of matters they regard as essentially within their own national prerogatives.

Challenge of Soviet Policy in UN

Nonetheless, UN public diplomacy provides a convenient vehicle for challenging Soviet mistreatment of Jews. More nations are actively represented at the UN than at any other world diplomatic site, promoting a climate of immediate and continuous communication. Focusing on Soviet antisemitism threatens the Kremlin's image and forces it to defend itself against allegations of persecuting Jews, while traditional diplomacy ("quiet" diplomacy, as it is sometimes known) is marked by behind-the-scene negotiation, the UN environment stresses open discussion and the value of world opinion. (In fact, the Preamble to the UN Charter takes the position that "We the peoples of the UN"—rather than of the sovereign nations—will promote human betterment.) The cutting of diplomatic ties between Israel and the Soviet Union, following the 1967 six-day war, which further tightened Soviet Jewry's isolation, enhances the UN's public exposure worth.

Public discussion is to the advantage of Soviet Jewry. According to Professor Thomas Hovet, Jr.:

> By focusing the spotlight of public opinion on a situation it is felt that this public exposure can freeze a situation and prevent a chain of events that might lead to conflict. At the same time there is a feeling that public discussion of an issue provides an opportunity for states not directly involved in the situation to make their influence felt in resolving the issue. The focus of publicity on the actions of a particular state threatening the peace may place that state not in an offensive but rather in a defensive position in which it must justify and explain its action.[1]

However, for all its strengths, the public spotlight does not necessarily resolve basic issues. Resolution ultimately arises from quiet diplomacy. In the human rights area, where UN enforcement is most unimpressive and nations tautly uphold domestic sovereignty, public diplomacy is especially weak. South Africa's snubbing its nose at the unending UN votes and resolutions condemning its policies in Southwest Africa is a classic case of the impotence of public diplomacy in this sphere.

Accordingly, the UN's usefulness in connection with Soviet antisemitism must be measured in perspective. It is no substitute for other forums—demonstrations, communications media, educational programs—in protesting Soviet injustice. To be sure, the UN has not always been used to challenge Soviet antisemitism. The five Black Years (*shwartse yoren*), 1948–1953, in which Stalin shut all Jewish theatres, schools, and publications, did not see the issue argued at the UN for two reasons:

The first, the inexperience of Jewish organizations with public diplomacy, and the resultant overall Jewish hesitancy to raise publicly charges of Soviet antisemitism was discussed by Ben Ami:

1. Thomas Hovet, Jr., "United Nations Diplomacy," in Maurice Waters, *The United Nations* (New York, 1967), p. 196.

> For generations the Jews maintained the dictum: "Do not provoke the gentiles." Taught by bitter experience, they were always afraid of making matters worse than they were. To raise an outcry, to protest, to stand up for their rights and lives, might make the gentiles all the angrier and provoke them into more violence and bloodshed . . . "sha, sha, don't make a row," frightened Jews would say when they learned of the bitter lot of their brethren in another town or another country. Rather than resort to open protest, the Jews developed a technique of peaceful intercession. This in time became the art of "Jewish diplomacy." The Jewish mediator would rush around discreetly and try through supplication, bribery, and self-debasement to moderate the ruler's decree. . . . A few years ago when Jewish leaders began asking themselves what to do about the problem of Soviet Jewry, many said "Sha sha." They claimed that every loud protest and outcry would serve to anger the Soviet and harm the Jews in the Soviet Union.
>
> Only when all attempts at discussions with the Soviet authorities failed and when the burden of eye-witness accounts continued to grow—only then did Jewish organizations, some slowly, others more rapidly, begin to raise their voices in behalf of the Jews of the Soviet Union.[2]

The second reason was the fear that denunciations would prove counterproductive. In his last years, Stalin was considered mad and unresponsive to foreign opinion on almost everything, including Soviet persecution of the Jews, and it was held that pressures from abroad would only further enrage him. By 1961 the UN began to appear as a safer forum for attacking Soviet anti-Jewish policy. The Communist party's "liberal" wing was then in power, and, as a result of its greater tolerance of pluralism, experts felt it opportune to raise the issue of Soviet Jewish rights.

Coincidentally and in response to a multinational outbreak of swastika daubings on Jewish and other property, the Sub-commission on the Prevention of Discrimination and Protection of Minorities surveyed antisemitic practices in the early 1960s. But since the sub-commission's central

2. Ben Ami, *Between Hammer and Sickle* (Philadelphia, 1967), pp. 295–96.

work is the preparation of human rights studies (rather than the enforcement of those rights), it could do little about specific antisemitic incidents.

Role of NGOs

However, this first UN investigation of antisemitism set a precedent for nongovernmental organizations (NGOs)[3]—the 206 private national and international groups accredited to the UN at the recommendation of the Economic and Social Council (ECOSOC) and in consultative status with it—to draw attention to Soviet Jewry's predicament, a factor hardly endearing them to Soviet UN representatives. But there are limitations to the effectiveness of NGOs challenging a member nation, especially a paranoid superpower such as the USSR; understandably, their criticisms are more muted than those of member nations.

NGOs have cited Soviet antisemitism in the context of debates on conventions dealing with racial discrimination and religious intolerance. But at least one official UN study also carries damaging material on Moscow's suppression of Jewish rights. Critical material submitted by the Coordinating Board of Jewish Organizations (CBJO; representing its constituents: B'nai B'rith, Board of Deputies of British Jews, and South African Jewish Board of Deputies) was incorporated in this document dealing with the right of everyone to leave any country including his own, and to return to his country. Significantly, this information remained in the study despite Soviet demands for its suppression.

Disclosures in 1967 that certain NGOs and their affiliates were recipients of Central Intelligence Agency grants sharpened Soviet hostility. In 1969 ECOSOC launched its first full investigation in 19 years of the NGOs. In this survey certain Jewish NGOs were assailed by Arab states for alleged support of Israel. The Soviet Union, too, denounced those NGOs claiming mistreatment of Soviet Jews. One question in the over-all inquiry of NGOs, used by the USSR to harass Jewish NGOs, was, "Have you in

3. Sidney Liskofsky, "The U.N. Reviews Its NGO System," *Reports on the Foreign Scene*, American Jewish Committee (January 1970).

the past 10 years criticized any government in which you have no constituency?" While other Jewish NGOs met the investigation's approval, the NGO investigatory committee refused to reach a final decision on the fate of the Coordinating Board of Jewish Organizations, one of the most outspoken critics of Soviet antisemitism.[4]

What impact has NGO participation had on the problem of Soviet antisemitism? NGOs sharply differ in estimating the extent. According to the Consultative Council of Jewish Organization *(CCJO;* represents Alliance Israélite Universelle, Canadian Friends of the Alliance Israélite Universelle and the Anglo-Jewish Association), Jewish NGOs abuse their privileges by being too concerned with "defending their own particular interests." In its view, "We can never, under existing regulations, present our case in an intelligent and meaningful way. All we do is to provoke the Soviet representatives and provide them with the opportunity to denounce us and libel us."

By contrast, the Coordinating Board of Jewish Organizations holds that Soviet Jewry will be aided only by a vigorous UN campaign. And, since governments do not generally supply critical information, CBJO argues, NGOs must spell out violations of human rights: "To the extent that NGO sources are not included, these studies will remain in the realm of abstraction."[5]

While NGO criticism has successfully put the Soviet Union on the defensive, the intensity of UN dialogue vastly increased, once member nations entered the arena. Critics of Soviet antisemitism could be classified in three categories: Israel, United States, other nations.

Role of Israel

Experience with UN bloc voting has given Israel a valid skepticism toward the organization's potential for fostering peace and security. Yet Israel is

4. In 1970 the NGO investigatory committee and ECOSOC voted to retain the consultative status of CBJO as a nongovernmental organization.

5. Ronald I. Rubin, "Soviet Jewry and the United Nations: The Politics of Non-Governmental Organizations," *Jewish Social Studies*, July, 1967, p. 149, 151.

not powerful enough either in its own right or as a signatory to any major military treaty to remain oblivious to UN action. Thus, Israel puts together a motley coalition of allies in the recurring Middle East disputes before the UN. What is more, Israel's invective against Soviet support of the Arabs further predisposes Moscow to dismiss its protests. After attacking us for helping "peace loving" Arabs (so the Russians must reason), how dare the Israelis hold forth on Soviet internal policies!

Yet Israel cannot treat lightly the plight of Soviet Jewry: personal, cultural, and historic ties bar indifference. And Jewish religious imperatives—crying out for oppressed brethren—rule out vacillation. For these reasons and more, the ordeal of the world's second largest concentration of Jews is a diplomatic priority for Israel.

As a rule, the UN treats human rights issues not from the perspective of resolving specific problems in particular nations, but with the purpose of setting forth general human rights principles. Israel has not missed opportunities to relate the fate of Soviet Jewry to such broader UN human rights concerns. Israel has raised the issue in connection with human rights conventions of religious discrimination and racial prejudice, as well as before the plenary of the General Assembly and the Security Council.

Most recently (November 10, 1969), upon a signed request of the petitioners, Israel submitted directly to UN Secretary General U Thant an appeal from 18 Jewish families living in Soviet Georgia, which accused the Soviet Union of preventing their emigration from the Soviet Union and settlement in Israel.[6] In the past, Israel refrained from taking such public initiative on behalf of Soviet Jews because it feared reprisals against Jews who had smuggled out such documents. In this instance, Israeli diplomats felt that the petitioners themselves had decided to overlook the prospect of reprisals.

6. Although Secretary General U Thant honored Israel's plea and circulated the document (A/7762) to every member nation of the UN, he refused to circulate other similar statements by Soviet Jews brought to his attention in 1970 by Israel Ambassador to the UN Yosef Tekoah.

When Israel first raised the issue of Soviet antisemitism, it was deliberately vague in accusing the Soviet Union. It deplored discrimination against "a certain large Jewish community," "a large section of the Jewish people," "a great and ancient Jewish community resident in one of the world's mightiest states." Subsequently, Israel decided to do away with diplomatic niceties and became more blunt, quoting excerpts from more egregious Soviet antisemitic publications, as well as condemnations by a number of Western Communist parties of Soviet anti-Jewish policy.

What charges has Israel leveled against the Soviet Union? It must be stressed that, while opposing Soviet antisemitism, Israel has never extended these criticisms to other aspects of Soviet life and Communist ideology. It has attacked emigration curbs on Jewish families torn apart by World War II; restrictions on the production of Jewish religious articles, prayer books, ritual foods *(matzot)*, and Yiddish literature and culture; the closing of synagogues and Yiddish theatres and the prohibition of private instruction in Judaism and Jewish culture; the singling out of Jews as economic criminals (especially in the early 1960s, when a disproportionate number of Jews were sentenced for alleged capitalist crimes); antisemitic references to Jews in the Soviet press: economic, political, social, and educational discrimination against Jews. Nevertheless, Israel has refused to exaggerate the suffering, never charging Moscow with physically persecuting Jews.

Israel also has appealed the plight of Soviet Jewry in the framework of UN human rights machinery. It has urged the appointment of a UN high commissioner for human rights who would receive public petitions on infringements, and conduct inquiries based on the information received. The appointment of a high commissioner was first recommended in the United States in December 1963 by Jacob Blaustein, and received wide support from international nongovernmental organizations concerned with human rights (AJYB, 1966 [Vol. 67], p. 469). Thus, Ambassador Joel Barromi argued in 1967:

> Israel has more than once drawn attention to the thwarted aspirations of the second largest Jewish community. . . . Such a situation constituted

> an appropriate field of action for the High Commissioner, whose role would be to rekindle international awareness of human rights and give impetus to the process which would lead to constructive and voluntary international solutions. The establishment of a post of High Commissioner would assuage the bitterness of individuals and groups who felt that they had been forgotten and would provide a stimulus for those who wished to improve and liberalize laws, practices and policies.[7]

Another goal championed by Israel is a more potent role for NGOs. As already mentioned, certain NGOs drew Moscow's condemnation for referring to Soviet antisemitism. Commending NGOs, Ambassador Haim Cohen said in 1965:

> . . . their reports might well be more objective than those made by governments, since they were made by private observers who had no interests at stake and were not actuated by considerations of prestige. The exceptions could not justify unfairness to the vast majority. Hence, the non-governmental organizations would be encouraged to submit reports which would assist the Commission to form an idea of the progress made in human rights; governments should be given an opportunity to comment if those reports implicated them.[8]

In 1968, Israel stepped up its attacks in an unprecedented move before the Security Council. Since human-rights problems are not debated in a vacuum, but in the politically charged atmosphere of the UN, Israel followed standard diplomatic procedure in introducing Soviet anti-Semitism into one of the perennial Security Council exchanges on the Middle East. [The following account of the dramatic exchange, based on the verbatim record of the May 6, 1968, Council session,[9] replaces an article used to present the information in Rubin's original paper.

7. E/AC.7/S.R. 572 (This and similar notations refer to official UN documents.)

8. E/CN.4/S.R. 842.

9. [The quotes and information for this new text are taken from S/PV.1422 unispal .un.org/unispal.nsf/o/dcfab68b7db3e6ac052567fc0056dd56?OpenDocument.]

Lord CARADON (United Kingdom and Northern Ireland), President of the Security Council, opened the session by inviting "the representatives of Jordan and Israel . . . to participate."

The first speaker was Mr. MALIK of the Soviet Union. "The Security Council is continuing its consideration of the situation which has developed in Jerusalem as a result of the acts of aggression committed by Israel against the Arab States," began his clearly anti-Israel, pro-Arab discussion.

" . . . the Israel aggressors are still pursuing a policy of tyranny and violence against the peaceful Arab population . . . depriving them of their fundamental rights. . . . [These] are acts of aggression, violating the United Nations Charter and the Universal Declaration of Human Rights. . . ."

Following Malik's detailed censure of Israel's many supposed transgressions, during which he compared Israel to "the Hitlerite annexationist" and reiterated the Soviet delegation's support of the Arab States, he turned the floor over to Mr. SHAHI (Pakistan) who presented *his* delegation's take on the situation.

When called upon to exercise his right of reply, Israel's representative, Mr. Y. TEKOAH, began, "Pakistan belongs to the group of counties of dubious distinction which deny the right of [Israel,] a Member State of the United Nations, to exist. . . . [Israel] challenges and rejects Pakistan's right to speak in the name of Charter principles . . . human rights . . . or . . . peace," citing numerous accounts of that nation's atrocities.

After pointing out the responsibility of Council members "towards peace and international security," Tekoah segued into his response to the Soviet Union. "The Middle East has . . . had a full taste of the Soviet Union's policy on these vital matters," he began, citing its vetoes of water development projects, freedom of navigation and "any attempt to censure the murder of Israeli citizens in Israeli territory," and ending, "The Middle East has not heard a single word from Moscow indicating that the Soviet Union is interested in a just and lasting peace."

Referring to "[Malik's] allegations regarding the conditions of life among the Arab inhabitants of Jerusalem," Tekoah was stating that, "The Security Council would undoubtedly be expected to consider any such allegations . . . were it not for the strange anomaly in the Soviet attitude towards human rights. The discrimination and disabilities from which the Jews suffer. . . . In Moscow alone . . . ," when Caradon abruptly cut him off, saying, "I give the floor to the Soviet Union on a point of order."

"What we are . . . discussing here is Israel's aggression and illegal activities in Jerusalem," MALIK argued. "The arrogant, and cynical intrusion . . . into the internal affairs of other States . . . is to divert attention . . . from all that Israel is doing to prevent a settlement in the Middle East. . . ."

When Malik finished, Caradon asked "the representative of Israel to continue . . . [but] to ensure that what we say in this debate is specifically directed to . . . our agenda."

Tekoah tried four more times to question the credibility of the Soviet delegate's, each time poignantly getting at least one new fact about Soviet anti-Semitism on record before being cut off. When he spoke for the sixth and last time, he appeared to be confining his comments to the subject on the agenda, speaking of the myriad freedoms and rights afforded Arab schools, religious institutions, clubs, inhabitants and citizens in Jerusalem, detailing a long list before cleverly adding, "When the Soviet Government grants similar rights to its Jewish citizens, we in the world at large shall be able to recognize its right to speak on behalf of human rights."]

Finally, Israeli accusations of Soviet antisemitism provoked responses from certain Arab nations, which fear appreciable Soviet Jewish emigration to Israel. While the Arabs do not necessarily endorse all Soviet human rights positions, they hardly pass up opportunities to take political swipes at Israel. They use the issue of Soviet Jewry to attack Israel's authority to represent world Jews, the alleged dual political allegiance of Jews and alleged Israeli mistreatment of Arab nationals. Typical are the following statements:

MRS. GHORBAL (U.A.R.): Furthermore, no one in the Committee spoke as the representative of Islam, Christianity, or Buddhism, and by the same token Israel was not entitled to speak for all the Jews in the world. Israel clearly sought to claim the double allegiance of Jews wherever they were, and to convince the world that all states were accountable to it for acts committed against Jews. It was even said that political

Zionism wishes to perpetuate the racial distinction theory in order to use it to further its political aims. . . .[10]

Mrs. Afnan (Iraq): Some delegations have advised the Soviet Union to allow Russian Jews to leave the country, but their own immigration laws would not welcome them. They were offering the homes of a million Arab refugees.

The Israeli representative had come to the Committee to complain of discrimination against Jews and said that one out of every ten Israelis was an Arab and that there was no discrimination against Arabs. Before Israel was established, out of ten Arabs only one was of the Jewish faith. In their own land, a majority of nine to one had been reduced to a minority of one to nine. And the Israeli representative had the cynicism to claim non-discrimination.[11]

Role of United States

A basic objective of United States foreign policy is support of the UN "to ensure the survival and prosperity of our political and social values in an era of protracted international disequilibrium."[12] The mutuality between UN human rights provisions and most American beliefs is clear-cut. The American political commitment to diversity and peaceful change lends force to the international application of this notion.

Strategically, references by the United States to Soviet antisemitism serve a dual purpose in its relations with the Kremlin. They promote the liberalization of Soviet society by exposing Soviet citizens, particularly the emerging young elite, to the advantages of personal freedom and an international philosophy of "live and let live." Additionally, they "neutralize the ideological thrust of Communism."[13] Through indirectly contrasting the

10. AC.3/S.R. 1168.

11. AC.3/S.R. 1171.

12. Lincoln P. Bloomfield, *The United Nations and U.S. Foreign Policy* (Boston. 1967), p. 44.

13. Ibid., p. 45.

freedom of American Jews to the plight of Jews in the Soviet Union, Washington shows that a free and open society "can yield more ultimate satisfactions than a totalitarian system."[14] By refusing to overlook these human rights violations and by stressing the security dangers stemming from them, the United States, in effect, rejects what might appear as a detente, and puts international reconciliation on a far more realistic footing.

American compassion for Russia's Jews is no recent phenomenon. Czarist pogroms shook the American conscience before the cold war and Stalin's contrived suspicion of an "international Jewish conspiracy" became political facts.[15] As for action on behalf of Soviet Jews, the State Department conceded the limitation of official governmental intervention. Its 1967 position paper, *The Jews in the Soviet Union*, stated:

> We have found from past experience that government-to-government approaches to Soviet officials at all levels are totally ineffective. Our approaches in the past have been brushed aside by claims that there is no antisemitism in the USSR and that, by raising the subject, we are attempting to interfere in the internal affairs of the Soviet Union for some "Cold War" purpose.

To be sure, the refusal of the United States to ratify, as of this writing, UN human rights conventions, despite presidential urgings, has not diminished American presidential support for more vigorous UN action. Since the early 1960s, when Soviet antisemitism was first confronted in the UN, the United States—second only to Israel—has pressed for the rights of Soviet Jews. At the outset, the United States, like Israel, was mild in voicing criticism in that it did not specifically name the Soviet Union.

> MRS. MEANS (U.S.A.). In countries where the Constitutions nominally guaranteed freedom of worship, religion, expression and thought,

14. Ibid.

15. In this connection, see Alex Littmann, "A Nation Outraged: American Response to the Mistreatment of Jews in Russia 1880–1891" (M.A. thesis, Department of History, New York University, 1968, unpublished).

> synagogues were stoned and desecrated without any attempt by the responsible authorities to apprehend the guilty and, together with other places of worship, were even closed. Jews were also discriminated against on the basis of nationality.[16]

However, like Israel, the United States has become increasingly outspoken in citing Soviet antisemitism. In its first references, the United States raised the situation of the Soviet Jews in the context of general human rights principles under discussion by different UN organs. Most recently, the United States representative to the Human Rights Commission sought a deliberate confrontation with the Soviet Union on the status of Soviet Jews. On November 25, 1969 Mrs. Rita E. Hauser, the American representative, made an independent statement on Soviet Jewry before the Third Committee of the UN General Assembly, the first time the United States raised this issue not in the context of some general human rights discussion. In addition to citing over-all harassment of Soviet Jews, Mrs. Hauser read a letter from Mrs. Elizaveta Isaakovna Kapshitzer of Moscow, addressed to the UN General Assembly, which had been brought to her attention by the American Jewish Conference on Soviet Jewry. In it, the writer accused the Soviet writer's union of ousting her son Vitold for asking to emigrate to Israel. He was later denied permission to leave the Soviet Union, and both he and his mother now were living on her pension, the equivalent of $40 a month.

Indicating their displeasure with this statement, the Soviet and Ukrainian delegates to the Third Committee interrupted Mrs. Hauser three times as she read Mrs. Kapshitzer's plea. According to Charles W. Yost, United States ambassador to the United Nations, the United States was pleased with the outcome of committee consideration of this case. He wrote to Congressman Jonathan B. Bingham on December 4, 1969, "The Soviets demonstrated exceptional sensitivity during the debate, and we feel that our efforts resulted in worthwhile publicity and a good measure of sympathy among other delegates, several of which also spoke out."

16. E/AC.7/S.R. 473.

The substance of United States criticism does not differ much from Israel's. The United States has publicly acknowledged consulting with Israel on Soviet antisemitism.[17] The United States took issue with Moscow's discrediting of all religions and then went on to cite specific hardships imposed on Jews. In UN conventions on eliminating racial discrimination and religious intolerance, the United States supported separate articles on antisemitism. It compared antisemitism with apartheid; it warned that antisemitism constitutes a present, as well as historic, danger; it challenged the notion (continually advanced by the Soviet Union) that antisemitism is peculiarly an outgrowth of Nazism.

The most interesting difference between Israeli and United States exchanges with Soviet diplomats is the personal framework occasionally marking the American presentation. The tenure of Morris B. Abram as United States Ambassador to the Human Rights Commission, while simultaneously serving as president of the American Jewish Committee, may account for this. Two examples are indicative:

Ambassador Abram argued that no political system provides absolute guarantees against intolerance. He cited the return to respectability of Trofim Kichko (who had been silenced since the world-wide condemnation of *his* vicious *Judaism Without Embellishment* in the early 1960s) in the wake of the 1967 six-day war (AJYB, 1969 [Vol. 70], p. 391). According to Abram, the [new] Kichko book contradicted a report of the Ukrainian Soviet Socialist Republic which maintained that there was no racial prejudice in that country. The report added that the Ukrainian criminal code provided for imprisonment for stirring up such discord, but that the law had no real function, since the younger generation was being educated in the spirit of understanding, and Socialism (Communism) was incompatible with racism.

17. For instance, in a reply of December 10, 1969, to a letter from Congressman Jonathan B. Bingham, H. G. Torbert, Jr., acting assistant secretary of state for congressional relations noted: "The U.S. Delegation to the (Human Rights) Commission will, as in the past, consult with the Delegation of Israel, which is also a member of the Commission, in order to determine the best course of action to follow on this matter."

Abram thereupon sent Boris S. Ivanov (the Soviet diplomat) a copy of the Kichko work,

> . . . pointing out that Mr. Ivanov had inveighed against all forms of discrimination and had voted to include ethnic and national discrimination among the forms of discrimination to be covered by the draft convention on the elimination of all forms of racial discrimination.
>
> After considerable delay, Mr. Ivanov had merely sent him a press release from the Soviet Embassy at Washington on "Jews in the Soviet Union" which disagreed with the author of the book on some points and stated that the work contained some slipshod formulations and that its make-up left much to be desired. He had then reiterated his questions to Mr. Ivanov, but had received no reply. Finally, he had written again soliciting a reply and suggesting that it might be useful for a delegation to visit the USSR with the same opportunities to observe facts at first hand as members of the Sub-Commission had had at Atlanta. That letter had also remained unanswered.[18]

While this episode lacked personal bitterness, the dialogue between Ambassador Abram and his Soviet counterpart, Ambassador Yakub A. Ostrovski before the 1967 meeting of the Human Rights Commission was heavy with antisemitic aspersions. The incident, which may well be one of the most antisemitic in the history of the UN, called forth formal representation to the UN Mission of the Soviet Union by Secretary of State Dean Rusk. Abram was attacked by Ostrovski simply because he was a Jew. The Soviet diplomat said Abram was conducting himself as though he were at a meeting of the American Jewish Committee, and members of the Human Rights Commission merited more respect. Subsequently, he accused Abram of serving two masters: the United States government and "the Zionist organization over which he presided." The inability of the Soviet ambassador to restrain himself, despite rigorous professional training, illustrates perhaps more than anything else how unsettling Moscow finds critical references to its antisemitism.

18. E/CN.4/Sub.a/S.R. 434.

Besides the formal use of UN organs for drawing attention to Soviet antisemitism, the UN also was increasingly considered as a forum for challenging Soviet policy by Americans concerned with this issue. A series of rallies were organized and advertisements placed by the American Jewish Conference on Soviet Jewry for December 11, 1967, the anniversary of the adoption of the Universal Declaration of Human Rights. The following year, on Human Rights Day, the Conference submitted to the UN a petition with 250,000 signatures, protesting the violation of Soviet Jewry's human rights spelled out in the Universal Declaration of Human Rights. In November, 1969, 59 members of the House of Representatives urged the State Department to support Israel's request that the UN act on the plea of the 18 Jewish families from Soviet Georgia who sought permission to emigrate to Israel. Of course, these activities do not include the numerous protests held at the UN on other occasions particularly involving youth under the auspices of the New York Conference on Soviet Jewry and the Student Struggle for Soviet Jewry (AJYB, 1969 [Vol. 70], pp. 113, 115).

Other Countries

Aside from the United States and Israel, other members of the UN took note of Soviet antisemitism only occasionally. Contrasted with ritualistic attacks on South African apartheid, the fate of Soviet Jewry seems of scant import. For smaller nations, motivated by humanitarian zeal, the UN offers an accepted public forum for challenging human rights violations. Privately, these powers probably would not dare call attention to internal Soviet racism.

Thus far, some 15 UN members, including Israel and the United States, have addressed themselves to the issue of Soviet antisemitism. Moral rather than political considerations apparently motivate those countries which speak out from time to time. The absence of consistent condemnation of Soviet antisemitism by the most ardent anti-Communist bloc in the UN, the Latin American countries—perhaps for fear of indirectly taking sides in the Arab—Israeli conflict-bears out this conclusion. Nations raising the problem included Australia, Austria, Canada, Dahomey [Benin], Denmark, Dominican Republic, France, Great Britain, Italy, Madagascar,

New Zealand, Sierra Leone, and Uruguay. What is most disappointing here is that the transcript of UN human rights exchanges on antisemitism, relating to conventions subsequently adopted by the Human Rights Commission, show many overlooked opportunities for condemning Soviet policy. Invariably antisemitism was linked to Nazi atrocities in World War II, and current Soviet injustice was not mentioned.

References to Soviet antisemitism were both subtle and direct, with the former tack dominating. Two examples of the subdued approach, in the context of the Kichko book, follow:

> Mr. Juvigny (France). Turning more specifically to the objectional publication mentioned by Mr. Abram, he said that if world public opinion had had to rely solely on Government sources of information, the publication in question would perhaps never have been known abroad. It could even be conjectured that no mean role had been played by world public opinion, aroused by articles in the press in influencing the authorities of the country concerned to suppress the publication in question.[19]

> Mr. Ermacora (Austria). In conclusion, his delegation believed that the commitments entered into on an equal footing by all States parties to the convention would be meaningless if the States concerned permitted the publication of pamphlets and books of the kind the observer from Israel had mentioned at a previous meeting.[20]

A general reference to Soviet antisemitism:

> "Mrs. Ramaholimihaso (Madagascar) said that she had listened with great interest to the statement made at the previous meeting by the representative of Israel, and, like him, welcomed the fact that, increasingly, ethnic minorities had freedom to preserve their cultures and traditions. She hoped there would be further progress in that direction."[21]

19. Ibid.
20. E/CN.4/S.R. 808.
21. AC.3/S.R. 1392.

By contrast, the following Australian statement was far more pointed. The date (1962) is worth noting because intensive Israeli and United States condemnations had not yet begun. Significantly, the Australian accusation stemmed in part from pressure brought by the Jewish community on the Foreign Office.[22]

> MR. WHITE (AUSTRALIA). I feel that I must also mention specifically the fact that the Jewish communities throughout the world have expressed concern at the treatment of Jews in the Soviet Union. Representatives on the Committee will already be aware, from material reaching them in the press and in other ways, of the grounds stated for this concern—for example, criticism in the press and radio, and even by some Soviet officials, against the Jews. Official restriction of Jewish religious observance—a recent example being the ban on public baking of unleavened bread for the 1962 Passover; and official action against individual Jews, such as the fact that out of the death sentences for economic offenses imposed lately in the Soviet Union, an unduly high proportion has been passed on Jews.[23]

Soviet Position

Self-righteously, the Soviet Union sees the UN's human rights forum as a channel for berating Western shortcomings, while never admitting any of its own. Ethnic harmony, religious tolerance, and national understanding are held forth by Moscow's diplomats as the image of Soviet diversity. The West, by contrast, is derided for discrimination and minority abuses. This stance is at variance with the human rights position of the United States, which concedes past and present imperfections, particularly in race relations.

22. The background of the Jewish community's role and the Australian intervention is explained in Isi Lieber, *Soviet Jewry and Human Rights* (Victoria, Australia: Human Rights Publications, 1963).

23. The verbatim text cited here was summarized in a press release of the Australian Mission to the UN; AC.3/S.R. 1170.

Even if the Soviet Union had not so reassuringly hailed its human rights record, Moscow's hostility to strengthening the implementation machinery of the UN would pit it against further international protection of Soviet Jewry. Suspicious of NGOs, opposed to a UN High Commissioner for Human Rights, whom it threatened to boycott, and vigilant of its domestic jurisdiction rights, the Soviet Union is in no frame of mind to bow to passing criticism by member nations of Jewish deprivations.

Although Communist commitment to scientific materialism sparks opposition to all religion, a whole cluster of circumstances cause Judaism and Jews singular hardship: Jewish individualism and legacy of freedom is anathema to Communist uniformity; Soviet Jewry's many relatives in the West arouse suspicion; cultural ties to Israel run counter to Soviet xenophobia; and the Jew is too convenient and indigenous a scapegoat—as he is for other East European regimes in suppressing liberalization—for the Kremlin to ignore.

And this is not discounting Arab admiration for Jew-baiting, although, in truth, the Arab position represents a dividend of, rather than incentive for, Moscow's racism. There is nothing especially new in harassing an ideology internally, while reaching an accommodation with it internationally. Even UAR President Nasser's public identification with Soviet foreign policy does not prevent the suppression of the Egyptian Communist party.

Yet foreign condemnation at the UN of Soviet antisemitism gets on Moscow's nerves. (The Soviet Union's sensitivity to such accusations voiced in other forums is indicated by the distribution in the free world of a steady stream of publications denying discrimination against Jews.) It has made the fundamental policy decision that these charges will not go unanswered. Increasingly, the Soviet Union has developed a more systematic response to such criticisms, one that has gone through three stages: Originally, attacks at the UN were ignored. Then they were challenged by the Soviet Union on the ground that they constituted interference in the USSR's internal affairs, and thereby violated the UN Charter; occasionally Soviet diplomats mildly took issue with accusations of Soviet antisemitism. Now they are elaborately contested by the Soviet Union. Soviet diplomats take the offensive in rebutting such accusations. Nations raising charges of

Soviet antisemitism are accused of attempting to subvert the Soviet Union by destroying its multinational character through the introduction of the poison of nationalism.

In rebutting allegations of antisemitism, Soviet delegates to the UN call on a mixed bag of arguments. As with many exchanges at the UN, their response has no relevance to the accusation. They cite carefully prepared statistics intended to do away with these charges. In taking the trouble to draw up these doctored arguments, Moscow shows it is disturbed.

It is revealing that Soviet UN denials of antisemitism contradict certain official admissions. On July 19, 1965, for the first time in decades, Premier Aleksei Kosygin surprised Soviet audiences by acknowledging the danger of antisemitism. On that occasion, the 25th anniversary of Latvia's "liberation" by the Soviet Union, he said that "nationalism, Great Power chauvinism, racism, and antisemitism . . . are completely alien to our society . . . and contradict our *Weltanschauung.*"

In an editorial on the "friendship of peoples" in the USSR. *Pravda*, on September 5, 1965, also deplored antisemitism on Soviet soil. However, that condemnation of antisemitism rested not on morality, but on the practical ground that such manifestations blacken the Soviet image abroad. After underscoring the "international obligations" of the USSR, the editorial stated:

> V. 1. Lenin, the great creator of the Communist Party and founder of the Soviet State, bade our Party hold sacred the friendship of peoples of the USSR. He wrathfully assailed any manifestations of nationalism whatsoever, and in particular he demanded an unceasing "struggle against anti-Semitism, that foul fanning of racial specialness and national enmity" created by the exploiting classes.[24]

No such admissions intended for internal Soviet consumption have ever been voiced at the UN.

24. Moshe Decter, "Soviet Jewry: A Current Survey," *Congress bi-Weekly*, December 5, 1966, p. 12.

The procedures of UN bodies involved with human rights make for the discussion of broad areas of social justice rather than of concrete cases of repressions. USSR references to the status of its Jewish citizens most often occurred in debates on declarations outlawing religious and racial discrimination. These can be divided into defensive and offensive statements.

Defensive Arguments

Here are characteristic defensive arguments regarding Soviet antisemitism as they were used by Soviet diplomats, as they were summarized in UN documents:

1. The problem does not exist in law. The Soviet Constitution and laws are cited as placing Jews on an equal footing with other Soviet citizens.

> No one was entitled to charge the USSR government with antisemitism when the USSR Constitution stipulated that any discrimination based on racial or ethnic origin was punishable by law.[25]

2. The problem does not exist in fact. Soviet diplomats further argue that anti-Jewish discrimination, at least so far as religious observance is concerned, is actually nonexistent in the USSR.

> On the other hand, many of the Jewish inhabitants of the USSR did not practice their religion, since the number of believers in any faith was declining rapidly in that country, as in many others.[26]
>
> It was regrettable that the delegation of a Member State should try to use for selfish and political ends an important discussion to which everyone should try to make a constructive contribution . . . the Israeli delegation was obsessed by a problem which existed only in its imagination and which it tried to relate to every question being dealt with by the different organs of the United Nations.[27]

25. E/CN.4/Sub.2/S.R. 416.
26. E/CN.4/Sub.2/S.R. 438.
27. AC.3/S.R. 1241.

3. Soviet Jews have no cause to complain. In attempting to show that Jews have no cause for complaint, Soviet representatives cite certain statistics of Jewish professional employment. They never concede existing discrimination in employment, particularly the bars against Jews in senior policymaking posts. Neither is mention made of the increasing difficulties for Jews to gain university admission, and of the pressure exerted on Soviet Jews after the six-day war to denounce Israeli policy. Most importantly, Soviet statements at the UN do not adequately answer charges that Jews are denied the essential religious and cultural institutions and other means for preserving their separate identity.[28]

> . . . 7,647 Jews were delegates to central and local public bodies and 290,707 had received diplomas from national universities or institutions of higher technical education; which meant that in the latter respect Jews ranked third after the Russians and the Ukrainians. Of Soviet scientific workers, 36,173 were Jews. In addition, more than 2,000 Jews had received doctorates in science and 13,000 had obtained advanced scientific diplomas; eighty Academicians or corresponding members of the Academy were Jews. Forty-two Jews had been given the highest awards for socialist labour and a large percentage of the members of various artistic and cultural associations were Jews. 14.7 per cent of Soviet physicians were Jews; 8.5 per cent were critics and newsmen; 10.4 per cent were prosecutors, lawyers and judges; 7 per cent actors, sculptors, etc. A Jewish-language cultural newspaper was published in Moscow. While Jews in Czarist Russia had lived in ghettos and had been subject to many measures of harassment, they were today better treated in the USSR than in most countries of the free world. Those facts proved how false the picture drawn by the Western Press was.[29]
>
> . . . [was] the United States representative . . . aware that in the Soviet Union there was not a single case in which a citizen had been prevented from taking part in elections—a frequent occurrence in the United States—and that in the USSR no one had ever been discriminated

28. In this connection see annual reviews of the USSR Jewish community in the *American Jewish Year Book.*

29. E/CN.4/S.R. 808.

> against in regard to his choice of dwelling, work or education—a form of discrimination which was widespread in the United States. In September 1959, in New York, Mr. Khrushchev, Chairman of the Council of Ministers, replying to a question asked him at a press conference, had stated that in the USSR all nationals, including Jews, enjoyed equal rights and lived in peace and that, moreover, a substantial number of Jews were high in the ranks of those who worked on interplanetary travel. That was a clear reply to the United States representative's question.[30]

Offensive Arguments

From an offensive position, Soviet diplomats maintain that:

1) Charges of antisemitism represent a smoke screen. This, they say, is used to conceal Israeli aggressive policies.

> The object of those remarks had been simply to spread a smoke-screen to conceal the situation in Israel and the occupation of Arab territories brought about as a result of Israel's aggressive policies.[31]
>
> . . . How could the United States representative dare to raise his voice in an appeal for the freedom of nations when the soldiers of his country were killing thousands of people in Vietnam? The United States representative should read the newspaper; he should be informed about the crimes against humanity committed daily by his country in Vietnam.[32]

2) Balance is needed in assessing antisemitism. While antisemitism is unjust, it is argued, it is no more loathsome than other types of racism including apartheid, Zionism and Nazism.

> Anti-Semitism was a manifestation of discrimination against one particular race. Consequently, *apartheid* and anti-Semitism could not be placed on the same footing. The former was a general form of racial discrimination which might be applied at any period and against any

30. AC.3/S.R. 1171.
31. E/CN.4/S.R. 979.
32. E/CN.4/S.R. 928.

> race. The latter was merely one manifestation of racial discrimination in a particular case.[33]

In this connection, the following episode is noteworthy. In drafting a convention in 1965 on the "Elimination of All Forms of Racial Discrimination," the United States and Brazil proposed before the General Assembly's Third Committee an article to "condemn anti-Semitism and take appropriate action for its eradication" (AJYB, 1966 [Vol. 67], p. 263). The USSR proposed instead the following amendment:

> States Parties condemn anti-Semitism, Zionism, Nazism, neo-Nazism and all other forms of the policy and ideology of colonialism, national and race hatred and exclusiveness, and shall take action as appropriate for the speedy eradication of those inhuman ideas and practices in the territories subject to their jurisdiction.[34]

Of course, the Committee turned down this absurd grouping. But the Soviet Union successfully used the ploy of grouping together antisemitism, Zionism and Nazism to bring about the rejection of the original amendment on antisemitism.

3) Antisemitism is peculiarly a product of Nazism; Zionism is the same as Judaism. Here is a favorite Soviet device of linking odious strawmen. Antisemitism is continually said to originate in West Germany—a nation posing a compelling threat to the Soviet Union—and thereby to augur a revival of Nazism. Also, Jews are never attacked as Jews, but for their professional, cultural, or religious ties. Thus, in scoring Jewish NGOs, the Kremlin does not cite their religion, but their political support of Israel (Zionism) which, for certain NGOs, represents only a part of their UN responsibilities.

> The wave of Nazi and anti-Semitic outbursts which, beginning in West Germany, had recently swept the whole of Western Europe and the

33. E/CN.4/S.R. 784.
34. Decter, op. cit., p. 11.

> United States of America, had focused world attention on the threat of a revival of Nazism and its terrible consequences. . . .
>
> Some United States Zionist organizations also tried to cover up the shameful situation by shifting the blame on the U.S.S.R. It was common knowledge, however, that the U.S.S.R. was one of the few European countries where there had been no manifestations of that kind and where Jews suffered no discrimination.[35]

4) Antisemitism is an American phenomenon. In an effort to undermine United States criticism of Soviet antisemitism, it is stated that the United States has no right to sit in judgment on the Soviet Union inasmuch as antisemitism is still deeply rooted in Americans.

> In regard to the Jewish question, which seemed to be of special interest to the United States representative, the book by Benjamin R. Epstein and Arnold Foster, *Some of My Best Friends*, published in 1962, showed that anti-semitism had not died with Hitler and was deeply imbedded in the American subconscious mind . . . that some 5.5 million Americans were discriminated against in various fields and particularly in the matters of education and accommodation.[36]

Conclusion

While the Soviet Union remains faithful to its aim of wiping out the Jewish identity, it does not turn a deaf ear to foreign criticism. Protests have at least slowed the Kremlin's timetable for cultural genocide. The visit of Moscow's Chief Rabbi Judah Leib Levin to the United States in 1968; the availability of *matzot* in many large cities; the termination of trials of Jews as "economic criminals," and the removal of Kichko's *Judaism Without Embellishment*, all show that the Soviet Union will not defy completely outraged world opinion.

Realistically, what is the UN's role in fighting Soviet antisemitism? The complexities of international relations make it impossible to assess the

35. E/CN.4/S.R. 686.
36. AC.3/S.R.1171.

actual effectiveness of the UN, as compared with other forums in which the Soviet Union has been assailed. Political interaction is hard enough to measure accurately nationally; it is 125 times more difficult to define in the UN organization. One can only point to the cumulative impact: Moscow's embarrassment with public attacks on its antisemitism.

Bolder use must be made of intergovernmental and interpersonal communication at the UN in drawing attention to the persecution of Soviet Jewry. Except for Israel and the United States, member nations have scarcely raised the question.

Its human rights apparatus makes the UN a natural milieu for sympathetic diplomats to raise again and again (as in the case of apartheid in South Africa) the tragedy of Soviet Jewry. Between formal sessions the UN also offers unique opportunities for personal contact. Face-to-face activity in this concentrated diplomatic setting—in the delegate's lounge, in the corridors, at cocktail parties, and receptions—will increase delegate awareness, while intensifying Soviet embarrassment.[37] The following comment by an East European diplomat illustrates the UN's potential in that area:

> The contact that you have here with other diplomats is ten or twenty times more than that which you should have in a national capital. This is especially true during the Assembly sessions. You have contacts every day not just with one person, but with many persons. Between sessions, there is still more contact here with diplomats from other countries than there would be in a national capital.[38]

Besides, UN diplomats are rotated to other posts and they will take with them their understanding of, if not compassion for, Soviet Jewry, derived from their experience of public exchanges and face-to-face contact.

37. Ronald I. Rubin's "The UN Correspondent," *The Western Political Quarterly*, December, 1964, discusses the communications opportunities at the UN, drawing largely on Chadwick F. Alger, "Personal Contact in Intergovernmental Organizations" in Robert W. Gregg and Michael Barkun, eds., *The United Nations System and its Functions* (Princeton, 1968).

38. Alger, ibid., p. 110.

The opinion of mankind, represented in part by the UN, is a crucial factor of today's international relations. An increasingly informed world public judges rivalries between the Communist world and the West by their respective adherence to publicly professed values. Of course, nations do not carry out foreign policy on the strength of world opinion polls. Certain interests are sacrosanct. Thus, despite a shocked world opinion, the Soviet Union invaded Hungary in 1956 and Czechoslovakia in 1968. But the crushing of Jewish identity, while convenient for Soviet politics, is not essential to it.

Moscow's vulnerability must be trumpeted. In vying with the United States in the nonaligned world, Soviet diplomacy patiently projects a humanitarian image. The Kremlin, too, condemns racism in its attempt to undermine the social fabric of the Western democracies. Harlan Cleveland notes the illuminating role of the UN in this context:

> Let no one believe that this is a pointless exercise, unrelated to political reality. Under the strong light of world opinion, a nation's prestige is engaged; and since national power is not unrelated to national prestige, governments are influenced by world opinion—even though it is hard to prove because they seldom admit it. The blended conscience of men of good will may wink at injustice in the dark; but when the lights are on, a good conscience must speak, or desert its possessor. No government anywhere is immune to the moral indignation of those, including its own citizens, who watch it at work.[39]

But even if the UN does not deflect the USSR from its oppressive course, even if all the verbal exchanges fail to move the Kremlin, the suffering of Soviet Jewry must be registered for the record. How ironic if the Jew, whose teachings of brotherhood and justice are at the bedrock of the UN, would remain as obscure today in the council of nations as he was earlier in this generation when silence greeted Hitler's gathering storm.

# # #

39. Harlan Cleveland, *The Obligations of Power* (New York, 1966), p. 133.

The New Style of Soviet and Other Jews
[*American Zionist*, May 1971]

The successful international protests of December, 1970, to avert the death sentences imposed by the Soviet Union on the alleged Leningrad hijackers is a landmark in the effectiveness of outside intervention on the Kremlin's domestic Jewish policy. As optimism mounts as to the eventual release of Jews seeking to emigrate to Israel, what has been the rule of the Kremlin's two main adversaries on this issue, United States Jewry and the Israeli Government?

Clearly, there has been a shift in protest tactics on the part of United States Jews and the Israeli Government, but this change was a reaction to an earlier more dramatic and more daring escalation by Soviet Jews themselves. Had Soviet Jews not intensified their protests, probably both American Jews and Israel would not have reacted similarly. Only after the death of Stalin does American Jewry—and the world—begin to see the enormity of the suffering of Soviet Jews. Until Stalin's death, Soviet Jewry lived largely in isolation. Appeals concerning the plight of Soviet Jews up to Stalin's death were essentially made through "quiet diplomacy" rather than through mass, public demonstrations.

In 1956, a delegation of United States rabbis visited the USSR, the first such official group in nearly 40 years. During the 1960s, the many great wrongs perpetrated against Soviet Jews never elicited the Jewish organizational commitment and international outrage of today. Why the greater awareness now?

For one thing, the past decade has seen an increase in international sensitivity to what were once regarded as purely domestic matters. The invitation recently by President Nixon to certain prominent Soviet intellectuals to attend the forthcoming trial of Angela Davis illustrates this shift. Who would have imagined, by contrast, John Kennedy ten years ago making a similar offer?

More particularly, in terms of American Jewry, there were also reasons why the Soviet Jewish cause did not receive substantial commitment in the 1960s. To be sure, the fate of three million Jews—the last important East European Jewish community—should have merited high priority.

But Israel was faced with great problems and too few American Jews had the stamina to fight both battles at the same time, particularly when Israelis were dying at the front and Soviet Jews were seemingly merely harshly discriminated against. American Jews who did care about Israel would hear direct reports from visiting Israeli representatives, or see things first hand during visits.

It was easier to excuse complacency regarding Soviet Jews. The few Jews who managed to leave the Soviet Union did not give public lectures on the problem, while the practice of successfully sending appeals from Russia to the outside world had not yet arisen. Thus, tourists were the chief direct channel of reports on Soviet Jewry, and in the 1960s few American Jewish tourists took this route.

Even those Jews who were concerned fought with the wrong weapons. During the 1960s the thrust of these efforts came from the elites, the opinion leaders, who did not activate the grassroots. Without questioning the value of mobilizing public support from such elite groups, it must be added that this approach was used essentially because it represented a continuation of traditional Jewish pressure tactics, and because it was easier and less expensive than developing systematic local campaigns.

Thus, in that decade the American Jewish public relations campaign on Soviet anti-Semitism stressed meetings with ranking political leaders and statements by such groups as intellectuals appealing to "world conscience." Jews were late to learn the confrontation tactics of the "New Politics" whereby political stands, however well-taken, go unheard without the supporting role of shoe leather and noise. Perhaps large-scale picketing of Soviet institutions in the United States on a continuous basis, or public advertisements urging boycotts of Soviet cultural performances, or pressure by academics to cancel international conferences slated for the Soviet Union would have alerted public opinion sooner to the issue. None of these approaches would have involved violence. (While picketing took place, it was rare; the major Jewish organizations also never officially sponsored boycotts, although smaller Jewish groups pursued this tack.)

A positive step in the campaign on behalf of Soviet Jews was the establishment in 1964 of the American Jewish Conference on Soviet Jewry, a coordinating body of more than 20 leading American Jewish organizations. The establishment of this body was commendable in that it represented a change from the traditional competition characterizing these organizations' individual efforts. Whatever success the American Jewish Conference realized, however, might have been enhanced had it been provided with more financial and personnel support.

The growing awareness displayed by American Jews of the Soviet Jewish problem was also encouraged by Middle East politics. As a result of the threat posed by the Soviet Union to Israel in the aftermath of the Six Day War, it became easier to see the enemy in his many guises. If Russia were a friend of Israel, or not an active ally of the Arabs, would she have been so scorned by Western Jews? Increasingly, Jews tend to assess the internal status of a given country's Jews on the basis of that country's relations with Israel. (Similarly, in the DeGaulle era, there was an upsurge in Jewish interest in the internal welfare of France's Jews.)

Accordingly, since the Six Day War, the mounting volume of appeals by Soviet Jews to the Israeli Government, the United Nations, and the like, also sensitized American Jews to Soviet anti-Semitism, particularly the desire of many Soviet Jews to emigrate to Israel.

The emergence of the Jewish Defense League as a factor in the American Jewish reaction is explicable on several grounds. By the time the JDL entered the scene in the late 1960s many different Jewish organizations advanced ways for treating the problem, but no one group seemed to have the answer. The fragmentation of American Jewish life also made possible the introduction of new groups. A growing fashionability of violence, the style of violence in public life in the late 1960s, accounted for its use by the JDL as a means of attracting public attention and, from some, even admiration.

Before Rabbi Meir Kahane turned to the Soviet Jewish issue, he was no stranger to controversial causes; previously the JDL took on the New Left and Black extremists. In addition to the JDL's seeming advocacy of violence, another basic difference between it and both "establishment" American groups and the Israeli Government positions is JDLs ideological framework in viewing the issue. According to the JDL, the situation of Soviet Jewry is not an isolated human rights problem, but a natural outgrowth of Soviet "tyranny" and Communist philosophy. Communism, in other words, is incompatible with freedom, including the freedom of Jews. By contrast, neither the American Jewish "establishment" nor the Israeli Government ever attributed anti-Semitism to Communist ideology.

Despite strong criticism of the JDL by both the American Jewish "establishment" and the Israeli Government, the organization is an important element in the protest campaign against Soviet anti-Semitism. Critics of the JDL argue that the exposure given to the group's tactics of harassment, sensationalism and violence does not necessarily mean that the predicament of Soviet Jews will be ameliorated.

Moreover, critics maintain, the Kremlin as well as Western Communist parties have been given an easy way of discrediting Soviet Jewish claims—they merely focus on JDL hooliganism. It is also stressed that Americans disregard causes identified with bombings and harassment. More serious is the claim that these tactics, by forcing the U.S. to apologize to the Kremlin, have the effect of vitiating the whole object of the protests: Finally, critics hold, the JDL was not necessary to win publicity for the problem, because world attention to it was steadily increasing.

In defense of the JDL, one might say that only unusual and sensationalistic activities succeed these days in gaining press notice. While such tactics may not be very respectable they have repeatedly captured headlines, and along with the headlines came background stories which filled in readers on the problem. Despite the rhetoric and statements of American Jewish organizations, JDL supporters claim, past protests were weak and as a result the public hardly recognized the problem.

Another useful aspect of JDL activity, defenders maintain, is that its sensationalism succeeded in pressuring the more traditional Jewish organizations to escalate their public protests and dramatization of the problem. It may be that more staid organizations were uncomfortable with the prospect of having their own activities appear less important when compared with JDL activity.

If any one source deserves credit for keeping the Soviet Jewish problem alive, it is the Israeli Government, but here too Israel's activity reflects a parallel to the escalation undertaken by Soviet Jews. In the 1950's, Israel felt a certain gratitude towards the early support given it by the Soviet Union at the United Nations. Although Golda Meir raised the issue of Stalin's "Doctor's Plot" at the United Nations, this accusation was more the exception than the norm.

With the worsening situation in the 1960s, Israel raised the issue more often at the United Nations. At first, Israel was purposely vague in accusing the Soviet Union, referring to discrimination against "a large section of the Jewish people," for example. In that decade, Israel cited the whole range of the Jewish plight, including cultural and religious deprivations as well as anti-Semitic references in the press.

The developing military confrontation with the Soviet Union brought home to the Israeli public the Soviet political threat, this theme being today one of the main points of Israel's foreign information services. The breaking of diplomatic relations by the Soviet Union was also a big blow to the few existing ties between Soviet Jews and the outside world. The emotional charge from the appearances of Israeli entertainers, well-known by now to concerned Jews, came to a halt.

Although Israel intensified its behind-the-scene and international efforts on this problem, it refused until well into 1970 to encourage recent Soviet Jewish emigres to speak out. Indicative of this position was the official stand regarding the public fast by the recent Russian emigré Yasha Kazakov outside the United Nations in March, 1970.

Although Kazakov's fast drew much public attention, the government logically feared that the embarrassment to the Soviet Union by such criticisms might force the Kremlin to dry up the trickle of Jews it had permitted to leave since the Six Day War. Israel's Cabinet issued a statement supposedly out of concern for Kazakov's health.

As 1970 rolled on, the government's opposition to such private criticism of the Soviet Union lessened, largely as a result of the irrepressible desire of many Soviet Jews to go for broke in their efforts to come to Israel. As Soviet Jews succeeded in parading the issue before the world, the feeling emerged in the Israeli Government that there was less and less to lose by abandoning previous restraint towards the Soviet Union on this issue.

Prior to this development, it was Israel's policy to maintain secrecy over the trickle of Jewish immigration from the USSR, although the Jews who left were given permission by the Communists ostensibly for family reunion. By publicly criticizing the Soviet Union, these emigres would discredit Communist claims that Soviet Jews are not anxious to leave for Israel, and would likewise create problems for Moscow with Arab client states who could charge the Kremlin with feeding Israel's war machine.

In its time, the policy of restraint had a certain success in that 1,000 Jews came from the USSR in 1970, although only 300 had been permitted to leave in the other two and a half years since the Kremlin broke diplomatic relations with Israel after the Six Day War.

Israel made the fundamental policy decision to capitalize on outraged world opinion relating to the Leningrad hijacking trial in the hope that such pressure would force the Kremlin to increase the number of emigres to Israel from 1,000 to perhaps tens and hundreds of thousands. Thus the Israeli Government held that the long-term risk of not permitting these emigres to speak out was greater to the hope of rescuing Soviet Jewry than the short term embarrassment their criticisms might cause the Soviet Union.

Thus, those Jews who protested against the Leningrad trial at the Western Wall, for instance, by wearing their Soviet labor camp and other identifications, were telling the world that they were protesting not simply as Jews but as recent emigres from the Soviet Union, any loss of face to the latter notwithstanding. Now, this tack had the full support and encouragement of the Israeli Government.

Since the Leningrad trials, Israel's publicity of the Soviet Jewish problem has grown. Golda Meir personally welcomed Soviet *olim* at the airport, and sent recent *olim* from the Soviet Union living in Israel to the Brussels Conference on Soviet Jewry.

The real initiators of the change in international reaction to the plight of Soviet Jews, therefore, were the Jews inside the Soviet Union. Their courage has set the framework for the escalation of worldwide protests which have since taken place. That these Jews are determined to reach Israel is clear, and it remains for those who march with them elsewhere to follow their leadership.

# # #

In 1973, Rubin had an opportunity to write some "propaganda" of his own. The next article was for all intents and purposes written for, rather than about, Soviet Jews. It was published in Russian by the Press and Publications Service of the United States Information Agency for distribution in the Soviet Union. Having only the printed (Russian) version of the article at hand, Rubin asked Professor Zhana Yablokova, a former student of his who is now an assistant professor of English at the Bureau of Manhattan Community College to translate it back into English for this anthology.

Sylvia Hirsch's Cheesecake
[*America Illustrated* (Moscow), November 1973]

Monsieur Andre studied the art of bakery in Switzerland and knew this business well. However, three years ago when he visited Miss Grimble Bakery he encountered something he did not expect. With great amusement he watched how the chef, Mrs. Hirsch, an ordinary fifty-three-year-old American woman, was mixing in cream cheese, eggs, and sugar for her famous cheesecakes. Everything she did was so different from the universally accepted rules of baking that Monsieur Andre could only silently shake his head. He had no doubt that there would be no cheesecake at the end.

But he was wrong. There was a cheesecake, and it was great. So were all the other cheesecakes Mrs. Hirsch baked. Since then Monsieur Andre has been a devoted admirer of this amazing woman, who single-handedly built her business regardless of the tough competition. Mrs. Hirsch started her business four years ago practically from scratch. Now she sells pastry in the amount of $250,000 a year, and her annual income is about $30,000.

How could she do that? Easily. She knew that her cheesecakes were very good and that cheesecakes and other pastry products were in great demand. Now her shop sells five to six hundred cakes daily to the hundred and twenty best hotels and restaurants in New York City.

Sylvia Hirsch was born in Texas. She attended public school in Dallas where she was hardly the best student. Her high school culinary teacher would just shake her head: "No, Sylvia will never become a good housewife." Sylvia's accomplishments in her sewing class were no greater. But years later, after Sylvia got married and became a mother of three, she decided that she needed to improve her culinary skills. "Most of the people who lived in Dallas used to bake their own bread and pastry," Mrs. Hirsch recalls. "Everything sold in the pastry shops they considered indigestible."

In 1965, her husband, Jay Hirsch, decided to sell his jewelry business and move to New York. By that time Sylvia had not only collected a whole pile of recipes but also acquired a reputation as one of the greatest cooks in town. She was particularly known for her cheesecakes, the recipe for which she herself had created about thirty years earlier.

In New York, Jay Hirsch had opened a Texas style restaurant, "Bronco Barbecue." In that restaurant the meat was grilled right on hot coals. The Hirsches hoped that New Yorkers would like their spiced grilled meat served with salad and corncobs. This dish became very popular in the 60s, at the time of Lyndon B. Johnson's presidency. The Hirsches believed that these types of restaurants were necessary in a big city like New York. However, "Bronco Barbecue" did not become a commercial success. Since the Hirsches did not have the money to hire a baker for their restaurant, Mrs. Hirsch started to bake her famous cheesecakes and serve them to the costumers. As luck would have it, the restaurant started to attract customers not so much for its grilled dishes, but rather for the cheesecakes that Mrs. Hirsch baked at home and then brought to the restaurant.

Mrs. Hirsch's cheesecakes became legendary. For some reason, New York has a reputation as a cheesecake capital, and, indeed, there is a multitude of them in New York. But Mrs. Hirsch's cheesecakes were unique. Like most culinary artists, Mrs. Hirsch is reluctant to share her secrets with others; however, some of these secrets are not secrets anymore: the filling of her cakes she makes from cream cheese, and for the crust she uses breadcrumbs. She also uses eggs. She uses, however, neither the flour nor potato starch that most recipes use. But she uses a lot of sour cream. According to Mrs. Hirsch, bakers in New York usually use German or Dutch recipes. These recipes suggest using cottage cheese rather than cream cheese. As a result, these cheesecakes become less tasty and soft.

The proof is undeniable. While describing the taste of Mrs. Hirsch's cakes, the renowned journalist Suzy Knickerbocker wrote that they are so good that they deserve "to be drowned in." Craig Claiborne, the head of the *New York Times* food and restaurant review column, was also astonished by Mrs. Hirsch's products.

Eventually, instead of sending flowers to the hostess of a well organized party one attended last evening it became popular in New York to send Mrs. Hirsch's cheesecakes. Her cakes also became popular among theater lovers who would often treat themselves to a nice dessert after a show. Of course, popularity is a very desirable thing in business, but there are limits to what one can do. Although Mrs. Hirsch's daughter was assisting her by that time, there were only so many cheesecakes they could make a day. It is very possible that their products were so popular because their supply was rather limited.

Meanwhile, Jay Hirsch's restaurant, "Bronco Barbecue," went out of business. Mrs. Hirsch, however, continued to supply a few restaurants and the most devoted customers with her cakes. One of the restaurants gave Mrs. Hirsch's cakes an incomprehensible but appealing name that reflected both the ambience of the restaurant and the atmosphere of the vibrant 1920s. Mrs. Hirsch's cheesecakes became known as "Miss Grimble Cakes."

Jay Hirsch once again returned to the jewelry business that he knew so well and thought that it was time for his wife to leave her cheesecakes alone and consider some other, more profitable, profession. "But we did not have enough money to try but something new," recalls Mrs. Hirsch. "The cakes, meanwhile, were still in demand."

Mrs. Hirsch continued to bake cheesecakes at home. She tried to save money on anything she could, except the quality of her cakes. "We would buy the cream cheese on Saturdays when it would go on sale," says Mrs. Hirsch. "Not a whole a lot, but a few cents we would manage to save. The store manager knew us well and would order more cream cheese specially for us."

By then, not only her daughter Linda was helping her but also her granddaughter. Every day the three of them would pack their cakes, take a subway train, and deliver the cakes to the customers.

Somehow, Mrs. Hirsch found time to become a co-author of a cookbook A *Salute to Chocolate* that discussed the role of chocolate in cooking and provided unique examples of how chocolate can be used in, for example, meat dishes. Thus, the book recommends using bittersweet chocolate in cooking meat Spanish style because it enhances the flavor of the sauce.

Mrs. Hirsch never really liked the constant turmoil in her kitchen. The family finally decided that it would be good for everybody if they opened a pastry shop. The opportunity arose in 1986 when some family friends lent them $7,500. Soon after, at 165 Columbus Avenue, Mrs. Hirsch opened her Miss Grimble Bakery.

"It was not an easy thing to do," recalls Mrs. Hirsch. "We didn't have enough money and our suppliers refused to deliver cream cheese if we wouldn't pay on time. But one of our customers, who considered our cheesecakes the best in the city, lent us some money."

Saving every penny, Mrs. Hirsch bought used appliances for her bakery. She bought a big table, two refrigerators, a big sink and a stove with an oven. In the first year, the bakery's gross income was $70,000.

In order to attract more customers, Mrs. Hirsch decided to start baking pecan pies in addition to her cheesecakes. She says that the pecan nut is the trademark of Texas, her home state. Texas Pecan pie, which had always been a favorite dessert in the South, now became as popular in New York as Miss Grimble's cheesecakes.

At first Mrs. Hirsch thought that she would deliver her cakes to restaurants and hotels only, but her old clients continued ordering her products as well. Sometimes a famous actor or an opera diva, or somebody who had tried her cake at a restaurant, would call in and ask Mrs. Hirsch to bake his or her favorite cake. As a result, Mrs. Hirsch continued selling her cakes retail as well.

A year later, Mrs. Hirsch's business was doing very well and she began thinking of a larger place. Soon she moved to 305 Columbus Avenue, where her pastry shop remains until now. Moving the business to a new place was not as hard as may have been expected; the old loan was already paid off by then and Mrs. Hirsch could take another one in the amount of $25,000, which was necessary in order to rent and equip the new place.

Officially, the company is called "Miss Grimble Inc." It belongs to Mrs. Hirsch, who is the company's president, and her daughter, who is its vice-president. Despite of his wife's success, Mr. Hirsch prefers not to intervene in the pastry business.

Aside from Mrs. Hirsch and her daughter, there are two other bakers working for the company. During Christmas time, Mrs. Hirsch temporarily hires one more baker. There are also a baker's helper, two stock workers, a dishwasher, and two truck drivers. Instead of buying the trucks, Mrs. Hirsch rents them from Hertz Car Rental. Since Hirsch signed a two-year contract with Hertz, the company agreed to replace their logo on the rented trucks with the logo of Miss Grimble Bakery.

Mrs. Hirsch is proud of the fact that she has not spent a cent on advertisement; her customers themselves are the best advertisement. Besides the people working with her in the bakery, she also has to pay an accountant who goes over her bookkeeping record once a month and does her income taxes once a year. Like most small-business owners she sometimes occasionally uses legal services, which also cost her some money.

Miss Grimble Bakery is located in a historical, multicultural part of New York City. Right next to it there is a department store. Across the street from it, there is a Spanish food store. The rent Mrs. Hirsch pays is not very high—about $600 a month. Just 20% of the sale is retail, but this is a very reliable part of the income. Mrs. Hirsch knows that her devoted customers will always find their way to her bakery, even if they have to cross the whole city in order to do so.

Mrs. Hirsch' pastry shop has its own unique ambience. The cakes are displayed in two glass showcase refrigerators. All over the walls, there are menus of the many restaurants that sell Mrs. Hirsch's products. There is also an office where Mrs. Hirsch and her daughter spend their time when they are not occupied by serving the customers and overseeing the work at the kitchen. Finally, there is a sparkling-clean kitchen, filled with a mouth-watering aroma flowing out of the big ovens where the cakes are baked.

Mrs. Hirsch's bakery is very busy. The place is not big enough, so Mrs. Hirsch is again in search of a more spacious place for her pastry shop.

Some of the supplies Mrs. Hirsch buys directly from wholesalers, which saves her some money. Once a week, for example, a milk farm delivers 500 kilograms of cream cheese packed in 30-pound containers. The ingredients that Mrs. Hirsch needs in small quantities, such as fruit, she buys in near-by stores.

The bakery is open six days a week, 9:30 a.m. to 7:00 p.m. Most of Mrs. Hirsch's customers pay their bills when they pick up the orders, but some receive bills from Hirsch once a week or once a month by mail. Today, in addition to the cheesecakes and pecan pies that Mrs. Hirsch was making when she just started her business, the bakery makes a variety of about fifteen different kinds of cakes, such as strawberry, raspberry, pineapple, and many others. Depending on the ingredients, an 8-inch cake costs between $4 and $6.50. Bigger, 10-inch, cakes cost between $8 and $12. Honestly speaking, Mrs. Hirsch's cakes are not cheap at all, but according to her, a cake like this is enough for a party of twenty.

The bakery also sells different kinds of muffins, such as lemon and chocolate muffins and muffins with British marmalade.

Lately, Mrs. Hirsch has begun selling pastry of European origin, such as Vienna chocolate cakes, cakes with chocolate cream, and French apple pies.

If the order is placed in advance, Mrs. Hirsch can make practically any dessert.

What are Mrs. Hirsch's plans? She is not really worried about competitors. Mrs. Hirsch is sure that her products are unique. She notes with pride that many professional bakers send her their recipes, asking her for suggestions on how to improve them. Nor is she worried that the relatively high price of her cakes may scare customers off. She is sure that there will always be people who are ready to pay more for a better product. Also, her long-time customers often express their gratitude that prices have not changed since the day the bakery opened.

Mrs. Hirsch's successful experience inspired one of her female relatives to open a branch of Miss Grimble Bakery in a small resort town in Westhampton, New York. Although the bakery is open only on weekends, it sells three to four hundred cakes a week. The quality of the cakes is the same, but the price at the Westhampton branch is slightly higher.

Mrs. Hirsch's high school culinary teacher would be surprised to find that her former student's cakes are being served at executive meetings at the Metropolitan Museum of Art as well as at many other important meetings. But what does Mrs. Hirsch herself think about all of it? She cannot stop wondering: "It seems to me that I am the happiest woman on earth. I can't believe all of it's happening in reality."

From time to time Mrs. Hirsch comes across new business opportunities. Thus a few big companies offered to buy her business. She rejected the offers because she is afraid that without her personal supervision the quality of the products will decline. Also, some airlines and cruise companies have approached Mrs. Hirsch with a proposal to be their supplier of cheesecakes and other pastry products. Mrs. Hirsch rejected these offers as well because she doubts she can manage such a big product line. So, Miss Grimble Bakery remains a small business in New York City.

To everybody who may want to open a food business that will become famous for the high quality of its products Mrs. Hirsch suggests, "Everybody can become as successful as I. What's important is that the products find their customers. What is even more important, however, is that the quality of these products is the very highest. When business becomes successful, it is very important not to start chasing the dollar. You should never lower the quality of your product; otherwise, people will stop buying it."

9
Education

In the 1970s Rubin wrote two op-eds about an educational issue impacting New York's multicultural (including Jewish) population. Because they are similar, the second, *CUNY's Future: It's All Politics* [*New York*, February 1977], is not included.

To Be Educated, or More Educated: That Is the Question
[*New York Times*, April 10, 1976]

In the next few months hard choices will be made concerning the future of the City University of New York [CUNY]—choices that go to the heart of the democratic nature of higher education and the types of programs that can most benefit a troubled city.

The debate about restructuring the City University not only involves money but, more fundamentally, who will find himself seated in a classroom or library next September, the minority-member high school graduate seeking to become a beginning civil servant or the doctoral candidate in Renaissance history. Funds are no longer available to support a New York public university trying to educate both types of students simultaneously.

Based on the restructuring proposals announced by the Board of Higher Education this week and still to be approved by the Emergency Financial Control Board, the emphasis is on protecting graduate programs. The City University Graduate School and University Center, in an ultramodern building on 42d Street, has barely lost a desk while certain of its sister community and senior colleges are scheduled to be shut down.

Instead, it might be more profitable to sharply scale down graduate offerings and close the Graduate Center. Cutbacks in these areas would provide for the survival of some of the admittedly less glamorous but utilitarian colleges marked for destruction.

Many colleges and universities boast of special identities and missions, but the City University is one of the really few to have any. In its own way the mission of the university is the mission of the United States and the portals of New York City—opportunity for the have-nots. What attracted hundreds of thousands of students to public municipal colleges here for a century and a half was not an awesome respect for graduate programs nor the possible presence of a National Book Award winner on the faculty.

These students came mainly because they were financially hard-pressed and the institutions were free, accessible, solid and respected. In view of projections of a continually declining middle-class population, for tens of thousands of future New York City high school graduates the choice clearly remains either the City University or a closed door to college.

In such an atmosphere, why should an economically disadvantaged student be denied a college education while facilities exist to train medievalists, physicists and Chaucerians? In these graduate areas, why should the university's relatively recent graduate programs compete with private, world-renowned universities here such as New York University and Columbia?

Let the City University instead concentrate on the undergraduate programs that are consistent with its mission and, as a result of such training, contribute directly to New York's future well-being.

To be sure, the City University is hardly alone among American colleges that are forced today to rethink educational priorities. Almost always, however, when the choices are made, the results favor the undergraduate curriculum. Brown University, for instance, recently disclosed plans to suspend graduate work in political science—a small contribution toward maintaining the integrity of its undergraduate offerings.

In defense of the City University's graduate programs, it is argued that the presence of a graduate faculty helps to benefit undergraduate instruction. The collegial interaction between graduate and undergraduate faculty, supporters say, sharpens the research awareness of the latter. This contact is said to benefit students who are kept abreast of recent scholarship. This proposition may well be correct. Yet there are many excellent colleges in all sections of the country that offer no graduate work and boast both scholars and students of the first rank.

The fact is that the City University is not Harvard, and even if certain elements of it ever sought to compete for that educational mantle, in these economically austere times they had better redirect their goals.

In the absence of money, basic educational standards at the City University's undergraduate level have been eroded; money to keep the teacher/student level at a decent size, to buy supplies, and to support libraries is rapidly drying up. In each of the foregoing areas cutbacks have severely reduced the university's stature.

The choice, however unfortunate, has boiled down to maintaining a far-ranging graduate program or closing down one or two senior or community colleges. This decision must rest on one factor alone: how it affects the welfare of current and future students.

Were we to shut some senior and community colleges, inevitably large numbers of students would find college inaccessible. Were the Graduate Center to close, the more resourceful and aware graduate student would readily find a home in a comparable graduate program elsewhere.

Regrettably we can no longer afford to support both. The greatest good for the greatest number is what CUNY is all about.

PART FOUR

The Turn of the Century, 1990–2008

10

Education, Continued

In the early 1990s Rubin wrote another "education" article, but this one was as much, if not more, about Jewish personalities and politics as it was about education. The *yeshiva* he wrote about—in the community in which he lives—has a very strong heritage, steeped in Jewish history and Judaism.

From Telshe-Lithuania to Riverdale
[*Yeshiva of the Telshe Alumni's Dinner Journal*, June 1993]

The Telshe Heritage

The penetrating sound of Kol Torah that one hears upon entering the Beis Hamedrash of the Yeshiva of the Telshe Alumni, in Riverdale, New York, extends back in time to the beginnings of the Jewish people. This give and take of Talmudic argumentation, engaged with enthusiasm and *Hasmada* by the 133 *talmidim* of the Yeshiva, gives assurance that Yiddishkeit is being passed on to yet another generation, in one more epoch in the migration of the Jewish people.

The watchword of the Yeshiva is the premise that Jewish survival without Torah represents an empty shell; indeed it is only through Torah learning that Jewish continuity is assured.

While we are fortunate in our current *Golus* that both yeshiva enrollment and Jewish learning are rising, few Torah institutions can point to the heritage of the Telshe name. In the world of education, as in other areas of human endeavor, experience, reputation and commitment are standards by which an undertaking is judged.

The Yeshiva of the Telshe Alumni, though in existence only a decade, extends back to 1875, to the town of Telshe, Lithuania. It was there that Rabbi Eliezer Gordon zt"l [may the memory of the righteous be for a blessing], one of the *gedolei Torah* of his era, founded the historic Telshe Yeshiva. In addition to serving as *Rosh HaYeshiva*, Rabbi Gordon was also the *Rav* of the 3,000 Jews in the community. What marked the Telshe Yeshiva then, and its Riverdale offspring now, is an intense commitment to Torah study combined with an emphasis on character development.

During its years in Lithuania, the Yeshiva attracted an international student body drawn by the Telshe approach stressing clarity of logic and reason in Talmudic study. Among the luminaries who assumed leadership of the Yeshiva after Rabbi Gordon, were Rabbi Yosaif Leib Bloch in 1910 and Rabbi Avrohom Yitzchok Bloch in 1930. At the outbreak of World War II, some 350 students were enrolled at the Telshe Yeshiva.

In the summer of 1941, Nazi troops marched into Telshe, murdering most of the rabbeim, *talmidim* and Jews of the town. The courage and defiance of Rabbi A. Y. Bloch, HY"D [may G-d avenge his blood], who proclaimed his faith in G-d to the Gestapo officers even as he was brutally beaten, is still remembered in the annals of *Kiddush Hashem* during the Holocaust.

The American Experience

Providentially, two of the most talented scions of Telshe—Rabbi Eliyahu Meir Bloch and Rabbi Chaim Mordechai Katz—had left for America, shortly before the Nazis captured the town. Their mission in America was to arrange for the relocation of the Yeshiva here. Although these two Rabbis lost almost everything—family, Yeshiva and community—their *emunah* survived. It was this faith that motivated them to reestablish in America. By 1941, Telshe became the first European Yeshiva transplanted to America, faithful to the European traditional standards of advanced Talmudic study and excellence. Cleveland, a city in the American heartland, was chosen as the new home.

At the outset, since few American students were prepared to undergo the demanding Telshe Yeshiva program, a *Mechina* Preparatory Academy was added, combined with a high school to satisfy their general study requirements. It was geared to students of high school age, culled from all levels of elementary Jewish education. By 1948 a Graduate Institute was founded for advanced studies. Eight years later, the Yeshiva moved to its current home, a modern, beautifully landscaped, fifty-three acre campus in Wickliffe, Ohio.

Presently, the Telshe Yeshiva is known as one of the main centers of Jewish learning in the world. Headed by Rabbi Mordechai Gifter, a native of Portsmouth, Virginia, and an alumnus of the Yeshiva in its Lithuanian home, Telshe is known for its commitment to developing the whole personality of a *talmid*—both in learning and in *midos*—a true *ben Torah.* Graduates of Telshe serve *Klal Yisroel* not only in the main metropolitan areas of the United States and Israel, but in smaller communities in Texas, North Carolina, Colorado and other parts of the country. *Rabbonim* who spent their formative years at Telshe also hold positions in Belgium, France, Argentina, Australia, South Africa, and most recently in the Ukraine, as Rav of the Jewish community in Kiev.

Telshe Branches Out

With the growth of the Jewish public that could appreciate the *derech* of Telshe, Orthodox Jewish families turned to the Cleveland Yeshiva with a request to establish branches in their communities. In 1960, the first branch began in Chicago upon the invitation of the local Jewish community, with the encouragement of the Cleveland *hanhala.*

The needs of Jewry on the Eastern Seaboard, the home of the vast majority of American Jews however, were still not fully addressed. By 1980, an estimated 1,000 Telshe alumni were living in the Greater New York area. In addition, many graduates of other traditional *yeshivos* welcomed the prospect of a New York Yeshiva based on the unique elements of the Telshe *derech.*

Telshe Moves Eastward

A group of these alumni, operating under the guidance and direction of the *Rosh HaYeshiva,* Rabbi Mordechai Gifter, decided to organize and establish a "Telshe" Yeshiva in close proximity to the greater New York area. A suburban site was considered ideal to develop a Torah atmosphere away from the bustle of the New York metropolis.

A three-building complex was purchased in the Bergen County community of Westwood, New Jersey. In the Fall of 1981, the Yeshiva of the Telshe Alumni opened its doors in Westwood, New Jersey. Despite the high hopes of the young Yeshiva's Administration, the three years in Westwood were marred by harassment, intimidation and violence. Reports of anti-Semitism perpetrated against the new Yeshiva were carried in both the Jewish and secular media, as every effort was made to drive the Yeshiva away. Physical attacks on the Telshe students grew so offensive that people of goodwill in the community volunteered their services and escorted the *talmidim.* United States Representative Robert Toricelli, sensitive to the plight of the innocent *bachurim,* urged the local police to provide additional security.

Instead, local officials sought to dislodge the Yeshiva by using the legal process to make life as difficult as possible. Ultimately they succeeded in driving the Yeshiva out by using the process of eminent domain, claiming that the school premises were needed for a municipal site. (Ten years later, the buildings are still boarded up, unused).

When the Yeshiva of the Telshe Alumni abandoned Westwood, enrollment stood at 35 students. Despite its first years of adversity in hostile surroundings, the Yeshiva's reputation was already well established in the world of Jewish education, and it was ready to move on.

The Riverdale Years

Although leaders of various Jewish communities in the New York area sought to attract the fledgling Yeshiva, people of foresight and commitment—led by an individual whose visionary generosity is matched by his desire for anonymity—prevailed upon the Yeshiva to choose Riverdale as its new home. The warmth of the Riverdale community and the public encouragement of its rabbinate made Riverdale an oasis that was greatly appreciated after the Westwood experience. The Yeshiva is housed in a structure of great architectural quality in a sylvan setting, opposite the

Wave Hill Nature Preserve, a location removed from the distractions of urban America. The Wave Hill site holds the dormitory, dining facilities, administrative offices and a *bais medrash*. The main *bais medrash* is situated a few blocks away at the Parkway campus.

The Yeshiva's 133 students hail from many communities in the United States and Canada. Although approximately half the student body comes from the Metropolitan New York area, large contingents also come from Los Angeles, Baltimore, and Toronto.

The Yeshiva's budget of nearly $1.2 million is only partially covered by the student's tuition, reflecting the fact that almost sixty percent of its students are sons of professional Jewish educators. Consequently, the Yeshiva must raise almost $600,000 annually for its scholarship program, which places an exceptional burden on the *Rosh HaYeshiva*.

The Yeshiva's Moving Spirit

Faithful to its origins, the Yeshiva of the Telshe Alumni concentrates on the development of the total *bachur*, in placing major emphasis on an individual *Rebbe-Talmid* relationship. The entering class consists of only sixteen boys, although many applicants compete for these openings. Other high school *shiurim* are limited to some twenty students each. *Rebbeim* are chosen not merely for their exceptional scholarship and skill in pedagogy, but also to serve as role models.

Insightful and understanding—their warmth and dedication to each and every *talmid* have become legendary. Although trained and educated at various *yeshivos* in the United States, the majority of Rebbeim studied in Telshe as well. All have furthered their education at the world-renowned Yeshivos of Brisk in Yerushalayim. As a result, the two great traditions of Telshe and Brisk have merged in Riverdale.

In the Yeshiva, the *Rebbe* serves a multi-faceted role. He guides his students in approaching the *Talmud* with well-loved analytical skills. Among his goals are the development of an approach to studying *Chumash* with the classical commentaries. But the interaction between *rebbe* and *talmid* is not limited to the classroom; the *rebbe* also serves as a counsellor in helping each student in his development of *midos* and in attaining moral sensitivities.

The *rebbe* seeks to form a close relationship with each of his *talmidim*. Scenes of *Rebbeim davening*, walking, and dining with *talmidim* in warm fellowship are part of the kaleidoscope of the Yeshiva. In this interaction, the *Rebbe* and *Talmid* discuss issues of *hashkafa*, personal relationships, and other topics that concern adolescents, as they struggle to move into adulthood. During *Shabbos*. students visit their *rebbeim*, experiencing the warmth of *Shabbos* in a home environment that they will strive to recreate as adults. In its academic program, the Yeshiva tries to develop rigor in learning, based on the students' mastery of a specific number of *blatt Gemora*. While each year the curriculum calls for covering some seventy-five *blatt*, the Telshe method emphasizes repeated review of the material studied. On each level, the *Rebbe* regularly gives *bechinos* to test the student's achievement. Four times a year, the *Rosh HaYeshiva* tests each student in a classroom setting. The auspicious nature of the *bechina* with the *Rosh HaYeshiva* is underscored by students dressed in their *Shabbos* clothing.

To develop each student's capacity for independent study, the Yeshiva sponsors a program that encourages *talmidim* to complete the *Mesechta* learned that year. At a special *Melave Malka*, each *talmid* attaining this goal is awarded $250.00 in *seforim*. Approximately half the students in the Yeshiva undertake this challenge—the Yeshiva devotes $10,000 to awarding such prizes.

In late afternoons, high school students take a full program of secular studies, in a program supervised by Rabbi Gershon Brafman, previously head of the Torah Education Institute in Israel. All major areas of study are completed in conformance with the requirements of the New York Board of Regents syllabus, with special emphasis on communication skills and other areas of future use. A unique feature of the afternoon curriculum is Jewish History, from the end of the era of the *Batei Mikdash* to current times, presented by the well-known author, Rabbi Zechariah Fendel.

Bais Medrash

Upon graduation from high school, most students elect to remain and enter the Yeshiva's highly advanced *Bais Medrash* for a full four-year program of intense Torah study. Here the *bachur* immerses himself in the *Yam Hatalmud,* drawing on the wisdom of the great commentators and Sages of our rich *Talmudic* heritage. Special emphasis is placed on developing in a *derech halimud* whereby the tools for independent study are finely honed. The key component for this is the unique *blatt shiur* patterned after the classic "Brisker" Approach—the highlight of the day. To this end, *bachurim* are divided into *chabura* groups where each *bachur* is expected to master a *sugya* with all its complexities; organize and structure a thesis, incorporating original insights and interpretations to deliver to his colleagues. The vigorous *Talmudic* discussions that ensue, sharpen the mind and result in a tremendous symphony of *kol Torah.* Not to be neglected is the development of a *derech hachaim,* an approach to life, where world events are viewed through the Torah perspective, and the life's problems approached guided by the rich Telshe tradition.

The Yeshiva and the Community

In keeping with the Telshe tradition, the Yeshiva has pioneered a truly innovative project in the field of adult education. Ever sensitive to the needs of the community and seeking to share the full richness of Torah with all who thirst for Torah knowledge, the Yeshiva has added a talented educator to its faculty. Rabbi Elimelech Kohn avails himself from early morning until late at night to accommodate a flexible program structured to suit each individual's level of Torah education and time availability. Subject matter covers the full gamut of our rich tradition. From basic *Chumash* to in-depth study and analysis of *Chumash* and *Nach;* beginning *Gemora* to advanced *Talmud* study, with relevant commentaries. *Shulchan Aruch* and practical halacha, as well as *hashkafa* and philosophy are given their due.

Classes at all levels are held for men, for women and for couples. Study sessions are held one-on-one or in small groups, allowing each individual to study at their own pace and maximize those precious moments spent in Torah study.

In short, the entire spectrum of Torah study is offered to those who wish to avail themselves of it.

The response has been overwhelming. People from all walks of life—businessmen, professionals, and college students—have enthusiastically availed themselves of this unique opportunity.

The program has enhanced the lives of all it has touched. For some, it is a chance to make up for the lost opportunities of their youth. For others, it is a chance to rejoin the intensive learning experience of their own yeshiva days. For the *baal teshuva,* it is a new opportunity to become an integral part of the Torah community uniting all in the pursuit of the common goal, Torah knowledge. Participants in the program have eagerly shared their experience with their own families and friends, expanding the impact of the learning experience and influencing others to join as well.

No longer a mere suburb of Manhattan, Riverdale is being turned into a Torah metropolis. The Yeshiva has become a magnet attracting scores of people from surrounding communities who are seeking to enhance their knowledge of our heritage. From Manhattan and Monsey, from Scarsdale, New Rochelle and Harrison, people are drawn to the focal point of Torah study and scholarship that is in Riverdale.

Twice yearly, the Yeshiva sponsors *Yoma d'Kallah* days which are attended by scores of participants from throughout the New York and New Jersey region. Scholars and laymen alike come to experience a day of intense learning at an advanced level. Sophisticated lectures are provided by acknowledged *talmidei chachomim* and members of the faculty, followed by lively discussions during question-and-answer sessions. The highlight of the program is a profound discourse and inspirational words of the *Rosh HaYeshiva,* making this a truly memorable day for all who participate.

The warm relationship that has developed between the community and the Yeshiva extends beyond the walls of the Yeshiva. A deep bond of friendship and profound admiration has blossomed between the Yeshiva and the local Rabbinate. Members of the Rabbinate partake in the Yeshiva functions and are frequently invited to address the student body. Yeshiva faculty members give classes and are called upon to lecture at the local shuls, occasionally delivering *Shabbos* sermons and talks. They *daven* there, actively participate in communal functions and celebrate each others *simchas.*

In addition to providing staff to promote communal learning, the Yeshiva also hosts the Riverdalc *Bet Midrash* at its Parkway Campus. Organized by local individuals and encouraged by the communal rabbinate, the Riverdale *Bet Midrash* attracts some 100 individuals weekly, directed by Rabbi Mordechai Willig and Rabbi Jonathan Rosenblatt. Administered by Rabbi Yerachmiel Barash, and Rabbi Elchonon Finkelstein as the Riverdale liaison, the Bet Midrash also brings young resource fellows from the New York area to offer learning opportunities to the *Bet Midrash* students. Classes are once a week, one-on-one, or in groups; material ranges from the elementary to advanced levels.

Thus, the *Bet Midrash* provides for the broader community what the Yeshiva provides for its students—the prospect to grow in Torah study and religious identity.

The New Chapter: The Opportunity Next Door

In these thirteen years of growth, the transplanted tree of knowledge represented by the Yeshiva of the Telshe Alumni has borne fruit, reproducing its *derech* in Riverdale, bringing Jews closer to their holy heritage. And the future holds promise for more. . . .

11

Connecting to Israel

Whether on sabbatical or on vacation, Israel is a frequent destination of Rubin's. While there, he finds ways to connect with the Jewish state. In Part III, he served as a senior visiting professor at one of Israel's top universities. Here he addresses first volunteering in the Israeli army and then being part of an organized group of people transported to Ben Gurion Airport to greet Israel's 200 newest citizens—immigrants from North and South America—who were arriving on the December 27, 2007 *Nefesh B'Nefesh* flight. *Nefesh B'Nefesh,* which literally means soul by soul, is an organization that helps Jews make *aliyah,* which literally means ascent and figuratively means immigration to Israel.

Serving in Army Helped Identity with Israel
[*Riverdale Press,* January 11, 1990]

Does the prospect of serving as a volunteer in the Israeli army stir your feeling of Jewish nationalism? Have you considered making a contribution to the state of Israel not in terms of money, but in terms of your time and talent?

If your answer to the above is yes, you may be a prospective candidate for Volunteers for Israel, the seven-year-old program which sends Americans to meet the critical manpower needs of Israel. Some 2,000 to 3,000 Americans are expected to sign up for the program this year.

Volunteers serve in their assignments for three weeks. They pay their airfare to Israel (receiving a slight subsidy), but food and board are provided by the host government.

I participated in this program last July and August, an experience which turned out for me to be a moving one and, I hope, a constructive way of showing my identity with Israel.

Living in Israel was not entirely a new experience for me. I spent a year there as a visiting lecturer at Haifa University and another on sabbatical in Jerusalem. Our daughter, Talia Bluma, 9, a student at SAR Academy was born in Jerusalem's Share Zedek Hospital.

During this trip, however, I wanted to help meet Israel's manpower needs. As a result of the intifada, thousands of Israeli reserve soldiers serve in the West Bank and in Gaza. Being in the reserves normally means leaving one's family and job for between 30 and 60 days a year.

What could an American Jew do to help Israel meet the great demands on its manpower pool?

That is where Volunteers for Israel enters the picture. Established in 1982, during Israel's war in Lebanon, Volunteers for Israel provides men and women to work in back-up positions on Israel's military bases, thereby freeing up the reserve soldiers for more strictly military endeavors.

Actually, participation in this program is not limited to Jews—one of the women in my group was a Christian school teacher hailing from Madison, Wisconsin. Also, volunteers serve in hospitals, social service agencies and kibbutzim, in addition to military installations.

My group of 17 consisted of 12 men and five women. In terms of background, the group represented various ages, professions and social experiences. I shared a room with a pediatrician from Georgia in his mid 50's, a resident of New Rochelle who recently graduated from Skidmore College and a black Jew from Brooklyn in his 60's (on his third go around with Volunteers) who studies during the year at a Lubavitch Yeshiva.

Among the women there were several college students, some recent college graduates, several school teachers, a dental assistant, a real estate broker and housewives. Two women hailed from Canada and one from Holland.

Since we signed up for this program with no pre-conceptions other than that of helping Israel, we were flexible in terms of what we expected for work assignments. Owing to security considerations, we were told not to publicize the exact location of our base, both in correspondence and in phone calls home.

Accordingly, we reported our base as being about 45 minutes traveling time from Jerusalem.

Our base was a warehouse base, meaning that military supplies for reserve units were stored there. These supplies had to be maintained in battle ready condition. Before Volunteers for Israel sent participants there on a regular basis, we were told that many more reserve soldiers were required to do the chores that we were assigned.

My job consisted of vehicle maintenance—an experience new to me given my sedentary academic background. Hundreds of military vehicles were stored at various sheds on the base—military half tracks, personnel carriers, supply trucks, repair trucks and ambulances.

During the height of fighting between Israel and Lebanon in the early 1980's, each of these vehicles, we were told, saw action. My work consisted of checking the air pressure of tires of those vehicles, changing the engine oil and removing gun turrets from half tracks. My partner in these tasks was a volunteer from Atlantic City, New Jersey, in his 40's who recently sold his beer distributionship [sic] and was seriously considering Aliya (emigration to Israel). By the end of the work day the military uniform I was issued was soaked with sweat.

The women of the group essentially did packaging of military spare parts and personal effects, cleaning and oiling of Uzi machine guns and painting of military vehicles. Our routine consisted of being awakened at 6 a.m. for breakfast at 7 a.m., and work beginning at 8 a.m. There would be a midmorning snack break, an hour for lunch and the work day ended by 4:30 p.m. In the evening, lectures were arranged for the group by outside speakers on subjects such as the nature of Zionism and the life of Hannah Sennesh, the Jewish heroine executed by the Nazis. We were taken on tours of the Northern part of Israel and of modern and historic Jerusalem. Fridays and Saturdays were days off.

Meals were all taken in the Army mess hall together with the Israeli soldiers assigned to the base. Not surprisingly, volunteers speaking Hebrew were at an advantage in socializing with the soldiers. I became rather friendly with my supervisor in the garage who showed me around the city of Yavne, about a half hour from the base where we lived.

According to administrators of the program some 14,000 people have thus far participated in this venture, with quite a few having served a few times. On a tour arranged for us by Volunteers, I met an attorney and his wife from Chicago who had participated as volunteers three times.

Does the program work? Clearly it frees up Israeli soldiers to serve in more pressing military capacities. It also sends a message to the people of Israel that Jews in the free world are willing to share their goal of maintaining the Jewish state. Each morning, together with the Israeli soldiers, all the volunteers would stand at attention for the ceremonial unfurling of the Israeli flag. While I was still simply a volunteer, at that moment I felt an identity with the State of Israel and with Jewish history that I will remember my whole life.

# # #

Welcoming Israel's Newest Olim
[*Jewish Press*, January 9, 2008]

Having spent earlier sabbaticals here in Israel, I knew the subject of *aliyah* loomed as a background issue but hardly expected the untold ways it would recast itself. Jerusalem's stylish German Colony, where we rent a furnished apartment, has seen an influx of French-speaking *olim*—so much so that when one of the Hildesheimer Street *shul*'s *Simchat Torah* honorees came forward, a chorus of "*La Marseillaise*" rang out. I once heard the congregation's black-frocked *rav* trying to explain a complex Talmudic point and then wondering aloud in Hebrew whether he should add some French to his vocabulary.

The *aliyah* theme surfaced again in a friend's e-mail announcing he planned to arrive the following month on a flight sponsored by Nefesh B'Nefesh (NBN), the *aliyah* service organization.

"Scary," he wrote, "but better scared than sorry."

After making a mental note of his December 27 arrival date, I was reminded once more of *aliyah* at the premiere showing of the film "Refusenik" at the Jerusalem Jewish Film Festival. This moving account, showing both the heroic Jews trapped in the Soviet Union desperate to emigrate to

Israel a generation ago and the daring activists in the United States who took up their banner, held personal meaning for me.

In 1968, I wrote one of the first books on their struggle (*The Unredeemed: Anti-Semitism in the Soviet Union*), and on three occasions visited these Prisoners of Zion. Whatever tears I shed during the movie were dwarfed by how I felt when Sharansky, Levin and some fifty other survivors of the Gulag (some now aided by canes and walkers) came onstage afterward to a five-minute standing ovation.

As though some master plan were at work, the next morning an ad appeared in newspapers inviting readers to welcome NBN's 31st chartered *aliyah* flight at Ben-Gurion Airport.

Two more experiences underscored the theme of *aliyah*. Less than a week before the trip to the airport, the Daf Yomi class I attend at the Hildesheimer *shul* finished the tractate *Ketubot*, the last few pages of which glorify the land of Israel to the extent of allowing husbands and wives to divorce spouses who refuse to settle there.

The world of the dreamers who trekked across Europe three centuries ago to board boats sailing to the Holy Land came alive, only a day before the NBN welcoming ceremony, during a tour to Tiberias run by the Orthodox Union's Israel Center. I saw the *shul* founded by the followers of the Baal Shem Tov, and in the city's old cemetery, the tomb of Rav Yisroel of Shklav, one of the students of the Vilna Gaon who made the precarious journey.

It was 5 a.m. and still dark when my wife and I boarded one of three chartered buses parked in front of Jerusalem's Binyanei Ha'uma for the ride to the airport. Among the passengers, many of whom carried homemade signs, were joyous teenagers and twentysomethings, parents with infants in tow, and Shulamith and Yehoshua Neaman, the seventyish couple who had led the previous day's Tiberias tour.

We sat behind alumni of an earlier NBN flight—a couple from Portland, Oregon, and their three babies—who'd made *aliyah* as they were becoming more religiously observant, because to their mind the choices were either a larger Orthodox community in America's Northwest or Israel. They were traveling to the airport to welcome a 21-year-old woman from Seattle who had just finished a pastry chef's course.

Arriving at El Al's Terminal 1, I went upstairs where a *minyan* was underway. What impressed me was the relatively large numbers of boys in the room who were in their early teens. I learned from their *madrich* (guide) that these 120 students from Kfar Saba's religious high school had set out early in the morning to fulfill the *mitzvah* of greeting Israel's newest arrivals.

At 7:30, the crowd of about one thousand ran outside to the tarmac and formed two parallel lines abutting the makeshift gate where the *olim* would pass. Fifty *chayalot* (female soldiers) waving Israeli flags stood at the front of the rows under the bright sun. Israeli music blared, a young man blew into a long, curled *shofar,* hand-drawn signs bobbed up and down, guitars sounded. Everyone was pressing to get a glimpse, or touch, or reunite with the new arrivals. It was a scene of joyous, triumphal pandemonium.

The first of three buses shuttling the *olim* from the plane drew closer, circling again, seemingly teasing the crowd to shout harder and wave more strongly. Finally, the heroes stepped down from the bus greeted by hugs, kisses, tears, *mazal tovs*, and handshakes. Fatigued, but apparently sure they had done the right thing with their lives, the newcomers smiled, cried, kissed loved ones, and even tried capturing the moment's emotions with camera photos of their own.

The 200 arrivals were a cross-section of age, dress, and religious observance. One couple came from Venezuela, a few from Canada. Some were Holocaust survivors; others were already preparing to serve in the Israel Defense Forces. The eldest was a woman of 93, the youngest a girl of three and a half months.

Anna Solomon, 24, born in Toronto and holding an MA degree in mathematical finance, felt she was living out her grandparents' dream. "My parents wanted to come," she said, "but couldn't do so after the war." Jeff and June Glazer were uncertain whether their three children in Teaneck, New Jersey, would follow their example.

Among the young, the pull of Israel was especially powerful. Atara Mark, 20, from Plainview, New York, aspired to teach English and was headed for Bar Ilan University. "It's all my parents' fault." she joked. "My father wanted to jump on the plane with me."

Simona Kogan, 25, who edited a website back in Metuchen, New Jersey, planned to settle in Ranana. "I feel very connected here. I could be Jewish in America, but my Jewishness is more fulfilled by being in Israel."

Jeff Daube, 57, a schoolteacher from Riverdale, New York, was excited at the prospect of launching a new career as the Israel representative of the Zionist Organization of America.

The lesson of the new *olim* is that an intense love of Israel and a deep desire to fulfill the *mitzvah* of *yishuv Eretz Yisrael* will surpass the pull of family, friends, habit and culture. Like the Soviet Jews who risked the Gulag, the pilgrims to Tiberias who risked persecution and poverty, even the French in my community who were far from certain the beachhead they established on Hildesheimer Street would be a success, these Jews came here because they see Israel as their home—and a glorious place in which to live.

May they be inspired by the spirit that drew them to Israel to accomplish great things for *Klal Yisrael*.

12

U.S. Foreign Policy, Terrorism, and the Middle East

Throughout the first decade of the twenty-first century, Rubin followed the travesty that was the United States' policy on terrorism and the Mideast, writing prolifically about the key players: Colin Powell, President George W. Bush, John Bolton, and Condoleezza Rice. Forever politically alert to news from the area, a *Wall Street Journal* article by Richard Haass of the Council on Foreign Relations in 2007 mandated that Rubin respond, which he did in the form of a "Letter to the Editor." The chapter ends with a look at the 2008 presidential and vice presidential contenders.

Dawdling Diplomacy Emboldens Terrorists
[*Forward*, "ForwardForum" column, February 2003]

When confronted by terrorism, action trumps inaction. So runs the conceptual underpinning of President Bush's case for military pre-emption. Despite such tough rhetoric, America's dawdling diplomacy regarding the liberation of Iraq makes it seem as though the president has failed to heed his own rule of statecraft.

Nearly half a year has passed since Bush made the case at the United Nations General Assembly for "disarming" Iraq. More than 100 days ago, Congress voted overwhelmingly in favor of going after Saddam Hussein.

In politics, as in life, everything is in the timing. Yet the administration's haggling with the U.N. Security Council over resolutions and its hectoring of the hapless inspectors serve both to embolden Saddam and those opinion elites who sanctimoniously reach for the moral high ground in covering up for the Iraqi dictator. The administration, as identified with prevaricating Secretary of State Colin Powell, seems ill fitted to play the game of cold-blooded power politics. Too bad the Democratic Party's base is weighted so much to the left, because next year's presidential primaries cry out for a challenge to a vulnerable chief executive from the foreign policy right.

At this stage of history, it has fallen to the United States to maintain the order of world civilization. According to Henry Kissinger's classic work "Diplomacy," such leadership is consistent with the rules of international relations. In every century in the modern era, Kissinger claims, one nation has emerged to put its stamp on world statecraft. "Almost as if according to some natural law," he writes, "in every century there seems to emerge a country with the power, the will, and the intellectual and moral impetus to shape the entire international system in accordance with its own values." Despite America's diplomatic destiny, Kissinger holds that no nation has been as reluctant as the United States to interfere in the affairs of other nations.

When political bullies and the variegated forces of anti-Americanism sense a disconnect between the rhetoric and action of a would-be crusader nation, the power of the latter languishes. As a result of Bush's diplomatic shuffle since last fall, American power has dropped. This image of an indecisive leadership threatens American security and world order. Thus, Osama bin Laden had no reluctance to resurface in a broadcast calling for renewed *jihad.* With a straight face, the North Korean despot Kim Jong Il threw out U.N. arms inspectors and admitted lying about not developing nuclear weapons. Yasser Arafat continues to dangle in power, somehow exempt from the calls for regime change in the Middle East.

Bush's uncertain leadership has laid the basis for the confluence of attacks on American intentions by the self-appointed representatives of public opinion. To be sure, it does not take much to ignite the latent anti-Americanism from the morally self-righteous, the jealous and the Muslim fundamentalists. But within the mob are those good and innocent people whose values will never be the same once they have acquiesced to the brazen insults directed at the world's main beacon of freedom. A resolute American-led invasion of Iraq would have avoided such self-doubt and embarrassment about this nation's intentions.

Domestically, Bush has also paid a price for his prevarication. The stock market meanders lower, Republicans in Congress are hesitant to come to the defense of his economic programs and only one Democratic senator has thus far embraced his tax cut proposal. Six Republican senators have had no fear to declare themselves opposed to the president's wish to drill for oil in the Alaskan wilderness. Nearly 100 of the nation's city councils have gone on record against military action in the wake of the president's perceived waffling.

The lesson of Bush's indecision is that there is a price to pay in the tough neighborhood of power politics and national self-interest if one insists on behaving like a consensus-driven nice guy. Those who gave us and died for the values of freedom deserve a more clear-headed leadership to execute Western civilization's precious legacy of moral prescriptions.

# # #

The New Powell Doctrine
[*Forward*, "ForwardForum" column, March 2003]

Regardless of how the war with Iraq unfolds, the six-month American dalliance with the United Nations over the future of Saddam Hussein represents one of this country's main post–Cold War diplomatic defeats. What makes this disaster even more aggravating is that the wounds were self-inflicted and avoidable.

Future historians will blame this fumbling exercise in statecraft on Secretary of State Colin Powell, who showed himself to be wedded to a romantic, outdated notion of great power collective security. If Powell were driven by instincts of *realpolitik* rather than illusions of diplomatic clubbiness, the issue of Saddam's fate would never had been brought before the U.N. The "coalition of the willing" would have vanquished Saddam months earlier. The forces of the free world would have sustained many fewer casualties than they are suffering now.

Before embarking on the imbroglio of the Security Council, Powell's subordinates should have briefed him on the expected cynical machinations of France. Most likely, Russia and China would have at worst abstained in the final vote in the absence of the implacable French veto.

Based on personal experience, Powell should have also known what sort of fiasco would emerge from an inspection process headed by an indecisive pedant such as Hans Blix, the chief U.N. weapons inspector. In the end, Powell ruled out a follow-up vote to Resolution 1441 with the aim of protecting the world body from the historical accounting that it deserved. American political interests would have been better served had the "whip count" that President Bush originally sought from the Security Council taken place. The culprits would have been exposed before the highly vaunted "world public opinion."

Moreover, such a vote would at least have put in perspective the humiliating photos of Bush, head of the world's only superpower, desperately "working the phones" imploring politically irrelevant countries such as Guinea and Cameroon for permission to go to war.

How did Powell trap the president into the diplomatic abyss of the U.N.? Surely, the tough-minded realists in Bush's inner circle were against this perilous path. And the world organization's failure to reign in Saddam over a period of a dozen years, its failures in Rwanda and in the Balkans, its knee-jerk advocacy of the Palestinian cause to Israel's detriment and the posturing of Secretary General Kofi Annan represented sound warnings for protecting this well-meaning but diplomatically inexperienced president from the U.N. morass.

Clues to Powell's thinking are found in Bob Woodward's 2002 book "Bush at War," in which the secretary of state is quoted as regretting that during the first Gulf War "he hadn't pressed his arguments that forcefully" for containment. Perhaps Powell really felt that what came to be ridiculed as a farcical inspection process would work. Perhaps he naively convinced himself that at this historical juncture the Security Council's permanent members would abandon power politics in their decision making. Perhaps containment was such an article of faith with Powell that when he met privately with the president in August in the Oval Office he threatened to resign were this noble position not tried.

The whole picture of Powell's pressures will only come to light some day with the publication of Bush's memoirs. But we do know that in the same month Powell willfully entrapped the president into pursuing the

U.N. option, Vice President Dick Cheney drew a virtual blank on his trip to the Middle East to round up diplomatic support for joint military action against Saddam. Why wasn't Cheney's rueful report factored into the abortive decision to go to the Security Council?

Two pillars undergirded Powell's theory of statecraft: the strength of international coalitions and the efficacy of the political containment of hostile nations. Both approaches proved feckless in confronting Saddam in the post–September 11 culture of terrorism. Coalitions meant the diplomatic security of the good ol' boys network of the transatlantic alliance and the supposedly rational permanent members of the Security Council engaged in harmonious conference diplomacy. Containment meant avoiding the use of military force and the reliance instead on sanctions and pressures by the "international community" in the form of inspectors, observers and peacekeepers.

In the best of times, both these diplomatically pat schemes would be doomed to failure in the absence of a recognized superpower whose role it was to enforce international order. But two dramatic changes undermined Powell's commitment to what historians term the old diplomacy. For one, the end of the Cold War signaled the rise of states that, no longer dependent on the United States for security, are seeking new places of glory in the international arena. Secondly, the onset of terrorism eroded the traditional Band-Aid schemes by which diplomats like Powell tried to keep the peace.

What made Powell's blindsiding of Bush even more astonishing was that the quixotic decision to invoke the higher authority of the U.N. was reached in the fall of 2002, around the same time the administration released what has come to be known as the "Bush Manifesto."

This document, intending to confront the peril that lay "at the crossroads of radicalism and technology," asserted the aggressive plan of preemptive self-defense against terrorists "to prevent them from doing harm against our people and our country."

While this muscular statement may have proven embarrassing to the negotiation-oriented bureaucrats in Powell's State Department, its recommendations mirrored the thinking of the national security realists in the administration. In order to restore his damaged credibility as leader of the world's beacon of freedom, this is the strategy that a hopefully more experienced president will follow.

###

Unilateralism Versus Post-Nationalism
[*Jewish Press*, May 19, 2004]

In the Western intelligentsia's indictment of the Bush administration's war on terrorism, no sin holds greater opprobrium than unilateralism. Despite the presence of some sixty nations in the American-led coalition in Iraq, the liberal battle cry roils against what the elites perceive to be a new smug level of triumphalism and quasi-imperialism.

To be sure, the likes of Dr. Howard Dean and university faculty club critics more or less agree that Saddam Hussein is not the sort of guy they would choose to take out to lunch. But at the same time, they denounce American unilateralism as arrogant and self-righteous—a threat to world order.

On the surface, this anger against alleged White House braggadocio manifests itself in political terms—the familiar charges that the administration is ignoring the international community, betraying America's traditional allies ("old" Europe), shunning the venerable route of multilateral diplomacy. But in truth, the Left's angst over President Bush's confident prescription for foiling terrorism is more cultural than political.

A main current of "progressive" thinking today is post-nationalism—i.e., narrow definitions of national self-interest are to be subordinated to the higher values of world community. Yes, the president's critics may proclaim their faithful devotion to this country's heritage, to its precious open and democratic society. But they resent the absolutist connotations of a fierce nationalism and what they denigrate as the cocky rigidity of an us-versus-them world-view.

Much has changed culturally in the "progressive" outlook since the disastrous presidential candidacy of George McGovern three decades ago. Then, opponents of this country's role in Vietnam cited the supposed corruption of our South Vietnamese allies, the prospects of an unwinnable jungle-based guerrilla war, or their belief in the Communists as a possibly redemptive force.

None of those arguments come into play in the Left's opposition to the American action in Iraq. Since McGovern's time, two important intellectual currents have gained prominence in normative "progressive" thinking, and in the process undermined traditional interpretations of national sovereignty—multiculturalism and moral relativism. Post-nationalism has come to the fore in an increasingly secularized American culture that takes issue with the traditional trinity of God, Mother and Country. When President Bush labels certain regimes in absolutist terms, charge the cognoscenti, he underscores the "yahoo" limitations of his simplistic frame of reference.

Adherents of post-nationalism reject a pre-emptive foreign policy as both bellicose and bourgeois. Even if the use of force is intended to end a despotic regime, the military option must be "authorized" to render it legitimate. Otherwise, the unilateral intervention represents a swaggering, morally wrong act, defying as it does the sacrosanct notion of "world opinion." Whether the "self-aggrandizing" President Bush cloaks his "unilateral schemes" in crusader orhumanitarian terms, antiwar critics claim the venture will engender Iraqi hatred rather than respect for the United States.

Israel's supporters have every reason to worry about the growing consensus in the Democratic Party in favor of multilateral diplomacy. Were the United States to formulate its foreign policy toward Israel based on the will of the world's main fulcrum of multilateralism—the United Nations—it would be bad news indeed for the Jewish state. Yet in his tortured reasoning, Senator John Kerry besmirches President Bush for pursuing a supposed unilateral policy regarding Saddam Hussein, while claiming he would not empower the United Nations to call the shots in the case of Israel. At least we must praise President Bush for the consistency of his world-view.

What is the alternative to the president's alleged hubris, his use of power politics, according to this post-nationalist mindset? The respectable forum for reducing tensions must, according to Kerry and Company, be the conference table. There, the moral high ground will remain assured against atavistic politicians resorting to war and force and assertions of national hegemony.

Techniques for this type of institutional diplomacy run the gamut from dialogue and neutral inspectors to peacekeepers, economic sanctions and boycotts. The "rule of law" rather than military might must be the instrument for settling international disputes. Accordingly, Dr. Dean in his abortive campaign for the presidency refused to pre-judge the guilt of Osama bin Laden for 9/11 barring any such finding by a court of law.

At bottom, the attack of the post-nationalists on the unilateral use of American power is not based merely on so-called bullying abroad, but is rather a manifestation of the ongoing cultural war. The question comes down to which side holds the morally superior position—the post-nationalists relying on the sagacity of a supposedly united world community, or a president imbued not in the brutal ways of Hobbes or Machiavelli, but with the sense of mission to use this nation's strategic might to preserve freedom against the barbarians that lurk.

# # #

Bolton Versus Powell: A Tale of Two Diplomatic Cultures
[*Jewish Press*, May 2005]

The confirmation theatrics in the Senate over John Bolton's nomination as this nation's United Nations Ambassador have featured not only the well-worn cast of Democratic Party leftists and old-line multilateralists from Foggy Bottom, but the behind-the-scenes accusation by Colin Powell—whose legacy as secretary of state is steadily going bust—about the nominee's alleged meanness. Powell's backbiting came as no surprise to those versed in Washington infighting.

Not much had been heard from Powell since President Bush unceremoniously dropped him from his second-term Cabinet without so much as telling him in advance that Condoleezza Rice would be taking over at State. The string of successes attributed to the much-maligned Bush Doctrine—the notion of democratic idealism espoused by administration heavyweight thinkers such as Bolton, Deputy Defense Secretary Paul Wolfowitz and Vice President Cheney, has served to underscore the failure of Powell's global consensus, negotiations-based legalistic approach to fighting terrorism.

On issues of terrorism and confronting authoritarian regimes, history will show that Powell's approach reflected a bygone era. He refused to call for regime change in North Korea, mistakenly relied on old-fashioned conference diplomacy in challenging Iran's mullahs, resisted the use of force to depose the Taliban, and naively turned to the United Nations to head off Saddam Hussein.

Ironically, Powell's one big success against the weightier strategic thinkers in the administration in winning over the president—taking the case against Saddam to the UN for the umpteenth time—led to the classic photo of him haplessly appealing to a dismissive Security Council about the Iraqi leader's lurking menace.

So was it surprising that Powell surfaced in a rear-guard effort (one clearly aimed at redeeming his place in history) by attacking Bolton for lacking a softer and gentler persona in dismissing the advice of disgraced State Department and CIA "intelligence" bureaucrats?

Powell was grudgingly forced to accept Bolton as one of his six undersecretaries based on Vice President Cheney's job recommendation. Years before, in his autobiography, Powell revealed his disapproval of a more muscular American diplomacy such that as championed by Bolton. In the administration of George Bush senior, charged Powell, Cheney and Wolfowitz had turned the Defense Department into "a refuge for Reagan-era hardliners."

In his two decades of diplomatic experience, Bolton distinguished himself for mustering support to end the UN's notorious Zionism is Racism resolution and for cobbling together a coalition at the international organization to enforce standards for Saddam to abide by following the first Gulf War. Bolton stood out among Powell's entourage in opposing the foreign-policy culture that saw diplomacy as a legalistic operation designed to buy time. In Bolton's view, the United States in the world arena should unapologetically use its power in pursuing its vital interests.

Specifically, the record of how a visionless Powell dealt with Yasir Arafat underscores the contrast between the Powell and Bolton approaches to statecraft. At best, Powell's performance might be excused for showing endless patience for that inveterate terrorist. But a more telling analysis would fault Powell for aimlessness, naiveté, an unwillingness to ostracize Arafat and a lack of intellectual honesty in his evenhanded criticism of the Palestinian and Israeli positions. Powell's ongoing attempts to negotiate with Arafat stood in stark contrast to President Bush's morally based refusal to even take a phone call from the Palestinian terrorist.

From the outset, Powell misjudged Arafat as a person subject to pragmatic arguments. In his first speech on the subject of terrorism as secretary of state, at the University of Kentucky two months after the chastening experience of 9/11, he tried convincing Arafat that terror was unproductive (note the absence of any denunciation of terrorism as "morally compromising" its perpetrators—subsequently a central point of President Bush's case against Arafat): "The intifada is now mired in the quicksand of self-defeating violence and terror directed against Israel."

In Congressional testimony later that month, Powell betrayed a startling lack of moral clarity in his understanding of the nature of terrorism by seemingly excusing the murder of Israeli civilians by Palestinians. "One man's terrorist," he declared, "is another man's freedom fighter."

Later that year, after his maiden trip to the area was greeted by a suicide bombing, Powell gave vent to the morally equivalent "cycle of violence" argument: "We've got to get beyond this period of suicide bombings and retaliatory actions or other defense actions."

Upon meeting Arafat in December, Powell tried a different tack, warning the terrorist that if he didn't go after Hamas, the fundamentalists would seek to kill him. Britain's Daily Telegraph (December 2, 2001) ran the conversation:

> "They are going to destroy you."
> "And he said, 'Yes, I know.'"
> "I said, 'you'd better do something.'"
> "And he said, 'I know.'"

In analyzing Powell's record on the Palestinian-Israeli conflict, one looks hard to find any moral condemnation of terrorism. What emerges is criticism of terrorism as ineffectual rather than illegitimate. Thus Powell warned Israel and the Palestinians to stick with the administration-backed road map peace plan because sustained violence would only take them to "a cliff that both sides will fall off."

Asked by Al-Jazeera television on June 23, 2003, whether "there is any legitimate resistance" by Palestinians against Israel, Powell again advanced the argument that terrorism had accomplished nothing for its perpetrators—and once more skirted the moral question of murdering innocent civilians:

> "What has this kind of resistance achieved for the Palestinian people, whether you describe it as legitimate or illegitimate, whether it is terrorism or resistance; whatever you call it, let me ask the question this way, what has it achieved for the Palestinian people?"

Was Israel justified in killing terrorists who murdered innocent Jews? Here, Powell made the case that terrorism begets more terrorism, a position popular in the type of conference diplomacy rhetoric eschewed by Bolton. On the ABC News program "This Week" (September 7, 2003), Powell condemned Israeli assassinations of Hamas terrorist leaders: "To kill one Hamas leader, but wound 9 children or 10 children in the course of this, who will grow up to become Hamas leaders or Hamas killers later, they have to consider the long-term consequences of this policy."

Ironically, Powell's statement contravened President Bush's address the same day (which might have been vetted by Bolton among others) in which he said, "We have learned that terrorist attacks are not caused by the use of strength. They are invited by the perception of weakness. And the surest way to avoid attacks on our own people is to engage the enemy where he lives and plans."

While Bolton and other non-sentimental strategists in the administration increasingly focused on sidelining Arafat, Powell pursued his own version of diplomacy. In retrospect, one wonders whether Powell was joking in August 2003, after Arafat had no doubt ordered a terrorist attack on Israeli civilians, when he issued the following appeal: "I call on Chairman Arafat to work with Prime Minister Abbas and to make available to Prime Minister Abbas those security elements that are under his control."

In September 2003, following Israel's announcement that it was severing all contact with the Palestinian Authority (some fifteen months after President Bush's condemnation of the "morally compromised" PA), Powell still refused to break relations. Falling back on Foggy Bottom's legalistic approach to diplomacy, Powell insisted, "Yasir Arafat is the elected head of the Palestinian Authority and reflects the leadership that the Palestinians wish to have. So he still has the authority, that mantle of leadership given to him by the Palestinian people, and we will continue to work with him."

Given the reformist wave represented by Bolton's muscular diplomacy, is it surprising that his increasingly discredited former boss sought to deligitimize him for meanness (read, moral certitude)?

# # #

Bush Can't Afford Another Blink

[*Jewish Press*, July 2006]

Based on his soaring rhetoric on the defense of freedom and the threat of terror, George W. Bush no doubt recognizes what is at stake if Iran goes nuclear—a sure high-tech escalation of that country's drive to impose Islamic rule over non-compliant infidels. Presumably, he also took the time to read the May letter from the Iranian president threatening the United States with war unless it followed "the true path," i.e., conversion to Islam.

Yet President Bush clearly blinked when Secretary of State Condoleezza Rice announced that the U.S. would join the European Union, China and Russia at the diplomatic table in order to convince the Islamic Republic to abandon its apocalyptic goals. The mullahs would drop schemes of nuclear jihad, goes the hope, if enticed by "incentives," a Mideast updating of Bill Clinton's failed touchy-feely diplomacy in the face of North Korea's nuclear quest.

If there was any doubt about how thoroughly sandbagged the president was by Foggy Bottom's accommodationist tack, it was erased by the surprise he expressed in Vienna at Iran's request for another two months to weigh the contents of Secretary Rice's incentives. Why should Iran, wondered the president out loud, need so much extra time to reply to his "reasonable offer"? In other words, the fanaticism of these holy warriors could be negotiated or finessed away (assuaged by "reason").

It is impossible not to contrast the president's succumbing to Rice's diplomacy of engagement with his standing up to the same conceptual framework advanced earlier in his administration during the stewardship of Colin Powell. As secretary of state, Powell saw the Israeli-Palestinian conflict in terms of moral equivalency—Palestinian terrorism precipitating an Israeli response sometimes resulting in Arab civilian deaths.

In condemning this "cycle of violence," Powell failed to distinguish between the former's deliberate targeting of civilians and the inadvertent casualties stemming from the Israeli counterattack. Powell, in urging a "peace process" and "confidence building" gestures, imagined that Arafat would modify his signature terrorism in response to diplomatic pressure.

Bush, to his credit, sent the State Department's aficionados of even-handed diplomacy on the Israeli-Palestinian conflict packing. He accused Arafat of betraying the interests of his people through his terrorism, and insisted that Israel was justified in refusing to make concessions as a result of such terrorism.

Given the president's strength in rebuffing the State Department on the Israeli-Palestinian conflict, one can't help but ask why he took Foggy Bottom's advice and blinked on Iran. Former Bush foreign policy insider Richard Perle, in a recent Washington Post op-ed, pointed to the move of Ms. Rice from the White House, where she served during Bush's first term as National Security Adviser, to the State Department, where, in Perle's words, "she is now in the midst of—and increasingly represents—a diplomatic establishment that is driven to accommodate its allies even when (or, it seems, especially when) such allies counsel the appeasement of our adversaries."

Though highly admired, Powell came to State identified with the cautionary, globalist, stability-oriented statecraft of the president's father. If George W. Bush had trouble understanding that Powell's "realism" stemmed from the conference diplomacy approach of James Baker or Brent Scowcroft, the neocons around the president were there to cut Powell down to size.

Rice, by contrast, came on the scene as George W. Bush's coach and tutor. Supposedly, her loyalties were to his muscular type of diplomacy, not to Foggy Bottom's diplomatic "engagement" school of thought. But that was then, and we've now seen indications that Rice has been co-opted by State's accommodationist mentality not only in her Iranian gambit, but in her response to North Korea's threat to test a nuclear missile. The North Koreans, she lamented, don't value the notion of "compromise."

The president's independence of mind on Palestinian terror is attributable to a number of factors, including his having personally seen, during a helicopter flight hosted by Ariel Sharon while Bush was still governor of Texas, the physically vulnerable nature of Israel.

Moreover, Arafat's lying to the president about the nature of the North Korean arms shipment seized at sea by Israel did not exactly serve to increase Bush's regard for the integrity of the Palestinian terror chief.

And electoral politics likely figured, to some degree, in the president's decision to ignore State's position on the Palestinians—he may have wished to satisfy his evangelical, pro-Israel base, or increase the level of support among Jews for the Republican party, or both.

The media beating the president has taken on the duration and cost of the Iraq war may help explain why he decided to handle the threat of a nuclear Iran in concert with the chimerical forces of old Europe, China and Russia.

His naïve offer to Iran notwithstanding, President Bush knows his legacy will be determined by how successfully he fought the forces of terror with the forces of freedom. He does not want to send a lesson that violence works, as Bill Clinton did by inviting Arafat to the White House more often than he did any other president or prime minister.

The strength of a great leader is the certitude of his moral vision—a resolve diminished by the slightest blink.

# # #

Do Palestinians Really Want a Permanent Peace with Israel? A Response to "The Gipper's Mideast Playbook" by Richard Haass [Letter to the Editor—*Wall Street Journal Online*, April 14, 2007]

Mr. Haass's restating of the tired Council of Foreign Relations' even-handed approach to the Israeli-Palestinian problem calls on President

Bush to "spell out" his vision, as though the absence of clarity from Washington underpins the dispute. In June 2002, courageously departing from the moral equivalence approach of both President Clinton and the elder President Bush, the incumbent White House occupant made his position very clear. President Bush ascribed the dispute at bottom to the terrorism initiated by Arafat, who he argued had fundamentally betrayed the hopes of his people.

Clearly, as long as terrorism—a mindset abetted in Palestinian schools and mosques—marks the approach of the Palestinians, President Bush could give speeches, appoint special envoys, call for summit conferences and fantasize about "political horizons," all to no avail. The most disturbing feature of Mr. Haass's piece, given his role as a centerpiece of the liberal foreign policy establishment, is his disingenuous reference to Arafat's alleged lack of "leadership" at Camp David. According to Mr. Haass, Arafat's failure to "compromise" stemmed from the absence of a "political environment" that would enable him to win the endorsement of other Arab states for his alleged peace-making intentions. Arafat was the terrorist par excellence, and recognition of the rightful existence of a Jewish state was a notion he fought to the death. The record of Oslo showed that while Arafat was soft-talking "engagement" oriented diplomats the likes of Mr. Haass, he was unremittingly engineering and paying for terrorist operations. On the same day that Arafat shook hands with Clinton and Rabin on the White House lawn, he in fact gave a speech in Arabic for the folks back home claiming that the Oslo enterprise was only a holding operation.

# # #

The Statecraft of Condi Clinton
[Unpublished—Written while in Israel, December 2007]

For those with long memories, Condoleezza Rice's pre-Annapolis persona, harkened back to the humiliating scene of her only female predecessor at Foggy Bottom, Madeleine Albright, physically running after Yasser Arafat at a Paris chateau in October, 2000, after the rambunctious terrorist fled negotiations underway between the two of them, plus Israel's Ehud

Barak. Albright never caught Arafat whose commitment at the time was more towards the intifada than the Clinton administration's chimerical "peace process."

In an updated version of this road-running analogy, a more fast-footed Rice aims to cross the diplomatic finish line dragging with her the hapless Israeli and Palestinian disputants.

For Rice, crunch time has come. In the concluding paragraph of his sympathetic biography, *Twice as Good: Condoleezza Rice and Her Path to Power* (2007), Marcus Mabry delineated the options facing her, "the skilled tactician who translated a bold foreign policy vision into the birth of a new Middle East, or the too loyal consigliore who failed to save an inexperienced and irresponsible president."

Though Rice's replacement of Colin Powell was greeted with high expectations, it could be argued that her tenure produced even greater diplomatic reversals than occurred under her predecessor. Rice shared with Powell the same flawed approach to the Israeli-Palestinian conflict stressing process over policy (appearances over reality), thus trying to fudge insoluble differences between the disputants. Conceptually, this cynicism represented a carryover of the finessed statecraft of Bill Clinton.

Thus Powell, in order to give the illusion of diplomatic progress, came up with the notion of a "provisional" Palestinian state that would achieve permanence following Palestinian good behavior. Similarly, Rice introduced the diplospeak "political horizons" for the void at the conference table.

More damaging, was the failure of both Foggy Bottom incumbents to think outside the box, focusing instead on by the book methods of statecraft. This Old School approach to international relations emphasizing structures, legalisms, and consensus building, might have been suitable in an age of emperors or as a way of resolving disputes between democracies. But in a climate of Islamist terrorism, these tacks lacked diplomatic creativity.

The legalism of an official Palestinian state was seen by Rice as a panacea for the Israeli-Palestinian conflict. No matter that such a new nation lacked a credible civic culture, failed to curb terrorist incitement, or refused to recognize Israel as a "Jewish" state. How to achieve a reduction in the enmity of the disputants? Again, Rice turned to a favorite tack of Powell's—confidence building

Ironically, though Rice and Powell were named to their posts to advance the president's agenda, especially pre-emption as a response to Islamist terrorism, both secretaries of state served more as ambassadors to the White House rather than as presidential advocates.

State's slowness to recognize the new era showed in its delay in dropping Clinton's Oslo "peace process." In particular, Powell's emphasis on the role of diplomacy in dealing with Arafat revealed the discrepancy between his interpretation and the president's interpretation in responding to terrorism. The Bush Doctrine urged making war on terrorists, whereas Powell insisted that Israel negotiate with confirmed terrorists, i.e. Arafat. Under Rice, State's career diplomats, largely ignored during Bush's first term because they stood for accommodationism, resurfaced.

Mabry's biography of Rice never directly compared her approach to diplomacy and that of Clinton. But personality-wise, they shared two hubris type similarities—firstly, neither was plagued by self-doubt, and secondly, the mutual refusal to accept personal defeat. In fact, in the book's last line, after spelling out Rice's Middle East diplomatic options, Mabry predicted, come what may, "she will move on, she'll get over it."

But beyond the personal, operational similarities marked both Rice and Clinton. Though Clinton intellectually grasped diplomatic complexities, details never much interested him. He was not adept at delegating. By contrast, Mabry cited criticisms of Rice's "dysfunctional" record as National Security Council director during Bush's first term: "Critics, both inside and outside the administration, describe policies that the NSC was to slow to handle, too muddled in its handling of, or never handled at all."

Strategically, the final comparison between Rice and Clinton was that neither had an overarching philosophy of diplomacy. To be sure, in her 2000 Foreign Affairs article, "Promoting the National Interest," Rice implicitly criticized Clinton's record, arguing the need for a "disciplined and consistent foreign policy" that separated "important from the trivial." Though Rice never came up with a fresh diplomatic doctrine, Mabry argued that she was actually "a realist who had been mugged by 9/11," The upshot of her epiphany was what she called "transformational diplomacy."

Thus, Rice's widely criticized observation during last year's Israeli-Hezbollah war predicting the "birth pangs" of a new Middle East. Her push for a Palestinian state under the governance of an impotent Fatah leadership was attributable to the same quixotic mindset that "failed states" could be repaired "through helping to build governance structures." Isn't this simply an updated version of the Clintonian realism that produced an Oslo agreement legitimizing meaningless structural-legal change in the absence of Middle East democratization?

###

Why Bush May Yet Shock Everyone and Bomb Iran
[*Jewish Press*, February 6, 2008]

Given his swaggered walk and ineloquent delivery, George W. Bush is an easy one to underestimate. But pundits and politicians do so at their own peril, cases in point being Al Gore and John Kerry, two gentlemen who like to think of themselves as high cultivated and erudite.

Despite his simplistic veneer, Bush belongs to the thin ranks of conviction politicians—leaders like Reagan, Churchill and Lincoln, who stand on core principles. Though members of this group at times find it necessary to zig and zag in order to remain politically viable, their brand of ideological commitment stands in stark contrast to the masters of finesse and the celebrity-seekers who dominate electoral office.

Since Islamofascist terrorism is the defining issue of his presidency, and Iran is the main perpetrator of this signature evil, it should come as no surprise if Bush chooses not to end his White House term with Tehran closing in on nuclear weapons. Conscious of his legacy, he would not want the record to show it was on his watch that the Islamic Republic went nuclear, or at the very least moved irreversibly down that road.

Two elements inform Bush's convictions—he is both a born-again Christian and a Texan. Based on this dual identity and the approaching end of his presidency, it is not all that outlandish to visualize Bush putting

Secretary of State Condoleezza Rice on notice that the diplomatic latitude she asked of him had proved a flagrant failure. High grades from the Council on Foreign Relations fail to win encomiums from this Beltway-wary Texan.

From his Christian faith, Bush draws the conviction that while freedom represents God's gift to humanity, cruel and evil tyrants are capable of building hells that raze civilizations. As a (swashbuckling) Texan, he sees it as his responsibility to protect the good guys from the local bullies. On both counts, Ahmadinejad must be stopped.

Though bombing Iran may seem remote (former UN ambassador John Bolton has described the prospect as nearly zero), some of Bush's key foreign policy moves have shown his capacity to act independently of the State Department and foreign policy establishment.

It was Bush, after all, who politely shelved the recommendations of the Baker-Hamilton Commission on Iraq and who went to war in Afghanistan and Iraq, overruling the advice of then-Secretary of State Colin Powell. Likewise, while Yasir Arafat was Bill Clinton's most frequent overnight White House guest, Bush would not even take a phone call from the Palestinian terror chieftain, again overruling Powell. In fact, Bush was so disenchanted with his secretary of state that he didn't bring him back for his second term.

While pinpointing the moment that Bush will give the order to strike is beyond this article's scope, constitutionally he can launch an invasion without going to Congress. A provocation might stem from another Iranian speedboat charge, or an attack on an American facility somewhere, or the use of Iranian-made explosives on the Iraqi battlefield.

Absent such provocations, the president has spent seven years already warning the world about Tehran's terrorism.

During Bush's recent visit to Israel, he gave hints as to how he sees the world and, indirectly, of the attack that may yet come. Why, he asked at Yad Vashem after viewing a 1944 aerial reconnaissance photograph of Auschwitz, did the United States fail to bomb the camps? The question's message was that principled leaders do not countenance the appeasement of evil.

Leaving the museum, the president signed the guestbook "God Bless Israel." This was extraordinary language from a man as laconic as Bush. On foreign trips he does not typically go around penning salutations asking divine oversight for, say, Saudi Arabia or Germany. With that statement, Bush did more than express support for a democratic ally. The most powerful person in the world was asking God to watch over the Jews in the Holy Land. Imagine, then, the revulsion he must feel at Iranian threats to blow this people off the face of the earth.

Finally, in a hardly noted aside during his airport arrival in Israel, Bush revealed the sense of mission he sees in his presidency. Though he had been to Israel once before, he said, he had never expected to return as president.

On the surface, a strange statement, but at the same time one that captured his understanding of the hand of Heaven. To my surprise, confessed this humble Christian, divine destiny brought me to the White House.

And for what purpose?

Based on his earlier statements, to fight terrorism and to preempt terrorism. What nation stands in the forefront of terrorism, and what nation would be its first target once armed with nuclear weapons?

Before this proud Texan and faithful Christian returns to the ranch to clear brush, possibly turning over the presidency to a successor with dubious motives, don't be surprised if he throws all his power behind the honorable course of attacking Iran.

# # #

How about Brownback for Vice President
[*Jewish Press*, April 9, 2008]

Though the ranks of single-issue pro-Israel Jewish voters (they comprise perhaps one-fourth of the Jewish electorate) have contracted as a result of mounting assimilation, those voters have nonetheless learned a lot over the past sixteen years.

Lesson number one: Bill Clinton's Democratic Party, based on Clinton's coddling of Yasir Arafat and his pussyfooting with Islamic terror, is not the comfortable home for pro-Israel Jews it was once thought to be.

Lesson number two: George W. Bush's Republican Party—based on Bush's shunning Arafat and his confronting Islamic terror—provides a more inviting home for advocates of a tight U.S.-Israel relationship.

Admittedly, single-issue Jewish voters are nowhere near being a dominant element in the still overwhelmingly pro-Democrat Jewish community. Yet signs are pointing to those voters favoring John McCain over either Hillary Clinton or Barack Obama in November. The reason? McCain's decades-long support for Israel's security and his tough approach to Islamic terrorism.

Certainly compared to the two remaining Democratic contenders, McCain's positions on the Middle East have not been subject to sudden shifts, as was the case with Hillary Clinton when she set out to run for the U.S. Senate in 2000 and Barack Obama as he revved up his presidential campaign.

McCain can only strengthen his appeal to Jewish voters for whom Israel ranks at the top of any list of concerns by selecting Senator Sam Brownback of Kansas as his vice presidential running mate.

For one thing, McCain's candidacy would be enhanced by Brownback's conservative bona fides and relative youth (the Kansan is 51). For another, the presence of such a strong pro-Israel duo would accelerate the movement into the Republican Party already underway on the part of Israel-oriented Jewish voters.

The appeal to the pro-Israel community of a Brownback vice presidential candidacy occurred to me recently while I sat listening to Brownback's keynote address at the Jerusalem Conference (where he was the only U.S. congressional figure in attendance).

As a political scientist, I had been aware of his Israel advocacy, both from strategic and spiritual standpoints (Brownback is a devout Catholic, having converted from evangelicalism in 2002). Even so, four things stood out in his speech: his opposition to creating a Palestinian state, preferring instead some form of West Bank Arab confederation with Jordan; his opposition to any division of Jerusalem, an argument he made to Prime Minister Olmert; his integrity in refusing to disclose Olmert's response after being badgered to do so from an audience heckler; and his introduction to the crowd of a yarmulke-wearing foreign policy legislative aide, an appointment surely made with no thought of pleasing his handful of Jewish Kansas constituents.

As McCain's running mate, Brownback would bring credentials important to the Republican base such as his staunch pro-life record and the congressional amendment he introduced banning same sex marriage.

And as a member of the Senate Appropriations Committee, he knows economics, an area where McCain needs strengthening. The conservative Club for Growth hailed Brownback's record: "On taxes, Social Security reform, school choice, and tort reform, Senator Brownback has demonstrated an outstanding commitment to fighting for American taxpayers. His record on trade, political speech, and government regulation of business is generally pro-freedom with a few exceptions."

To be sure, Brownback is hardly a "hard core" conservative. He shares McCain's rather liberal leanings on immigration and he supports stem cell research. Though he opposed the Iraq troop surge, a position McCain notably championed, he voted against Democratic propositions for imposing war deadlines.

So far, no obvious favorite has emerged as a potential McCain running mate. South Carolina Governor Mark Sanford and Minnesota Governor Tim Pawlenty are among those who've been mentioned, but they disagree with McCain on immigration and campaign finance reform while lacking Brownback's strongly conservative economic credentials. And Kansas adds a regional balance to the Arizonan's ticket not much different from Minnesota or South Carolina.

Given Brownback's strong intellect, vigor, and exemplary position on Israel, his position on the McCain ticket in November could spell the difference in key Electoral College states such as Florida, California, New Jersey, Ohio and Pennsylvania.

Moreover, the existence of such a ticket, so strongly committed to a secure Israel, might spur many Israel-centered voters who've voted Republican in recent presidential elections but still identify as Democrats to fully align with the GOP by changing their party registration, and perhaps even one day running for public office themselves as Republicans.

13

Political and Communal Personalities and the Jewish Community

Rubin continues to look at contemporary figures and their impact on the Jewish community. In addition to the many articles he wrote about "personalities" during this time period, Rubin's third book was also "personality" focused. *Rudy, Rudy, Rudy: The Real and the Rational*, his book of quotes from NYC Mayor Rudolph Giuliani, was published by Holmes & Meier in October 2000.

Clinton's Example
[*Jewish Week*, November 1998]

So we should overlook President Clinton's staggering illegal and immoral acts because his administration is good for the Jews. This is the thrust of Rabbi Irving Greenberg's argument ("Public successes outweigh private failures," Oct. 9).

But is Clinton good for the Jews? Oslo flounders, Pollard rots in jail, Hillary endorses a Palestinian state and Saddam thumbs his nose. More broadly, are Jews immune from moral erosion when the president lies while swearing under oath to God, when he lies to everyone in sight about his liaisons, when he tampers with witnesses?

Some corrections to Rabbi Greenberg's points: Clinton never yet "apologized' for his perjury. The apology was only for the "inappropriate relationship" with Monica. King David, unlike Clinton, never lied about his sexual misconduct, was not a career adulterer, not a self-styled victim.

Ironically, on the same page as Rabbi Greenberg's piece, an ad appears for a woman's class on the Laws of Niddah. The theme of these laws is the holiness of marriage and the sex act. In an open society, aren't those of us with a Torah perspective trying to observe such a holy lifestyle inevitably sullied by the presence of a pervert in the White House?

# # #

Prince of Ethnicity

[*Forward*, October 1999]

[Editor's Note: This article was published before health reasons prompted Giuliani to withdraw from the Senate race.]

Despite Hillary Rodham Clinton's Democratic label and New York's Democratic reputation and despite the celebrity hype she can enjoy as she moves closer to announcing her candidacy, Rudolph Giuliani will nonetheless wind up persuading more New Yorkers that it is he who merits becoming the next junior senator from the Empire State. Decisive to the mayor's victory will be the Jewish vote.

It's a question of mathematics. Mr. Giuliani will hold Mrs. Clinton to a maximum of 50% of Jewish votes, and that will mean the election for him. Indeed, Mrs. Clinton's staff seems to recognize the importance of the Jewish constituency, as evidenced by her statements about Jerusalem, her efforts to have the Federal Bureau of Investigation reopen the case of the chasidic youth shot on the Brooklyn Bridge in 1994, Ari Halberstam, and her plans to visit Israel this fall.

The fact is that no Democrat in recent elections has gone to the U.S. Senate from New York without running well ahead among Jews, who account for some 10% to 15% of the electorate. Senator Schumer held Senator D'Amato to less than a quarter of votes by New York's Jews. Jewish ballots will prove particularly important next year based on the expected loyalties of other blocs.

Mr. Giuliani is ahead among middle-American white ethnics in the suburbs and upstate not only because New Yorkers see him as the true "first fan" of the New York Yankees, but because of his record in taming the untamable city. In black, Hispanic and other minority communities, the first lady holds the lead, but we are not talking here about a monolithic vote. In his most recent mayoral campaign, Mr. Giuliani won 40% of the Hispanic vote, and he is still fairly popular in that community. The wishy-washy way that the Clintons handled the FALN clemency issue did not win over to Mrs. Clinton's side a significant number of Hispanic voters.

The mayor also pulled 20% of the black vote in 1997, a major increase over the 5% he drew in 1993 in defeating Mayor Dinkins. In both these minority constituencies, Mr. Giuliani will be sure to play up the themes of New York City's transition—the drop in crime, job growth, fiscal restraint and the virtual passage into oblivion of the squeegee men.

Thus, the arithmetic of the contest dictates that Mrs. Clinton must run superbly in the minority communities, hold Mr. Giuliani to a small lead among white non-Jewish voters and capture something like two-thirds of the Jewish vote. Yet harvesting such results among Jews will prove tough for the first lady. Jewish voters in New York today are far less embedded in Democratic Party liberalism than they were a generation ago when Commentary's Milton Himmelfarb quipped that Jews are the only group on the American political landscape having the socio-economic status of Episcopalians and the voting profile of Puerto Ricans.

True, indigenous liberalism remains—support for abortion rights and more government aid for schools and medical costs. But this liberalism is basically background music. More pressing for Jews today is the feeling of being beleaguered by terrorists, whether Muslim "youth marchers," Arab nationalists or white supremacists. Jews also worry about the nation's moral decadence.

New York's Jews have shown that it is not *treyf [i.e., it is kosher!]* to vote for Republicans. This switch began in 1980 when Ronald Reagan captured 40% of the Jewish vote and climaxed in 1997 with Mr. Giuliani winning 75%. In between, Mr. D'Amato pulled some one-third of that vote in his best Senate election campaigns.

In point of fact, there is not one "Jewish vote" in New York state, but three. In one bloc, Mrs. Clinton faces big *tsores [aggravation]*, in the second she will find *simcha [joy]*, but in the third and pivotal group, Mr. Giuliani is blessed with greater *mazel ["luck"]*.

Among the first constituency, call it the Orthodox-ethnic, the mayor has built up so much capital that God himself might not be able to vanquish him. These traditionally inclined voters support the mayor's no-nonsense commitment to civic standards. The mayor's record of throwing Yasser Arafat out of Lincoln Center, apologizing to the Jews of Crown Heights for the "pogrom" that took place there during the Dinkins administration, supporting government money for parochial schools, threatening the funding of the Brooklyn Museum of Art for displaying trashy, blasphemous "art," taking trips to Israel in the wake of terrorist bombings, directly attacking anti-Semitic demagogues—that is a record Mrs. Clinton can't beat among this bloc. Whatever fallout Mr. Giuliani experienced from the shooting by cops of the mentally ill Jewish man in Boro Park, Gary Busch, it will not last long, given the mayor's strong anti-crime suit.

The second Jewish bloc is Mrs. Clinton's. These are the secular, advocacy-oriented (police brutality), politically correct liberal Jews. More concerned about universalistic, "progressive" causes, these voters will find nothing disingenuous about the sudden disclosures of Mrs. Clinton's Jewish step-grandfather or nothing contradictory about her support for a Palestinian state and her commitment to the indivisibility of Jerusalem as the "eternal" capital of Israel.

These two groups each account for about 20% of the Jewish electorate, thus canceling each other out. The remaining 60% of the Jewish vote constitutes the third group. It is among these voters that the fiercest battle for Jewish support will be fought.

On the surface, most voters in this bloc might be seen as more apt to vote for a Democrat than a Republican. Someone like Mr. Schumer illustrates the political persona of candidates favored by these moderately liberal Jewish voters. Mrs. Clinton's main plus with this constituency are the strides she has made for women's activism in the public policy arena.

Yet Mrs. Clinton should lower her sights with this group. At a minimum these voters hold a grudging respect for Mr. Giuliani's record in improving the civic culture of Gotham. Less victimized by crime, more upbeat about the city's spirit, they are willing to concede to the mayor his contentious, stubborn demeanor.

Moreover, Mrs. Clinton will be unable to castigate Mr. Giuliani as a right-winger, her epithet for those who pursued the story about President Clinton's relationship with Monica Lewinsky. These highly informed Jewish voters will not be taken in by such flippant labeling; they know about the mayor's support for gay rights, gun control, abortion rights and rights for illegal aliens.

The first lady will also have to figure out how to handle the Jonathan Pollard hot potato, the case of the Jewish intelligence officer serving a life sentence for spying for Israel. Jewish pressure on the president will continue to mount to pardon Pollard following the release of the FALN terrorists. But Mr. Clinton's political capital in the pardoning arena is sharply limited given the opportunistic motives ascribed by the public to his freeing of the FALN convicts. If the Clintons try to take both sides of a Pollard pardon, as they did with the FALN, the first lady will be subject to "character" accusations again.

To win two-thirds of the overall Jewish vote, Mrs. Clinton would need 47 points of the 60 available from this third group; those points could be added to the 20 she'll get from the other group. But 47 out of 60 is more than 75%. Given the records of the two candidates and the sympathies of this middle group, Mrs. Clinton stands little chance of seeing that kind of support (she'll more likely wind up with no more than 30 of the 60 points) and so is destined to do worse than she needs to among Jews to pull out a victory.

In a nutshell, that is why the next senator from New York will be Rudolph Giuliani.

###

Olmert's Liberal Mindset to Blame for Lebanon Fiasco
[*Jewish Press*, August 2006]

Clichéd postmortems analyzing Israel's failure to deal Hizbullah a clear defeat miss the point in blaming Prime Minister Olmert's lack of military experience or native ineptness. The key reasons for Israel's poor performance are deeper and far more ideological.

True, Olmert lacked the military background of certain of his predecessors. But defending a country is more an issue of strategic judgment than a question of whether or for how long a person wore fatigues. Ronald Reagan, who never saw battle, defeated the Soviet Union in the Cold War. Moreover, Olmert, a calculating man, is hardly inept or disorganized.

Rather, Israel lost—or at least did not win—the war because the core liberal-secular beliefs of its leaders made them too militarily cautious in confronting the cult of death represented by Hizbullah. Morale, more so than Merkava tanks, determines which side better understands the end game of war and accordingly musters the nerve to make the necessary sacrifices. In other words, modern guerrilla warfare is as much about ideology as F-16s, which is why Hizbullah fanaticism triumphed over Olmert's secular mindset.

Like all thinking people, Olmert is driven by basic political and social values. While believing himself strongly committed to the security of Israel, he is also very much a product of contemporary Western culture—its notion of acceptable nationalism, its emphasis on diplomatic rather than military solutions, its distaste for military violence.

Since Olmert is not an observant Jew, his understanding of political right and wrong in a global culture is similar to that of respectable secular-minded American Jewish liberals. One group speaks and thinks in Hebrew, the other in English—but both operate under the same assumptions and reach the same conclusions in the articles penned by their academics and the reporting and editorializing in their elite newspapers and opinion journals.

(In my despair during the fighting, I amused myself by substituting Olmert with certain American Jewish liberals whose reputations are marked by a reluctance to take the battle too forcefully to the enemy, i.e., Michigan Senator Carl Levin and Clinton National Security Adviser Sandy Berger.)

"White guilt in the West," writes historian Shelby Steele (*Wall Street Journal*, August 22, 2006), prevents the Left from facing up to Islamic extremism. "The West is so terrified of being charged with its old sins of racism, imperialism, and colonialism that it makes oppression an automatic prism on the non-Western world . . ."

How much was this endemic sense of liberal guilt responsible for Olmert's failure to use the full force of the Israeli military? What was the relationship between his advocacy of convergence (withdrawal from parts of the West Bank from which future rocketing of Israel could take place in exchange for nothing from the other side) *while battles were still underway*, and his complacent use of infantry on the ground? Did he feel some doubt about the rightness of annihilating the invaders for fear of being called an oppressor?

Olmert's ideologically liberal mindset provides a context for understanding Israel's inability to defeat an extremist enemy with a take-no-prisoners mentality. Throughout the fighting, Olmert's message cast doubt on the legitimacy of Israel's cause. Given Hizbullah's apocalyptic commitment to the mass murder of the infidel Jews, Olmert's deliberately limited response (reminiscent of Lyndon Johnson's defeatist "limited war" strategy in Vietnam), the case could be made that he was worn down at some level by trendy liberal support for "oppressed" peoples.

A militarily committed prime minister would never have handed over the Ministry of Defense to a union boss holding Peace Now credentials. In response to Hizbullah's act of war, Olmert's original puny goal was to secure four villages and a strip of territory six miles wide and 2.5 miles along the border. Instead of threatening Hizbullah's Syrian arms supplier, Israel repeatedly made clear that it would not attack Damascus. The decision to call up reserves came only after public pressure.

Even so, Olmert's deputy prime minister, the tiresome Shimon Peres, voted against the plan to move thousands of troops into Lebanon, arguing that Israel should rely on diplomacy, the liberals' favorite tack for dealing with military violence. Not to be outdone, Olmert also showed his penchant for diplomacy over military force when, after a public outcry, Israel finally called up some 30,000 troops.

While everyone knew the clock was about to run out, Olmert ordered the soldiers to hang around for three days instead of hunting down Hizbullah fighters.

The most revealing example of Olmert's lack of moral clarity was his response to criticism of the accidental bombing in Kana. An embarrassed Israel announced a two-day bombing suspension. If Olmert believed

Israel's cause was just, why did he cede the moral high ground because of an unfortunate accident?

In the end, Olmert confirmed his servitude to the liberal mindset by assigning the fate of the two kidnapped Israeli soldiers—whose plight triggered the war—to some hoped-for diplomacy down the road. Sadly, this hapless concession illustrated, more than any other of his numerous mistakes during the war, the degree to which Olmert relies on ideological dreams at the expense of real power.

14

Jewish Personalities

Joe Lieberman

Political Orthodoxy
[*Wall Street Journal*, Letter to the Editor, August 16, 2000]

Michael Medved wants it both ways when he attacks Sen. Joseph Lieberman's politics as well as the teachings of Orthodox Judaism. He takes issue with Sen. Lieberman's attitudes toward abortion and homosexuality. Then, he arrogates to himself Rabbinic authority criticizing the Orthodox positions on intermarriage and feminism.

Mr. Medved compares Orthodox teachings on those issues to the ban on interracial dating at Bob Jones University. Orthodoxy has no such interracial social bans. Moses's wife was black, and in modern day Israel it is not uncommon to see marriages between recently arrived black Ethiopian Jews and white Israelis.

Orthodoxy simply holds different prayer requirements for men and women. Since women are seen as the main child caregivers, they are not required to pray communally as are men. Yet they are encouraged to pray at home. At synagogue, the sexes are separated not because of alleged superiority or inferiority. Prayer is a sensitive, personal experience. Mingling of the sexes is seen as distracting experience, given our human, physical drives.

Mr. Medved may have been a synagogue president for fifteen years, but my guess is that he was often dozing off during the rabbi's sermons.

###

Getting to 'President Joe'
[*Forward*, "ForwardForum" column, August 3, 2001]

If Senator Joseph Lieberman of Connecticut does indeed make a run for president in 2004, several current political trends may help him become the first Jewish resident of the White House.

Mr. Lieberman's ascent to the vice presidential nomination last year was predicated on his being his party's most formidable critic of President Clinton. Mr. Lieberman's Senate speech berating the president's dalliances was the cover Al Gore needed to protect him from George W. Bush's expected moralistic onslaught.

During the 2000 presidential campaign, Americans got to know that the measured Connecticut senator was an observant Orthodox Jew and, in retrospect, this identity did not hurt the Democratic ticket. True, Mr. Lieberman's disheartened moderate supporters remember how quickly he shed centrist positions on affirmative action, school vouchers and Hollywood filth. Jews also were antagonized by his kind words for the Reverend Louis Farrakhan and his interpretation of Judaism as not opposing interfaith marriage.

Now, as Mr. Lieberman campaigns for the presidency, ironically enough he must thank George W. Bush for defining the issue that could serve to vault him ahead of his competitors for the 2004 Democratic nomination. When the president added faith-based charities to his agenda, he afforded Mr. Lieberman the chance of turning what would normally be a liability (his Jewish Orthodoxy) into a positive.

No Democrat has better credentials from which to press this issue. Although secular Democratic Party stalwarts may rail against government aid for faith-based charities, Americans mostly favor this innovation. Such attention to faith figures in Mr. Lieberman's campaign to reorient his party: "We have too often dismissed and disparaged the importance of faith in American life and made the faithful feel unwelcome in our party, particularly if they are open and outspoken about their religion," he has said.

These "wise words," as *The Wall Street Journal* termed them, position Mr. Lieberman within the American mainstream. But will they help him gain the Democratic nomination? Although the Connecticut Senator is clearly positioning himself as a candidate, judging by the evidence of his sundry travels and fundraising, there remains his pledge not to run should Mr. Gore seek another shot.

Other than the chance of the former vice president losing stomach for another go, Mr. Lieberman's prospects depend on whether the barracudas of his party—especially its money people—are willing to sit down with Mr. Gore for a talk.

If the message Mr. Gore takes away from such a meeting is praise for his place in history, what do the polls show about other would-be nominees? Senator Hillary Rodham Clinton of New York ranks as a second choice, but most handicappers advise her to continue shedding baggage in preparation for a try in 2008.

Which leaves Mr. Lieberman as the next favorite. Strategically, his candidacy would build on the Democratic Party's blue-collar base while sending the message that he is not part of its elitist, effete liberal hierarchy. Adding to the prominence he has gained from faith-based issues, Mr. Lieberman stands to gain visibility from his new post as head of the Senate's Committee on Government Administration. Given his proclivity for seizing on issues, the Connecticut senator will not pass up chances to badger the White House from his new bully pulpit.

The field of his likely opponents pales by comparison. Senator Tom Daschle of South Dakota and Rep. Richard Gephardt of Missouri are busy either retaining or seeking power for themselves in Congress. Senator John Kerry of Massachusetts exudes an aristocratic air that conjures images of the Democratic limousine-liberal. North Carolina's Senator John Edwards, a neophyte compared to Mr. Lieberman, seems too Southern at a time when the country wants to put Clintonism to rest.

The political primary schedule also favors Mr. Lieberman's candidacy. New Hampshire voters might be partial to a fellow New Englander. In the prized early Southern primaries, Mr. Lieberman might gain sway for his tradition-based persona from Southern Baptists who are committed to family values. A likely victory in New York's April primary would add to his credentials.

If Mr. Lieberman is the Democratic standard bearer, count on him to replay the script he used in winning election to the Senate over incumbent

Senator Lowell Weicker in 1988. In that contest, Mr. Weicker did not know what hit him as Mr. Lieberman attacked simultaneously from the right and the left. If national morals continue to falter, Mr. Lieberman's faith orientation positions him for an assault on the right. A slowing economy, too much environmental deregulation or an accelerating energy crisis might leave Mr. Bush vulnerable on the left.

Electoral College arithmetic also may work to Mr. Lieberman's advantage. There is scant likelihood of defections by New York, California or the big Midwestern industrial states that Mr. Gore won in 2000. Finally, the choice of Mr. Edwards as running mate holds the possibility of adding a few Southern states, including Florida, to the Democratic column. Since Mr. Gore's Electoral vote in the South was zero, such a showing would mean the election.

# # #

Joe Lieberman's Jewish Inreach
[*Jewish Press*, March 24, 2004]

As a Jew and a political scientist, what intrigued me about the ill-fated presidential run of Senator Joseph Lieberman was not the question of whether he would make it to the White House, but rather how his candidacy forced American Jews to face their spiritual selves.

Based on a steady media focus, Jews and political junkies of all persuasions were reminded about a couple of the more colorful aspects of this otherwise dull Democratic presidential campaign—Joe Lieberman's Sabbath observance and kosher eating.

The anomaly of this Orthodox Jew's presidential quest was no less striking than the conflicted social landscape of American Jewry which spawned him. Given this country's openness and meritocracy, Jews have risen to heights and felt a sense of cultural belonging unprecedented in their history. But precisely because of such comfort levels, Jews who sensed no need to hold on to Joe Lieberman's Judaism were intermarrying and assimilating at record rates. As a result, the American Jewish population was no longer growing and probably in a state of decline.

In what spirit did America's Jews relate to Mr. Lieberman's devotion to Orthodoxy—a devotion, according to various studies, shared by no more than ten percent of his co-religionists? (To make his religious observance seem less forbidding, the Connecticut senator labeled himself "observant" rather than Orthodox.)

Much inner searching about values is underway in our nation, as highlighted by the moral dimension in the debate over going to war with Saddam and the subsequent military occupation. Thoughtful but disillusioned Jews were looking for refreshing alternatives to an admittedly cynical and materialistic culture. In that context, does it take much imagination to guess that Senator Lieberman's piety confronted other Jews, at least on some level, with challenges, curiosity and, perhaps, doubts about their basic life choices?

The Jew most removed from Senator Lieberman's devoutness was the secular, acculturated type, proudly non-observant and most likely intermarried, who perceived a disconnect between his pursuit of the American Dream and a commitment to the traditions and suffering of the Chosen People. Joe Lieberman's refusal to turn on a light on Saturday? A clear throwback to the superstitions of this man's black-hatted European grandfather.

Yet given the media play about Mr. Lieberman's Orthodoxy, is it far-fetched to imagine this non-practicing Jew's Christian wife admiringly making mention over dinner one night of the senator's independence of mind and courageous sense of spirituality? Or his teenage child asking innocently about kosher food laws? After all, someone as cultivated and as respected as Joe Lieberman cannot be dismissed as some sort of fanatic or relic of antiquity.

The Jew committed to moderate religious observance was the one most likely to have been impacted by the senator's candidacy. Though this Democratic politician did not double as a religious outreach professional, his example was certain to have motivated the middling Jew to more serious commitment. This type of Jew, already believing in his faith's main tenets, will study more, observe more and affiliate with his people more based on Joe Lieberman's positive role model.

Ironically, the constituency on which Mr. Lieberman held the least sway was his fellow Orthodox Jews. While at first proud of the senator's vice presidential nomination in 2000, many held him to high religious standards as that campaign wore on—so much so that a spokesman for Agudath Israel reminded Jews that Joe Lieberman was running for vice president, nor chief rabbi.

Whether or not Joe Lieberman's Orthodoxy would have translated into Jewish votes this year is another topic. Some Jews worried about the dangers of a Jew in the White House. Others agree with Ariel Sharon that no American president has been a greater friend of Israel than George W. Bush.

For me, the main story about Joe Lieberman's historic candidacy had nothing to do with whether he got nominated or elected. By forcing Jews of all persuasions (true bipartisanship) to come to terms with their spirituality, he fulfilled his assignment in this world. In the race of life, Joe Lieberman won the vote of the true Commander in Chief.

# # #

Why Lieberman Will Lose
[*Jewish Press*, August 2, 2006]

I hate making this call about my Orthodox Jewish brother Joe Lieberman, but he almost certainly will lose next week's Connecticut Democratic Senate primary. He will be defeated, as predicted by the polls and pundits, primarily because of his support for the Iraq war and his refusal to join in the demonization of George W. Bush.

Lieberman will also go down because he is a man of faith, an Orthodox Jew, a believer in an overarching religious authority. His strong religious convictions (from which stem his commitment to the human rights of Iraqis) put him at a clear distance from an increasingly secularized Democratic Party activist base. And he may not be the only Democratic politician to suffer from being on the wrong political side in this cultural divide.

Democratic Illinois Senator Barack Obama recently warned of the peril awaiting a political party tagged with such a religiously indifferent identity. A study comparing church attendance of both Republican and Democratic delegates to the 2004 presidential nominating conventions showed that the GOP scored much higher in the worship criterion.

While Lieberman has compiled a reliably liberal voting record in his eighteen-year Senate career, there are enough Connecticut Democrats who will go to the polls on August 8 in order to self-righteously congratulate themselves for voting to remove this decent man.

While Lieberman is far from preachy about his Orthodoxy, it's not a secret that he prays and studies Torah on a daily basis, and that he refuses to engage in any politicking or traveling on the Sabbath. Such values establish him as a fundamentalist outsider to an increasingly relativistic "do your own thing" Democratic electorate. While his stand on Iraq serves as the foremost reason for liberal activists to oppose him on primary day, Lieberman's religious commitment has never endeared him to Democratic Party secularists.

To be sure, national security was Lieberman's main motive for originally concluding that Saddam had to go and national security is why he refuses to get behind his opponent's arbitrary deadline for withdrawing American troops. But Lieberman's support for the war is also attributable to his religious conviction that the biblical ideals of freedom and equality belong to all God's creatures, not just Yale professors and yuppie Westporters.

As a man of religious faith, Lieberman believes in man's responsibility to make the world God created a better place by helping to spread the gift of liberty, however imperfectly the results may first appear.

Ironically, a case can be made that the infamous kiss the president bestowed on Lieberman on the floor of the House of Representatives was more a reflection of the kinship they share as men of faith than a token of affectionate gratitude for Lieberman's carrying the ball against the antiwar Left. Bush and Lieberman are both sustained by the belief that despite the attacks of the elite media, their ultimate accountability as to how they used this nation's power will be to their Creator.

Politically, it would have been far less costly for Lieberman to join the guilt-ridden "illegitimacy of military power" wing of his party. But to overlook the brutality of hate-filled fanatics would be to betray his bedrock religious principles and expose this country and the Middle East to an even more likely terrorist threat.

The conclusion to be drawn from Lieberman's pending defeat is that his party's self-styled "progressive" human-rights base is ideologically bankrupt when it comes to fighting the most bigoted enemy of our time.

15

Jewish Personalities

Fred Lebow, Holocaust Survivor and Creator of the New York City Marathon

During the 1990s, Rubin focused most of his writing energies on his biographies of Fred Lebow and Rudolph Giuliani. *Anything for a T-Shirt: Fred Lebow and the New York City Marathon* was published by Syracuse University Press in November 2004 and was cited by *Runners World* as one of the top 10 running books of that year.

Letter from the New York Marathon: Homage to an Unlikely Impresario [*Forward*, October 1999]

When the New York City Marathon marks its 30th run on Sunday, November 7, the vision of its founder, the charming showman Fred Lebow, will shine once again as urban theater in sneakers. In going the distance—26.2 miles through the city's five boroughs—the 30,000 runners and plodders will give the Big Apple one of its most exciting, inspiring and unifying days of the year. Among the 2 million spectators who energize the marathoners with their cheers, some will ask themselves whether they have the fortitude to go the distance. That such fantasies stir within the everyday men and women who line the route, as well as those who cross the Central Park finish line, is the best proof that Lebow's vision of a people's race lives on.

Before Lebow, who died five years ago at the age of 62, the marathon was an obscure, sweaty enterprise focused on elite runners. Lebow's approach consisted of hyping the race as a party so that the ordinary plodder would not be discouraged by the fearsome prospect of such a feat. Bands, banners, T-shirts, medals for all finishers and a rose to every woman, a pre-race carbo-loading party at Tavern on the Green, a post-race dance—these were part of Lebow's shtick, designed to enhance his street theater and broaden the appeal of the event. A 100-person team of mental-health professionals was even put into action at the race's Staten Island start to counsel jittery runners.

In the process of creating the modern marathon, Lebow may have been relying on his own Jewish sensibility and exposure to Jewish culture. Indeed, this is what the research I've done for a biography on Lebow suggests. While he could fairly be considered the impresario of the running world, he could as easily be seen merely as a deeply Jewish Holocaust survivor out to make it in America.

Growing up as Fishl Lebowitz in Arad, Romania, he and his immediate family of Orthodox Jews somehow survived the war. After vagabonding around Europe, he arrived in America in 1951, enrolling at Brooklyn's Yeshiva Torah Vodaath. Finding the environment too confining, he moved to the Midwest and worked as a television salesman and later as an owner of a small improvisational nightclub. By 1962, when he returned to New York to work as a garment center knitter, he had long since shed the Orthodoxy of his youth.

Originally, he took up running, Lebow joked, to improve his tennis game. Along with the rest of America, he had joined the fitness movement of the late 1960s. But the leaders of the New York running scene hardly shared Lebow's emerging populist strategy. Marathoning, to be sure, was only for the most dedicated runners.

Beginning in 1970, Lebow—together with Vince Chiapetta—directed the New York City Marathon in Central Park, where it remained for the next five years. Participants, who at the time numbered only in the hundreds, were considered a strange breed. Lebow's breakthrough came with the 1976 Bicentennial, when a five-borough marathon was staged for the first time.

Among the ethnic communities that—somewhat unwittingly, perhaps—would host and help showcase the new marathon were the chasidim, centered on a stretch along Bedford Avenue in Williamsburg, the race's

10-mile point. For Lebow, leading the race as he did each year in his pace car, the passage through this area was a Journey back in time. "*Lommen herren*"—"Let's hear it!" roared Lebow in Yiddish from his bullhorn, encouraging the chasidim to cheer the oncoming pack.

On the hot 1984 Marathon Sunday, Lebow was worried about dehydration of the runners. As he rode through Williamsburg, he shouted to a handful of chasidic roadside spectators, "*Die loyfer darfen vasser!*"—"The runners need water!" The chasidim returned with seltzer.

Yet Williamsburg must have underscored the pain that this cosmopolitan bachelor in some sense felt in having distanced himself from the insular life-style of his family and his past. According to *New York Times* reporter George Vecsey, "it took me years to even sense Fred was spooked by the impassive stares of the chasids, almost as if they were judging him."

In interactions with his staff, signs of the nation's most visible race director's Jewishness appeared, and not only in his frequent use of Yiddishisms. In conversations with his technical director and successor, Allan Steinfeld, Lebow would use Jewish expressions freely. A public relations associate, Laura Leale, said she learned terms such as *meshugene* (crazy), *treyf* (nonkosher) and shiksa (non-Jewish woman), from Lebow.

Publicly, Lebow claimed he was a vegetarian, but he kept kosher following his own personal formulation. According to Mr. Steinfeld, "Whenever we would go anywhere, he would always order a vegetarian plate. Actually, he kept kosher."

In a telling answer to the question of who would be running among his 18,000 marathoners in 1984, Lebow cited "Roc Dixon, Grete Waitz and Charlie Rosenthal from Brooklyn." Why link this obscure Charlie Rosenthal with these two marathon stars? Lebow was underscoring the everyman nature of his race; but significantly he chose an overtly Jewish name to make the point.

In a vivid example of Lebow's desire to add new shtick to his race, he once offered $1,000 to any chasid running in earlocks and extended religious fringes who completed the race. No takers appeared.

As the only marathon in the world with a Jewish prayer service, the New York City Marathon was unique. The sight of some 100 runners standing in shorts, warm-up outfits, prayer shawls and tefillin invariably drew crowds. Each year, Lebow congratulated the runners who were praying in a tent prominently located in the race's staging area. During the service, marathoners developed the tradition of shouting aloud the blessing that thanks God for "giving strength to the weary."

Himself a marathoner as well as race director, Lebow competed in 69 marathons in more than 30 countries. His most serious nod to his Jewish roots may have been his thinking during 1983 Berlin Marathon. Here, the locale's associations with the Holocaust apparently spurred him on to show his hosts his running prowess: "The start was on the actual lawn of the historic Reichstag building, rebuilt after the war," Lebow said. "I thought, 'This country is responsible for the Holocaust, [which] screwed up my childhood and family life. I'm running on their turf—I'm going to show them.' When at last I saw the finish banner and clock right in the middle of Berlin, I saw I had a chance to break 3:40. I began a long sprint, driving myself. I finished in 3:39:02, my best time in more than 10 years. And then I threw up."

After he was stricken with brain cancer in 1990, Lebow became more reflective. In this reassessment of his life, family and a return to the religion of his youth emerged as priorities.

Two hours before the start of that year's marathon—the event Lebow had fine-tuned for an entire year—the race director quietly entered the tent at the Fort Wadsworth staging area where the marathon minyan prayer service was underway. "Fred was so thin that when I put my arm around him, I could feel he hardly filled out his running suit," said Rabbi Jim Michaels, who was also planning to run that day. After Lebow prayed with the minyan for a few minutes, Rabbi Michaels interrupted the service, reciting the Hebrew prayer for the ill. Spontaneously, the marathoners broke into Hebrew songs asking God's blessings for the people of Israel. "There were tears in everyone's eyes," recalled Peter Berkowsky, cofounder of the Marathon Minyan.

Although Lebow's new outlook did not mean a return to Orthodoxy, he went to temple, read about Jewish topics and became involved with cancer victims, both Jews and non-Jews. Beginning in 1992, he attended luncheons of the Israel Cancer Research Fund and was the organization's honoree in 1993. He attended the affair dressed in tuxedo, sneakers and signature running cap.

This writer, who sweated his way to six marathon finish lines, illustrates the type of person who responded to Lebow's challenge. A few years back, the prospect of my completing a marathon was no less outlandish than swimming across the Atlantic. I was one of those joggers in shorts emblematic of Lebow's pop-culture revolution.

Little by little, my recreational running gave way to more ambitious schemes. Remember, we're not talking about great athletic style here, just plodding along mile after mile at one's own pace. Lebow realized that it was more than an athletic goal that motivated his marathoners. He once remarked that for his 23,000 finishers, there were 23,000 different reasons why they ran.

At the start of one marathon I ran, the mood at the Staten Island staging area was festive. Crossing the two-mile-long Verrazano-Narrows Bridge and glancing at my fellow marathoners, most of whom looked far more fit than me, I wondered what chutzpah brought me to that assemblage.

When I passed the chasidic stretch of the race, I tried to establish some identity with the onlookers. "*Shalom al Yisroel!*" I shouted, "Peace on Israel!" Mostly, I was ignored, but one chasid did respond: "*For vus loifst du vi* a *meshugener?*"—"Why are you running like a *meshugener?*" Maybe it was a good question.

With a few different turns in his life, the spectators in Williamsburg might have included a Fishl Lebowitz. Lebowitz's beard would be fuller, a long black coat would have replaced the warm-up outfit and a black hat would have taken the place of his John Hancock bicycle cap. But if Lebow had not taken the route he did, relying on his Jewish sensibilities to create this "people's race," I might not have the pride I now have for having run "like a *meshugener*" through the streets of the Big Apple.

# # #

A Marathon Man's Answer to the Nazi
[*New York Post*, Nov 03, 99]

How would Fred Lebow, the late founder of the New York City Marathon, have handled the prospect of Joerg Haider, the Austrian neo-Nazi parliamentarian, running in Sunday's race?

Some Jews urged the marathon either to disqualify Haider or to reroute the race to avoid passing the Hasidic community's turf along Brooklyn's Bedford Avenue, where many Holocaust survivors and their families reside. I'm convinced that, though Lebow (a Holocaust survivor himself) would have detested Haider's views, he'd also have refused both options.

Politicizing the marathon was precisely the opposite of his inclusive vision. Lebow not only tried to enlist the ordinary plodder as well as the elite athlete in the spectacle he created, he also sought as international a field as possible. He even went behind the Iron Curtain at the height of the Cold War to recruit Soviet and Polish athletes for his race.

And this publicity-minded race director would have quickly sensed the promotional value of the Haider affair. Controversy held benefits, felt Lebow, because it generated more interest in the marathon, thereby drawing more people to think of the running lifestyle. Spurring the uninitiated to take up running was the mission of Lebow's life.

But in addition to being a showman, Lebow was a Jewish survivalist. He confronted anti-Semitism not by tuning it out but by proving himself, by undermining his detractors. He ran the Berlin Marathon in 1983 despite the city's painful associations with the Holocaust. "I'm running on their turf—I'm going to show them," was the way Lebow defined his challenge. (After finishing the race in his best time in more than 10 years, he threw up.)

How best to demonstrate the failure of Haider's neo-Nazis? By affirming life and the ability to rise again. Defying Nazi bestiality, Williamsburg boasts a living, thriving—if colorful—Jewish community. Let the Hasidim turn out en masse for the marathon, showcasing their large families—the best sign that they have triumphed over the Holocaust. Let Jewish pride assert itself.

At the same time, the media-savvy Lebow would [have] urged the Hasidim to display placards denouncing Haider so as to influence whatever remains of decent public opinion in Austria.

The marathon's trip through Williamsburg held a special meaning for Lebow. It was a reminder of the destroyed world of his Holocaust childhood. But for 30,000 runners from 100 nations who trailed behind his pace car, this little, otherworldly enclave provided an exposure to his own resilient people, as well as the Big Apple's ethnic richness.

The Hasidim's proud message to Haider and other Jew-haters is no different than what they are telling other marathoners: Le Chaim—To Life.

# # #

Fishl's Marathon
[*Jewish Press*, November 3, 2004]

When 35,000 marathoners spring across the Verrazano-Narrows Bridge this Sunday, November 7, at the thirty-fifth running of the New York City Marathon, they will be reenacting the dream of Fred Lebow, the heavily-accented Transylvanian who convinced the plodders and shleppers of the world that they could go the course's 26.2 mile distance.

Before Lebow—born Fishl Lebowitz in 1932—came on the scene, marathoning was limited to only the most skilled athletes. Now, as a result of Lebow's vision, some 500,000 Americans annually ignore their strained Achilles tendons and sore knees in what has been transformed from an austere race into a form of street theater.

But in addition to creating the fun festival that the modern marathon has become, Lebow, whose tenth yahrzeit [anniversary of his death] is observed this year, at bottom was always aware of who and what he was: a Jew.

He arrived in the United States after surviving the Holocaust as a boy and gravitated to New York's garment industry where his entrepreneurial nature took him from an entry level position on the knitting machines to owner of his own knockoff design company. He was introduced to running as a way of improving his tennis game. Although he was never good at it—he came in next to last in the first marathon he ran—running gave him a feeling he wanted the world to share.

Having suffered through the horrors of religious persecution and separatism, he was intent on making marathoning, which had theretofore been an exclusive sport, an inclusive activity—a people's race. His marathon included everyone: world-famous record-setting elite runners, everyday middle and back-of-the-pack shleppers like himself, valiant members of the Achilles Track Club for disabled athletes, and people such as the Vietnam veteran with no legs who took four days to finish the race "running" on his hands.

While Lebow promoted this populist vision, his shtetl background, his Yiddish, and the religious observance of his youth (which his siblings had not abandoned as he had) were always part of him. He participated in a special Passover seder for New York Road Runners Club staff and friends, and lit Chanukah candles with them in his office. He usually spent the High Holidays with his Orthodox family, mostly with his sister in Monsey, New York.

Lebow felt a special connection with the part of his marathon's route that took him and the runners through the chassidic area of Williamsburg in Brooklyn. He would shout in Yiddish to chassidic spectators, "lommen heren (let's hear it)" and "die laufer darfen vasser (the runners need water)" as he led his pack of runners through their streets. As soon as he recognized the need for a Shacharit [morning] service at the marathon staging area, he set up a tent for what still is the world's only marathon minyan.

In 1992, Lebow, by then a brain cancer patient in recovery, decided to run his marathon creation for the first time in his life to prove to himself and other cancer survivors that he was able win the race within. Before the marathon's start, he slipped away from his handlers and prayed with the minyan, donning tefillin as he asked for strength to cross the finish line.

On April 28, 1994, his cancer worsening, the *New York Daily News* reported that Lebow had "started the process of reverting to his original name." Explaining his move, Lebow said, "I've always observed the Jewish holidays and always been proud of my heritage and it's time I return to my original name."

Fishl Lebow died Sunday, October 9, 1994—the day of his marathon's pre-race tune-up. His tombstone reflects the dichotomy of his identity—the running world impresario and the Jew from pre-war Transylvania. In capital letters on the tombstone's slope it says, "FRED LEBOW" with the inscription "He was humble in his greatness." And chiseled between his dates of birth and death is a big apple with a runner in the middle, the symbol of the New York Road Runners Club.

The Hebrew lettering on the tombstone's face shows that it is indeed Ephraim Fishl Lebowitz buried below. Beneath the Hebrew name are four Hebrew lines, each beginning with a letter from the name Fishl. Translated, the inscription reads: (F) His mouth abounded in truth; (I) He was beloved by all; (SH) His name was universally known: (L) His heart as his name, so he was. Lebow, in Hebrew, means "his heart."

# # #

Fred Lebow and Pol 101
[*Jewish Press*, October 2006]

Thanks to Fred Lebow, founder of the New York City Marathon, some 500,000 Americans will run in marathons this year. In my book *Anything for a T-Shirt: Fred Lebow and the New York City Marathon, the World's Greatest Footrace* (Syracuse University Press, 2004), I show how Lebow, a Holocaust survivor, changed the notion of this 26.2 mile race, which this year will be held on Sunday, Nov. 5, from a grueling, sweaty showcase for elite runners into a people's competition.

Though the book was well received by the running community, I wanted to use it as a learning tool. As a political scientist at an urban community college, I asked some 150 students to analyze how this race director dealt with power—the main conceptual standard in my field—in transforming the marathon race. How did Lebow use power to wrest the keys of the city, to entice race sponsors, to manipulate the media, and to recruit top athletes?

My students—multi-ethnic and heavily foreign born—found Lebow's story appealing. Born Fishl Lebowitz in 1932, he arrived in the United States after surviving the Holocaust as a boy and gravitated to New York's garment industry where his entrepreneurial nature took him from an entry level position on the knitting machines to owner of his own knock-off design company.

He was introduced to running as a way of improving his tennis game. Although he was never good at it—he came in next to last in the first marathon he ran—running gave him a feeling he wanted the world to share.

In addition to creating the fun festival that the modern marathon has become, Lebow, whose twelfth *yahrzeit* will be observed on October 26 (he died of brain cancer on Oct. 9, 1994—4 Cheshvan, 5755) was always intensely aware of who and what he was: a Jew.

He felt a special connection with the part of his marathon's route that took him and the runners through the chassidic area of Williamsburg in Brooklyn. He would shout in Yiddish to chassidic spectators, "*lommen heren* (let's hear it)" and "*die laufer darfen vasser* (the runners need water)" as he led his pack of runners through their streets. As soon as he recognized the need for a *Shacharit* service at the marathon staging area, he set up a tent for a *minyan*. Though none of my assignment questions dealt specifically with the race director's Jewishness—and I doubt there were even five Jews enrolled in my classes—my students were quick to relate to the Jewish themes in Lebow's life.

Some students picked up on Lebow's Holocaust experience as background for his transformative populist version of the marathon. They noted that his experience with the Nazis resulted in his disdaining elite categories and other stratifications. Furthermore, the very fact that Lebow made it through the Holocaust showed adaptability and a skill in living by his wits. Improvising, or coming up with new shtick, was basic to Lebow's marathon promotional schemes.

One woman attributed Lebow's relentlessness to the emphasis put on the individual's responsibility to strive (*shteig*) he heard both in his Orthodox home and *cheder [Jewish day school]*.

As is often the case, Fred Lebow's childhood played an essential role in shaping the man he would become. As a Jew growing up in the Holocaust era, the idea of *shteig*—meaning to continually climb or strive—was deeply embedded in his psyche. It was taught, quite understandably, that one must persevere in order to validate his existence. This belief would play an enormous role in Fred's life—from his early days in Europe, to his tenure in the garment center, and throughout the direction of his marathon. It would also serve as a representation to the "ordinary" people whose participation he sought in the race: a little *shteig* could go a long way in running a marathon.

The most moving book report was written by my one blind student, William R, a middle-aged man who sat in front of the classroom accompanied by Victoria, his devoted black Labrador, and a note taker supplied by student services. He found Lebow's struggles a metaphor for many obstacles he faced. The heroics behind Lebow's vision of this challenge of self-discovery gave William new inspiration:

> In 1986, I was hired to work at a corporate law firm as a mailroom supervisor. The senior partners . . . were very successful Jewish men who specialized in corporate law. As I started to familiarize myself with the company's interior, I admired the impressive paintings and antique furniture. However, it was one particular framed picture that most captured my attention and curiosity because it had nothing to do with the concept and law theme of the company.
>
> The framed picture belonged to one of the senior partners, M. S. It was a poster of the New York City Marathon which he ran and proudly displayed. Mr. S. once told me that he was a Holocaust survivor who fled from Germany when he was a little boy to escape the atrocities that would follow the millions of Jewish people in Europe. . . .
>
> Years later, this gentleman went to college and to graduate school and succeeded in becoming a senior corporate lawyer. . . .
>
> What I found fascinating was that the poster of the marathon he ran in contained the number of his entry which to him was the crowning achievement as significant as his accomplishments in law and his personal life. Although he never explained why that achievement was so monumental to him, he proudly wanted to be given recognition for it. . . .
>
> After I assessed all of the tribulations and successes of this man I finally understood why running in the marathon was an accumulation of the total achievements, successes and triumphs of his life. That shining moment when he reached the finish line was for him a total validation that would be with him for the rest of his life, and that New York City Marathon poster, which represented his participation, tied it all together.

After dealing with the questions I posed in my assignment, William brought his paper to a personal close:

> Being a blind person who lost his sight 13 years ago, I've been faced with many challenges throughout these recent years. I know what it is to hold some dreams and to lose others. However, just like my former boss who proudly displayed his New York City Marathon poster, I know what it is to enter a race of challenging issues that we face in life. It now blows my mind as I write this because this book has inspired me to run in the next New York City Marathon. . . .
>
> I think this (almost fifty-year-old) blind man has a lot of chutzpah planning to run in the marathon. I may be probably the last one to cross the finish line, but the experience will cap the goals of others who enter with disabilities and limitations. I've suffered many disappointments and denied opportunities since I lost my vision. I want to run in the race because I not only feel as a New Yorker I should take advantage of the opportunity, but because like my former boss, I want to make it one of my crowning successes.

Clearly, my multiethnic students identified with Fred Lebow's humanistic vision of renewal and inclusiveness. Hopefully, the story of this magical marathon—created by a Holocaust survivor no less humbly born than they—will spur their own dreams about also becoming King of New York for a day.

16

Jewish Personalities

Abraham Karp

Learning from the Master: My Debt to America's Greatest Judaica Collector [*Jewish Press*, April 2005]

I was introduced to the world of Judaica collecting in 1990 by the late Abraham Karp, who'd moved to my New York City neighborhood of Riverdale for his retirement years. I knew his name even before he came to Riverdale, due to my familiarity with his works on American Jewish history and his past presidency of the American Jewish Historical Society.

Previously I had defined myself as an observant Jew with a rather limited academic interest in the Jewish historical experience. The aesthetic element in this Jewish journey was something very foreign to me.

But walking into the Karp living room opened up a new world of culture and beauty. Thousands of books and manuscripts, some decorated in gilt pages and held together by clasps that were hundreds of years old, lined the shelves. Some books were miniatures meant to be carried in a pocket on the way to synagogue or study class. Others, with their heavy leather binding and thick pagination, had to be taken with both hands.

Many of these works were first editions or early editions of biblical and talmudic commentaries. I imagined the hands that held these books, the gas-lit lights by which they were studied, the sacrifices made to preserve them, and the limited numbers in (and great expense with) which they were originally printed centuries back.

When Abraham Karp was in his early teens growing up in the Bronx, he traveled by subway on shopping trips to the Jewish book dealers on the Lower East Side with his father, Aaron, a furrier who never had much money. The elder Karp, who in his youth had tackled intricate talmudic passages at Lithuania's famed Slobodka Yeshiva, wanted to transmit to his son his love of Jewish books. These were the depression years of the 1930's, when for the Karps a dollar or two spent on an eighteenth century Hebrew book represented a major purchase.

By the time he died in 2003 at age 82, Abraham Karp had amassed two of the great Judaica collections in modern times. The more distinguished of these collections, consisting of some 3,500 items of Americana Judaica, he gave to the Jewish Theological Seminary in 1990. Professor Arthur Kiron, curator of Judaica Collections at the University of Pennsylvania Library, called Karp's Americana material "perhaps the finest private collection of its kind ever assembled." In addition to books and manuscripts, the collection included ritual and ceremonial objects, paintings, synagogue records, newspapers and diaries.

Highlights from his other great collection were auctioned off earlier this month at the gallery of Kestenbaum and Company. The sale featured Bibles, liturgical works, rabbinics, Latin-Hebrew grammars, and books on chassidism and the Holy Land.

What made Karp's career as a Judaica bibliophile unique was not his success in accumulating items of rarity and beauty. Any collector with time and money (plus at least a minimal aesthetic sense) could put together a library of value. But Karp ranks as the greatest grassroots collector of Judaica in modern history.

"Grassroots" in this collecting context means that Karp's acquisitions were not made in the venerable oak-paneled halls of Sotheby's or Christie's under the tutelage of high-priced consultants. "What fun would there be if you had to pay a lot of money?" Karp would ask, dismissing the uncreative auction house approach to amassing collections. In 1980, after nearly a half century of collecting, Karp boasted that he rarely paid more than five dollars for any one volume.

Instead, Karp, though a courtly and impeccably dressed figure himself, excelled in off-the-beaten-path ways in his detective-like searches for literary treasures. Flea markets, dank basements, garbage dumps, theological seminary downsizing sales, dust-filled shelves in out-of-the-way antiquarian shops, neglected, unopened and unsorted boxes of books—these were the sites where Karp discovered the rarities which sold for thousands and tens of thousands of dollars at the Kestenbaum sale.

One item that Karp's widow Deborah, an English literature medievalist, has refused to put up for auction is a pair of lions of Judah probably carved by a German-trained coppersmith in the late nineteenth century. Karp found this treasure in a refuse dump outside a synagogue under demolition in Kansas City, Missouri, where he served as a rabbi in the 1950's. These lions, willed to New York's Jewish Museum, will also be featured at a Judaica show later this year at the New York Museum of Folk Art.

Karp, who graduated from Yeshiva College and was ordained by the Jewish Theological Seminary, brought to his collecting pursuits an encyclopedic knowledge of Jewish bibliography, enabling him to identify major finds. To be sure, Karp was not the only scholar of his era equipped with vast erudition to assess ancient Judaica. Other historians and librarians also were familiar with bibliography, bindings, printing records, library holdings and the like. But what set him apart was that his knowledge bridged both great literary worlds—the span of Jewish publishing going back to medieval Europe, North Africa and Spain as well as the entire field of Jewish Americana.

At the time of his death, Karp was the only scholar in the world whose knowledge encompassed both vast bibliographical subjects. He was as much at home with the culture of eighteenth century Jewish Amsterdam (at the time the center of international Jewish book publishing) as he was with the five hundred-member Charleston, South Carolina Jewish community of the same era.

Thus, Karp's unrivaled knowledge of Judaica bibliography, combined with his populist approach to collecting (meaning his willingness to get his hands dirty unearthing a treasure at the bottom of some neglected book pile) explains why he accumulated a collection worth millions today.

But in fairness to the modern-day neophyte Jewish book collector—especially one operating on budget as sparse as Karp's was—it is impossible to amass anything approaching what Karp put together beginning in the 1930's. He understood that he appeared on the scene at a period auspicious for a Judaica collector, and never denied the need to spend fortunes more today for, say, the 1796 first edition of Sefer Likutei Amarim, the fundamental exposition of Chabad chassidic philosophy, or for a sixteen volume calf-bound pocket Renaissance Hebrew Bible printed in Paris in 1543 by Robert Estienne the Elder (two of the items from Kraft's library that were sold at the auction).

In terms of timing, two Jewish social transformations were underway in mid-20th century America that brought to the fore Karp's cleverness as a collector: Suburbia was on the rise, and in moving to their new homes Jews routinely disposed of memorabilia from grandparents that had been gathering dust for decades in unopened boxes. Similarly, many of the immigrants coming to Israel to build new lives did not take seriously the old books and other religious Judaica they brought with them.

What the American and Israeli social transformations shared was a greater emphasis on secular lifestyles, which caused people to look more askance on the religiously oriented ancient books and memorabilia they'd inherited. Where would these unwanted volumes, scrolls of Esther, nostalgic biblical scenes and menorahs be disposed of?

The Jewish book dealers on the Lower East Side and Jerusalem's Mea Shearim served as outlets for this abandoned Judaica. Those merchants, with their haggard persona and meagerly appointed stores, are long gone. But some forty and fifty years ago, Abraham Karp scoured their unadorned shelves, their basements and storefront sales. This was a time when serious Jewish book-collecting hardly existed and would-be collectors were unable to match Karp's prodigious homespun knowledge.

Karp's collecting was also helped by his geographic relocations. As a rabbi, he served congregations in Swampscott, Massachusetts (a suburb ten miles north of Boston), Kansas City, and Rochester, New York. Each community served as a base for book acquisitions.

Sometimes Karp traded volumes with the librarians of local Christian theological seminaries. More often, he went on buying forays into the countryside. A visiting professorship at Dartmouth College made accessible the small towns of New Hampshire and Vermont. Thirty years back, recalled Karp, each New England town still housed its local antiquarian book shop. A nineteenth century Jewish marriage contract; a newspaper carrying a front-page obituary of Mordechai Noah, whom Karp called America's first Zionist; an advertisement from Haym Solomon's loan company—these were examples of overlooked collectibles that Karp's innocent queries or enterprising searches would ferret out.

May the devotion of this pioneering grassroots collector spur our curiosity in the Jewish printed book.

Conclusion

Two articles about three personally meaningful "endings" were selected for concluding this anthology of Rubin's works to date.

Two Finish Lines
[*Jewish Journal of Greater Los Angeles*, March 2005]

What is the touchstone that unites a 26.2-mile marathon with a *Siyum Hashas* celebration of completing the 7.5-year-page-a-day Talmud cycle?

The concept shared by both events is human striving—or in the language of the Lithuanian yeshiva, the commitment to shteig, to stretch one's limits. Someone who studies one page of Talmud a day, Daf Yomi, logs text pages; the marathon runner logs miles. Trappings of mortality bedeck the starting line—the Talmudist seeking better understanding of his mortality, and the marathon runner physically defying that same mortality.

This unlikely comparison of both fetes of transcendence occurred to me, based on my bicoastal participation at a Siyum and a marathon. One night, in early March, I was at New York's Madison Square Garden celebrating the completion of the Talmud cycle; the following afternoon I was flying to the Quality of Life Expo prior to the Los Angeles Marathon, the nation's fourth-largest long-distance race.

Adding my voice to thousands of my fellow Daf Yominiks at the Garden, I passionately and thankfully shouted, "May His great name be blessed for now and for eternity," and swayed to the musical beat of the chasidic songs.

At the three-day expo preceding the marathon, I manned a booth together with my editor, Peri Devaney, promoting my book, whose theme is also one of striving. This first biography of the founder of the New York City Marathon (*Anything for a T-Shirt: Fred Lebow and the New York City Marathon, the World's Greatest Footrace,* Syracuse University Press) shows how an impresario convinced the plodders and shleppers of the world that they could go a marathon's seemingly fearsome distance.

The similarity between these two enterprises crossed my mind during a low patch Thursday afternoon where, viewing a large-screened film clip in the auditorium of past L.A. marathons, particularly the slow runners and the wheelchair athletes, my thoughts somehow turned to the simcha I reveled in only a day and a half earlier in New York. Both of these events, I thought, were triumphs over human ordinariness and complacency.

True, on the surface, there was no hashava (the Talmud's word for common denominator) between these two enterprises—and a God-fearing Jew would be best off uttering a lehavdil (a statement of demarcation) before drawing similarities between a siyum and a marathon. After all, one undertaking is spiritual; the other, physical. The marathon represents a legacy of a hedonistic ancient Greek culture; the Talmud, a work of faith and holiness.

But is there any question about the commonality of obstacles facing the student of the daily page of Talmud and the marathon runner in training? Both often launch their daily trajectory at dawn, defy sleep, knowingly cut into family time and are undeterred by inclement weather and life's distractions. Many runners mark their miles in the company of other runners, encouraging one another. The Daf Yomi learner also tackles his talmudic page in a shiur, a group setting, rather than by himself.

While the runner's gear is his sneakers, and the Daf Yomi stalwart his Talmud, each striver calls on aids making the challenge more manageable. For instance, the runner applies breathing strips to his nose, eats protein bars (some of which hold kosher certification) and carries instruments measuring his speed. The talmudist not only cites other commentaries helping him to understand the sugya (topic) at hand, but brings in visuals and diagrams (the layout of the Temple in Jerusalem, the anatomy of a bull) to clarify an obscure text.

In my Riverdale, N.Y., Daf Yomi group I see daily examples of discipline and modesty on the part of the text's presenter, but this should not be surprising since immersion in holiness enhances character traits. But in this, my first experience in manning a booth, I also was exposed to real examples of humility.

Marathon officials had arranged to give gift copies of my book to some 300 "legacy" runners. These were finishers at the 19 earlier marathons and honorees, in a sense, at the marathon's 20th anniversary. Two of these legacy runners came to my booth carrying copies of my book asking for my autograph. Both were men probably in their 50s. I learned that one worked as an air-traffic controller and the other in the county court system. The air-traffic controller told me that he had completed a total of nearly 50 marathons. What stood out was the modesty from both these marathon runners in response to my compliments; neither of the two seemed boastful or truly regarded themselves as exceptional.

To be sure, the Talmud uses the metaphor of running in stressing superiority of Talmud study over ephemeral, worldly pursuits.

"We run, and they run," states the Talmud in celebrating the completion of a tractate. The Jew "runs" toward eternal life, the others pursue vanity. Without minimizing the spiritual superiority of the Daf Yomi goal, the marathon runner also obeys the Torah's edict "to watch carefully one's soul," interpreted by Jewish commentators as including health and physical fitness.

In competing against themselves, both the Daf Yomi student and the marathon runner are testing their limits and proving something about their core identities. May they both be blessed with the faith and energy to cross the finish—the Daf Yomi learner to go m'chayil l'chayil (from strength to strength), and the marathon runner to "go the distance."

###

An Unforgettable Forty-Year Shabbos Journey
[*Jewish Press*, December 13, 2006]

At the restaurant farewell dinner, Professor Dov Zlotnick asked the dozen or so students of his forty-year-running Saturday afternoon Talmud *shiur* to continue their learning despite his approaching retirement to Jerusalem.

Though he would be putting a cap on his career at the Jewish Theological Seminary, Professor Zlotnick promised to rejoin the *shiur* during his occasional return visits to its Riverdale, Bronx base. But not long afterward—due to the loss of its "rebbe" and the advancing age of its students—the *shiur* came to an end.

Since talmudic etiquette calls on those who finish a tractate to pledge a return to its holy pages rather than bid goodbye, it is worth exploring why this *shiur* succeeded both as a learning enterprise and as a warm *Shabbos* experience.

Most members of the *shiur* were Modern Orthodox, but the paths they'd traveled prior to settling in Riverdale were far from homogeneous. Some were European born and, having attended venerable yeshivos, sprinkled talmudic references with Yiddish. By contrast, a medical doctor in the group had no formal yeshiva learning whatsoever.

Among the group there was the academician of Libyan ancestry, teased by Professor Zlotnick for his prowess with colloquial Yiddish. When *yekkes* in the *shiur* failed to arrive on time, Professor Zlotnick needled them, citing punctuality as a virtue of their German forbears. Naturally, over the years there were losses due to deaths and people moving away.

Professor Zlotnick wanted the *shiur* to be a learning experience rather than a lecture. Though he could easily have filled the hour with erudite discourse, relying on the thousands of mishnaic chapters he knew by heart, his goal was for us, his students, to recite and grapple with the text.

What that meant pedagogically was that we were not there to be spectators entertained or awed with his knowledge or subtleties, but instead to do the necessary preparation ourselves. He emphasized that the journey to becoming a *yodea sefer* (a knower of the book, i.e., conversant with rabbinic literature) demanded not only time but also review and intense concentration. Osmosis was not the way to talmudic mastery.

"You can attend *shiurim* for twenty years, but unless you prepare the text yourself," warned Professor Zlotnick, "your level of learning won't increase."

As he went around the table calling on readers, he corrected when necessary our mistakes in pronunciation or translation, continuously throwing out questions: "Who was that *amora*'s (scholar's) teacher? In which academy did he study? Where else in the Talmud is this word found, this argument used?"

Often he came to the *shiur* armed with comparative texts illustrating a literary point or something intriguing or inspirational about a talmudic sage. Over time, he recognized our relative skills, purposely trying to avoid embarrassment by not assigning a reader who he felt was inadequate to the task.

In addition to its format, what made the *shiur* distinctive was its physical setting. Rather than being located at one fixed site, it rotated to a different home each *Shabbos*. These changes in locale meant rejuvenating afternoon walks both to mansions in Fieldston and modest apartments on Henry Hudson Parkway.

For me, the act of hosting involved a few hours of preparations—duplicating the talmudic text and carefully studying the material, transporting the Torah ark, arranging for prayer books for the afternoon *Mincha* prayer service, food shopping.

Determined to capture the spirit of *Shabbos menucha*, Professor Zlotnick saw his *shiur* not simply as a talmudic study session but rather as an integral element in the day's celebratory character. For that reason, *Mincha* was followed by *seudah shlishit*, the traditional third *Shabbos* meal. Profusely thanking the hostess, he would joke before taking his place at the table that the upcoming meal was really the highlight of the program. Cuisine varied depending on the calendar, with more elaborate meals served on the longer days of spring.

Though officially we came together for the *Shabbos* learning experience, strong social bonds were forged during the meals. This was the case despite our varied personalities, professions and income range. We celebrated and danced together at life-cycle events. Support was also there in unhappy times.

In my own case, invitations and advice from members of the *shiur* softened the pain of my divorce. They opened their homes with receptions for my wife-to-be when she came to town. In more mournful moments, the *shiur* consoled bereaved family members. Following the death of a twenty-five year veteran of the group, we placed an obituary notice in *The New York Times* signed "Professor Zlotnick's Talmud Shiur."

Once the eating was over, the host would briefly discuss the week's Torah portion. Professor Zlotnick would then shift the agenda to politics—not politics in a generic sense, but more specifically the past week's events as they related to the well-being of the Jewish people, particularly in Israel.

Professor Zlotnick followed the news closely. He saw news through an ideological prism—Jewish survival depended on political strength. He reserved special ire for secular Jewish liberals for what he considered their self-destructive illusions.

Similarly, he objected to relativism in religious standards, complaining about the leftward drift in Conservative Judaism, at whose seminary he taught, especially its decision to ordain women rabbis.

Though most members of the *shiur* seemed at least tacitly to agree with his politics, he was not unchallenged. One retired professor and bibliophile strongly stood his New Deal ground. When the amiability of the previous two hours seemed threatened, *shiur* participants could be counted on to wisely drown out debate by spontaneously singing the introductory verses to the *benching* (Grace after Meals), thereby bringing the meal to a close.

Now that the *shiur* belongs to the ages, I pursue my Talmud study most Saturday afternoons by attending the *Daf Yomi* class at the Riverdale Jewish Center. Since a lot of text must be covered each day in order to fulfill this group's seven-year cycle of completing the Talmud, I feel a sense of nostalgia for the graceful rigor with which Professor Zlotnick guided us in grappling with complicated concepts (quite a few of which were over my head), and for the camaraderie provided by those in the *shiur* who accompanied me on an unforgettable four-decade *Shabbos* journey.

Postscript

The Obama Years: On Whom Can We Rely?

PERI DEVANEY, *with assistance from* DR. RON RUBIN
(July 2011, with December 2012 Addendum)

Since mid-2008, after more than fifty years of prolifically putting his political opinions, concerns, and predictions and his deep connection to Judaism and Israel in writing, Rubin's pen has been virtually silent. He has been devoting his free time to family, a sixth book, and working more directly to impact the political and social areas he had been writing about. Instead of publishing articles to inform large numbers of people, he has been informing a more targeted group, working with people and organizations directly involved in securing the future for Israel and the Jewish people.

Rubin is today a very active member of NORPAC, the Political Action Committee (PAC), and the American Israel Political Action Committee (AIPAC). He is a frequent participant in missions to Washington, D.C. And he continues to spend his between-semester breaks in Israel, keeping abreast of the political and emotional climate and further strengthening his ties.

Rubin's move to a more hands-on involvement is due, in part, to a rapid growth in threats to the security of Israel and the Jewish people. Since his last published article: U.S.-Israel relations have become less secure; terrorist activity is on the rise; the situation in the Middle East—especially regarding Iran and Egypt—does not bode well; and as Steven Windmueller, a fellow of the Jerusalem Center for Public Affairs and Dean of the Hebrew Union College–Jewish Institute of Religion, Los Angeles, wrote (July 2009, e-JewishPhilanthropy.com), the "impact of the economic dislocation has already generated *a significant increase in anti-Semitism globally*," and two years later the global economic situation remains dire.

U.S.-Israel Relations

U.S.-Israel relations became worrisome for a large number of American Jews, mostly from Orthodox and more ethnic groups, just one day after Senator Barack Obama clinched the Democratic nomination as presidential candidate. During a June 4 address to the 2008 AIPAC Conference he declared, "Let me be clear; Israel's security is sacrosanct. . . . And Jerusalem will remain the capital of Israel and it must remain undivided," only to turn around the next day and apologize, saying "undivided" was a poor choice of words and repeating his apologies in several interviews over the weeks that followed. Despite this "faux pas," Obama won 78% of the Jewish vote, including large percentages of both the liberal and Orthodox communities.

Two months after the 2008 election, President Obama chose to give his maiden speech in Egypt, as a sign of his efforts to engage the Muslim world. And engage he did. For the next two years he berated Israel, especially the notion that Israeli "settlements" were at the root of its problems with the Palestinians. On May 19, 2011, he delivered a policy statement that began a six-day tap dance with Israeli Prime Minister Netanyahu and resulted in growing apprehension in the Jewish community concerned about Obama's possible pro-Palestinian leaning. His stand cost him a 20% drop in polls of the Jewish community.

The tap dance began May 19 with Obama's remarks, titled "A Moment of Opportunity," in which he declared, "The borders of Israel and Palestine should be based on the 1967 lines with mutually agreed swaps so that secure and recognized borders are established for both states. The Palestinian people must have the right to govern themselves, and reach their potential, in a sovereign and contiguous state."[1]

1. http://www.whitehouse.gov/the-press-office/2011/05/19/remarks-president-barack-obama-prepared-delivery-moment-opportunity.

The next day, at a White House press conference following a private meeting with Obama, Netanyahu stated, "I think for there to be peace, the Palestinians will have to accept some basic realities. The first is that while Israel is prepared to make generous compromises for peace, it cannot go back to the 1967 lines—because these lines are indefensible. . . .

"Remember that before 1967," Netanyahu continued, "Israel was all of nine miles wide. It was half the width of the Washington Beltway. And these were not the boundaries of peace; they were the boundaries of repeated wars, because the attack on Israel was so attractive."[2]

On May 22, Obama addressed AIPAC's 2011 Annual Policy Conference, stating, "Since my position has been misrepresented several times, let me reaffirm what '1967 lines with mutually agreed swaps' means.

"By definition, it means that the parties themselves—Israelis and Palestinians—will negotiate a border that is different than the one that existed on June 4, 1967. That's what mutually agreed-upon swaps means," Obama maintained. "It is a well-known formula to all who have worked on this issue for a generation. It allows the parties themselves to account for the changes that have taken place over the last 44 years.

"So long as there are those who long for a better future," the president went on, "we will never abandon our pursuit of a just and lasting peace that ends this conflict with two states living side by side in peace and security. This is not idealism; it is not naïveté. It is," he concluded, "a hardheaded recognition that a genuine peace is the only path that will ultimately provide for a peaceful Palestine as the homeland of the Palestinian people and a Jewish state of Israel as the homeland of the Jewish people."[3]

On May 23 it was Netanyahu's turn to address AIPAC. He talked about visiting D.C.'s "majestic memorials" and quoted "Jefferson's timeless words, '. . . all men are created equal'" and "Lincoln's immortal address, '. . . of the people, for the people, by the people'" and continued "Israel is the cradle

2. http://www.whitehouse.gov/the-press-office/2011/05/20/remarks-president-obama-and-prime-minister-netanyahu-israel-after-bilate.

3. http://www.whitehouse.gov/the-press-office/2011/05/22/remarks-president-aipac-policy-conference-2011.

of our common civilization. It's the crucible of our common values . . . founded precisely on these eternal values . . . [its] more than one million Muslims enjoy full democratic rights . . . [it is] the only place in the Middle East where Christians are completely free to practice their faith. . . . And this is why Israel, and only Israel, can be trusted to ensure the freedom for all faiths in our eternal capital, the *united* city of Jerusalem.

"What the people of Israel want is for the people of the Middle East to have what you have in America, what we have in Israel—democracy. So it's time to recognize this basic truth. . . . *Israel is not what's wrong with the Middle East. Israel is what's right about the Middle East.*

"My friends," Netanyahu added, "we want peace because we know the pain of terror and we know the agony of war. . . . We know the blessings peace could bring . . . to us and to our Palestinian neighbors. But if we hope to advance peace with the Palestinians, then it's time that we admitted another truth. This conflict has raged for nearly a century because the Palestinians refuse to end it. They refuse to accept the Jewish state."[4]

And finally, on May 24, the tapping ended with Netanyahu's address to the United States Congress: "Israel has no better friend than America. And America has no better friend than Israel. We stand together to defend democracy. We stand together to advance peace. We stand together to fight terrorism. Congratulations America, Congratulations, Mr. President. You got bin Laden. Good riddance!

"Of the 300 million Arabs in the Middle East and North Africa," he added, "*only Israel's Arab citizens enjoy real democratic rights.* I want you to stop for a second and think about that. Of those 300 million Arabs, less than one-half of one-percent are truly free, and they're all citizens of Israel!

"This startling fact reveals a basic truth," he continued, once again declaring that, "*Israel is not what is wrong about the Middle East. Israel is what is right about the Middle East.*"[5]

4. http://www.pmo.gov.il/PMOEng/Communication/PMSpeaks/speechaipac230511.htm.

5. http://www.pmo.gov.il/PMOEng/Communication/PMSpeaks/speechcongress240511.htm.

In Rubin's opinion, at this point it was clear Netanyahu won the "dance" as confirmed by Congress's overwhelmingly enthusiastic response. The Jewish community's concerns were put in abeyance when the United States government did not follow through on Obama's "ultimatum" to Netanyahu to accept a return to the pre-'67 borders as the basis for peace negotiations or risk losing U.S. support. However, a large segment of the Jewish community feared that if Obama would win the Democratic Party nomination, capture the 2012 election, and have another four years in the White House, Israel would no longer be able to count on strong U.S. support. As Glenn Kessler put it in his title of an article posted on the *Washington Post* website, July 11, 2011, "Obama and Israel: Stalled Diplomacy or 'Suspicion and Distrust'?"

And even if Israel could regain complete confidence in U.S. support, just what would that mean should the United States lose its place as the strongest nation in the world, a frightening possibility that looms large given the current financial crises and the rapid strengthening of China's position as a world leader in 2011?

In his address on May 19, as a lead-in to his statements about the Israel-Arab peace process and "return to the '67 borders," Obama had broached several other issues of interest to Israel and the global Jewish community. He talked about the "huge blow" we dealt al-Qaeda by killing Osama bin Laden, very briefly about Iran, and extensively about the "extraordinary change [that has taken] place in the Middle East and North Africa" over the prior six months, "and how [the United States] can respond in a way that advances our values and strengthens our security."

The Threat of Terrorism

After pointing out exactly what he thought of bin Laden as a person, Obama went on to say that "even before his death, al-Qaeda was losing its struggle for relevance, as . . . people saw that the slaughter of innocents did not answer their cries for a better life. . . . Al-Qaeda's agenda had come to be seen by the vast majority of the region as a dead end." The problem with Obama's premise is that by that point al-Qaeda was no longer dependent on the ideals of "the region" to wreak its terror. The group was already adept at using the Internet to spread its poison, recruit members from around the world, arrange "hits" and "deploy" cyberattacks.

Computer Weekly correspondent Kathleen Hall, in an article posted July 12, 2011, quoted "a senior Whitehall spokesman [who] said al-Qaeda has called for the use of more cyber terrorism." The article noted that "tools such as Google Earth and Street View are being used for planning, and the terrorist attacks in Mumbai in 2008 were directed by people using off-the-shelf secure communications technology." According to a June 16, 2011, article at FoxNews.com, "[al-Qaeda–linked] jihadist websites posted a 'hit list' of American executives, officials and companies . . . around the same time that American-born al-Qaeda spokesman Adam Gadahn released a video in which he called on Muslims in the United States to kill Americans, [prompting the Feds to send out an alert]." And when not being used *by* terrorist groups, the Internet is still disseminating news *about* terrorist attacks and an ever-increasing toll of death and destruction.

Iran

In his 2008 address to AIPAC, Obama spent considerable time on the problems of Iran, highlighted by his saying, "there's no greater threat to Israel or to the peace and the stability of the region than Iran. . . . The Iranian regime supports violent extremists and challenges us across the region . . . pursues a nuclear capability that could spark a dangerous arms race and raise the prospect of a transfer of nuclear know-how to terrorists. Its president denies the Holocaust and threatens to wipe Israel off the map." Yet in his May 19, 2011, policy speech he barely mentioned Iran, remarking simply that, "Our opposition to Iran's intolerance—as well as its illicit nuclear program, and its sponsorship of terror—is well known." He did not tie it back to the threat to Israel, give an update on Iran's efforts to develop nuclear warheads, or discuss new concerns arising out of the many recent changes in the Middle East framework.

Iran's nuclear program took a big step forward in May 2011 when it signed a deal with Turkey and Brazil, and it would have taken an even larger step had the March 2011 tsunami not interfered with Japan's plan to come on board as a partner in building Iran's nuclear power plants and to provide nuclear fuel rods. The Western nations continue to disbelieve Iran's claims that their nuclear program is strictly for peaceful purposes, certain that the enriched uranium they have been negotiating for is a clear indication that they are gearing up for the eventual development of nuclear warheads. The UN Security Council continued to impose sanctions on Iran for its nuclear program, adopting yet another new sanctions resolution in June 2011.

In October 2010, in February 2011, and then again in July 2011, Iran reportedly conducted covert ballistic missile tests according to British Foreign Secretary William Hague, and a UN Panel of Experts. These missiles, with ranges from 560 to 1,240 miles, are believed to be capable of carrying nuclear warheads and can reach Israel as well as U.S. bases in the area.

While the threat of Iran's possession of nuclear missiles is predicted to still be a couple of years away, a newer Iranian threat to Israel and to U.S. installations in the area could be imminent. In February 2011, two Iranian warships were granted passage through the Suez Canal by Egypt's new military rulers, just one week after taking power from Hosni Mubarak. As FoxNews.com reported, Israel clearly viewed this development as a provocation. Scores of electronic and print newspapers and magazines around the world including *The New York Times* quoted Prime Minister Netanyahu as saying Israel viewed the Iranian move "with utmost gravity" and that Iran was trying "to exploit the situation that has been created in order to expand its influence by passing warships through the Suez Canal," the "situation" being the overthrow of Mubarak, Israel's ally for the past thirty years.

A Changing Middle East

The largest portion of Obama's May 2011 policy statement focused on his plans to respond to the recent changes in the Middle East and Northern Africa, the final part of his plan being his "pre-'67" peace policy already discussed. To begin, the president spoke about relieving a "democratic" Egypt of up to $1 billion of debt and guaranteeing an additional $1 billion for rebuilding the country's infrastructure; creating Enterprise Funds to invest in Tunisia and Egypt; having OPIC (the U.S. government's Overseas Private Investment Corporation) launch a $2 billion facility to support private investment throughout the region; launching a comprehensive Trade and Investment Partnership Initiative; and more. "Just as EU membership served as an incentive for reform in Europe, so should the vision of a modern and prosperous economy create a powerful force for reform in the Middle East and North Africa," he noted.

While Obama's concerns for the region were ensuring financial stability and peace for the newly "democratic" nations, of much more immediate concern to the Jewish world was, as always, survival. The "extraordinary changes" Obama referred to were the result of what came to be known as "Arab Spring"—a series of revolutions in 2011 in which several Middle Eastern and North African countries overthrew existing regimes. While ostensibly positive moves toward democracy, these revolutions were *not* rebellions that had been in planning over a long time by organized groups ready to take over, or at least they didn't seem to be. (There is some speculation that they were all actually incited by groups, possibly one group, with an underlying agenda.) The ousting of the ruling governments left voids that could, and some would, be filled by fundamentalist groups whose governments would in the long run be no more democratic than the ones replaced and who would be a lot more hostile toward Israel.

"Arab Spring" began with the December 2010 revolution in Tunisia sparked off when a street vendor, Tareq al-Tayyib Muhammad Bouazizi, set himself on fire in protest of police corruption and ill treatment. President Zine el-Abidine Ben Ali was ousted and on January 14, 2011, he left the country. Prime Minister Mohamed Ghannouchi created an interim government of unity but resigned February 27 following complaints he was too close to Ben Ali. As of July 2011, Tunisia was still in a state of complete unrest, with elections originally planned for July moved to October.

According to a *New York Times* blog updated June 20, 2011, polls showed the ultraconservative Islamic Party Ennahda, which had been banned by Ben Ali as subversive terrorists, having the most support. There were already rumors of attacks on unveiled women and artists, and many of the activists and politicians among the country's coastal elite worried that the secular revolution of January might see the birth of a conservative

Islamic government. In a July 2011 op-ed, Hamadi Redissi, a professor on the faculty of law and political science at the University of Tunis and president of the Tunisian Observatory for a Democratic Transition, wrote that to "placate the West, [Al Nahda] wants to fashion itself in the image of Turkey's ruling Justice and Development Party [the A.K.P.]." But whether it would stay moderate and prove Tunisia's revolution to be "a triumph of liberalism" or revert to radical Islamism proving the revolution to have been "an open door for extremists," Redissi noted, would "depend on the willingness of new leaders to chart a responsible course" and on the secular and moderate parties' ability to stand up to pan-Arab and Islamist groups.[6]

On January 25, 2011, galvanized by Tunisia's success, Egyptians took to the streets in protest. When it was Mubarak's turn to step down, the Muslim Brotherhood—which former Pulitzer Prize finalist and award-winning correspondent David Wood described as "a secretive Islamist organization that has raised troops to fight Israel and called for global jihads against infidels and martyrdom for its youth"[7]—stepped in. (According to Wood, it was a Muslim Brotherhood gang that assassinated former Egyptian President Anwar Sadat for making peace with Israel. The Brotherhood maintains links with Hamas, Islamic Jihad, and al-Qaeda.) It was the Muslim Brotherhood that opened the Suez Canal to two Iranian warships.

On February 17, 2011, riots to oust Moammar Gaddafi began in Libya. On February 28, during an interview with Christiane Amanpour for *ABC Nightline*, Gaddafi blamed al-Qaeda for encouraging young people to seize arms from military installations and claimed that the people who had taken over Benghazi in eastern Libya were terrorists and al-Qaeda operatives. While most of what he said for the rest of the interview made it difficult to accept his words as more than the rantings of someone not quite in touch with reality, his al-Qaeda references might not have been far from the truth. According to a May 22 Reuters update by journalist

6. "The Revolution Is Not Over Yet" by Hamadi Redissi, http://www.nytimes.com/2011/07/16/opinion/16redissi.html.

7. David Wood, "After Egypt's Mubarak: The Muslim Brotherhood," *Politics Daily*, www.politicsdaily.com/2011/02/01/after-egypts-mubarak-the-muslim-brotherhood/print/.

Mohammed Abbas, "An Islamic revival is taking hold . . . after decades of tough curbs on worship by Muammar Gaddafi, but clerics say this will not be a new source of religious extremism as the West may fear." However, given conditions in the region, these assurances were weakened somewhat as Abbas continued, "Libyan society remained religiously conservative in character and that is now flowering anew," speaking of rebels with longer beards, ostentatious public prayer, an increase in sales of religious books, and plans for more centers for studying sharia (Islamic law). In his report he quotes Osama al-Salaaby, a well-known cleric and professor of sharia in Benghazi: "The situation in free Libya will revert to its natural state . . . the practice of religion in life, in the morals of the people, their ways, their return to the mosques." Gaddafi left Tripoli following UN sanctions and military actions to protect the Libyan people, and on July 15, 2011, the United States recognized Libya's rebel National Transitional Council as a legitimate government after assurances were offered that it would pursue a process of democratic reform.

Protests began in Syria in March 2011 and quickly escalated. Hoping to quell the protests, the government released dozens of political prisoners after which President Bashar Assad dismissed the government and accused the protesters of being Israeli agents. In response to Syria's bloody crackdown on the protests, in April 2011 the U.S. administration starting adding sanctions to those already in effect, and on May 18 they added sanctions to Assad and froze his accounts and those of six other officials. On July 11, 2011, after the U.S. Embassy, French Embassy, and American ambassador's residence in Damascus were attacked by Assad loyalists, and with there still being no show of willingness to dialogue with protesters or end the brutal crackdown on Assad's part, the United States removed all support. Secretary of State Hillary Rodham Clinton remarked, "From our perspective, he has lost legitimacy. He has failed to deliver on promises . . . [and has] sought and accepted aid from the Iranians as to how to repress his own people." The administration stopped short of demanding he step down.

An article in *The New York Times* the next day reported that Clinton's remarks appeared to be a response to criticisms about the "striking difference" between the U.S. response in Syria and Libya. The administration said it had no choice in Libya because of threats made by a very unpredictable Gaddafi. In Syria's case there was no chance of military remedy because of NATO's lack of interest in Syria and the UN Security Council's inability to pass a resolution similar to the one being enforced in Libya.[8] According to an earlier article in *The Jerusalem Post*, "veto-holding Russia has said it opposes any such council measure . . . [and] world powers have shown no appetite for any Libya-style military intervention in Syria."[9]

The *Times* article further pointed out that Syria is a force in the region while Libya isn't, and that the administration had thought Syria could be pulled away from Iran's influence and made a part of the Israeli-Palestinian peace accord. Naïve as some critics believed, it wasn't long before then that some American officials felt having Assad in power was better than risking creating a power vacuum that was proving to threatening other nations' stability and the security of Israel. But, the article continued, quoting a single senior official, "[Now that Mr. Assad] 'has shown definitively he has no interest in reform, the rationale for holding on to him has evaporated.'"

So as of mid-July 2011, Assad was still in power, looking to Iran for help to overpower the protesters, with Russia and others in effect condoning Assad's brutality, and relations with the U.S. cut off . . .

Anti-Semitism on the Rise

Anti-Semitism in the years 2008–2011 took on some fearsome characteristics. Similar to Holocaust Revisionists, there are whole groups of people involved with the "De-legitimizing of Israel."

As administrator at a organization called Jews for Judaism, a high profile name that frequently gets our public e-mail addresses on mass-emailing lists, I process a staggering number of "junk" e-mails from

8. Mark Landler and David E. Sanger, "White House, in Shift, Turns Against Syria Leader," *The New York Times*, July 12, 2011, http://www.nytimes.com/2011/07/13/world/middleeast/13policy.html?pagewanted=1.

9. Reuters, "Thousands of Syrians flee into Turkey . . . ," *The Jerusalem Post*, June 9, 2011, http://www.jpost.com/MiddleEast/Article.aspx?id=224342.

organizations intent on informing and warning the U.S. public about U.S.-Israel conspiracies, falsified Israeli histories, fantastic stories about how Israel is taking over the world . . . a twenty-first-century virtual version of the blood libel.

Much of today's anti-Semitism is hidden in rhetoric—as is the case with San Francisco's 2011 ballot to ban circumcisions under penalty of large fines. The question is whether or not the preponderance of medical reasons favoring circumcisions at an early age had anything to do with the bill's failure.

Much of this new anti-Semitism is direct. When Israeli Ambassador Michael Oren came to the University of California–Irvine (UCI), UCI's Muslim Student Union planned an elaborate scheme to disrupt his presentation and announced publicly that they resented the law school and political science department for inviting him to speak. To his credit, Oren completed his presentation despite being interrupted ten staggered times by men shouting at him and an eleventh time by a pre-planned mass exit; those that had come to hear him remained until after 6 p.m. to hear him and were, unfortunately, deprived of a scheduled question-and-answer session because of the delays.

Anti-Semitism, along with anti-Zionism, on college campuses throughout Canada, is a threat that has been escalating since 2009, and the divide between anti-Israel and anti-Semitic is lessening. The Canadian Parliamentary Coalition to Combat Anti-Semitism released a report in July 2011 following two years of hearings. It found that anti-Semitism *is* on the rise in Canada, especially in universities, and several recommendations were made. According to an article by Sara R. Horowitz posted on the former Canadian Jewish Congress's website, there are three classic anti-Semitic strategies: scapegoating, demonizing, and isolating Jews. Horowitz reported that some scholars of anti-Semitism have begun to refer to its latest manifestation as "Judaeophobia" and "Israelophobia" to make clear to progressive groups on campus—who actively oppose such phenomena as homophobia and Islamophobia—that current anti-Israel discourse reflects an irrational fear that leads to hatred and discrimination.

Hate crimes are also on the rise. A December 2010 article in the *New York Post*, by State Editor Frederic U. Dicker, noted that "[h]ate crimes across New York State jumped 14 percent in 2009, led by an increase in attacks on Jews and Jewish institutions, state records released yesterday show." A March 2010 article at WashingtonTimes.com talked about a Swedish Jew who was forced out of Malmo, where his family had had deep roots, by hate crimes. And a December 2010 article in the *LA Times* advised that "Hate crimes were down in Los Angeles County in 2009 compared with the year before, *but such crimes against Jews spiked almost 50%*, according to a report released Tuesday" (emphasis added).

At the June 2011 annual meeting of the Board of Governors of NCSJ (Advocates for Jews in Russia, Ukraine, the Baltic States & Eurasia)—and several other conferences throughout 2011—Hannah Rosenthal, the U.S. Department of State's Special Envoy to Monitor and Combat Anti-Semitism, spoke about six significant trends in anti-Semitism:

> First: "Anti-Semitism is not History, it is News. . . . [It did not end] when Hitler killed himself. [It is] evolving into new, contemporary forms of religious hatred, racism, and political, social and cultural bigotry." She gave examples: A synagogue defaced with "the Holocaust is a myth," "Adolf was right," and "Death to the Jews;" swastikas painted on 89 gravestones in Latvia by neo-Nazi youths in December 2010; updated "blood libel" accusations claiming Jews kidnap children to steal their organs; conspiracy theories about Jews being involved in executing the 9/11 attacks; "The Protocols of the Elders of Zion" continuing as a best seller and taught to religious students as truth; a declaration by a Russian Duma roundtable blaming the "international Zionist financial mafia for genocide against the Russian people;" and, in Belarus, the state press continues to publish anti-Semitic literature.
>
> Second: Holocaust denial "is being espoused by religious leaders, heads of State, such as in Iran, in academic institutions, and is a standard on hateful websites and other media outlets."
>
> Third: "[a] parallel trend of . . . Holocaust glorification and the growth of neo-Nazi groups . . . especially virulent in a variety of Middle Eastern media . . . calling for a new Holocaust to finish the job.
>
> Fourth: "Holocaust relativism—where some governments, museums, academic research and the like are conflating the Holocaust with other terrible events."

> Fifth: "Blurring the lines between opposition to the policies of the State of Israel and anti-Semitism. What I hear from our diplomatic missions, and from non-governmental organizations alike, is that this happens easily and often."
>
> And Sixth: "Growing nationalistic movements which target 'the other'—be they immigrants, or religious and ethnic minorities—in the name of protecting the identity and 'purity' of their nation. Over the past two decades, anti-Semitism has continued to form the ideological basis of many right-wing ultra-nationalist organizations."[10]

Rosenthal then reported on some of what they are doing in the State Department, and before detailing statics noted, "If we don't chronicle it, if we don't name it, we can't fight it," and ended on a possible up note, saying that "Even though the news is grim, we *have* seen *some* improvement throughout the former Soviet Union."

Perhaps the most publicized act of anti-Semitism from mid-2008 to mid-2011 was "26/11" (the November 26, 2008, terrorist attack on Mumbai). Ten locations were assailed and more than 150 people killed. Six of those killed were Jews who perished in the Nariman (Chabad) House, in and of itself not a staggering number. However, that this one segment of "26/11" was indeed a crime of hate was stated clearly in an article in the *Times* a year later: "For the terrorists themselves, Nariman House was different. It was the only Jewish target, and the terrorists would be told by their handlers in Pakistan that the lives of Jews were worth 50 *times* those of non-Jews."[11]

The Jewish world, strongly united as it only is during times of tremendous sorrow, fear and joy, watched with emotions running high when they heard news about the young boy, Moshe, newly orphaned by the attack, but proof that "Am Yisroel Chai"—the people of Israel lives!

10. http://www.humanrights.gov/2011/07/25/special-envoy-rosenthal-on-anti-semitism-in-the-former-soviet-union/.

11. "Mumbai Terror Attacks: And Then They Came for the Jews," *The Sunday Times (London)*, November 1, 2009, www.timesonline.co.uk/tol/news/world/asia/article6896107.ece.

Addendum

Much has transpired between August 2011 and this book's going to press. Several more chapters could be filled with commentary, more than belongs here, in this Postscript. However, given the timing, we would be remiss in not commenting on three news items from November 2012 that are certain to greatly impact the Jewish world and Israel in the years to come.

On November 6, 2012, President Barack Obama was reelected for a second term. His level of pressure on Israel continues to exceed that of any former president. Despite the lack of success of any of his attempts to use sanctions to force Iran to suspend their bellicose policies and stop their nuclear production, he is still trying to engage them diplomatically and maintains his promise that they will never have a nuclear bomb during his era. And he continues to deliberately follow a policy in the international arena of "leading from behind," stepping back from what had always been accepted as the United States's manifest destiny as guardian of democratic values globally.

From November 14 to November 21, 2012, "in response to incessant rocket attacks from the Gaza Strip, the IDF [Israel Defense Forces] launched a widespread campaign against terror targets in Gaza. The operation, called Pillar of Defense, had two main goals: cripple terror organizations in the Gaza Strip and defend Israelis living under fire."[12]

> On November 14, "President Shimon Peres . . . updated President Obama about the situation on Israel's southern border and said, 'The head of the military force of Hamas was killed half an hour ago. He was a most extreme man and was in charge of all the attacks and assassinations from Gaza against Israel. . . .
>
> For days, day and night, they are shooting rockets at Israel. Women cannot fall asleep. I was today there with the children. You know, there are limits. So I want you to know and I wanted to explain our motives.'"[13]

12. http://www.idfblog.com/2012/11/22/operation-pillar-of-defense-summary-of-events/.

13. http://embassies.gov.il/san-francisco/Newsandevents/Pages/Israel-strikes-terror-targets-in-Gaza-Nov-2012.aspx.

As has been their policy, the IDF gave advance warning to citizens in the areas being targeted:

> "Thursday, November 15: 8:45 a.m.: In addition to the leaflets dispersed by the IDF over the Gaza Strip, over 20,000 phone calls have been made to warn the residents of the Gaza Strip to stay away from Hamas and other terror organizations' operatives and facilities that pose a risk to their safety."[14]

Unfortunately, this information—and reports from independent sources that the Hamas interior ministry spokesman was on radio urging Gaza citizens to ignore the IDF warnings as propaganda—did little to allay the global outrage against Israel for the large numbers of civilian casualties, and Israel has been more isolated than ever since then.

So it was not surprising that on November 29, 2012—the sixty-fifth anniversary of the UN General Assembly's approval of the Partition Plan—the General Assembly voted overwhelmingly to "accord to Palestine non-member observer State status" despite the United States's vocal disapproval. The irony of date is clear to those familiar with the Partition Plan which in 1947 split what is now mostly Israel into two parts—one for a Jewish state and the other for an Arab state. The Jews accepted, and less than a year later the State of Israel was born. The Arabs refused, and it took another sixty-five years for them to become a "State" with many more limitations than it would have had sixty-five years ago. What the impact of this UN decision will be on the State of Israel and the Jewish people worldwide has yet to be seen.

In Summary . . .

The centrality of political power as a tool for Jewish survival and the importance of keeping a finger on the political pulse—Rubin's ongoing theme for more than fifty years—remain crucial for *netzach Yisroel*, the continuity of Israel and the Jewish people.

14. http://www.idf.il/1283-17570-EN/Dover.aspx.

Today, some three years after Rubin wrote his "Introduction," there is an even greater need to hope that "a more politically seasoned Jewry will come to better understand the precarious survival mechanisms for overcoming the daunting challenges that lie ahead" and to underscore Rabbi Soloveitchik's bold words from *Kol Dodi Dofek*, "*dam Yisroel eino hefker*" . . . "Jewish blood is not for the taking."

In the title of this Postscript the question is asked, "On whom can we rely." In *Mishnah Sotah* 9:15 that same question is asked and answered: "On Our Father in Heaven." But the Mishnah prefaces the question with a long, bleak list negating all possible human avenues, with no honor, no truth, no morality, no wisdom, none to offer reproof, our own families as our enemies, and more. As alarming as the challenges facing Israel, the Jewish people and the world today might be, the situation is nowhere near as bleak as that.

Today we are still able to rely on the skills, intelligence, and resources "Our Father in Heaven" has given us—and we have a responsibility to do so. Ron Rubin and I have attempted to present you with a resource that advocates a more politically savvy and proactive Jewish community that defends its right to exist and thrive—and that invites all people of good faith to be part of "what's right" in the Middle East and around the world. We hope we have succeeded.

Bibliography — Index

Bibliography

The works cited in *A Jewish Professor's Political Punditry* fall into four groups. The first includes those cited by Dr. Rubin in the Introduction he wrote specifically for this anthology. The second section lists those of Dr. Rubin's works reprinted herein. The third comprises the numerous works Rubin used when he created the materials being anthologized; however, it does not include the expansive list of people he interviewed during the fifty years covered. The last group includes the sources cited by the editor in the Postscript and other items written specifically for this volume.

Introduction

Halkin, Hillel. Review of *The Oslo Syndrome: Delusions of a People under Siege. Commentary*, Sept. 2005.

Hazony, Yoram. *The Jewish State*, 101. New York: Basic Books, 2000.

Karp, Abraham J. *Haven and Home: A History of the Jews in America*, 371. New York: Schocken, 1988.

Lederhendler, Eli. *The Road to Modern Jewish Politics: Political Tradition and Political Reconstruction in the Jewish Community of Tsarist Russia*, 33–34. Cary, NC: Oxford University Press USA, 1989.

Levin, Kenneth. *The Oslo Syndrome: Delusions of a People under Siege*, 77. Lyme, NH: Smith & Kraus, 2005.

———. "Diaspora Jews Embracing the Indictments of Their Enemies." *Jerusalem Center for Public Affairs*, jcpa.org, Feb. 1, 2007.

Peres, Shimon. *The New Middle East*, 80. New York: Holt, 1993

Rosenfeld, Alvin. *"Progressive" Jewish Thought and the New Anti-Semitism*, 16. New York: American Jewish Committee, 2006.

Soloveitchik, Rabbi Joseph B. *Kol Dodi Dofek (Listen—My Beloved Calls)*. Edited by Jeffrey R. Woolf. Translated by David Z. Gordon. New York: Yeshiva University Press, 2006.

Windmueller, Steven. e-JewishPhilanthropy.com, Jul. 2009.

Wisse, Ruth. "The Brilliant Failure of Jewish Foreign Policy," *Azure, Ideas for the Jewish Nation*, Winter 2001, 119, 120.

The Anthologized Works

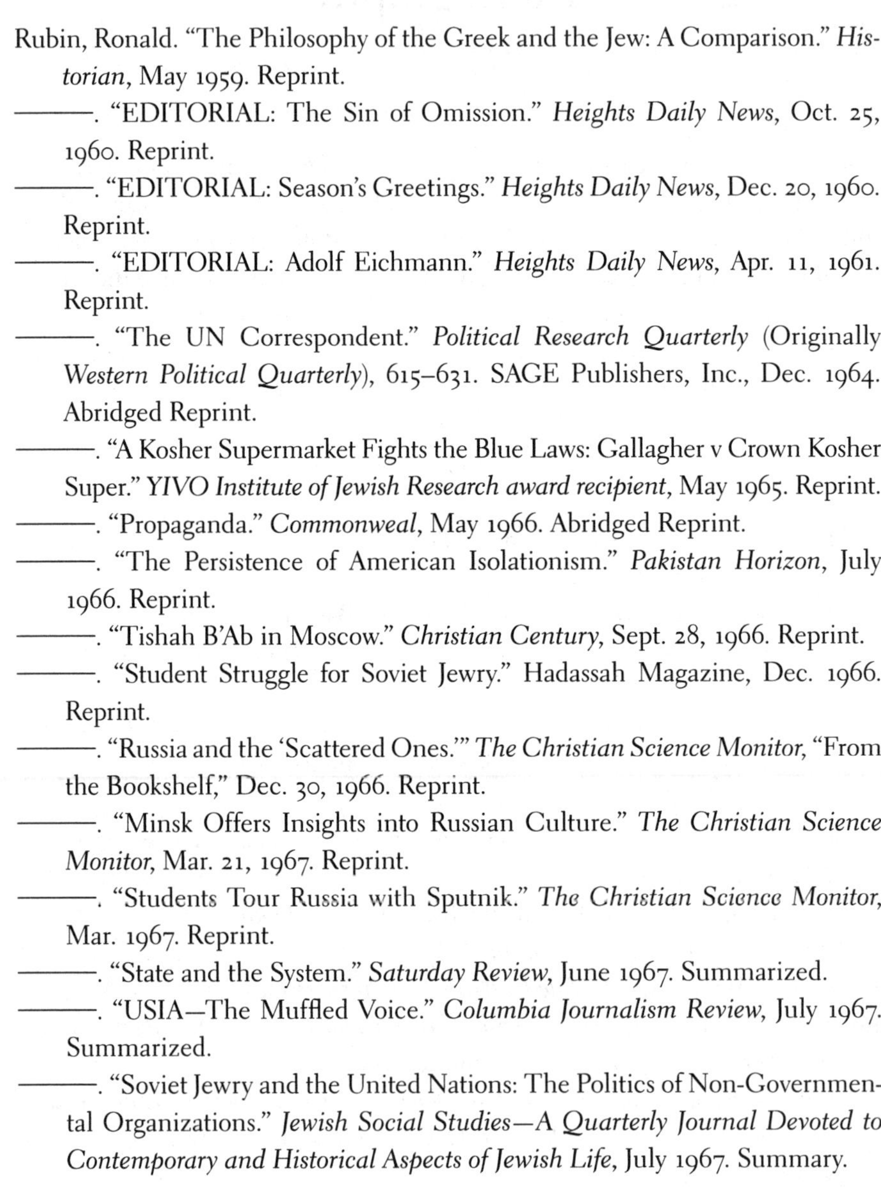

Rubin, Ronald. "The Philosophy of the Greek and the Jew: A Comparison." *Historian*, May 1959. Reprint.

———. "EDITORIAL: The Sin of Omission." *Heights Daily News*, Oct. 25, 1960. Reprint.

———. "EDITORIAL: Season's Greetings." *Heights Daily News*, Dec. 20, 1960. Reprint.

———. "EDITORIAL: Adolf Eichmann." *Heights Daily News*, Apr. 11, 1961. Reprint.

———. "The UN Correspondent." *Political Research Quarterly* (Originally *Western Political Quarterly*), 615–631. SAGE Publishers, Inc., Dec. 1964. Abridged Reprint.

———. "A Kosher Supermarket Fights the Blue Laws: Gallagher v Crown Kosher Super." *YIVO Institute of Jewish Research award recipient*, May 1965. Reprint.

———. "Propaganda." *Commonweal*, May 1966. Abridged Reprint.

———. "The Persistence of American Isolationism." *Pakistan Horizon*, July 1966. Reprint.

———. "Tishah B'Ab in Moscow." *Christian Century*, Sept. 28, 1966. Reprint.

———. "Student Struggle for Soviet Jewry." Hadassah Magazine, Dec. 1966. Reprint.

———. "Russia and the 'Scattered Ones.'" *The Christian Science Monitor*, "From the Bookshelf," Dec. 30, 1966. Reprint.

———. "Minsk Offers Insights into Russian Culture." *The Christian Science Monitor*, Mar. 21, 1967. Reprint.

———. "Students Tour Russia with Sputnik." *The Christian Science Monitor*, Mar. 1967. Reprint.

———. "State and the System." *Saturday Review*, June 1967. Summarized.

———. "USIA—The Muffled Voice." *Columbia Journalism Review*, July 1967. Summarized.

———. "Soviet Jewry and the United Nations: The Politics of Non-Governmental Organizations." *Jewish Social Studies—A Quarterly Journal Devoted to Contemporary and Historical Aspects of Jewish Life*, July 1967. Summary.

———. "The Promised Land Grows Dim." *Saturday Review*, Sept. 2, 1967. Reprint.

———. "The Real Shtetl." *Hadassah Magazine*, Nov. 1967. Reprint.

———. "Protests at Soviet Rabbi's Hunter Talk." *The New York Times* "Letters to the Editor," June 1968. Reprint.

———. "The Politics of the Aswan Dam; A Reappraisal: I." *Jewish Frontier Magazine*, June 1968. Reprint.

———. "The Politics of the Aswan Dam; A Reappraisal: II." *Jewish Frontier Magazine*, July–Aug. 1968. Reprint.

———. "The Plight of Soviet Jews." *Thought: A Review of Culture and Idea—Fordham University Quarterly*, Aug. 1968. Reprint.

———. "America's Voice in Israel." *Jewish Life*, May 1969. Reprint.

———. "Israel's Propaganda War." *Jewish Life*, Mar.–Apr. 1970. Reprint.

———. "Crock of Presidents." *Jerusalem Post*, May 1970. Abridged Reprint.

———. "American Jews and Soviet Jews." *Jewish Life*, Sept. 1970. Reprint.

———. "The Soviet Jewish Problem at the United Nations." *American Jewish Year Book*, 1970. Reprint.

———. "Broadcasting in Israel." *Jewish Life*, Mar.–Apr. 1971. Reprint.

———. "The New Style of Soviet and Other Jews." *American Zionist*, May 1971. Reprint.

———. "Israel's Foreign Information Program." *International Communication Gazette* [Originally *Gazette (International Journal of Mass Communications*, Amsterdam. Second Quarter 1973)]. New York: SAGE Publishers, Inc., May 1, 1973. Reprint.

———. "Where Have All The Liberals Gone?" *Jewish Life*, Oct. 1973. Reprint.

———. "Sylvia Hirsch's Cheesecake." *America* (Moscow), Nov. 1973. Reprint.

———. "The New Jewish Ethnic." *Tradition: A Journal of Orthodox Jewish Thought*, Dec. 1973. Reprint.

———. "To Be Educated, Or More Educated: That Is the Question." *New York Times*, Apr. 10, 1976. Reprint.

———. "Help for the Republicans: The Jewish Vote." *New York* Magazine, "The City Politic" Column, Dec. 1976. Reprint.

———. "Brooklyn's Hasidim: The Yiddish Connection." *New York* Magazine, "The City Politic" Column, Mar. 1977. Reprint.

———. "Republicans Court the Jewish Vote: GOP? Couldn't Hurt." *New York* Magazine, "The Capitol Letter" Column, July 1978. Reprint.

———. "The Most Powerful Rabbis in New York," *New York* Magazine, Jan. 22, 1979. Reprint.

———. "Israel's Word War," *Forum*, Jan. 1983. Abridged Reprint.

———. "Israel Center Library Dedicated in Memory of Young Oleh." *Jewish Action, Magazine of the Orthodox Union in Israel*, Summer 1983. Reprint.

———. "From Telshe-Lithuania to Riverdale." *Yeshiva of the Telshe Alumni's Dinner Journal*, June 1994. Reprint.

———. "Serving in Army Helped Identity with Israel." *Riverdale Press*, Jan. 11, 1990. Reprint.

———. "Clinton's Example." *Jewish Week*, Nov. 1998. Reprint.

———. "Prince of Ethnicity." *Forward*, Oct. 1999. Reprint.

———. "Letter from the New York Marathon: Homage to an Unlikely Impresario." *Forward*, Oct. 1999. Reprint.

———. "A Marathon Man's Answer to the Nazi." *New York Post*, Nov. 3, 1999. Reprint.

———. "Political Orthodoxy." *The Wall Street Journal* "Letter to the Editor," Aug. 16, 2000. Reprint.

———. "Getting to 'President Joe.'" *Forward*, "ForwardForum," Aug. 3, 2001. Reprint.

———. "Dawdling Diplomacy Emboldens Terrorists." *Forward*, "ForwardForum," Feb. 2003. Reprint.

———. "The New Powell Doctrine." *Forward*, "ForwardForum" column, Mar. 2003. Reprint.

———. "Joe Lieberman's Jewish Inreach." *The Jewish Press*, Mar. 24, 2004. Reprint.

———. "Unilateralism versus Post-Nationalism." *The Jewish Press*, May 19, 2004. Reprint.

———. "Two Finish Lines." *Jewish Journal of Greater Los Angeles*, Mar. 2005. Reprint.

———. "Learning From The Master: My Debt To America's Greatest Judaica Collector." *The Jewish Press*, Apr. 2005. Reprint.

———. "Bolton versus Powell: A Tale of Two Diplomatic Cultures." *The Jewish Press*, May 2005. Reprint.

———. "Bush Can't Afford Another Blink." *The Jewish Press*, July 2006. Reprint.

———. "Why Lieberman Will Lose." *The Jewish Press*, Aug. 2, 2006. Reprint.

———. "Olmert's Liberal Mindset to Blame for Lebanon Fiasco." *The Jewish Press*. Aug. 2006. Reprint.

———. "Fred Lebow and Pol 101." *The Jewish Press*, Oct. 2006. Reprint.

———. "Response to 'The Gipper's Mideast Playbook' by Richard Haass." *The Wall Street Journal Online*, Apr. 2007. Reprint.

———. "The Statecraft Of Condi Clinton." Unpublished. Dec. 2007.

———. "Why Bush May Yet Shock Everyone and Bomb Iran." *The Jewish Press*, Feb. 6, 2008. Reprint.

———. "An Unforgettable Forty-Year Shabbos Journey." The Jewish Press, Dec. 13, 2006. Reprint.

———. "How About Brownback for Vice President?" *The Jewish Press*, Apr. 9, 2008. Reprint.

———. "Welcoming Israel's Newest Olim." *The Jewish Press*, Jan. 9, 2008. Reprint.

Rubin, Ronald, and Evelyn Rubin. "Friends in Need of Votes, Friends Indeed?" *Shma: A Journal of Jewish Responsibility*, Oct. 1976. Reprint.

Rubin, Shulie. "Letter to Russia." *Young Israel Viewpoint*, Feb. 1985. Reprint.

Works Cited within the Anthologized Works

Books and Articles

Alger, Chadwick F. "United Nations Participation as a Learning Experience." Evanston, IL: Northwestern University, 1962.

———. "Personal Contact in Intergovernmental Organizations" in *The United Nations System and its Functions* edited by Robert W. Gregg and Michael Barkun. Princeton: Princeton University Press, 1968.

Ami, Ben. *Between Hammer and Sickle*, 295–96. Philadelphia: Boss, 1967.

Beard, Charles A. *The Open Door at Home*, 318–19. New York: Macmillan, 1934.

———. *A Foreign Policy for America*, 32–33. New York: Alfred K. Knopf, 1940.

Bloomfield, Lincoln P. *The United Nations and U.S. Foreign Policy*, 44, 45. Boston: Little Brown and Company, 1967. Second edition.

Case, Belle and Fola La Follette. *Robert M. La Follette*, vol. 2, 993. New York: Macmillan, 1953.

Cleveland, Harlan. *The Obligations of Power*, 133. New York: Harper and Row Publishers, 1966.

Cole, Wayne S. *America First: The Battle Against Intervention 1940–41*. Madison: University of Wisconsin Press, 1953.

Decter, Moshe. "Soviet Jewry: A Current Survey," 11, 12. *Congress bi-Weekly,* Dec. 5, 1966.

Dewey, John. *Intelligence in the Modern World,* 590. New York, 1939.

Dulles, Foster Rhea. *America's Rise to World Power 1898–1954,* 114. New York, 1954.

Goldman, Eric F. *Rendezvous with Destiny: A History of Modern American Reform,* 218, 293, 295. New York, 1952.

Greenberg, Rabbi Irving. "Public Successes Outweigh Private Failures." *The Jewish Week.* Oct. 9, 1998.

Hoover, Herbert. *The Memoirs of Herbert Hoover: The Cabinet and the Presidency,* 377–378. New York, 1952.

Hovet, Thomas, Jr. "United Nation Diplomacy" in Maurice Waters, *The United Nations,* 196. New York, 1967.

Hyde, Grant M. *Newspaper Reporting,* chapter 15, 178. New York, 1952.

Johnson, Walter. *The Battle Against Isolation.* Chicago, 1944.

Kramer, Meyer. "Is America a Christian Country," 5, 12. *Tradition,* Fall 1961.

Kruglak, Theodore E. *The Foreign Correspondents,* chapters 3 and 8. Geneva, Switzerland, 1955.

Lawrence, Gunther. *Three Million More?* Garden City, NJ: Doubleday, 1970.

Levy, Mark, and Michael Kramer. *The Ethnic Factor: How America's Minorities Decide Elections.* New York: Simon and Schuster, 1973.

Lieber, Isi. *Soviet Jewry and Human Rights.* Victoria, Australia: Human Rights Publications, 1963.

Lippmann, Walter. "Weapon of Freedom." *Life,* 56, no. 9 (1940): 28.

Liskofsky, Sidney. "The U.N. Reviews Its NGO System." *Reports on the Foreign Scene.* American Jewish Committee, Jan. 1970.

Littmann, Alex. "A Nation Outraged: American Response to the Mistreatment of Jews in Russia 1880–1891." M.A. thesis, New York Univ., 1968.

Mabry, Marcus. *Twice as Good: Condoleezza Rice and Her Path to Power.* New York: Rodale Press, 2007

Pfeffer, Leo. *Church, State and Freedom.* Boston: Beacon Press, 1953.

Rice, Condoleezza. "Promoting the National Interest." *Foreign Affairs.* Council on Foreign Relations, vol. 79 (2000): 1.

Roosevelt, Franklin D. *The Public Papers and Addresses of Franklin D. Roosevelt, 1941 Volume,* 187–190. Edited by Samuel Rosenman. New York: Harper, 1950.

———. *F. D. R., His Personal Letters 1928–1945,* 1159. Edited by Elliot Roosevelt. New York: Duell, Sloan and Pearce, 1950.

Rosenman, Samuel. *Working with Roosevelt*, 167. New York: Harper & Brothers, 1952.

Rubin, Ronald I. "Soviet Jewry and the United Nations: The Politics of Non-Governmental Organizations," 149, 151. *Jewish Social Studies*, July 1967.

———. *Anything for a T-Shirt: Fred Lebow and the New York City Marathon, the World's Greatest Footrace*. Syracuse: Syracuse University Press, 2004.

Shapiro, Leon. "Eastern Europe: Soviet Union," 391. *American Jewish Year Book 1969*. New York: American Jewish Committee, 1969.

Singer, Howard. *Bring Forth the Mighty Men: On Violence and the Jewish Character.* New York: Funk and Wagnalls, 1969.

Steele, Shelby. "Life and Death." *Wall Street Journal*. Aug. 22, 2006.

Swift, Richard M. "The United Nations and Its Public." *International Organization*, vol. 14 (Winter 1960).

Thomas, Hugh. *Suez*. New York: Harper & Row, 1967.

Woodward, Bob. *Bush at War.* New York: Simon & Schuster, 2002.

Print and Electronic News Media, Periodicals, and Journals

"This Week," *ABC News*

Akher Siah, Egypt

Al Matzor, Egypt

American Jewish Year Book

Christian Science Monitor

Commentary

Daily Telegraph, Great Britain

The Jerusalem Post, Israel

Jewish Press

Kadima

Maariv, Israel

New York Daily News

The New York Times

The Pilot

Religious News Service

Reuters

The Springfield Globe

United States Law Week, May 29, 1961

The Wall Street Journal

Official Government Documents

United Nations. *Report of the Secretary General to the World Organization (A/65)*, 45. Lake Success: United Nations, June 30, 1946.

———. *Annual Report of the Secretary General on the Work of the Organization (A/930)*, 140. Lake Success: United Nations, 1949.

———. AC.3/S.R. 1168, Circa 1968.

———. E/AC.7/S.R. 473. Circa 1954.

———. E/AC.7/S.R. 572. 1966.

———. AC.3/S.R. 1170. 1962.

———. AC.3/S.R. 1171.

———. AC.3/S.R. 1241.

———. AC.3/S.R. 1392.

United Nations Commission on Human Rights. E/CN.4/Sub.a/SR. 434.

———. E/CN.4/S.R. 686. 1953

———. E/CN.4/S.R. 784. 1959.

———. E/CN.4/S.R. 808. 1960.

———. E/CN.4/S.R. 842. 1962.

———. E/CN.4/S.R. 928. 1967.

———. E/CN.4/S.R. 979. 1968.

———. E/CN.4/Sub.2/S.R. 416.

———. E/CN.4/Sub.2/S.R. 438.

United Nations Correspondents Association. *United Nations Correspondents Association 1962 Directory*, 2. New York: United Nations, 1962.

United States Senate. "Comment by Henry A. Kissinger." Committee on Government Operations. U.S. Senate: Mar. 3, 1970.

Case Law

Commonwealth of Massachusetts. *Commonwealth v. Has*, 122 *Mass.* 40. 1877.

———. *Davis v. City of Somerville*, 128 *Mass.* 594. 1880.

———. *Commonwealth v. White*, 190 *Mass.* 578, 77 N. E. 636. 1906.

———. *Commonwealth v. McCarthy*, 244 *Mass.* 484. 1923.

———. Appellate Brief re *Gallagher v. Crown Kosher Supermarket*. Circa 1960.

Crown Kosher Supermarket. Appellees' Brief re *Gallagher v. Crown Kosher Supermarket*. Circa 1960.

Massachusetts Legislative Documents. "Observance of the Lord's Day," section 5, 6. *Massachusetts General Laws*, chapter 136. 1954.

———. "Labor and Industries," section 48. *Massachusetts General Laws*, chapter 149.

New York Court of Appeals, *New York v. Friedman*, 302 N.Y. 75. 1950.

Supreme Judicial Court of Massachusetts. *Commonwealth v. Chernock, Massachusetts* A.S. 1057. Nov. 13, 1957.

United States Supreme Court. *Reynolds v. United States*, 98 *U.S.* 145. 1878.

———. *Soon Hing v. Crowley*, 113 *U.S.* 703. 1885.

———. *Hennington v. Georgia*, 163 *U.S.* 299. 1896.

———. *Petit v. Minnesota*, 177 *U.S.* 164. 1900.

———. *Cantwell v. Connecticut*, 310 *U.S.* 296. 1940.

———. *Thornhill v. Alabama*, 310 *U.S.* 88. 1940.

———. *Prince v. Massachusetts*, 321 *U.S.* 158. 1944.

———. *West Virginia State Board of Education v. Barnette*, 319 *U.S.* 624, 639. 1944.

———. *Thomas v. Collins*, 323 *U.S.* 516. 1945.

———. *Friedman v. New York*, 341 *U.S.* 907. 1951.

———. *Zorach v. Clauson*, 343 *U.S.* 306. 1952.

———. *Braunfeld v. Brown*, 366 *U.S.* 599. May 29, 1961.

———. *Gallagher v. Crown Kosher Supermarket*, 366 *U.S.* 617, May 29, 1961.

———. *McGowan v. Maryland*, 366 *U.S.* 420. May 29, 1961.

———. *Two Guys from Harrison-Allentown, Inc. v. McGinley*, 366 *U.S.* 582. May 29, 1961.

Works Cited by the Editor

Books, Articles, and Blogs

Abbas, Mohammed. Reuters, May 22, 2011.

Dicker, Frederic U. "New York Sees a Surge in Hate: Crimes Up 14%." *The New York Post*, Dec. 31, 2010. Accessed at http://www.nypost.com/p/news/local/ny_sees_surge_in_hate_IM7xmcNGdIopEowrCRZZII.

Gee, Alastair. "Mumbai Terror Attacks: And Then They Came for the Jews." *Sunday Times (London)*, Nov. 1, 2009. Accessed at www.timesonline.co.uk/tol/news/world/asia/article6896107.ece.

Hall, Kathleen. "Cyber Terrorism Set to Increase After al-Qaeda Calls for More Cyber Attacks, Says Government." *ComputerWeekly.com*, July 12, 2011. Accessed at http://www.computerweekly.com/news/2240105012/Cyber-terrorism-set-to-increase-after-al-Qaeda-calls-for-more-cyber-attacks-says-government

Hoenig, William R. *Eye to Eye: Facing the Consequences of Dividing.* Alexandria, VA: About Him, July 2008. Revised edition.

Horowitz, Sara R. "Confronting Campus Anti-Semitism," 10. *Canadian Jewish News*, Feb. 26, 2009. [As posted on the Canadian Jewish Congress website shortly before the organization became part of the Centre for Israel and Jewish Affairs and the site no longer available.]

Kessler, Glenn. "Obama and Israel: Stalled Diplomacy or 'Suspicion and Distrust?'" Washingtonpost.com "Fact Checker" column, Jul. 11, 2011. Accessed at http://www.washingtonpost.com/blogs/fact-checker/post/obama-and-israel-stalled-diplomacy-or-suspicion-and-distrust/2011/07/08/gIQAwJwa4H_blog.html.

Landler, Mark, and David E. Sanger. "White House, in Shift, Turns against Syria Leader." *The New York Times*, July 12, 2011. Accessed at http://www.nytimes.com/2011/07/13/world/middleeast/13policy.html?pagewanted=1.

McTernan, John P. *As America Has Done to Israel.* Whitaker House, Apr. 2008.

Redissi, Hamadi. "The Revolution Is Not Over Yet." newyorktimes.com, July 16, 2011. Accessed at http://www.nytimes.com/2011/07/16/opinion/16redissi.html.

Reuters. "Thousands of Syrians flee into Turkey. . . ." *The Jerusalem Post*, June 9, 2011. Accessed at http://www.jpost.com/MiddleEast/Article.aspx?id=224342.

Windmueller, Steven. "The Unfolding Economic Crisis: Its Devastating Implications for American Jewry." e-JewishPhilanthropy.com, July 20, 2009. Accessed at http://ejewishphilanthropy.com/the-unfolding-economic-crisis-its-devastating-implications-for-american-jewry/.

Wood, David. "After Egypt's Mubarak: The Muslim Brotherhood." *Politics Daily*, Feb. 2, 2011. Accessed at www.politicsdaily.com/2011/02/01/after-egypts-mubarak-the-muslim-brotherhood/print/.

Electronic News Media, Periodicals, and Journals

ABC Nightline (abcnews.go.com/nightline)

Computer Weekly (ComputerWeekly.com, United Kingdom)

Fox News (FoxNews.com)

The Jerusalem Post (jpost.com)

The Los Angeles Times (latimes.com)
The New York Times (nytimes.com)
The Washington Times (WashingtonTimes.com)

Official Government Documents

Canadian Parliamentary Coalition to Combat Anti-Semitism. July 2011.

United Nations. S/PV.1422. New York: May 6, 1968. Accessed at http://unispal.un.org/unispal.nsf/0/dcfab68b7db3e6ac052567fc0056dd56?OpenDocument.

U.S. Department of State. "Special Envoy Rosenthal on Anti-Semitism in the Former Soviet Union." June 28, 2011. Accessed at http://www.state.gov/j/drl/rls/rm/2011/167738.htm.

Index